Studies in the German Drama

UNC | COLLEGE OF ARTS AND SCIENCES
Germanic and Slavic Languages and Literatures

From 1949 to 2004, UNC Press and the UNC Department of Germanic & Slavic Languages and Literatures published the UNC Studies in the Germanic Languages and Literatures series. Monographs, anthologies, and critical editions in the series covered an array of topics including medieval and modern literature, theater, linguistics, philology, onomastics, and the history of ideas. Through the generous support of the National Endowment for the Humanities and the Andrew W. Mellon Foundation, books in the series have been reissued in new paperback and open access digital editions. For a complete list of books visit www.uncpress.org.

Studies in the German Drama

A *Festschrift* in Honor of Walter Silz

EDITED BY

DONALD H. CROSBY AND

GEORGE C. SCHOOLFIELD

UNC Studies in the Germanic Languages and Literatures
Number 76

Copyright © 1974

This work is licensed under a Creative Commons CC BY-NC-ND license. To view a copy of the license, visit http://creativecommons.org/licenses.

Suggested citation: Crosby, Donald H., and George C. Schoolfield, editors. *Studies in the German Drama: A Festschrift in Honor of Walter Silz*. Chapel Hill: University of North Carolina Press, 1974. DOI: https://doi.org/10.5149/9781469657325_Crosby

Library of Congress Cataloging-in-Publication Data
Names: Crosby, Donald H. and Schoolfield, George C., editors.
Title: Studies in the German drama : A Festschrift in honor of Walter Silz / edited by Donald H. Crosby and George C. Schoolfield.
Other titles: University of North Carolina Studies in the Germanic Languages and Literatures ; no. 76.
Description: Chapel Hill : University of North Carolina Press, [1974] Series: University of North Carolina Studies in the Germanic Languages and Literatures. | Includes bibliographical references.
Identifiers: LCCN 74170290 | ISBN 978-1-4696-5731-8 (pbk: alk. paper) | ISBN 978-1-4696-5732-5 (ebook)
Subjects: German drama — History and criticism.
Classification: LCC PT615 .S8 | DCC 832

CONTENTS

FOREWORD ix
TABULA GRATULATORIA xi
WALTER SILZ xvii
THE WRITINGS OF WALTER SILZ xxi

*

Edwin H. Zeydel (1893—1973)
HROTSVIT VON GANDERSHEIM AND THE ETERNAL WOMANLY   1

Clifford Albrecht Bernd (Davis, California)
CONSCIENCE AND PASSION IN GRYPHIUS' *CATHARINA VON GEORGIEN* 15

George C. Schoolfield (New Haven, Connecticut)
JAKOB MASEN'S *OLLARIA*: COMMENTS, SUGGESTIONS, AND A RESUMÉ 31

Theodore Ziolkowski (Princeton, New Jersey)
THE IMPERILED SANCTUARY: TOWARD A PARADIGM OF GOETHE'S CLASSICAL DRAMAS 71

Harold Jantz (Baltimore, Maryland)
CAVEAT FOR FAUST CRITICS 89

Donald H. Crosby (Storrs, Connecticut)
ONCE MORE *AMPHITRYON*: LINES 1564—1568 103

Robert M. Browning (Clinton, New York)
KLEIST'S *KÄTHCHEN* AND THE MONOMYTH 115

George Reinhardt (Storrs, Connecticut)
A READING OF FRANZ GRILLPARZER'S *SAPPHO* 125

Hugo Schmidt (Boulder, Colorado)
REALMS OF ACTION IN GRILLPARZER'S *EIN BRUDERZWIST IN HABSBURG* 149

Franz H. Mautner (Swarthmore, Pennsylvania)
KONZENTRIERTER NESTROY: ZU DER KOMÖDIE *FRÜHERE VER-HÄLTNISSE* 163

André von Gronicka (Philadelphia, Pennsylvania)
DER UNBEHAUSTE MENSCH IM DRAMA GEORG BÜCHNERS . . 169

Otto W. Johnston (Gainesville, Florida)
THE INTEGRATION OF FICTIONAL PATTERNS IN HEBBEL'S DRAMATIC STRUCTURES 179

E. Allen McCormick (New York, New York)
GERHART HAUPTMANN'S *VELAND*: TOTAL TRAGEDY AS FAILURE OF TRAGEDY 199

Edson M. Chick (Williamstown, Massachusetts)
STERNHEIM'S *1913* AS SATIRE: FANTASY AND FASHION 213

Henry Hatfield (Cambridge, Massachusetts)
CAVE MATREM: THE BATTLE OF THE SEXES IN ERNST BARLACH'S *DER TOTE TAG* 225

Steven Paul Scher (New Haven, Connecticut)
BRECHT'S *DIE SIEBEN TODSÜNDEN DER KLEINBÜRGER*: EMBLEMATIC STRUCTURE AS EPIC SPECTACLE 235

FOREWORD

This volume has been compiled as a tribute to Walter Silz, Gebhard Professor of Germanic Languages and Literatures, Emeritus, Columbia University; it thus becomes an expanded complement to the special issue of the *Germanic Review* published in his honor in January, 1963.

In order to give equitable representation to Professor Silz's many well-wishers in the profession, the editors felt compelled to limit contributions to former students and to colleagues who had actually worked with him at the universities he served; in the end, these guidelines were relaxed slightly in order to accommodate several old friends whose exclusion would have seemed capricious.

In light of Walter Silz's fruitful research in three major genres — lyric poetry, the *Novelle*, and the drama — the concentration of this volume on one genre, the drama, may appear overly restrictive. Conspicuous among the strengths of Walter Silz's own scholarship, however, was its eminent usefulness; and it was in emulation of this virtue that the editors elected to eschew the usual *Festschrift*-format in favor of a unified theme. Their intentions will be well served if this volume is found to reflect the instructiveness of the scholar to whom it is dedicated.

The editors are pleased to express their gratitude to the Research Foundation of the University of Connecticut for a grant to help defray publication costs; to Professor Siegfried Mews of the University of North Carolina "Studies" for his patience and good counsel; and to Professor George Reinhardt of the University of Connecticut for untiring and invaluable editorial assistance.

Storrs and New Haven, Connecticut,
December, 1972

Donald H. Crosby
George C. Schoolfield

TABULA GRATULATORIA

Theodor W. Alexander
Texas Technological University
Lubbock

Walter A. Baber
St. Peter's College
Jersey City, New Jersey

Jacques Barzun
Columbia University
New York, New York

Carl F. Bayerschmidt
Columbia University
New York, New York

Joseph P. Bauke
Columbia University
New York, New York

Frederick J. Beharriell
State University of New York
Albany

Clifford A. Bernd
University of California
Davis

Hermann Boeschenstein
University of Toronto
Toronto, Ontario, Canada

Elaine E. Boney
California State University
San Diego

Frank L. Borchardt
Duke University
Durham, North Carolina

Robert M. Browning
Hamilton College
Clinton, New York

Arthur Burkhard †
Cambridge, Massachusetts

Carl E. Carrier
Ohio University
Athens

Edson M. Chick
Williams College
Williamstown, Massachusetts

Frederic Edward Coenen †
University of North Carolina
at Chapel Hill

Alan P. Cottrell
University of Michigan
Ann Arbor

Donald H. Crosby
University of Connecticut
Storrs

Liselotte Dieckmann
St. Louis, Missouri

Ingrid Otto Duckworth
Wellesley College
Wellesley, Massachusetts

Leonard L. Duroche, Sr.
University of Minnesota
Minneapolis

Martin Dyck
Massachusetts Institute of Technology
Cambridge

Waldemar Eger
University of North Carolina
at Chapel Hill

Esther N. Elstun
George Mason University
Fairfax, Virginia

John Francis Fetzer
University of California
Davis

Seymour Flaxman
Graduate Center
City University of New York

Norbert Fuerst
Indiana University
Bloomington

John Gearey
City College
City University of New York

Lalla E. Gorlin
New York, New York

Reinhold Grimm
University of Wisconsin
Madison

Diether H. Haenicke
Wayne State University
Detroit, Michigan

Carl Hammer, Jr.
Texas Technological University
Lubbock

Henry C. Hatfield
Harvard University
Cambridge, Massachusetts

Robert R. Heitner
University of Illinois
at Chicago Circle

Erich Heller
Northwestern University
Evanston, Illinois

Hertha Dithmar Heller
University of Alabama
Huntsville

Heinrich Henel
Yale University
New Haven, Connecticut

Valentine Charles Hubbs
University of Michigan
Ann Arbor

Raymond M. Immerwahr
University of Western Ontario
London, Ontario, Canada

Harold Jantz
Johns Hopkins University
Baltimore, Maryland

Otto Johnston
University of Florida
Gainesville

Klaus W. Jonas
University of Pittsburgh
Pittsburgh, Pennsylvania

George Fenwick Jones
University of Maryland
College Park

Ludwig W. Kahn
Columbia University
New York, New York

John Theodore Krumpelmann
Louisiana State University
Baton Rouge

John W. Kurtz
Oberlin College
Oberlin, Ohio

Victor Lange
Princeton University
Princeton, New Jersey

Herbert Lederer
University of Connecticut
Storrs

Wolfgang Leppmann
University of Oregon
Eugene

Frederick R. Love
Brown University
Providence, Rhode Island

Franz H. Mautner
Swarthmore College
Swarthmore, Pennsylvania

William Harold McClain
Johns Hopkins University
Baltimore, Maryland

E. Allen McCormick
Graduate Center
City University of New York

John Frederick McMahon
Lawrence University
Appleton, Wisconsin

George J. Metcalf
University of Chicago

Fritz Metzger
Bryn Mawr College
Bryn Mawr, Pennsylvania

Siegfried Mews
University of North Carolina
at Chapel Hill

Heinz Moenkemeyer
University of Pennsylvania
Philadelphia

Walter Müller-Seidel
Seminar für deutsche Philologie II
München

Kenneth Negus
Rutgers University
New Brunswick, New Jersey

John Edward Oyler
University of Calgary
Calgary, Alberta, Canada

J. Alan Pfeffer
University of Pittsburgh
Pittsburgh, Pennsylvania

Ferdinand Piedmont
Indiana University
Bloomington

Heinz Politzer
University of California
Berkeley

Paul F. Proskauer
Herbert H. Lehman College
City University of New York

William Webb Pusey III
Washington and Lee University
Lexington, Virginia

Helmut Rehder
University of Texas
Austin

Walter A. Reichart
University of Michigan
Ann Arbor

Eberhard Reichmann
Indiana University
Bloomington

George Reinhardt
University of Connecticut
Storrs

Henry H. H. Remak
Indiana University
Bloomington

Ernst Rose
New York University

Jeffrey L. Sammons
Yale University
New Haven, Connecticut

Steven Paul Scher
Yale University
New Haven, Connecticut

Hugo Schmidt
University of Colorado
Boulder

George C. Schoolfield
Yale University
New Haven, Connecticut

H. Stefan Schultz
Durham, North Carolina

Willy Schumann
Smith College
Northampton, Massachusetts

Harry E. Seelig
University of Massachusetts
at Amherst

Oskar Seidlin
Indiana University
Bloomington

Goetz F. A. Seifert
University of Tennessee
Martin

Johann and Renate Seitz
New Haven, Connecticut

Helmut Sembdner
Stuttgart

Alfred Senn
University of Pennsylvania
Philadelphia

Walter Herbert Sokel
University of Virginia
Charlottesville

Marion W. Sonnenfeld
State University of New York
Fredonia

Peter Spycher
Oberlin College
Oberlin, Ohio

Israel Stamm
Rutgers University
Newark, New Jersey

Taylor Starck
Harvard University
Cambridge, Massachusetts

Henri Stegemeier
University of Illinois
Champaign

Jack M. Stein
Harvard University
Cambridge, Massachusetts

Samuel L. Sumberg
City College of New York

Ransom T. Taylor
Marquette University
Milwaukee, Wisconsin

Gordon L. Tracy
University of Western Ontario
London, Ontario, Canada

André von Gronicka
University of Pennsylvania
Philadelphia

Ernest and Ellen von Nardroff
City College of New York
and Upsala College

Margaret E. Ward
Wellesley College
Wellesley, Massachusetts

Paul K. Whitaker
University of Kentucky
Lexington

Edwin H. Zeydel †
Cincinnati, Ohio

Theodore Ziolkowski
Princeton University
Princeton, New Jersey

Otto J. Zitzelsberger
Rutgers University
Newark, New Jersey

Department of German
Barnard College
New York, New York

Department of Modern Languages
Brooklyn College
City University of New York

Department of German
Brown University
Providence, Rhode Island

Department of German
University of California
Davis

Canisius College Library
Buffalo, New York

Colorado College
Colorado Springs

Connecticut College Library
New London, Connecticut

Deutsches Haus of Columbia University
New York, New York

Franklin and Marshall College Library
Lancaster, Pennsylvania

Furman University
Greensville, South Carolina

Gettysburg College Library
Gettysburg, Pennsylvania

University of Houston
at Clear Lake City
Houston, Texas

Department of Germanic Languages
Indiana University
Bloomington, Indiana

Department of Germanic and Slavic
Languages and Literatures
Kent State University
Kent, Ohio

Department of Germanic Languages and
Literatures
University of Michigan
Ann Arbor, Michigan

Department of German and Russian
Michigan State University
East Lansing, Michigan

German Department
Middlebury College
Middlebury, Vermont

German Department
University of Minnesota
Minneapolis

Department of Germanic and Slavic
State University of New York
Buffalo, New York

Department of Germanic Languages
University of North Carolina
at Chapel Hill

Department of German
St. Olaf College
Northfield, Minnesota

Sojourner Truth Library
State University College
New Paltz, New York

Swarthmore College Library
Swarthmore College
Swarthmore, Pennsylvania

Department of Languages
University of Utah
Salt Lake City

Victoria College Library
Victoria College
University of Toronto
Toronto, Ontario, Canada

Wake Forest University Library
Wake Forest University
Winston-Salem, North Carolina

WALTER SILZ

In 1922, at the close of a review of Walter Silz's first published monograph, *Heinrich von Kleist's Conception of the Tragic,* his former teacher at Harvard, Kuno Francke, wrote in *Modern Language Notes* as follows: "I cannot conclude this brief analysis of Dr. Silz's monograph without expressing the hope that this young scholar of mature insight and deliberate judgement will someday come to stand in the front rank of our profession."

Like most mortals, Germanists make poor prophets, but the hopeful sentiments expressed by Professor Francke were to become so splendidly fulfilled that this redoubtable scholar may well have possessed the gift of clairvoyance. Before many years had passed, Walter Silz had indeed come to stand in the front rank of our profession; it is a place he has filled with distinction for over four decades, continuing even into an unusually active retirement.

Heinrich von Kleist was an early love — it was to prove an enduring one — of the "young scholar," and in 1929 Silz's research bore fruit in a second, more ambitious study which explored Kleist's relation to the *Frühromantik*: *Early German Romanticism. Its Founders and Heinrich von Kleist.* The two Kleist-monographs, framing shorter studies on Kleist, Freytag, Raabe and Otto Ludwig, marked an initial scholarly decade rich in promise and accomplishment. Common to these publications were virtues which have come to be associated with Walter Silz: painstaking attention to the text; dispassionate evaluation of evidence; a refreshing freedom from cant; a lean and muscular scholarly prose. Still another common — one is tempted to say un-common — denominator for Silz's articles and books was a certain Yankee pragmatism, a reluctance on the part of the scholar to lose himself in abstractions and to becloud the lucidity of his arguments. Inevitably, Silz was to become regarded in some quarters as a bit "old-fashioned," a label he was willing to accept under his own understanding of the term: faithfulness to the text and to the author's intentions.

The 1920's and 30's were spartan times for our profession, as for others, and slow advancement through the various professorial ranks was the rule rather than the exception. Walter Silz is fond of jesting about the "princely sum" — it shall go unrecorded here — which constituted his beginning salary back in 1922; later he was often moved to chuckle good-naturedly over news of the precipitate advancement of one or another former pupil in the "boom years" of the 1960's. Yet his loyalty to Harvard was strong, and only in 1936 did he respond to the administrative challenge of a chairmanship at Washington University. In 1939 he accepted a similar position at Swarthmore College, a move which brought him back to the East, where he has made his home ever since. The years at Swarthmore were happy ones for Walter Silz, who warmed at once to the flexibility, the informality, and the high academic standards of this excellent college. His experience was enriched by the presence on the teaching staff of his gifted wife Priscilla, herself a fine *Germanistin* and a congenial partner in what students of that era recall to have been a remarkable teaching "team."

In 1949 Walter Silz accepted an appointment as head of the German Section of what was then the Department of Modern Languages at Princeton University, a position he was to hold for the next five years. This was a period of post-war recovery for American *Germanistik*, and graduate study at Princeton was an experience quite different from the impersonal "processing" characteristic of many programs in the post-*Sputnik* years. Seminars were small and resembled tutorial sessions at English universities. For all its academic advantages, this intimate relationship between professor and student had — at least for the latter — an obvious drawback: because there was no place to hide, students seldom ventured into Walter Silz's no-nonense seminars unfortified by a liberal dose of midnight-oil preparation. Academic rigors were nevertheless more than balanced by the genuine interest vested in each student by Walter Silz and his departmental colleagues. The door of the handsome house at 60 Laurel Road stood open and the gracious hospitality of Walter and Priscilla Silz added a human dimension to graduate study for the small band of graduate students and their wives. Candor compels the editors — both students of Walter Silz at Princeton — to admit that memories of civilized conversation around the crackling fireplace, of Priscilla Silz's *Weihnachtsgebäck*, and of good fellowship at *Adventkaffees* have proved more durable than, say, their exposure to the *Ablaut*-series of Middle High German verbs.

The assumption of administrative responsibilities inhibited neither the quantity nor the quality of Walter Silz's scholarship during the "middle period of his career; on the contrary, his most significant contributions during these years reveal a widening range of intellectual curiosity. Articles on Keller, Ludwig, Droste-Hülshoff and Storm adumbrated a deepening interest in a genre which Silz was to find especially congenial, the German *Novelle*. A triad of articles, including an interpretation which bids fair to deserve the adjective "definitive," was devoted to a favorite play, Kleist's *Prinz Friedrich von Homburg*. An analysis of Goethe's "Auf dem See" still stands as a model of sensitive yet sensible re-creation of lyric poetry — an exercise which looked ahead to later analyses of the poetry of Klopstock, Schiller, and Storm. Silz's research in the *Novelle* culminated, in 1954, in the publication of his best-known book, *Realism and Reality*. A collection of brilliant interpretations of nineteenth-century *Novellen*, this volume has become a classic in its own time.

In the fall of 1954 Walter Silz was called to Columbia University as Gebhard Professor of German Literature to fill a chair once occupied by such distinguished predecessors as Calvin Thomas and Robert Herndon Fife. Electing to keep his home in Princeton, where he and Priscilla, much like their lovely garden, had "taken root," Silz turned the necessity of commuting into the virtue of course preparation, dissertation reading, and fruitful study of the literature he continued to serve. Despite Silz's substantial editorial commitments to *PMLA*, *The Germanic Review*, and a heavy burden of dissertations, the Columbia years produced a remarkable scholarly *Spätlese*: articles on Goethe, Schiller, Hölderlin, Grillparzer, Droste-Hülshoff and Storm. In the "Kleist-Year" of 1961, a volume appeared crowning forty years of close reading: *Heinrich von Kleist. Studies in His Life and Works*. Silz's tenure in the tradition-rich Department at Columbia constituted his final permanent appointment, although visiting professorships at Indiana University, Brown University and Queens College, C.U.N.Y., were to follow for the still-vigorous Emeritus.

In recent years the poet Friedrich Hölderlin, a kindred spirit of Heinrich von Kleist, has come to occupy something of the position that Kleist held for the young Walter Silz, and the year 1969 saw the publication of a full-length study of Hölderlin's *Hyperion*. The habits of a lifetime of scholarship have not been abridged by the mere formality of retirement, and at regular intervals our professional journals are still enriched by well-turned essays informed by that "mature insight and deliberate judgement" which Kuno Francke discerned so long ago.

For all his impressive scholarly achievements, Walter Silz was no aloof, impersonal scholar but rather a representative of an earlier, less specialized generation which held that a professor's primary responsibilty is toward his students. How deeply Walter Silz felt this responsibility may perhaps be appreciated from the following anecdote recalled by a former student. A bitter late-winter blizzard exceptional for New York City had made transportation hazardous, and classes at Columbia had been canceled. Yet in mid-afternoon a solitary, slightly stooped figure could be descried trudging briskly through the snow-covered walks of the near-deserted campus. It was, of course, Walter Silz, with briefcase in hand and a three-hour, fifty-mile journey behind him. Asked by a bemused student — a few hardy souls had turned up, despite the cancelation — why he had made the long trip in such foul weather, Silz answered simply: "I was afraid somebody might be disappointed."

Walter Silz has disappointed few people during his long and distinguished career. As a student and later as a teacher he reflected credit on his *alma mater*, Harvard; he was an energetic and cooperative colleague in the various departments he served; he has been a tireless "man of the profession" who has given unstintingly of his time to our professional associations and journals. Yet the greatest debt to Walter Silz is owed by his students, many of whom have been privileged to come to know him as a colleague and friend. Speaking for the countless students who, through the years, have risen to the challenge of his undergraduate classes; for those who have benefited from the discipline and direction of his graduate courses; for those who were fortunate to have him for a *Doktorvater*; for all of us — students, colleagues, and friends — who have been touched by Walter Silz's dignity, dedication, and integrity, the editors express best wishes for a continued active retirement, *herzlichste Grüsse* and — *herzlichsten Dank.*

D. H. C.

G. C. S.

THE WRITINGS OF WALTER SILZ

The following abbreviations have been used:
AGR   *American-German Review*
GQ   *The German Quarterly*
GR   *Germanic Review*
JEGP   *Journal of English and Germanic Philology*
MfdU   *Monatshefte für deutschen Unterricht*
MLN   *Modern Language Notes*
MLQ   *Modern Language Quarterly*
PMLA   *Publications of the Modern Language Association of America*

I. BOOKS AND MONOGRAPHS

1. *Heinrich von Kleist's Conception of the Tragic.* Hesperia, No 12. Baltimore: Johns Hopkins Press, 1923.
2. *Early German Romanticism. Its Founders and Heinrich von Kleist.* Cambridge: Harvard University Press, 1929.
3. *German Romantic Lyrics. Selected and Edited with Introduction and Notes.* Cambridge: Harvard University Press, 1934.
4. *Realism and Reality. Studies in the German Novelle of Poetic Realism.* UNCSGL&L, No. 11. Chapel Hill: University of North Carolina Press, 1954, [4th printing 1966].
5. *Heinrich von Kleist. Studies in His Works and Literary Character.* Philadelphia: University of Pennsylvania Press, 1961.
6. *Hölderlin's "Hyperion." A Critical Reading.* Philadelphia: University of Pennsylvania Press, 1969.

II. ARTICLES AND NOTES

1. "Rational and Emotional Elements in Heinrich von Kleist," MLN, 37 (1922), 321-327.
2. "Freytag's *Soll und Haben* and Raabe's *Der Hungerpastor*," MLN, 39 (1924), 10-18.
3. "Pessimism in Raabe's Stuttgart Trilogy," PMLA, 39 (1924), 687-704.
4. "The Kinship of Heinrich von Kleist and Otto Ludwig," PMLA, 40 (1925), 863-873.
5. "Wieland's Letter to Kleist," MLN, 40 (1925), 514.
6. "Nature in the Tales of Otto Ludwig," MLN, 41 (1926), 8-13.
7. "Motivation in Keller's *Romeo und Julia*," GQ, 8 (1935), 1-11. [Earlier version of Chapt. 7 of No. I, 4].
8. "Kleist's *Prinz Friedrich von Homburg*, Lines 172-174," MLN, 101 (1936), 93 f. [Embodied in No. I, 5, pp. 256-258].
9. "On the Interpretation of Kleist's *Prinz Friedrich von Homburg*," JEGP, 35 (1936), 500-516. [Earlier version of Chapt. 8 of No. I, 5].

10. "A 'falsified verse' in Kleist's *Homburg?*," MLN, 105 (1940), 505-508.
11. "The Place of German in American Liberal Education," *Schoolmen's Week Proceedings*, 27 (Philadelphia 1940), 355-362.
11a. Reprinted in: AGR, 8 (Oct. 1941), 9-12.
12. "On *Homburg*, and the Death of Kleist," MfdU, 32 (1940), 325-332.
13. "Goethe's *Auf dem See*," *Studies in Honor of John Albrecht Walz*. Lancaster, 1941, pp. 41-48.
14. "Heine's 'Synaesthesia'," PMLA, 57 (1942), 469-488.
15. "A Note on Kleist's Verse Style," MLN, 108 (1943), 351-355.
16. "Otto Ludwig and the Process of Poetic Creation," PMLA, 60 (1945), 860-878.
17. "Theodor Storm's *Schimmelreiter*," PMLA, 61 (1946), 762-783. [Parts embodied in Chapt. 9 of No. I, 4].
17a. In German translation in: *Schriften der Theodor-Storm-Gesellschaft*, Nr. 4 (1955), 9-30.
18. "The Poetical Character of Annette von Droste-Hülshoff (1797-1848)," PMLA, 63 (1948), 973-983.
19. "Problems of 'Weltanschauung' in the Works of Annette von Droste-Hülshoff," PMLA, 64 (1949), 678-700.
20. "The Library's Goethe Exhibition," *Princeton University Library Chronicle*, 10 (1948-49), 193-196.
21. "A Recent Gift of Goetheana," *Princeton University Library Chronicle*, 13 (1951-52), 165-167.
22. "On Rereading Klopstock," PMLA, 67 (1952), 744-768.
23. "Schiller's Ballad *Der Taucher*," GR, 30 (1955), 252-259.
24. "Longfellow's Translation of Goethe's 'Über allen Gipfeln...'," MLN, 72 (1956), 344 f.
25. "Ambivalences in Goethe's *Tasso*," GR, 31 (1956), 243-268.
26. "A 'Tassosplitter'," MLN, 72 (1957), 128 f.
27. "Chorus and Choral Function in Schiller," *Schiller 1759/1959*, ed. John R. Frey. Urbana, 1959, pp. 147-170.
28. "Schiller After Two Centuries," AGR, 26 (1959-60), 3 ff.
29. "Antithesis in Schiller's Poetry," GR, 34 (1959), 165-184.
30. "The Achievement of the German Novelle," *Schoolmen's Week Proceedings*, 46 (Philadelphia 1960), 119-137.
30a. Augmented German version: "Geschichte, Theorie und Kunst der deutschen Novelle," *Der Deutschunterricht*, 11/Heft 5 (1959), 82-100.
31. "Zur Bühnenkunst in Kleists *Prinz Friedrich von Homburg*," *Der Deutschunterricht*, 13/Heft 2 (1961), 72-91. [Substantially, a translation of Chapter 7 of No. I, 5].
32. "*Das Erdbeben in Chili*," Kleist-Issue of MfdU, 53 (1961), 229-238. [Earlier version of Chapt. 1 of No. I, 5].
33. "Hölderlin's Ode *Heidelberg*," GR, 37 (1962), 153-160.
34. "Goethe: *Der Wandrer*," *Stoffe, Formen, Strukturen. Hans Heinrich Borcherdt zum 75. Geburtstag*. Ed. Helmut Motekat and Albert Fuchs. München, 1962, pp. 139-150.
35. "Annette von Droste-Hülshoff, *Der Tod des Erzbischofs Engelbert von Köln*," Heffner Issue of MfdU, 55 (1963), 216-224.
36. "Hölderlin, *Der gefesselte Strom/Ganymed*," *Studies in German Literature. Presented to John T. Krumpelmann*. Ed. Carl Hammer. Baton Rouge, 1963, pp. 85-94, 160 f.
37. "The Character and Function of Buttler in Schiller's *Wallenstein*," *Studies in Germanic Languages and Literatures. In Memory of Fred O. Nolte*. Ed. Erich Hofacker and Lieselotte Dieckmann. St. Louis, 1963, pp. 79-91.
38. "The Scholar, the Critic, and the Teacher of Literature," GQ, 37 (1964), 113-119.
39. "Grillparzer's Ottokar," GR, 39 (1964), 243-261.
40. "C. F. Meyer, *Der Heilige*," *Deutsche Erzählungen von Wieland bis Kafka*. Inter-

pretationen IV. Fischer Bücherei Nr. 721. Frankfurt am Main, 1966, pp. 260-283. [Translation of Chapt. 8 of No. I, 4].
41. "Kleist, *Das Erdbeben in Chili,*" *Heinrich von Kleist: Aufsätze und Essays.* Ed. Walter Müller-Seidel. Wege der Forschung 147. Darmstadt, 1947, pp. 351-366. [Translation of Chapt. 4 of No. I, 5].
42. "Die Mythe von den Marionetten," *Kleists Aufsatz über das Marionettentheater: Studien und Interpretationen.* Ed. Helmut Sembdner. Berlin, 1967, pp. 99-111.
43. "Theodor Storm: Three Poems," GR, 42 (1967), 293-300.
43a. In German translation in: *Schriften der Theodor-Storm-Gesellschaft,* Nr. 19 (1970), 25-34.
44. "Storm-Forschung in den Vereinigten Staaten," *Schriften der Theodor-Storm-Gesellschaft,* Nr. 17 (1968), 41-46.
45. "Hölderlin: *Unter den Alpen gesungen,*" GQ, 43 (1970), 24-34.
46. "Theodor Storm's *Über die Heide,*" *Studies in German Literature of the Nineteenth and Twentieth Centuries. Festschrift for Frederic E. Coenen.* Ed. Siegfried Mews. Chapel Hill, 1970 [2nd ed. 1972], pp. 105-110.
47. "Hölderlin and Wordsworth: Bicentenary Reflections," GR, 45 (1970), 259-272.
48. "Werther and Lotte at the Well," *Traditions and Transitions. Studies in Honor of Harold Jantz.* Ed. Lieselotte E. Kurth, William H. McClain, Holger Homann. München, 1972, pp. 125-131.
49. "Hölderlin: Two Domestic Poems," GR, 48 (1973), 5-20.

III REVIEWS

1. Julius Petersen, *Die Wesensbestimmung der deutschen Romantik* (1926). MLN, 42 (1927), 207 f.
2. Roger Ayrault, *Heinrich von Kleist* and *La Légende de Heinrich von Kleist* (1934); Walther Linden, *Heinrich von Kleist* (1935), GR, 11 (1936), 280-282.
3. *Heinrich von Kleists Werke,* 2nd ed. (1937), ed. Georg Minde-Pouet. GR, 12 (1937), 285 f.
4. *Letters of Ludwig Tieck,* ed. E. H. Zeydel, P. Matenko, and R. H. Fife (1937). GR, 14 (1939), 145-147.
5. Alexander Gode-von Aesch, *Natural Science in German Romanticism* (1941). MLQ, 3 (1942), 498-501.
6. Hölderlin: *Gedichte,* ed. August Closs (1942). JEGP, 42 (1943), 597 f.
7. E. L. Stahl, *Hölderlin's Symbolism* (1943); Agnes Stansfield, *Hölderlin* (1944), JEGP, 45 (1946), 114 f.
8. E. L. Stahl, *Heinrich von Kleist's Dramas* (1948). GR, 26 (1951), 62-64.
9. Franz Anselm Schmitt, *Beruf und Arbeit in deutscher Erzählung,* (1952). GQ, 26 (1953), 294 f.
10. Johannes Klein, *Geschichte der deutschen Novelle von Goethe bis zur Gegenwart* (1954). GQ, 28 (1955), 69 f.
11. *Klopstock: Werke in einem Band,* ed. K. A. Schleiden (1954). GQ, 29 (1956), 58.
12. Heinrich Henel, *The Poetry of Conrad Ferdinand Meyer* (1954). MLQ, 16 (1955), 370-372.
13. Max Freivogel, *Klopstock, der heilige Dichter* (1954). JEGP, 55 (1956), 329 f.
14. René Wellek, *A History of Modern Criticism: 1750-1950,* vols. I and II (1955). GR, 31 (1956), 307-309.
15. *Goethe: Selected Letters,* ed. Barker Fairley (1955); *Eckermann, Gespräche mit Goethe,* ed. Fritz Bergemann, (1955). GR, 32 (1957), 154 f.
16. Franz Stuckert, *Theodor Storm* (1955). GR, 32 (1957), 223-225.

17. Hans Pyritz, *Goethe-Bibliographie*, Lfg. 1 and 2 (1955 and 1956). GR, 33 (1958), 74 f.
18. Fritz Lockemann, *Gestalt und Wandlungen der deutschen Novelle* (1957). GR, 34 (1959), 153-155.
19. Stuart Atkins, *Goethe's Faust, a Literary Analysis* (1958). GR, 35 (1960), 137-144.
20. Friedrich Koch, *Heinrich von Kleist* (1958). GR, 35 (1960), 307-311.
21. Eva Rothe, "Kleist-Bibliographie 1945-1960," *Jahrbuch der deutschen Schillergesellschaft* (1961). GR, 38 (1963), 174 f.
22. *Heinrich von Kleist, Sämtliche Werke und Briefe*, 2. Aufl., ed. Helmut Sembdner (1961). GR, 38 (1963), 182-185.
23. Walter Müller-Seidel, *Versehen und Erkennen: eine Studie über Heinrich von Kleist* (1961). JEGP, 62 (1963), 182-185.
24. Fritz Martini, *Deutsche Literatur im bürgerlichen Realismus, 1848-1898, and Forschungsbericht zur deutschen Literatur in der Zeit des Realismus* (1962). GR, 39 (1964), 68-71.
25. W. H. Bruford, *Culture and Society in Classical Weimar, 1775-1806* (1962). GR, 39 (1964), 310-312.
26. Hellmuth Himmel, *Geschichte der deutschen Novelle* (1963). JEGP, 64 (1965), 134-136.
27. Benno von Wiese, *Novelle* (1963). GQ, 39 (1966), 107-109.
28. Lawrence Ryan, *Hölderlins "Hyperion": Exzentrische Bahn und Dichterberuf* (1965). GR, 41 (1966), 306-308.
29. *Heinrich von Kleist: Werke in einem Band*, ed. Helmut Sembdner (1966). GQ, 40 (1967), 257.
30. *Kleist-Bibliographie 1803-1862*, ed. Helmut Sembdner (1966). GQ, 40 (1967), 424 f.

HROTSVIT VON GANDERSHEIM
AND THE ETERNAL WOMANLY

Edwin H. Zeydel †

It is a curious fact that Hrotsvit von Gandersheim, one of the earliest writers of Germany documented by name (all of her works are written in Latin) and the earliest woman poet not only in Germany but in all of Europe, is perhaps entitled to more superlatives and "firsts" than any other writer. In his introduction to the most recent German edition of her works, *Hrotsvit von Gandersheim: Sämtliche Dichtungen*,[1] Bert Nagel, already noted for two other publications on her,[2] sums up some of these superlatives and "firsts." In addition to those just mentioned, Nagel reminds us that she was the first dramatic writer in the entire Christian world, producing a historical drama (*Gallicanus*; *Dulcitius* would qualify too), several middle class dramas (*Calimachus*, *Abraham* and *Pafnutius*), tragedies (*Dulcitius* and *Sapienta*) and an occasional comic scene (e.g., in *Dulcitius*); she was the first to imitate Terence; the first woman historiographer (in her two epics); one of the earliest, if not the first, to describe the medieval Christian heroic type; and the first delineator and representative of the "emancipated" woman. Nagel writes: "Ja, als erste *emanzipierte Frau*, als die sie die deutsche Frauenbewegung feiert, weist sie sogar über das Mittelalter hinaus auf die neueste Zeit. Sie war tief vom Selbstwert des Frauentums durchdrungen."[3]

Another achievement to this learned woman's credit which should be mentioned is the fact that, like Sebastian Brant's *Narrenschiff* (1494), her dramas have passed into the stream of Western European literature. This occurred late, to be sure — not until the nineteenth century — but when it came the echo was heard in England, France, Italy, Denmark and the United States.[4] Her plays have been discussed, studied, translated or performed either "live," in radio presentations, or as puppet plays, or used as the basis of new works. Besides, London has had a "Roswitha Society" since 1926 and New York a "Roswitha Club" since 1944.

It is Hrotsvit's championship of woman in her dramas on which I intend to focus attention in this study. And since her defense of women is intimately connected with the international renown she enjoys, some attention has also been given to the latter.

Already in the *Praefatio* of Book II, containing the dramas, where she mentions herself in the famous reference *ego, Clamor Validus Gandeshemensis*,[5] Hrotsvit refers pointedly to women as the principal subject of her plays. She would imitate Terence in diction, she says, but also turn her attention to women bad and good, morally weak and strong. Both *turpia lascivarum incesta feminarum* (disgraceful unchaste conduct of lewd women) and the *laudabilis sacrarum castimonia virginum* (the praiseworthy pureness of holy virgins) are to be depicted without discrimination. But this estimable task, she is ashamed to add, makes it necessary to deal, by way of contrast, with men in all their base, amorous villainy, madness and evil love-sick talk (*detestabilem inlicite amantium dementiam et male dulcia colloquia*). The stronger the senseless amorous temptation (*blanditiae amentium*), the greater will be the glory of the divine helper (*superni adiutoris gloria*), and the more illustrious the victory of the triumphant, when womanly frailty conquers the brute violence of men and confounds them (*virilis robur confusione subiaceret*).

In a closing paragraph Hrotsvit unburdens herself of an abject apology for her shortcomings as a writer. Insofar as she offers excuses for her stylistic inferiority to Terence, this apology is justified: *huius vilitas dictationis, multo inferior, multo contractior, penitusque dissimilis eius quem proponebam imitari.*[6] Of this she is not ashamed because it was not her purpose to write better Latin than Terence. She wanted to confute his pagan approach and philosophy. But she goes on to assure her readers that she has no intention of invading the province of men, who, she knows, far exceed her in ability; she would not venture to vie with even the least of them: *ipsis tamen denuntio, me in hoc iure reprehendi non posse, quasi his vellem abusive assimilari, qui mei inertiam longe praecesserunt in scientia sublimiori. Nec enim tantae sum iactantiae, ut vel extremis me praesumam conferre auctorum alumnis.*

Such a confession of inferiority seems utterly uncalled for. Intellectually and stylistically she bears comparison with the best male writers of her time. In profundity and breadth of scholarship she reached the highest pinnacle attainable during the Ottonian Renaissance. And as a canoness (not a nun) in the rarified atmosphere of Gandersheim she enjoyed the full favor of the Ottonian court, which commissioned her to write her epic on the deeds of the emperor. We have good reason, therefore, to suspect that she must have been conscious of her station in life and her ability. Her *supplicii mentis devotio* (humble consciousness of inferior intellect) is but an example of a literary pose not uncommon in medieval German writers.

In the Epistle dedicated to some of the learned patrons of her work, she carries this practice of disparagement to extremes, heaping upon herself one depreciative epithet after another, such as: *mei opusculum vilis mulierculae* (the slight work of me, the inferior little woman), *mei muliebre ingenium* (my woman's mind), *rusticitatem meae dictatiunculae* (the boorishness of my prating), *vilitas meae inscientiae* (the baseness of my lack of knowledge). Perhaps there is in her assumed humility a veiled reproach against those men who deemed her inferior. Like Hrotsvit, Einhard, the friend and biographer of Charlemagne, hardly more than 130 years earlier, had humbly belittled his own talent and qualifications in speaking of his *ingeniolum, quod vile et parvum, immo paene nullum est* (bit of intellect, which is inferior and poor, nay almost nil).

We turn our attention to Hrotsvit's plays. Since she has arranged all her works in the order in which they were written, we may proceed in that sequence. Her first play, *Gallicanus*, in two parts, takes us into the world of the Christian emperor Constantine, who ruled from 306 to 337, and his general Gallicanus, the titular hero. Part I shows us this pagan warrior's conversion to Christianity — one of Hrotsvit's favorite motifs. He is in love with Constantia, the emperor's daughter, an ardent Christian like her father. The latter tells her of Gallicanus' suit for her hand but, tolerant and considerate as he is, leaves the decision to her. He is her father but she is not his chattel. This affords her, a very clever girl, an opportunity to practice her wit. Although opposed to marrying any pagan, and resolved to live her life in chastity, she still feels that she cannot turn down Gallicanus outright because he is about to leave on a mission of war in the imperial cause. So she plans a ruse, to be revealed to the reader later. It is bold and does not merely consist in putting him off. She instructs her father to tell Gallicanus that she looks upon his proposal with favor. Then with divine and human assistance, but chiefly through shrewd scheming on her part, she, the wit and soul of Part I, succeeds in helping achieve Gallicanus' victory in battle and his voluntary conversion to a Christian life of renunciation and celibacy. After all is said and done, Gallicanus confesses: *Non contraluctor, non renitor, non prohibeo, sed vestris in hoc votis libens concedo, in tantum, ut nec te, mea Constantia, quam haut segniter emi vitae pretio, aliud, quam coepisti, velle cogo.*[7]

It is clear that throughout Part I Constantia, and not Gallicanus, the titular hero, is the real protagonist. She is kind, indulgent, but not without firmness of character and a touch of cunning and sly humor. Vergil's famous dictum: *Dux femina facti* fits Constantia as well as it does Dido.

In the brief Part II, Emperor Julian (the Apostate, 361-363), a nephew of Constantine, appears. He became emperor twenty-four years after Constantine's death. Hostile to Gallicanus, who is still active in spite of the long interval, Julian would have him, and indeed all Christians, put to death. Gallicanus appears only in one short scene, which is, however, very effective. In it he speaks but a few words: *Ne fatigemini, o milites*, he says to the hostile warriors of Julian, *inutilia suadendo, quia in aestimatione aeternae vitae flocci facio, quicquid habetur sub sole. Unde patriam desero et exul pro Christo Alexandriam peto, optans ibidem coronari martirio.*[8] One of Julian's counts has him killed, and he becomes a Christian martyr. Constantia is not even mentioned. She does not have to be. It is her Christian steadfastness that inspires Gallicanus' martyrdom. As often in Hrotsvit's plays, *virginitas, conversio* and *passio* lead to the very gates of Heaven under the guidance of a chaste, noble woman. And as always in Hrotsvit, retribution is visited upon all the wrongdoers who would foil the plans of God and his Christian followers. Only the penitent are forgiven and baptized. The fact that the time of this historical play is a critical period in history, in Hebbel's sense a turning point in the affairs of men which brings about the dénouement, and the further fact that the characters are representatives of the ruling class, make the action all the more impressive.

The next play, *Dulcitius*, also deals with a historical event, the persecution of the Christians during the reign of Emperor Diocletian (284-306), who had preceded Constantine on the throne. It is a drama of sacrifice and martyrdom and of steadfastness in the cause of Christianity. As in *Gallicanus*, the hero Dulcitius is only the titular protagonist. Actually there are three heroines, lovely young maidens who have dedicated their lives to chastity and service to God. They are Agapës (Love), Chionia (Purity) and Irene (Peace). Diocletian himself urges the apparently noble-born trio to renounce their vows and the Christian religion, and to return to the paganism of their forebears. They refuse. Irene, the youngest, sums up the feelings of all three in the words: *Hoc optamus, hoc amplectimur, ut pro Christi amore suppliciis laceremur* (This is our desire, this we embrace: to be subjected to torture for the love we feel for Christ). Angrily the emperor has Dulcitius, his lustful governor, confine them in irons to a dungeon. Dulcitius, tempted by their beauty, would seduce them and has them locked up in the basement behind the castle in quarters adjacent to where the kitchen utensils are stored. There he plans to visit them undetected. This leads to a famous comic scene, to be sure not acted out before our eyes but effectively related to her sisters by Irene peering through a chink in the wall when a loud clattering is heard. She sees Dulcitius, his senses apparently numbed by some higher power, kissing a pitcher and embracing the sooty pots and cauldrons, mistaking them for the maidens, and then returning to his soldiers as black as a Moor. They take him for a minion of the devil and toss him headlong down a stairway.

In disgrace and reviled by his wife, he angrily commands the soldiers to undress the maidens. But their clothes cling firmly to their bodies. The emperor, incensed over the discomfiture of his governor and the recalcitrance of the victims who defy the Roman gods, bids Count Sisinnius to submit them to torture. Should this fail to crush their defiance, they are to be put to death. Sisinnius confronts Agapës and Chionia first. Since they remain adamant, he has them burned. To the amazement of all, fire only releases their souls; their bodies and garments remain unseared. Now Irene is summoned. She too taunts Sisinnius. He has his men escort her to a brothel, but on the way two mysterious strangers tell them of new orders from Sisinnius: these strangers are to escort Irene to a hilltop nearby. Hearing of this deceit, Sisinnius on horseback, followed by his henchmen, hastens to the hill. A srange paralysis prevents them from ascending it. In desperation Sisinnius has one of his men shoot an arrow at the "evil" maiden (*maleficam*). Since there are no stage directions in the Emmeram-Munich codex, we are not told if she was wounded. Sisinnius believes she is dying: ... *te morituram haut dubito*, he exults. But she belies this with her triumphant words that the palm of martyrdom and the crown of virginity, not death, awaits her, while he will be condemned to hell (*in tartara dampnaberis*).

We cannot agree with the early French critic Magnin that *Ducitius* is "une farce religieuse, une bouffonnerie devotée, une parade sacrée."[9] Only one scene fits this description, and that is narrated and not represented. Otherwise it is a serious play, ending with the Ascension of the three martyred heroines. In effect the drama is a paean on the nobility of pure womanhood. Neither indignities nor persecution at the hands of wicked tormentors — in this case pagan tyrants — neither fire nor arrow daunts the maidens, for they know that martyrdom is vouchsafed them. Nowhere in literature before Goethe has a dramatist pleaded or depicted the cause of pure womanhood — the Eternal Womanly — with such earnestness and conviction as Hrotsvit did in *Dulcitius*.

Hrotsvit's third play, *Calimachus*, may well be weakest of her six. None the less it is significant. The unique plot concerns the desecration of the dead body of a beautiful young woman by a lover she has rejected. Her reason for spurning him is twofold: she has dedicated her life to chastity, and she is married, though for religious reasons she is no longer sharing her husband's bed. To cap the climax, we are shown the awakening of three corpses from the dead. As in the first two plays, it is again a woman around whom the action revolves, although the titular hero is a man. But the woman alone gives the play distinction. Hrotsvit's source, as usual, is legendary or a hagiography (now among the Apocrypha of the New Testament). With such literature the library of Gandersheim was well stocked.[10] This was welcome to Hrotsvit, for in her eyes legend had the validity of history.

Calimachus, a young Ephesian, is in love with Drusiana, the wife of Andronicus. Although aware that her teacher, John the Apostle, has dedicated her to a life of chastity and renunciation, Calimachus cannot control his passion. In a scene he expresses this love, but she rejects him: *discede, discede, leno nefande* (go, go, evil seducer). She assures him that, having refrained from consorting even with her husband, she would not entertain the thought of loving any man. This does not cool his ardor. He vows that the will win her by stratagem: *non desistam, donec te captuosis circumveniam insidiis* (I will not rest until I have outwitted you by trick).

Now Drusiana is in a quandary. If she reveals the evil intentions of Calimachus, it may lead to civil strife; if she conceals them, she will be involved in a diabolical intrigue. So she prays Christ to let her die. Her wish is granted forthwith.

At the tomb of Drusiana, Calimachus confers with Fortunatus, a servant of Andronicus, about viewing the body. Although Fortunatus voices no objection, he solicits a bribe from Calimachus. Both enter the tomb. On the point of desecrating the body Calimachus says to the dead woman: *Nunc in mea situm est potestate, quantislibet iniuriis te velim lacessere.*[11] Before the foul deed is done, however, a poisonous snake stings Fortunatus, and he dies. Calimachus merely dies of fright (*ego commorior prae timore*) after placing all the blame for what has occurred upon Fortunatus (quite unjustly), for having "deceived" him and "incited" him to commit the crime (*cur me decipisti? cur detestabile*

5

scelus persuasisti?). Nothing in the preceding scenes between the men indicates either deception or incitement on Fortunatus' part. His acceptance of the bribe is his only culpable act. Calimachus was clearly the instigator; indeed, he had threatened Drusiana with trickery when she rebuffed him.

In the next scene we are surprised by the appearance of the Lord. He accosts John the Apostle and Andronicus as they are about to visit Drusiana's tomb. Even before they know what has happened the Lord announces that He has come for the resurrection of Drusiana and Calimachus, *quia nomen meum in his debet gloriari* (because my name is to be glorified in them). It would have made this scene easier to understand if Hrotsvit had preceded it by some hint of an intercession on the part of John in favor of the pair and by some suggestion that Calimachus was now contrite. As it is, we are not prepared for the Lord's message any more than they are. Drusiana, I submit, deserves the highest reward Heaven has in store for men. Not so Calimachus.

The final scene is longer than all the rest together. It too takes place at the grave. John and Andronicus are alone but are later joined by Calimachus and Drusiana, restored to life through John's intercession. Calimachus, though still reviling Fortunatus, has experienced a complete transformation and is now devoted to a life of chastity and sanctity, like Drusiana. Fortunatus, however, *infelicissimus...diabolicae amaritudinis felle plenissimus* (most wretched...overflowing with the gall of devilish bitterness), as John describes him, repudiates life and chooses to die again rather than to see Drusiana and Calimachus wallowing in purity and virtue (*malo non esse quam in his tantam habundanter virtutum gratiam sentiscere*).

As already indicated, the play suffers from flaws, chiefly of structure and characterization. Andronicus is completely colorless, John's role is principally that of an intercessor. At first Fortunatus plays a passive part and seems completely free of guilt or wrongdoing, except for the bribe. But later he becomes a scapegoat and is called an archvillain. It is Fortunatus who is stung by the snake; Calimachus dies merely of fright. This seems to upset the balance of values and of guilt. Calimachus, maddened by passion and about to commit a heinous crime, dies, is warned after death by Heaven, repents, and is forgiven. His resurrection and God's forgiveness can only be explained by the words of John on Christian charity and forgiveness: *neminem...sprevit* [referring to Christ], *neminem suae gratia pietatis privavit, sed se ipsum omnibus tradidit suique dilectam animam pro omnibus posuit*. To this Andronicus replies: *Si innocens non occideretur, nemo iuste liberaretur*.[12]

Both of the two leading male characters who further the action, Calimachus and Fortunatus, are wrongdoers and sinners in varying degrees as Hrotsvit describes sinners in the *Praefatio*. Calimachus is given life anew, Fortunatus cynically prefers not to live again. Drusiana, however, like Constantia in *Gallicanus* and the three maidens in Dulcitius, is unblemished from beginning to end, chaste, steadfast in her ideals, noble in all her motives, sympathetic to those who are troubled, and ready to lay down her life to spare others. In a play marked by many weaknesses she stands out as worthy of a place beside Goethe's Iphigenie or Schiller's Maid of Orleans — a true representative of noble womanhood.

In *Abraham*, which might just as well have been called *Maria*, we meet a woman of a different kind. She is almost eight years old (*duas olympiades*) when the play opens and in her mid-twenties when it ends. An orphan, she is being reared by her uncle Abraham, a hermit bringing her up as an anchoress. At the age of twenty-two[13] a seducer disguised as a monk lured her away, and she escaped through a window of her cell. Abraham is heartbroken over this turn of events and tells his fellow hermit Effrem of his misfortune. Abraham had been warned of her flight by a dream. But failing to grasp its meaning, he had not noticed her stealthy departure until it was too late. He adds that he is sending out a friend, not bound by vows, to try to find her. Once she is found, Abraham plans to disguise himself as a soldier, play the part of a roué, and eat meat and drink forbidden a hermit, in short to make every sacrifice in order to bring her back to a life of renunciation and purity.

After two years Abraham's friend returns with the news that he has found Maria in an innkeeper's (*stabularii*) brothel, where she enjoys great popularity.

In the next scene Abraham has arrived at the brothel provided with his soldier's disguise, a hat to conceal his tonsure, some money to pay for the "services" of Maria, and an assumed jovial manner to suit the role he is playing. He gives the innkeeper a coin and asks that the *praepulchra, quam tecum obversari experiebar, puella* (this very pretty girl I hear you have here) be bidden to the meal. As soon as she kisses and embraces him as her next lover, she senses a mysterious urge to renounce her life of sin at last: *Ecce, odor istius flagrantiae praetendit flagrantiam mihi quondam usitatae abstinentiae.*[14] Once they are alone she proceeds to take off his shoes. But when he doffs his hat revealing his tonsure and calls her *meae pars animae* (part of my *soul*) she recognizes him, and a tearful reunion follows. Immediately she confirms that she is most unhappy. Her remorse is complete: she confesses her sins in contrite repentance. He comforts her with the words: *Humanum est peccare, diabolicum est in peccatis durare; nec iure reprehenditur, qui subito cadet, sed qui citius surgere neglegit*).[15] God in His mercy, he assures her, will pardon the sinner.

When they have reached home, Abraham advises her to enter the lower cell, where she will be safer from the viper of sin, should it arise to attack her again. To his friend Effrem he speaks joyfully of the severe penance she is doing, more stringent even than he had hoped for.

Many critics believe that *Abraham* is Hrotsvit's best drama. From the modern point of view its chief flaw is the suddenness of Maria's change of heart at the end. A realist might wonder too if she could not have undertaken any steps to end her life in the brothel sooner. The striking theme is as old as literature. In the Old Testament the Hebrew prophet Hosea takes a harlot for his wife. We are reminded too of Joseph and Potiphar's wife, and in Greek literature of

Hippolytus and Phaedra. In more recent literature the theme is a commonplace. Forgiveness — *remissio* — is very frequent in Hrotsvit's plays. The possibility that Hrotsvit herself might have had a past, as some writers in France and Germany have guessed, has no basis.

Maria, an orphan reared as an anchoress, lured into harlotry but rescued from debauchment to become once again a holy — and a wiser — woman, traverses a full circle of human experience until she finds rest once more in the care of that holy anchorite for whom no sacrifice was too great on her behalf. Of all the men we have thus far encountered in Hrotsvit, Abraham is the most striking — a man of sterling quality, holy from the start, one worthy of ministering to this noble penitent. But however important his role in the play, Maria, a prototype of repentant and forgiven womanhood, is the real heroine.

Certain parallels, though not altogether precise, can be drawn between *Abraham* and Hrotsvit's fifth play *Pafnutius*, based upon an old Greek tale (of Near Eastern origin) related in Latin and French versions and then in the *Acta Sanctorum*. Whereas the theme of *Abraham* was *re-conversio* by a hermit-uncle, the theme in *Pafnutius* is the *conversio* of the hardened courtesan (*meretrix*) Thais by the titular hero, also a hermit, but a stranger to her. Both Abraham and Pafnutius are holy men of untarnished character. Both undertake the hardships of a long journey in disguise to achieve their purpose. Through temptation the one girl has fallen from grace, while the other had never wished to enjoy the favor of Heaven. If "saving" a woman of the latter kind would seem the more difficult, Pafnutius might deserve even greater credit than Abraham. At any rate, Pafnutius is the second (and last) holy man of sterling mold to be found in Hrotsvit's dramas.

Pafnutius opens with a long scene in which the hermit demonstrates his expertise as an expounder of medieval dialects and scholasticism, then just budding. He discusses with a student the theory of numbers, the contrariety but eventual harmony of the "four elements," also the nature of music as one phase of the quadrivium, displaying his, or rather Hrotsvit's, knowledge of Boethius, Macrobius and other late Latin and early Christian writers. A reference to 1 Corinthians 1, 27 that "God hath chosen the weak things of the world to confound the things which are mighty" brings him to the theme of the play: *Quaedam inpudens femina moratur in hac patria* (a shameless woman tarries in this country). Rich and poor alike have been stripped of their possessions by her wiles. So Pafnutius decides to disguise himself as a lover in an attempt to convert her to a Christian life of renunciation.

No sooner has Pafnutius found and accosted her when he learns to his joy that in his presence she is ready to believe in the Christian God and to regret having lured many men to destruction. He assures her that she can be forgiven if she will repent and do penance. She declares her willingness even to destroy all the wealth she has meretriciously accumulated. This she does in the market place, burning all the precious gifts from her lovers, much to their surprise and chagrin. She explains her actions with the words: *finis instat peccandi tempusque nostri discidii* (this is the end of sinning and the time for our departure).

Now Thais is ready to obey Pafnutius' every word. He takes her to a convent and tells the abbess that he wishes to leave in her care: *capellam semivivam, dentibus luporum nuper abstractam* (a kid only half alive, just snatched from the teeth of wolves). A cell is prepared for her with only a small window through which she can be provided with food. Thais admits that after the luxury she has been enjoying, this new life will be arduous: *Mens assueta haut raro inpatiens est austerioris vitae* (A mind used to lechery often cannot bear a very austere life). She also brings up a surprisingly practical and realistic point — the sanitary and hygienic condition of the cell, and the foul air that will follow, but she is reminded hat conditions in hell may be much worse. And, regardless of this, her most important task will be to achieve mercy through tears and contrition.

Three years have elapsed. Pafnutius, eager to know if Thais has meanwhile found forgiveness, visits his fellow-hermit Antonius. Just then one of the latter's novices, Paul, reports a dream foretelling the redemption of Thais: *Thaidi meretrici servanda est haec gloria* (This glory of salvation is to be bestowed upon Thais, the courtesan). The last two scenes of the play are devoted to the protagonists Thais and Pafnutius. He greets her with rapture and tells her that in fifteen days her soul will ascend to Heaven: *Post quindecim namque dies hominem exies et tandem, felici cursu peracto, superna favente gratia, transmigrabis ad astra.*[16] This comes to pass. With the prayers of both winging skyward, she dies.

Again, as in *Abraham* the remorse and contrition of the heroine come too easily for our psychological and dramatic instincts. But we must bear in mind that in Hrotsvit's eyes both Abraham and Pafnutius are divinely inspired messengers, and that the change in Maria and Thais is wrought by God, not men. At any rate Hrotsvit has here succeeded in limning an impressive portrait of another exemplar of the Eternal Womanly, redeemed by the untiring devotion of the noble hero Pafnutius, and Thais' own torturing sense of guilt and penitence. It should be noted too that in both plays, depicting what in her *Praefatio* Hrotsvit has called *turpia lascivarum incesta feminarum*, the *lascivae feminae* find salvation through the help of the only two holy men of sterling character we find in her plays.

In my article, "Were Hrotsvitha's Dramas performed during her Lifetime?" we read:

> Anatole France, the most noted man of letters since Conrad Celtes and Johannes Tritheim to discuss Hrotsvitha, devotes sprightly little chapters to her in his essays *La vie littéraire*. He was apparently familiar with Magnin and Chasles and their views, and had witnessed marionette performances of *Abraham* and *Pafnutius* (which to be

sure he calls *Panuphtius*), also *Calimachus*. Anatole France was delighted with the success of the marionette performances...[17]

In 1888 France wrote his first article on the plays, published in *Le Temps*, urging marionette performances. The Signoret troupe carried out the suggestion, and the three plays mentioned were performed. In 1889 France published a second article in *Le Temps* praising the performances. We also have a letter by France of the same time to his friend Madame de Caillavet reporting that he has an idea for a new novel he conceived from his familiarity with "Hrosvitha" — a novel about a monk who converted a courtesan and *himself was converted*.[18] The novel came out in 1890.

One of France's most famous novels, it retains the name of the cenobite Pafnutius (now no longer incorrectly spelled as in *Le Temps*), changes Antonius to Palémon, and keeps Paul. He mentions Alexandria as the locale (as also in the *Acta*) and changes the plot to suit his purpose, as the letter just referred to indicates. In having Thais die as a converted sinner, he follows Hrotsvit. But Pafnutius, now a repulsive vampire at the end, is consumed by passion for her after converting her. This is indeed a radical change in the plot, which has been criticized by some as doing violence to a saint. France's final words sum up the fall of Pafnutius: "Un vampire, un vampire! Il était devenue si hideux qu'en passant la main sur son visage, il sentit sa laideur."[19]

Thais however, in France as well as in Hrotsvit, dies with thoughts only of Heaven. In Hrotsvit she prays: *Qui plasmasti me, miserere mei et fac felici reditu ad te reverti animam quam inspirasti.*[20] In France her last words are: "Deux séraphins viennent à moi. Ils approchent...qu'ils sont beaux...Je vois Dieu."

Four years after the appearance of this novel, Jules Massenet's opera of the same name, with a libretto by Louis Gallet based upon France's work, was performed for the first time in Paris. It immediately became one of the most popular in the French repertory. The plot follows the novel closely but changes the name of Pafnutius to the musically more adaptable Athanael. Palémon is kept, and Nicias represents Thais' lovers: he sets fire to her house when she follows Athanael to the desert — an echo of Thais' bonfire in Hrotsvit? When she is exhausted and ill, Athanael leaves her in the care of the abbess of an oasis convent but confesses that he lusts for her. Hearing a report of her death some time later, he rushes to the convent in a storm and finds her dying in the garden. Even now he still tries to rekindle the old passion in her. But it is too late. She dies, and he, in anguish, collapses beside her.[21]

It is clear, then, that to the many distinctions noted, we may add that Hrotsvit inspired not only one of Anatole France's most famous novels, but indirectly also a renowned opera by Massenet. Although discussed by Evangeline Blashfield (see n. 3) and O. R. Kuehne in his dissertation, *A Study of the Thais Legend, With Special Reference to Hrotsvitha's Pafnutius* (Philadelphia, 1922), the importance of this impact of the German tenth-century canoness upon two modern masterpieces has, to my knowledge, never been stressed sufficiently. In his scholarly little work on Hrotsvit (1966)[22], Bert Nagel does not mention it at all, although he discusses performances of Hrotsvit's plays.

The sixth and last play, *Sapientia*, is the only one in which a woman is mentioned in the title. Its theme reverts to an old Greek legend, retold in the *Acta Sanctorum*, and reminds us of *Dulcitius*. Sapientia, a Greek princess and a devout Christian, has brought her three young daughters Fides (Faith), Spes (Hope) and Caritas (Charity), twelve, ten and eight years old, as she explains in the abstruse language of Boethius, to Rome. They come to the notice of the Emperor Hadrian, who gives them an audience. Bidden by him to return to the worship of the old pagan gods, they boldly defy him and are confined to a dungeon. This only arouses the renewed scorn of the four resolute women. Again they are summoned before Hadrian, and the three children are cruelly tortured one by one, Fides with lashes of the scourge, removal of her breasts, fire, boiling in pitch and finally decapitation. But no word of complaint or cry of pain issues from her lips, for in her faith she is impervious to the pain of torture. Sapientia stands by and encourages her daughter in her martyrdom. Then Spes is flogged and lacerated with hooks. When she is to be boiled in oil, grease and wax, the vat bursts and some of the Emperor's henchmen suffer death. Finally she is beheaded. Again all this is of no avail and elicits only scorn and defiance. Now Caritas is led off to be cremated alive. But the flames of her pyre devour five thousand Romans and inflict no harm upon the eight-year-old girl: *Ludens inter flammivomos vapores vagabat et illaesa laudes deo suo pangebat* (she played among the devouring flames and, unharmed, intoned praises to her god). Finally she is executed by the sword — according to Hrotsvit the only possible method of ending the temporal life of a Christian martyr.

Now we see Sapientia, bereft but undaunted, taking the earthly remains of her three daughters, embalmed with spices, for burial. She is accompanied by a group of Roman women. Reaching a certain point on the road from Rome, she thanks the kind women and dismisses them with the words: *Grates vestrae humanitati pro solamine, quod contulistis meae orbitati* (Thank you in your kindness for the solace you have offered me in my bereft state). She kneels and after a long prayer to Christ, imploring Him to let her join her daughters in Heaven, dies.

The action, then, involves the martyrdom and Ascension of four noble women, faithful to their ideals unto death. *Virginitas, conversio* and *passio*, though playing their essential parts, yield to the high point once before reached in *Dulcitius*: *constantia* or *firmitas* as the happy consequence of *passio*.

More than any of Hrotsvit's other plays, *Sapientia* exemplifies the epic nature of her theatre. Like Brecht's, hers is a didactic theatre, one of ideological demonstration.[23] Brecht's *Verfremdungseffekt* — the technique of *distantiation* — is applicable, in a sense, to Hrotsvit too. In her, as in Brecht, the reader or listener is asked, as it were, not to identify with the actors, but to keep his distance and reflect upon the lessons they teach. Nor would an analogy between

Sapientia and Brecht's *Mutter Courage*, spanning a period of almost a millenium of theatre, be amiss, however far Brecht's political and humanitarian concerns are removed from Hrotsvit's Christian teachings. Sapientia lives by her Christian faith, Mutter Courage by war. Both alike sacrifice their three righteous children to the behemoth of evil.

Stripped of the medieval imagery with which Hrotsvit could not but invest her women, they seem to us just as real and warm as though they were living now. Whether remaining steadfast in their ideals, or discovering or rediscovering them after bitter experience, they end as "emancipated" women, to use Nagel's expression, but emancipated not from socio-political taboos but from the dross and thralldom of meretriciousness and sham. Contemplating these women in this higher sphere in which they all end, we are reminded of the immortal words of Goethe:

> Das Unzulängliche,
> Hier wird's Ereignis;
> Das Unbeschreibliche,
> Hier ist's getan;
> Das Ewig-Weibliche
> Zieht uns hinan.

NOTES

1 (München: Winkler, 1966). Although not noted on the title page, the Legends and the brief Apocalypse of John were translated by Otto Baumhauer, the dramas presented in the old 1850-1853 rendering of Bendixen, and the two epics given in the translation of Theodor Gottfried Pfund. Bendixen's practice of using tedious doggerel for Hrotsvit's *Reimprosa* is to be regretted. In the *Praefatio* and *Epistula* the meaning is sometimes obscured by this treatment.

2 *Hrotsvit von Gandersheim.* Ruperto-Carola, 15 (Heidelberg, 1963); *Hrotsvit von Gandersheim.* Sammlung Metzler, 44 (Stuttgart, 1965).

3 *Hrotsvit: Sämtliche Dichtungen*, ed. B. Nagel, p. 34.

4 The plays were translated into English in 1923 by Christopher St. John (a pseudonym for Christabel Marshall), and in the same year by H. J. W. Tillyard. The latter is to be preferred. In France the plays were translated much earlier by Charles Magnin in 1845 (see n. 9 below), with an excellent discussion, and the legends by V. Rétif de la Bretonne in 1854. Hrotsvit was discussed by Philarète Chasles in several works between 1854 and 1876. Anatole France's interest will be discussed in this article. In Italy S. Dolenz translated the plays in 1926 and Barozzi da Vignola discussed them in 1926-1927. In Denmark *Gallicanus* was translated in 1938 for a radio program, and the Russian Boris Jarcho has published articles on Hrotsvit in Germany and the United States. In the United States Evangeline W. Blashfield discusses Hrotsvit in *Portraits and Backgrounds* (1917), Sister M. Gonzalva translated her non-dramatic works in 1930, and Sister Mary Bernardine Bergman *Liber Tertius* in 1943. Eva May Newman's *The Latinity of the Works of Hrotsvitha* (1939) is noteworthy, as are Sister Mary Marguerite Butler's *Hrotsvitha, the Theatricality of Her Plays* (1960), and the recent

work edited by Anne L. Haight (1965). Several American scholars, including myself, have published numerous articles.

5 This is usually translated as "I, the strong voice of Gandersheim" or the like. But in view of the fact that *hrôt svith* (or *svinth*) does not mean "strong voice" but rather "strong in fame," I incline to the view that Hrotsvit had another meaning of *clamor* in mind: *acclamation, applause, reputation,* found in Vergil, Cicero, Horace and Tacitus, and doubtless familiar to Hrotsvit. See the *Harper Latin Dictionary* under *clamor*, B.: "Enjoying great applause," "strong in acclamation," "strong in reputation" — definitions which fit *hrôt svith* much better than the accepted rendering.

6 "This poor diction, much inferior, much more crabbed, quite different from his whom I took it upon myself to imitate." All Latin quotations are from the Karl Strecker edition of 1930.

7 "I do not oppose, I do not resist, I do not gainsay, but willingly yield to your vows in this. I do it to such a degree that I would not want to urge you, o my Constantia, whom I wooed with all my heart, to swerve from your resolution."

8 "Don't wear yourselves out, o soldiers, in useless persuasion. In contemplation of eternal life I care not what happens under the sun. Hence I leave the fatherland and make for Alexandria as an exile for the sake of Christ, hoping that there I will be crowned as a martyr."

9 *Le Théâtre de Hrotsvita* (Paris, 1845), pp. XL-XLI.

10 The question of Hrotsvit's sources was long ago studied carefully by Magnin in the work referred to in note 9. See pp. XXXIX-LV and 459 ff. See also Sister Mary Marguerite Butler in the work referred to in note 4 above, pp. 124 ff. A principal source is the *Acta Sanctorum*. But while her sources furnished the plots, Hrotsvit contributed the interpretation and value judgments.

11 "Now it is in my power to visit upon you any indignities I wish."

12 "He [i.e., Jesus], spurned no one, he deprived no one of the gracious benefit of His piety, but offered Himself to everyone, placing His beloved soul at the disposal of all." Andronicus: "If He had not died guiltless, no one would be saved with just reason."

13 Maria was about two, we assume, when Abraham adopted her. He says he had her *bis bina lustra* (twice two five-year periods). That made her twenty-two when she escaped and entered the brothel. Now two years have elapsed since then. Bendixen's note at the head of this third scene, "Zwanzig Jahre später," is misleading. He means twenty years since her adoption, not twenty years since the previous scene.

14 "Behold, the scent of those warm kisses reminds me of the scent of an abstinence that was once my wont."

15 "It is human to sin but diabolical to persist in it; he cannot justly be censured who falls once, only he who fails to rise again promptly."

16 "After fifteen days you will leave the human state, having finished your happy course here, and at last with the blessing of Heaven pass on to the stars."

17 *Speculum*, 20/4 (October 1945), 444.

18 Jacob Axelrad, *Anatole France. A Life without Illusion, 1844-1924* (New York and London, 1944), pp. 179 f. The more recent biography of Tylden-Wright (London, 1967), does not mention the matter.

19 Anatole France, *Thaïs* (Paris: Calmann-Lévy, n.d.), p. 359.

20 "Thou who hast fashioned me, take pity upon me and let my soul into which Thou hast breathed life, return happy to Thee."

21 To these treatments of the Thais story we may add a four-act American drama by Paul

Wilstach, *Thais*, "the story of a sinner who became a saint and a saint who sinned." It appeared in Indianapolis in 1911. In 1918 an American film on Thais also came out.
[22] Cf. n. 2.
[23] On this subject see Marianne Kesting's *Das epische Theater* (Stuttgart, 1959).

CONSCIENCE AND PASSION IN GRYPHIUS' *CATHARINA VON GEORGIEN*

Clifford Albrecht Bernd

I

In the numerous general studies treating Andreas Gryphius, and in those few which address themselves particularly to *Catharina von Georgien*,[1] much has been said that is illuminating. But one important clue to the understanding of this drama, first published in 1657, has not received the attention it deserves. We are referring to what we think is the key sentence in Martin Opitz' *Buch von der Deutschen Poeterey* (1624). It can be found at the beginning of the second chapter of the essay, and it reads as follows: "Die Poeterey ist anfanges nichts anders gewesen als eine verborgene Theologie / und unterricht von Göttlichen sachen."[2] What the father of German baroque literature wishes to state here is that poetic literature, in the widest sense of the term, has been and should continue to be a form of theology; the justification for its existence is to be found in the fact that it teaches man about the law and world of God.

We know that Gryphius was familiar with Opitz' work.[3] It can be fairly safely assumed, therefore, that he also knew Opitz' statement about literature being a "hidden" (or "poetic" — in contrast to "pastoral") theology. But even if this hypothesis were not true, and Gryphius had only become acquainted with Opitz' concept of literature through a secondary source, his play *Catharina von Georgien*, nevertheless, becomes exceedingly meaningful when interpreted as a work of "hidden" theology. The play offers a specific theological message. The reason why the message is given in a "hidden" or "poetic" manner is because Gryphius wishes to let his audience see what cannot be seen through the eyes of the world. He wishes to make visible in the play that which is only visible to the eye of God and which would otherwise, if the poetic structure did not reveal it, remain "hidden" to man. Only a poet (or more especially: a dramatist with the capabilities of Gryphius) could succeed in raising this veil. It is raised superbly in *Catharina von Georgien*.

The play treats, above all, the dramatic conflict between conscience and passion. Gryphius seeks to show that man must choose between the two; and he also wishes to make clear the consequences of this choice. In stressing the conflict between conscience and passion Gryphius was not unique in his age. At the same time, scores of works of pastoral theology sought to point to the necessity for man to choose between following the dictates of his conscience or of his emotions. One need only check the word *conscientia* in the *Bibliotheca realis theologica omnium materiarum, rerum et titulorum*, edited by M. Martin Lipenius (Francofurti ad Moenum, 1685),[4] to discover more than one hundred titles of books by pastoral theologians about conscience and passion. But if Gryphius was not unique in insisting on this dichotomy, his attempt to unveil this topic in a work of poetic rather than pastoral theology was unusual; and his success in giving his poetic theology a dramatic exposition was extraordinary.

II

Looking at the play itself, we note that its entire artistry is centered on an obtrusive dichotomy which, as we shall see later, serves to underline the dualism between conscience and passion. There is, first of all, the double title: *Catharina von Georgien Oder Bewehrete Beständigkeit*. It tells us that the play is about something both personal and general, about someone specific and something abstract.

The next artistic element that quickly prepares us for the play's inherent dichotomy is the rhyme scheme. Quite frequently we can discover in the play a strict adherence to the Alexandrine with its characteristic caesura. In addition, each foot of verse is divided in two by a short and a long syllable. Verse I, 99[5] may be taken as an example:

$$v - / \ v \ -/ \ v \ \ - / \ \ v \ -/v \ \ - / \ v \ \ -$$
Bejammert und betraur't. Wer wolte nicht dem Tod

Such a line, moreover, forms a couplet by rhyming with the next verse:

$$v \ \ - \ \ / \ v \ -/ \ v \ \ \ - \ / \ \ v \ - / \ v \ -/ \ v \ \ -$$
Getrost entgegen ziehn / dafern die ehrne Noth

A larger unit of two couplets results when these two verses are seen to correspond to the two following verses. Verses I, 99 and I, 100 each contain twelve syllables with a masculine rhyme; verses I, 101 and I, 102 have thirteen syllables with a feminine rhyme:

$$v \ \ - \ \ \ / \ v \ \ -/ \ \ v \ \ - / \ v \ \ -/v \ -/ \ v \ \ -/v$$
Vor euch solch Opffer wolt' O Königin der Frauen

$$v \ -/ \ v \ \ - / v \ - \ / \ \ v \ \ - / \ \ v \ -/v \ \ \ -/ v$$
Die je der Tag bekrönt kont auff der Erden schauen!

As a contrast, we can find units of four verses consisting of two sets of interlocking rhymes, instead of two rhymed couplets. One pair consists of two short lines with a masculine rhyme, while the other pair has two long lines with a feminine rhyme. Verses I, 1 to I, 4 may serve as an illustration:

> O Die Ihr auff der kummerreichen *Welt*
> Verschrenkt mit Weh' und Ach und dürren Todten*beinen*
> Mich sucht wo alles bricht und *felt* /
> Wo sich Eu'r ichts / in nichts verkehrt / und eure Lust in herbes *Weinen*!

The same fundamental dichotomy is brought out by another dualistic rhyme scheme. In the verses IV, 265 to IV, 272, for instance, we notice two corresponding stanzas, each containing two verse pairs. They, too, interlock; but instead of the first verse rhyming with the third and the second with the fourth, as we saw above, the first verse rhymes with the fourth and the second with the third. Since the first and fourth verses also have a feminine rhyme and the second and third a masculine rhyme, the feminine pair encloses the masculine one. This even becomes apparent visually, for the masculine pair is indented and the feminine one not:

> O Haupt und Feldherr deiner Glider!
> > Der du den Kampff für uns versucht /
> > Und durch dein Blut / was Gott verflucht /
> Gesegnet: für dir fall ich nider!

Many other external features in the drama give further evidence of its dichotomic structure. The dialogue between the two protagonists, Catharina and Chach Abas (a woman and a Christian on the one hand; a man and a heathen on the other) is revealing in this respect. Beginning with verse I, 763, for example, each character speaks a line which alternates with a line spoken by the other person. Two lines of dialogue between Catharina and Chach Abas form a couplet with feminine rhyme. This couplet is followed by another couplet of dialogue between the same characters with masculine rhyme. Verses I, 763 and I, 764:

> Cath. Und schlägt den schwachen Kahn an ungeheure Klippen /
> Chach. Man schwam ans Land / ging gleich das Wasser an die Lippen

contrast with verses I, 765 and I, 766:

> Cath. Diß Schif ist durch den Sturm zuscheittert auff der Flut
> Chach. Der Schipper fast / ob gleich der Mast zusprungen / Mutt.

The identical rhyme scheme is repeated until verse I, 787, when it is broken by two long stanzas in a dialogue between Catharina and Chach Abas. Once again a dichotomy becomes apparent: this time because the words of Catharina and the corresponding ones of Chach Abas each comprise equally long stanzas of sixteen verses. In addition, the dichotomy represented by this dialogue is made visible by virtue of its juxtaposition with the immediately preceding dialogue. Whereas in the earlier dialogue Catharina spoke first and Chach Abas replied to her, we now find the situation is reversed: Chach Abas speaks first and Catharina replies. These two long stanzas of dialogue (I, 819 ff.) are followed by a dialogue according to the same pattern as in the preceding dialogue. In contrast, however, to the earlier dialogue in single lines, Chach Abas speaks first and Catharina replies. The two sets of dialogue in individual lines not only enclose the two long stanzas of dialogue but also are of equal length. This again makes for a dichotomic situation in the same manner as we had seen beforehand in the analysis of verses IV, 265 to IV, 272.

Contributing also to the portayal of a dichotomy in the play is the dualistic way in which the action unfolds. The play progresses in part through the use of dramatic scenes in which everything is told to us in a *dialogue* between two characters. However, the drama also progresses at times through the use of scenes in which we are enlightened by means of a *monologue*. Thus, two forms of speech are employed intermittently: dialogue and monologue.

Closely related to these two ways in which the drama's action unfolds is the alternating use of narrative statement and dramatic action. On occasion, we are informed of what took place by means of a *narrative* statement; at other times, events are made known to us through the play's *dramatic* action. For instance, long before Chach Abas appears on the stage for the first time (I, 727), we are made thoroughly acquainted with his character through the detailed descriptions contained in the earlier dialogue between Catharina and Demetrius. His passions were not revealed to us in a *scenic* or *dramatic* way but rather in a *narrative* or *epic* way. However, when he appears on the stage, we learn more about him directly through his speech and actions. As a consequence of this alternate use of narrative and drama, it may be said that a dual method of presentation is employed to unfold the action to us.

Another important external division which is readily apparent in the play comes to the fore by means of an artistic contrast between realistic and unrealistic scenes. The very first scene, for instance, is completely allegorical and therefore exceedingly unrealistic. Eternity, in the form of a person, speaks to the audience (I, 1-88). This unrealistic scene is immediately followed by a conspicuously realistic one, in which the two real characters Demetrius and Procopius discuss topical political events (I, 89 ff.). Even the settings of these two scenes are visibly unrealistic and realistic. The stage directions at the beginning of the first allegorical scene state: "Der Schauplatz lieget voll Leichen / Bilder / Cronen / Zepter / Schwerdter etc. Uber dem Schau-Platz öffnet sich der Himmel / unter dem Schau-Platz die Helle. Die Ewigkeit kommt von dem Himmel / und bleibet auff dem Schau-Platz stehen." The setting of the following scene is realistic. The stage directions tell us: "Der SchauPlatz verendert sich in einen Lustgarten." This alternation between realistic and unrealistic scenes continues throughout the play and is particularly conspicuous when the speech and actions of such life-like characters as Catharina and Chach Abas are interrupted by choruses of abstract figures such as those at the end of the fourth act, viz.: *Die Tugenden, Tod, Libe.*

A dichotomy is further apparent in the drama's language. In contrast to the dialogue between two realistically described characters we are, at times, confronted with a language that differs radically from anything a real character would use. Catharina's exclamations of joy when she realizes that she will be liberated by death from the yoke of this world are a good example of this artificial language which contrasts so greatly with the language of the real world:

> O freudenvolle Schrifft! O auffgelöste Bande!
> O uberreichte Cron. O abgelegte Schande!
> O Freyheit meiner Seel! O längst verhoffte Ruh!
> O ewig Königreich! O Vaterland! glück zu. (IV, 241-244)

Other linguistic devices, not specifically related to the antithesis realism-non-realism, also serve to make us aware of the play's inherent dichotomy. In one verse, for instance, we are referred to the dichotomy *Thron — Kercker* (I, 280), in another scene *Thron* is contrasted with *Bar* (I, 418-419), and in a third scene *Thron* is juxtaposed to *Staub* (IV, 316).

But the most dramatic means of all that is employed in *Catharina von Georgien* to make the audience aware of a dichotomy is the portrayal of characters. They are divided into two sets, forming two opposing forces. The one set is headed by the Christian queen Catharina, the other by the heathen king Chach Abas. On Catharina's side are Salome, Serena, Cassandra, Der Königin Frauen Zimmer, Procopius, Demetrius, and the priest Ambrosius. On Chach Abas' side we find Seinel Can, Iman Culi, Ein Diener, and Der Blutrichter.

The Russian envoy is an intermediary between these two forces. The fact that he functions as a go-between strengthens the existence of the two opposing camps. This dualism becomes all the more firmly rooted in the audience's mind when it discovers that in the course of the drama all of the ambassador's efforts at mediation are ineffective. In other words, in spite of his great abilities as a negotiator, which he certainly must have had as a chosen diplomat of the Czar of Russia, he could not bridge the chasm between the two opposing forces. That, of course, emphasizes all the more the dichotomy evoked by the presence of these two camps.

Another character plays an active role in the drama: *Die Ewigkeit*. Since this character is allegorical and since she represents the infiniteness of eternity in contrast to the short lives of all the temporal characters, another dichotomy becomes manifest. It could be said that since this allegorical figure of eternity is but one character and that there are fourteen real temporal figures, no genuine balance of figures exists here, and because of this specific character constellation, one could not actually speak of the use of a dichotomy. We would reply that for Gryphius one figure representing the weight of all eternity certainly can effectively counterbalance fourteen temporal figures. Furthermore, if Gryphius intended to impress his audience with the concept of dichotomy by means of this juxtaposition, as we believe he did, then he had to create this numerical imbalance. Otherwise, fourteen eternal figures would have far outweighed an identical number of corresponding ephemeral figures in the temporal sphere.

In contrast to the fifteen active characters in the play there is also an unspecified number of inactive characters. Both the number and the role of these *Stumme*

Personen, as they are called, are ambiguous. This too reveals further evidence of a dichotomy in the drama.

But returning to those active characters who have the chief responsibility for the portrayal of the drama's message, we discover that it is the dramatist's unquestionable intention to divide them into black and white figures. The good ones are those who are on the side of the Christian queen Catharina; the bad ones are the followers of the heathen king Chach Abas. The narrated preface makes this clear before the dramatic action begins. With regard to Catharina we are told:

> Die von mir begehrete Catharine trit nunmehr auff den Schauplatz unsers Vaterlandes / und stellet dir dar in ihrem Leib und Leiden ein vor dieser Zeit kaum erhöretes Beispiel unaußsprechlicher Beständigkeit / die Crone Persens / die Ehr deß Siegreichesten und Berühmtesten Königes / die Blüthe der Jugend / die unaußsprechlichen Wollüste / die Freyheit so höher zu schätzen als das Leben / die schreckliche Marter / die Gewalt der Parthen / die Art deß Todes / so grauser als der Tod selbst / die Thränen deß Mitgefangenen Frauenzimmers / das Verlangen nach ihrem Thron / Kind / und Königreich bekriegen eine zarte Frauw / und müssen überwunden unter ihren Füssen ligen. Mit kurtzem: die Ehre / Tod und Liebe ringen in ihrem Hertzen umb den Preiß / welchen die Liebe / nicht zwar die Irrdische und Nichtige / sondern die heylige=Ewige erhält / der Tod aber darreichet und versichert. So kräfftig ist der in dem schwächsten Werckzeuge / dessen Ehre diese Königin mit ihrem Blut außstreicht / diß einige beklage ich; daß meine Feder zu schwach / so hohe Geduld / so hertzhafte Standhafftigkeit / so fertigen Schluß das Ewige dem Vergänglichen vorzuziehen / nach Würden herauß zustreichen.

The villainy of the king is made equally clear in the narrated preface. Moreover, fewer words are used to describe him than was the case with respect to Catharina's goodness, which in itself is indicative of the narrator's intentions. Chach Abas' villainy is made further clear by means of a contrast with the innocence and goodness of Catharina:

> CATHARINE... nach dem Sie ruhmwürdigst ihr Königreich wider den grossen König in Persen zu unterschiedenen malen beschützet / ihres Schwehers und Ehegemahls Tod gerochen / und endlich von dem König auß Persen mit unüberwindlicher Macht uberfallen / hat Sie sich in eigner Person in das feindliche Läger begeben / umb Frieden zu bitten: Alda sie stracks in gefängliche Hafft genommen / nach Schiras der Persischen Hoffstadt verschicket. Und von dem verliebten Könige verwahret worden. An welchem Ortt nach etlicher Zeit / als Sie dem in unkeusche Liebe entbrandten Könige die Ehe abgeschlagen / und bey Christi Bekändtnüß verharret... die erschreckliche Marter der glüenden Zangen standhafftig außgestanden / und ihr jammervolles Leben voll freudiger Geduld / auff dem Holtzstoß vollendet.

III

Turning now from the narrated preface to the action of the drama, we note a fundamental difference in the portrayal of the actions of the two opposing characters. The good forces symbolized by Catharina appear passive in comparison with the activity of the villain Chach Abas. The reason for this, as we further discover, is that Chach Abas' actions are the product of raving passions, whereas Catharina's lack of activity is a result of her unwavering appeal to her conscience. Throughout the drama Catharina is portrayed as a prisoner; she never enjoys the freedom to make any other than purely spiritual moves. Chach Abas, on the other hand, not only has complete freedom to act as whim might dictate, but he also appears to possess the means to pursue every opportune temptation. Because of their external circumstances Catharina is restricted chiefly to her inner world while Chach Abas has complete freedom. In practically every scene in which she appears she is more narrator than an actor. In only two scenes is she active: in the dialogue with her adversary Chach Abas (I, 727-831) and in a subsequent dialogue with her adversary's representative, Iman Culi (IV, 82-264). In every other scene she merely narrates past events or comments on the present. Even the scene in which only her ladies-in-waiting appear is marked by a lack of activity. Their function, too, is restricted to passive commentary (V, 1-104). In the two scenes in which Catharina really does act all that is apparent is her resigned but unfaltering will to follow conscience. Any physical activity on her part, be it but a change in facial expression, is absent. Twice she is presented with the opportunity to be freed from imprisonment, and each time she firmly but calmly refuses. Twice the heathen king Chach Abas offers her freedom and riches if she would marry him, but because he is a murderer (I, 680, II, 379), a thief (I, 476), and an adulterer (I, 780) her conscience will not permit her to deny her Christian faith by marrying him:

>....... Der König beut uns an
>Was ewig Catharin nicht willens zu empfangen.
>Und nicht empfangen muß. Wir wündtschen vol Verlangen
>Daß Abas uns erhör. Bricht er die Kett' entzwey /
>Und schenkt uns Gurgistan; so sind wir warlich frey /
>Und fallen ihm zu Fuß und küssen seine Hände /
>Und schweren Trew' und Dinst biß zu deß Cörpers ende
>Doch wil er daß der Geist nicht Christlich sich erklär;
>So wird die Freyheit uns mit Persens Cron zuschwer.
>Wir rühmen sein Gemütt / das uns zu hoch wil ehren;
>Doch leider kan der Geist von keiner Freyheit hören /
>Die uns von disem trent / der sich mit uns vermählt /
>Der uns diß Leben gab und unser Har gezehlt.
>Vil besser daß diß Fleisch verschmacht in tausend Schmertzen!
>Vil besser daß diß Blut auß auffgeschlitztem Hertzen
>Die Erd' und Hencker färb'. Als dises Reich verschertzt
>In dem kein Elend herrscht das in der Welt uns schmertzt! (IV,108-124)

Uncompromisingly, therefore, she clings to the dictates of her conscience:
> Nicht deß Gewissen Recht... verletzen. (IV, 150)
> Doch seelig die...
> Die ihr *Gewissen* nicht... beflecket (IV, 37-38)

In dramatic contrast to Catharina's lack of activity, as a result of her tenacious desire to remain faithful to her conscience, stands the vehemence of activity on the part of Chach Abas. He boldly brushes aside the world of conscience, as Catharina unmistakably makes clear when, describing his actions, she states:
> Ach! kan der Zepter Durst so die Vernunfft bethören!
> Ach kan der Cronen Geitz die Seele so entehren!
> Daß sie Verwanthes Blut / wenn dise Pest erwacht /
> Und deß *Gewissens* Grimm blind setzen auß der acht. (III, 125-128)

Instead, he lets himself be guided by the violence of his unbridled passions. Catharina also makes this clear when she goes on to say:
> [Wir begaben] uns recht zu deß *Tyrannen* Füssen
> Und wolten seine Faust in tiffster Demut küssen.
> Er / dem der *schwere Zorn durch alle Sinnen kracht /*
> *Erhitzt in geiler Brunst* / als wir der grausen Macht
> Mit Thränen zugesetzt / als wir mit eigner Leichen
> Uns den *gereitzten* Grimm erboten zuerweichen.
> Die offt verkehrte Rött' im Angesicht entdeckt;
> Wie *hefftig seine Seel durch Rach und Lib entsteckt.* (III, 341-348)

From a dramatic standpoint the characterization of Chach Abas as a man of unrestrained passion is further emphasized when Catharina's description of him is interrupted at various intervals by exclamations of horror on the part of the Russian ambassador. On one occasion he is so shocked by what Catharina has to say about Chach Abas that he questions whether the king is really as unrestrained as Catharina reports:
> Hat Abas diß getrieben? (III, 130)

Another time he can hardly believe what he hears:
> Was hör ich! Himmel hilff! (III, 221)

On a third occasion he just gasps and exclaims:
> O Himmel! solte diß ein Mensch von Abas dencken! (III, 277)

Even Chach Abas himself reveals in dialogue how much his actions are determined by passion. He states bluntly that he finds himself motivated by a restless feeling of passionate love, by a desire for power, and by a mad feeling of revenge:
> Verzeih' es heisse Lib die Rachgier steckt uns an!
> Halt in / Rach halt! die Lib ists / die uns hindern kan. (III, 399-400)
> Rach / Lib und Zepter sind die unser Hertz bekrigt.
> Rach / Lib und Zepter sind die uber uns gesigt. (III, 447-448)

The extent of Chach Abas' passion becomes most apparent when, in the character portrayal of him, we notice the number of telling references made specifically to his anger, rage, and wrath:

>Der Er *in heissem Zorn* das Leben hat geschenckt (I, 140)
>Da Abas wider uns *in tollem Zorn* entbrand (I, 472)
>Hiß er *in heissem Zorn* Printz Alovassa binden (I, 478)
>Chach ward *nach langem Wütten* (I, 490)
>Er wolte selbst ins Feld / und hub an *scharff zu toben* (III, 325)
>Er hiß *in tollem Grimm* den Curtzi Bassi prügeln (III, 329)
>Er *biß ... ihr erhitzt / die Finger von der Hand* (III, 331-332)

In addition to the character portrayal, the plot of the play acquaints us with Chach Abas as a man who knows only the world of passion. When he is first introduced, he has a passion for political revenge (I, 525). Subsequently, he gives expression to his passionate love for Catharina (I, 727 ff.). Particularly in the verse:

>Die Libe steckt diß Hertz mit heissen Flammen an (I, 789)

this passion becomes obvious. All other events in the plot are keyed to these two passions burning in the heart of Chach Abas.

A further important dramatic element pointing to Chach Abas' passionate character is dialogue. It intensifies those two passions responsible for all of Chach Abas' thoughts, words, and deeds. The more he tries to persuade Catharina to return his love and the more staunchly she refuses him, the more his passions are aroused. The scene of dramatic dialogue between the two protagonists begins with Chach Abas' attempt to woo Catharina with a delightful metaphor:

>Hir finden wir die Sonn' es mag der Himmel prangen
>Mit seiner Flammen Glantz! (I, 727-728)

and ends with his determination to break her adamant will:

>man bricht wol Diamant I, 830)

The next act begins with another dialogue — this time, however, between Chach Abas and his advisor Seinel Can — in which Chach Abas tells his confidant about his passion for Catharina:

>Ein innerlicher Brand hat unser Marck verzehret (II, 38)

Seinel Can, in reply, seeks to temper his king's passions:

>...Der Fürst schlag auß der acht
>Das angenehme Bild (II, 120-121)

But this only serves dramatically to quicken them. They are now even more inflamed than at the end of the previous dialogue. With fury retorts:

>...Ha! schlechte Phantasey!
>Läst sich wenn Haus und Dach entbrand die Flamme decken?
>Läst sich der lichte Blitz bey trüber Nacht verstecken?
>Ein Wort / ein schneller Blick / ein Seufftzer macht zu nicht
>Was ein erdichtet Haß und falscher Zorn verricht. (II, 124-128)

As a result of the third dialogue in which Chach Abas takes part, between the Russian envoy and himself, his passion reaches a dramatic climax. The envoy asks Chach Abas to free Catharina (II, 161). Chach Abas immediately grants his request (II, 180), a flash of baffling generosity. We should have expected the king to wish to reflect a while before he made a difficult choice: whether to maintain friendly relations with Russia or to indulge his personal desire for Catharina. But since Chach Abas does not weigh his decision, he acts altogether irrationally. This absence of reason indicates once more how his actions are determined by passion. This becomes even more apparent in the next scene: no sooner has Chach Abas made his hasty decision to free Catharina than he regrets it (II, 206-207). Again we see the unstable mind of a man who knows only passion. But this opinion, too, is hardly expressed when it is once more reversed: he reaffirms his earlier decision to free Catharina from her imprisonment and thus to placate the Russian Czar and envoy, but he does so only because another thought has suddenly occurred to him. By granting her freedom he can, at the same time, give her the freedom to choose whether she wishes to become his bride on the very same day or to die. Thus the dialogue with the Russian envoy has finally given him a way to satisfy a passion quickly: either he will consummate his desire for Catharina by forcing her to marry him that very day or he will slake his thirst for revenge by punishing her refusal with death. In his mad rage he sums up the decision he has suddenly made with the following words:

... Sie sol auch sterbend fühlen
Wie heiß der Zorn entbrand / den nicht ihr blut zu kühlen (II, 217-218)

A climax in the portrayal of Chach Abas as a man of passion has been reached, and the three successive dialogues have made this climax visible in a way that could only be possible in a drama.

IV

Until now we have endeavored to show how the entire artistry of this play is centered on an obtrusive dichotomy, and that this dichotomy becomes most visible in the drama's two leading characters, one of whom represents the world of conscience, the other the world of passion. So clearly delineated are these two worlds in the drama that the purpose of the play's inherent dichotomy can only be to stress the existence of these two worlds. But we would not be doing justice to the drama if we were to content ourselves with directing attention towards this dichotomy. The play is designed, above all, to give the audience a theological message. This message is revealed when the consequences of leading a life either dictated by conscience or determined by passion become apparent to the audience.

From the beginning of the play the dramatist's theological position is indicated clearly. As we are told in the preface: those who, like Catharina, obey their conscience and reject the world of passion turn their faces "von dem was Vergänglich auff die ewigherrschende EWIGKEIT." But those who, like Chach Abas, become slaves to their passions are so blinded, we hear (I, 5), that they will never find eternity:

> Ein Irrlicht ists was Euch O sterbliche! verführet
> Ein thöricht Rasen das den Sinn berühret. (I, 9-10)

Particularly deceptive, the allegorical figure of Eternity states, are the passions for fame, riches, and love:

> Wie mancher steigt durch Rauch des falschen Ruhms verblendet
> Nach hoher Ehr und fält /
> Wenn der Gewächsten Flügel schwung bey gar zu naher Sonnen endet.
> In höchste Schmach / und wird ein Scheusal aller Welt.
> Ach thörichte! der vor euch sinckt auff beide Kni
> Wündtscht offt euch da zu sehn wo nichts denn Tod und Müh.
> Ihr die ihr euch in Gold verliebt
> Und Süd und Ost durchrennt umb andre reich zu machen;
> Wo bleibt ihr wenn man alles übergibt?
> Wenn eine Stunde schleust die Reitung aller Sachen?
> Wer Jahre zehlt denckt der wol je an mich?
> Wehn liebliche Gestalt betreuget /
> Wehm seiner Wangen Farbe leuget
> O HErr O Himmels HErr helt er sich schöner wol als dich? (I, 43-56)

The rewards for following these passions are death and dust:

> ... Vor mir liegt Printz und Crone
> Ich tret auff Zepter und auff Stab und steh auff Vater und dem Sohne.
> Schmuck / Bild / Metall und ein gelehrt Papir /
> Ist nichts als Sprew und leichter Staub vor mir. (I, 67-70)

But in addition to making his own theological position clear, the dramatist wishes to offer to his audience a "hidden" theology. In fact, it would appear as if it were his foremost objective to unveil to his audience those consequences of deciding between conscience and passion that are hidden from the eyes of the world and are only visible to the eye of God. Everything in the drama, we believe, leads up to this revelation.

The consequences are made particularly visible in the dramatic portrayal of Chach Abas, who is punished for having dedicated his life to satisfying his passions. Consistent with the dramatist's intention to present a "hidden" theology, the drama unveils to us the punishment accorded to Chach Abas that would otherwise remain hidden from the eyes of the world because it occurs within him.

Hardly have we heard that Catharina has suffered the death of martyrdom as a result of her refusal to accept the hand of Chach Abas, than we become a witness to a scene in which the king, in an evident fit of madness, is inwardly tormented to such an extent that he quickly resolves to spare her life (V, 145).

Then, as he is unable to soothe the torment gnawing at him because she is already dead, he seeks to purge the feeling of guilt torturing him by casting the blame on the man who had carried out the king's order to murder Catharina immediately if she did not accept the royal marriage proposal. Iman Culi, he insists, did not exercise the proper prudence when he carried out the king's command so rapidly (V, 150-153) and consequently must die for his failure (V, 161). However, Chach Abas does not admit to himself that he had earlier ordered Iman Culi either to carry out his command or be beheaded (III, 445 ff.), and that Iman Culi, therefore, had no alternative but to obey. He thus seeks in vain to lighten the burden of guilt tormenting him. Iman Culi makes this clear to the audience:

> ...O frembder Fall der Dinge!
> Indem ich / was der Fürst so scharff befahl / vollbringe;
> Fällt dieser Sturm auff mich. Er reumet was er kan
> Durch unser Hände weg / und greifft uns selber an
> So bald die That vollbracht / wir freveln ihm zu gutte:
> Er wäscht von eigner Schuld sich rein mit unserm Blutte! (V, 161-166)

To the eyes of the world, however, Chach Abas is freed of all guilt. The Russian ambassador, representing the Czar and the entire Russian nation, is convinced by Chach Abas' spokesman, Seinel Can, that Iman Culi is the real murderer. The ambassador is willing to relieve Chach Abas of all responsibility for what happened in the kingdom, provided the king executes Iman Culi for the deed that has been committed (V, 341 ff.). The Russian envoy's wish is fulfilled when Iman Culi is beheaded (V, 344). By making it appear that he has brought the murderer to justice, Chach Abas succeeds in convincing the mightiest nation in the world that he bears no guilt. But any crime that can be successfully hidden from the eyes of the world cannot, as the theology of this drama makes visible, remain hidden from the eye of God. The drama's final scene reveals to the audience what the eyes of the world did not see: that Chach Abas did not succeed in convincing himself that Iman Culi was Catharina's murderer, and, above all, that God knew the identity of the real murderer. In an admission which Chach Abas makes to the dead Catharina (in other words: to himself), he states:

> Princessin schau! Princessin wir bekennen
> Entzeptert! auff dem Kny! und mit gewundnen Händen /
> Daß wir unrechtmässig dich betrübet /
> Daß wir ein Stück an dir verübet /
> Welches aller zeiten Zeit wird grausam nennen.
> Princessin heische Rach!
> Ach! Ach! Ach!
> Laufft! bringt die Mörder umb / die Hand an sie geleget!
> Weg Zepter weg! Chach hat hir selber Schuld! (V, 410-418)

By convincing the Russian ambassador of his innocence, and by thus placating the mighty Russian Czar, Chach Abas succeeds in escaping all earthly punishment for the criminal way in which he tried to satisfy his passion, but he cannot succeed in escaping God's punishment, the punishment of the burning fires of hell:

> Ist Catharina Tod und Chach ist noch bey Leben!
> Und wil der Himmel nicht /
> Gewaffnet mit der Glut von Schwefel=hellem Licht
> Feuer nach dem Kopffe geben? (V, 345-348)
> ...die Scharen auß der Hellen
> Gehäret mit Schlangen / gerüstet mit Plagen /
> Die haben Holtz zu diser Glut getragen /
> Und uns gesucht ins Grab durch deinen Tod zu fällen! (V, 371-374)
> Feuer! Feuer! Feuer! Feuer! Feuer kracht in disem Hertzen!
> Wir verlodern / wir verschmeltzen angesteckt durch Schwefel=Kertzen!
> (V, 408-409)

To be absolutely certain about the "hidden" theological message the dramatist wishes to convey with these references to punishment by fire and brimstone, one need only compare these verses with those verses in Luther's Bible (the one with which Gryphius was most familiar[6]), in which we are told how God uses the identical elements of fire and brimstone to punish those who only follow the dictates of their passions. Of great similarity, for instance, is the way in which, according to Luther's translation of the Old Testament, God punished Sodom and Gomorrah for their sins of passion:

> Da liess der HERR Schwebel und Fewr regenen von dem HERRN vom Himel er ab...(1. Mos. 19)[7]

No less striking, however, is the punishment recorded in the New Testament that is given to those who live a life based on passion. According to Luther's translation we hear:

> Wer überwindet / der wirds alles ererben / und ich werde sein Gott sein / und er wird mein Son sein. Den verzagten aber / und ungleubigen / und greulichen / und Todschlegern / und Hurern und Zeuberern / und Abgöttischen / und allen Lügenern / der teil wird sein in dem Pful / der mit fewr und schwefel brennet. (Offb. 21)

In much the same way that the consequences of choosing between conscience and passion are revealed in Chach Abas' character portrayal, the tragedy of Catharina proves instructive. The difference is that instead of our seeing how God punishes those who have chosen to follow their passions, we now see how God rewards those who have taken care to obey their conscience. In Catharina's character portrayal, too, a "hidden" theology is unveiled, for the rewards that accrue to her are also visible only to God. The drama, however, makes visible to us what would otherwise remain invisible.

This "hidden" theology of Catharina's dramatic portrayal reveals an astonishing fact: Catharina, who, as far as the eyes of this world could see, was a prisoner, is actually quite free (I, 83; III, 508; IV, 55, 243, 300, 305); she does not feel imprisoned at all because she has at her disposal the resources of the entire infinite kingdom of eternity (IV, 244). Chach Abas, by contrast, who in the eyes of the world apparently enjoyed the sovereign freedom to move about in his entire kingdom, is actually a prisoner; he is the prisoner of his passions, for all his actions and thoughts are governed and tormented by these passions. The ruler who to outward appearances wears the crown is, in the last analysis, a poor and pitiful wretch. Catharina, who appears utterly impoverished, may be said to wear a crown which is far more splendid than anything this world could see: the crown of the kingdom of eternity (IV, 244, 263, 298, 370; V, 178). Chach Abas, putatively lord over all he surveyed, actually suffers the unbearable tortures of the burning fires of hell (V, 407-409); but Catharina, who according to the eye-witness accounts of her ladies-in-waiting is burned alive (V, 1-118), does not really feel the pain of any fire at all (V, 12, 20, 35).

To reinforce our earlier observation regarding the certainty of the "hidden" theological message contained in the references to Chach Abas' punishment by fire and brimstone, we can turn again to Luther's Bible for verification of the "hidden" theological message that is now dramatized in Catharina's reward for her faithfulness to her conscience. In Luther's translation of the Epistel of St. Paul to the Romans we read:

> Denn so die Heiden / die das gesetz nicht haben und doch von natur thun des gesetzes werck / dieselbigen / dieweil sie das gesetz nicht haben / sind sie jnen selbs ein gesetz / damit / das sie beweisen / des gesetzes werck sey beschrieben in jrem hertzen / Sintemal jr Gewissen sie bezeuget / da zu auch die gedancken / die sich unternander verklagen oder entschuldigen / auff den tag / da Gott das verborgen der Menschen / durch Jhesum Christ / richten wird / lauts meines Evangelij. (Röm. 2)

NOTES

[1] Strangely, there exist only two essays which claim to be interpretative studies of this drama: Clemens Heselhaus, "Gryphius. Catharina von Georgien," *Das deutsche Drama*, ed. B. von Wiese (Düsseldorf, 1958), vol. I, pp. 35-60; and Hans-Jürgen Schings, "Catharina von Georgien. Oder Bewehrete Beständigkeit," *Die Dramen des Andreas Gryphius*, ed. G. Kaiser (Stuttgart, 1968), pp. 35-72. In neither of them is *conscience* (*Gewissen* or *conscientia*) ever mentioned.

[2] The quotation is taken from: Martin Opitz, *Buch von der Deutschen Poeterey* (Breßlaw, 1624). A copy of this work, without page numbers, is located in the library of the University of Kiel.

[3] Cf. Eberhard Mannack, *Andreas Gryphius* (Stuttgart, 1968), pp. 29, 31; Willy Flemming,

Andreas Gryphius (Stuttgart, 1965), pp. 29, 123; Marian Szyrocki, *Andreas Gryphius* (Tübingen, 1964), pp. 22-23.

4 A copy of this work is located in the library of the University of Kiel. The word *conscientia* is found in vol. I, pp. 409-412.

5 These Roman and Arabic numbers, and all such subsequent ones in our essay, refer to acts and verses in the play. Quotations are taken from vol. VI of Andreas Gryphius: *Gesamtausgabe der deutschsprachigen Werke*, ed. H. Powell (Tübingen, 1966). Italics are our own.

6 Cf. Willy Flemming, *Andreas Gryphius*, p. 114.

7 All quotations from Luther's Bible are taken from the one printed in 1546 by Hans Lufft at Wittenberg.

JAKOB MASEN'S *OLLARIA*:
COMMENTS, SUGGESTIONS, AND A RESUMÉ

George C. Schoolfield

I

The Jesuit Jakob Masen (1606-1681) is known to Milton scholars because of the good possibility that his epic on the fall from grace, the *Sarcotis*, provided "the idea and some of the scenes," as Faber du Faur puts it, for *Paradise Lost*.[1] To students of the German Baroque, he is — before all else — the author of a work on dramaturgy, the third part of his poetics, the *Palaestra Eloquentiae Ligatae*.[2] His own dramas, adduced as examples in the same third part, have received less attention; only recently, with the essay of Harald Burger on Masen's *Rusticus imperans* — the Jesuit's treatment of the "king for a day" theme — and Burger's critical edition of this most frequently performed of Masen's plays, has interpretive attention been given to Masen as a practicing dramatist.[3] Burger follows the instructive method of showing, with copious quotations from the dramatic theory, how Masen practiced what he preached: what Burger has written is of essential importance, both for the study of a major Baroque comedy and for the investigation of Masen's manual for playwrights. The present essay has the aim of calling attention to another of Masen's seven extant plays, the *Ollaria*, of making a few proposals and conjectures about it, and of attempting to place it in what may be called a thematic context; for it treats, as the title would indicate, a popular dramatic figure, the avaricious man — the man who hides his fortune in a pot in order to preserve it.

II

We do not know when Masen wrote his plays; it has been concluded on the basis of a statement to the reader of the *Palaestra* — the statement is placed between the "pure" comedies (*Ollaria, Rusticus imperans,* and *Bacchi schola eversa*) and the tragedy (*Mauritius Orientis Imperator*) on the one hand, and the "mixed" plays on the other (*Josaphatus, Androphilus, Telesbius*) — that some plays from Masen's hand were given for the delegates at the Congress of Münster in 1647 and 1648:

> Hactenus in purè Comicis Tragicisve substitimus, nunc & mixtas comico tragicoque argumento actiones... in scena proponemus, avidè aliàs, cum in theatro spectarentur, prae superioribus exceptas, idque potissimum Monasterii Westphalorum, quando armis hoc seculo anni 1647, & 1648, diversorum regnorum collisione serventibus, legatis per Europam eodem confluentibus, de pace universali disceptatum, et denique conclusum fuit.[4]

That Masen's plays were given at Münster under such brilliant circumstances, however, provides no argument at all that they were composed in the later 1640's; indeed, in order to have been given before so illustrious an audience, they must have acquired a certain reputation already. Johannes Müller has sidestepped the question of the date of the plays' composition by his statement that "Seine Dramen erscheinen in den letzten Kriegsjahren auf den rheinischen Bühnen und finden bei den katholischen Friedensgesandten in Münster Beifall"; Bernhard Duhr is not much more helpful with his note that the yearly reports of the Münster Jesuits speak of many comedies being played between 1642 and 1648, particularly comedies by Masen.[5] In his own introduction to the plays, Masen himself implies that they are "youthful" works: "Siquid inveneris neglectiori expolitum pumice, juvenili studio, quo haec pleraque fudi, ignosce."[6] These youthful plays may well have been written during the decade coming directly after Masen's entrance into the Jesuit order at Trier, on 14 May 1629, years which he seems to have spent as a schoolman at Trier, Cologne, and Emmerich.[7] Even as a student at Cologne he had tried his hand as a dramatist, writing a play, *Vitus et Modestus*, which embarrassed the adult Masen as he remembered its highflown style; it had been acted by him and his school-fellows ("cum meis coætaneis") once upon a time (*Palaestra* III, p. 46).

As for the sequence in which the plays were written, we are once again constrained to do guesswork.[8] The fact that *Ollaria* is given first position among the three comedies (and, indeed, among the collected plays) may be an indication of its early composition; still another sign pointing in the same direction is the extreme simplicity of its structure and content, a characteristic rather repetitiously noted by the few commentators on Masen's dramatic production: "Die Ollaria, die Heilung eines jungen Geizhalses nach einer Erzählung Petrarcas, baut sich mit regelmässiger, steigender Entwicklung, Höhe im dritten und heiterer Lösung im fünften Akte sehr einfach und ganz nach Masens Theorie auf."[9] To which must be added, of course, that, whatever theory Masen may have had in his head at the time of composition, he had not yet put it on paper; the essay on dramaturgy was written after the plays had been completed, and as Masen states [p. 129], he learned by doing: his instructions to would-be playwrights end with the words "expertus didici."[10]

As compared to the more subtle and complex comedy of the drunken peasant and the duke,[11] and the attempt, in the *comedia fabulosa, Bacchi schola eversa*, to make a comedy on a plot of the author's own devising,[12] the straightforwardness of *Ollaria* would make it a first publishable and playable effort; Masen is unwilling to fly too far or too high. Still another argument that may be presented for the dating of *Ollaria* before the *Rusticus* is the frequency with which the latter is mined for examples in the two *Libri poesis dramaticae* of the *Palaestra*; *Rusticus* is mentioned ten times, including one very long example, while *Ollaria* is cited but twice.[13] Probably the theorist Masen felt that *Ollaria*, with its beginner's simplicity, was less happy a hunting ground than his later works. If Masen's plays are his "juvenile studium," then *Ollaria* is in all likelihood the most youthful product among them.

III

The two instances in which Masen mentions the *Ollaria* have both to do with simple aspects of the simple play. The first (p. 37) tells how the poet has tried, in *Rusticus imperans* and *Ollaria*, "to correct the archaic quality of [Plautus] by means of the purity and moderation of [Terence]," and, yet, "to animate the mildness of [Terence] by means of [Plautus'] genial strength at representing manners, all the while remaining within the bounds of refinement, which, in his pursuit of the character of the basest of men, [Plautus] has sometimes exceeded."[14] In other words, Masen will attempt to write a comic language both philologically and morally unimpeachable (as he must, for school use), yet with the vigor and colorfulness necessary for capturing an audience and making a forceful point; an effort he recommends warmly, then, to would-be dramatists. The second mention of *Ollaria* is to be found in Chapter 13 of the Second Part (p. 102), under Masen's discussion of the "productio dramatum, eorumque errores, ficti an veri esse debeant" ("the prolongation of the dramas, and their misapprehensions, whether these ought to be true or invented"). The misapprehension, to Masen's mind, is a main tool of the dramatist, and Chapters 9 through 22 of the Second Part are devoted to it. The core of the event must be true, Masen says:

> It will be the poet's job to compose his material in so truthful a way that it is able to serve the enjoyment [of the spectators]. Thus, in *Ollaria*, the truth of the matter consists in the fact that the son has buried money beneath the ground (for which the father has then substituted stones). Prudently, [the son] accepts the father's admonition, that he should be just as concerned with the stones beneath the ground as with a lump of silver. Whoever will have set forth this material with his own additions, complexities, and many other events, will not destroy the story in the drama, he will ornament it; and, unless he narrates it ingeniously, he will win less credence for the truth of his account.[15]

Once having come upon the proper stuff, it is the poet's task to dress it up properly, so that he may more readily persuade the audience, even as he entertains it, of the rightness of his argument. The *errores* may be devised by the poet himself; by means of them, he lengthens his play, making the tale of the treasure's concealment and exchange both worth listening to and convincing.

The tale itself is taken from Petrarch's *De remediis utriusque fortunae*, Book II, Dialogue 13.[16] Masen, who evidently was fascinated by the material, used it once again in his tractate on the Christian use of wealth, *Aurum sapientum sive ars sine scelere et cum virtute ditescendi* (Cologne, 1661), where he retold Petrarch's tale at some length (pp. 23-25); the tractate was translated into German in 1666, as *Aurum sapientum, d.i. Kunst, christlich u. ohne Sünde reich zu werden, aus hl. Schrift*.[17] The tale, as it appears in the tractates, is a severe reduction of the Petrarchan text, of whose many details Masen had made skillful use, some twenty or thirty years before, in the composition of his *Ollaria*. In Petrarch's dialogue between Ratio and Dolor, Ratio tells a story in illustration of his point that possessions bring woe in their wake:

> Lately, among the Italians, there was a certain noble and distinguished man, wealthy enough in his ancient properties, wealthier in virtue, but not in money, so that he had learned to be accustomed to the role not of money's guardian, but its steward and its master. His first-born son, exceedingly zealous in business matters, had acquired great wealth and a large amount of gold by watchful care and great stinginess; and it was a wonder to behold, the youthful generosity of the old father, and the ancient frugality of the youthful son. Often the father exhorted him not to betray his own nature, not to be forgetful of piety and reputation, nor to let the respect properly owed him and his natural rights be debased for the sake of money's acquisition. In short, he should wish that his riches would be of some value to himself and his aged mother, and to his younger brothers and his relatives, and his friends, and to the poor. Wealth was made for these ends, and not merely for guardianship and torment: thus far the father. But a song is sung in vain to the deaf or to the miserly. At length it came about that the son was absent on public business, and with some select men undertook a journey to the Pope at Rome. While he was absent, the father, straightway taking advantage of the situation, made his entry with new keys of the treasure chamber and the cask, and removed the treasure, useful to no one, from its place of hiding, and clothed himself and his wife and the whole family most exquisitely. He bought horses most handsomely caparisoned, silver vessels, fine furniture, and at length a spacious house, but one only a little elegant, which he enlarged with new additions, and adorned it with distinguished pictures and made it seem smaller with all those things which a generous and elegant and abundant life requires, furthermore giving much to the poor. But he put back those sacks, in which his son had kept his gold, filled and stuffed with sand and pebbles from the river, returning them to the place they had been before, and everything was bolted shut. All these things were done in a very short time, because both the intention of the distinguished old man and the money itself were ready. The brothers went out to meet the returning son on the way; he stood rooted to the spot at their approach, astonished by a manner of dress he had not seen before, and he asked whose the horses might be, and where the clothes came

from; and, happily and with a boyish ignorance inexperienced in all things, they said that they belonged to the lord their father, and that they had many other horses at home in the stable, and that their parents had a varied and royal dress; and he said "I have begun to be more and more astonished at each and every thing." Then, when he reached the threshold of the paternal dwelling, he hardly recognized his parents and hardly recognized the walls themselves, and now filled not with simple wonder but with amazement, and beside himself, he approached the chamber and the cask swiftly, where, since he saw nothing changed on the outside, he grew calm in his spirit for a little while. And realizing that the presence of his comrades and haste allowed him to do no more, he quickly opened the chest, and, having looked at the sacks and ascertaining that they were swollen and obtruding in their usual manner, he went away, soon, with some public matters having been taken care of, to return home, where he closed himself into the chamber, opened the casket, inspected the sacks, and, finding the gold turned into sand, cried out. His father ran in and said: "What's the matter, my son, why are you lamenting, why are you weeping?" "I have lost," he replied, "the money which, acquired by so many vigils, by so much labor, I had put aside in these sacks. I am despoiled in your own home, father." To this his father replied, "Why do you say you are despoiled? Do I not see that the sacks are full?" And he, weeping: "It is sand, father, not gold.' As soon as he said this, he showed his father the open sacks. "Yes," the old man said, betraying no emotion, "What does it matter to you whether the sacks are filled with sand or money?" A memorable statement, a remarkable thought. Because money lies idle in the hands of many people, doing naught save to occupy a space and a spirit, in some people's hands it is used evilly and dishonestly, and, finally, it is employed fruitfully by but a few.

To which Dolor replies: "I have lost the money which I love.' And Ratio says:
> You are undone by an evil love. For the love of money is avarice. The less you have of it, the less you wish it. For that satirical fact has become known by experiment, that one desires those things less which one does not have. Moreover, that loss is greatly to be desired; for money is a thing of great good, to which a greater evil is inseparably joined. *Dolor*: I have lost the sweet defence of my life. *Ratio*: How do you know that it is not rather its bitter destruction? Many more people have perished on account of wealth than for poverty's sake.

What qualities in this anecdote from Petrarch's consolatory reader attracted Masen? Plainly, as the schoolman-dramatist he was, he saw the opportunity for extending a chain of *errores* from the seriously meant prank undertaken by the good father: as in Plautus' *Aulularia*, a treasure first hidden and then removed afforded a large opportunity for the construction of misapprehensions. (What some of these misapprehensions were will be demonstrated later on, in the discussion of *Ollaria* proper). Also, Masen perceived the chance the tale afforded for the addition of amusing servant-figures, patterned after those of Roman comedy: both the father and son would have retainers. But, before all else, the tale in Petrarch presented Masen with a new twist on an old comic theme; a reversal of the traditional roles of father and son. Indeed, Petrarch himself had given admiring attention to this feature of his story: "Erat illi filius

35

primogenitus, fori negociis apprimé industrius, qui vigili cura & parsimonia ingenti magnas opes multumque auri quaesierat: & *erat mirum visu, in patre sene juvenilis largitas, in juvene filio senilis tenacitas*" (italics added). Using Petrarch, Masen could, and did, make an instructive reversal of the familiar pattern in Plautus and Terence, where the miser is the old man, the *senex avarus*, and the young man is the *juvenis prodigus* or, at least, *largus*. The great misers of Roman comedy are old Euclio of Plautus' *Aulularia*, and, somewhat less radically shaped, old Theopropides of Plautus' *Mostellaria* and old Demipho of Terence's *Phormio*. As for the young man, interested in life (and girls) rather than gold, he is Lyconides, who will have his Phaedria, whether or no, in the *Aulularia*, (where, to be sure, he is not Euclio's son but his would-be son-in-law), Philolaches, Theopropides' son, enamoured of Philematium in the *Mostellaria*, and Antipho, Demipho's son, desirous of making an honest woman of Phanium, in the *Phormio*. (In fact, the young man is doubled here; Antipho is aided by his cousin, himself lusting after a music-girl).

Even as he employed the same Plautine-Terentian sources as so many other dramatists of his time,[18] Masen thus created what appears to be a *unicum* in the dramatic portrayal of the miser in the sixteenth and seventeenth centuries.[19] In the Italian comedy of the Renaissance, the lead of the Palliata is followed very closely: in Lorenzino de' Medici's *L'Aridosia* (1536), Aridosio is the old and tight-fisted father ("un vecchio avaro"), and Tiberio is his son, in love with the slave-girl Livia (no slave-girl after all, it happily turns out). There are three youths in the play who mix passion and honorable intentions. Erminio, Tiberio's cousin, wants to get his pregnant Fiammetta out of a nunnery; Cesare wants to marry Aridosio's daughter Cassandra, but cannot because Aridosio will not provide her with a dowry; and Cesare's father will not let him marry a girl without one. In order to embellish the already involved intrigue of his play,[20] Lorenzino also borrows the detail of the haunted house from the *Mostellaria*, of which Masen would make use in *Ollaria*: Tiberio and Livia have a tryst in Aridosio's house, and the old man is persuaded to believe that devils inhabit it; afraid to enter, he is characteristically concerned about the treasure hidden inside. Lorenzino was imitated, in turn, by Pierre Larivey in France, with *Les esprits* (1579), in which still greater space is given to the story of the haunted house; the line can then be readily followed to Molière's *L'Avare*, which draws on both Plautus and Larivey,[21] and from Molière to the five comedies on miser-figures by Goldoni. As the figure develops in this Romance tradition, the account of the amusement caused and the damage done by avarice is adorned by complications of intrigue, or by giving the miser some special additional trait apparently incompatible with his stinginess (as in *L'Avare*, with the marriage plans of Harpagon, or in de la Hoz y Mota's *El Castigo de la Miseria*, where the miser has the hidalgo's pride); but the generation-roles remain constant throughout, "vecchio avaro" and "giovan innamorato."

Another factor remains constant as well: the plays about the old miser are all comedies, and the worst overt punishment the old man gets is ridicule. Giovambattista Gelli's Ghirigoro de' Macci, in *La Sporta*, is genuinely happy about the infant addition to his family, his "nipotino," even though it has cost him some money; and, while Harpagon will spend the remainder of his days isolated by his avarice, he does have, after all, the thing he loves best, "ma chère cassette." It is left up to the spectator to decide whether or not he is a tragic figure (as Rousseau believed he was); the essential good humor of the Roman comedy, which did not moralize about the damage the miser did to his family and friends, is never lost. However, it may well be that Molière's comedy comes closest to tragedy of all the plays in the Plautine-Terentian tradition, just because Molière is particularly aware of the Scriptural admonition: "He that is greedy of gain troubleth his own house" (Proverbs 15:27), and surely that is what Molière's Harpagon has done. Should some scholar undertake the task of writing a comparative study on the miser-figure in the drama of the Renaissance and Baroque, and its continuation in Goldoni's theater, he might want to contrast the "happy" end of the miser-plays which stick close to the Roman pattern with the savage ending of those plays which do not, and which, indeed, regard the unrepentant avaricious man as deserving of dreadful punishment. In such plays, to be sure, the miser has been given additional and complicating traits: Marlowe's Barabas, boiled alive at the end of *The Jew of Malta* is, of course, a Jew and a man who wants revenge for his loss of money at least as much as he wants the money itself — as Shylock does; Jonson's *Volpone*, finishing "sick and ill indeed," loves money for its own sake but loves woman's flesh and sheer trickery too; the rich man in the plays "vom reichen Manne und armen Lazaro" (see, for example, Georg Rollenhagen's), crying out for mercy, which he does not get, has withheld his money from charity but spent it willingly to make a show. Yet all these fellows have been guilty of the deadly sin of avarice, perhaps the worst sin of all: "For the love of money is a root of all kinds of evil" (I Timothy 6: 10),[22] and, in the cases of Barabas, Shylock, and the rich man of the parable, they "trouble [their] own house." Here, too, a remarkable play by the Danish pastor and playwright, Hieronymus Ranch, should be mentioned; in *Karrig Niding* (1599), the eponymous hero practices his vice to the distinct disadvantage of his wife, his children and his servants — starvelings all. Locking up his gold and the household provisions, he sets off on a trip to acquire more money, in clear illustration of avarice's insatiable nature: "He that loveth silver shall not be satisfied with silver; nor he that loveth abundance with increase: this also is vanity. When goods increase, they are increased that eat them; and what advantage is to the owner thereof, save the beholding of them with his eyes?" (Ecclesiastes 5: 10-11). In his absence, the clever tramp Jep Skald appears, persuades Niding's wife to break open the larder, and, after all have eaten their fill, Skald takes the willing Fru Niding to bed — evidently, Niding has kept her on short rations here, too. When Niding returns, he is confronted by a conspiracy of wife, lover, and servants. Now, he is the beggar in fact, and has lost not only treasure and family, but even his identity. It is the subtlest and perhaps the cruellest punishment a stage-miser receives.[23]

In the *Ollaria*, Masen would appear to belong to the Roman-comical line; he need but adhere to Petrarch's text in order to achieve a very happy ending — the young man is mocked (mildly), is cured, and is restored to the family. But in the *Ollaria*, as in another Jesuit comedy on the miser-theme, Jacob Bidermann's *Jacobus usuarius* (1615-1618?), a terrible punishment — the most terrible punishment — is avoided in the nick of time, or, in Bidermann's play, at time's end. In Bidermann, old Jacobus is about to be taken off to hell, when the Blessed Virgin, summoned by the miser's *Angelus custos*, recalls that he has said the rosary in her honor daily, and so he is saved. Whatever we may think of Bidermann's main argument, we must remember that he, too, has taken the pattern of *senex avarus / juvenis prodigus* to make his point; much of the comedy of the play's first four acts, precisely as in Plautus and Terence, depends on the efforts of the son's servant, and the parasite Hericlo, to get money for the boy. But Bidermann is aware, as Masen would later be, of the root of the trouble. The boy has been afraid to approach his skinflint father: Jacobus, again, has "troubled his own house," and richly deserves the fate he almost gets. Just so, Petrarch's skinflint son (it is made abundantly clear) has done great damage to his own family; and Masen, reading the anecdote, saw with equal clarity the abyss into which the son's vice would have led him, had he not been converted. Thus, Bidermann and Masen both, while using the Roman tradition and ending their miser-plays happily, come close, by implication, to the harshness of the line of plays described in the preceding paragraph.

It is scarcely surprising, of course, that the Jesuits held damnation at the ready in their miser-plays; they were clergymen. And, it is worth noting, a special factor in their training had made them particularly keen to the harm avarice could do. In the Second Week of the *Spiritual Exercises* of St. Ignatius, a meditation for the Fourth Day is devoted to the proper attitude toward money, and that attitude's role in salvation. There are three "couples" of men in St. Ignatius' example: the first pair may wish to get rid of their passion for money, but take no steps toward that end until it is too late; the second pair will want to have a union with God and yet keep their money too; the third "wish to remove the attachment, but so wish to remove it as also not to be tied by any affection to the thing acquired, or the not keeping of it; but wish solely to will that thing, or to will it not, according as God our Lord shall put it into the will, and according as shall seem better to the person concerned for the service and praise of His Divine Majesty."[25] Bidermann's Jacobus, not a very bright man, is like the bunglers of the first pair: luckily for him, he accedes to the wish of the Virgin Mary, that he become generous, in Act V, Scene 3, providing at least some basis (apart from his mariolatry) for his salvation in Scene 12.[26] Reading Petrarch, Masen may well have detected a representative of the second class in the skinflint son (who must have been a sanctimonious sort, since the summons of the

Pope made him leave his treasure), and a representative of the third class in the father, who practiced and preached the correct use of wealth — the subject to which Masen would later address an entire book, the *Aurum sapientum*. The *Ollaria*, therefore, is the youthful Masen's compact, dramatic statement on a matter whose importance had been made very plain to the novice of the Jesuits; the *Aurum sapientum*, in which the Petrarchan tale is retold at the very outset, is the aging schoolman's reflection on the same topic. Petrarch's tale had fallen on fruitful ground, and ground well-prepared by Masen's teachers in Cologne and Trier.

Finally, one more element in Petrarch's tale spoke to Masen, spoke, we should guess, both to the Jesuit and the dramatist. It is, quite simply, the resemblance between the account of the good Italian nobleman and his tight-fisted son, and the parable in Luke 15 of the good father and his wastrel offspring. Masen was aware of the extensive use to which the parable had been put in the drama of the previous century, and in his own.[27] Its popularity rested on a variety of factors: 1) the opportunity it afforded for an introduction into "Christian" drama of the Plautine-Terentian parasite, as in Macropedius' *Asotus* (1507?, printed 1537) and Gnaphaeus' much imitated *Acolastus* (1529), and then, by extension, the chance it gave for a detailed depiction of low life to a high purpose, as in Wickram's *Der verlorene Sohn* (1540); 2) its ready employment in confessional polemics, as in Burkhard Waldis' Low German and Lutheran play (1527) and then in Hans Sachs' (1556), in which faith very patently gets the palm over good works, and, from the other side, in Hans Salat's Catholic drama, where, in his preface, the Lucerne clerk expresses the hope that the time's "vil verlorne sün und kinder" will return "zum rechten vater" (1537); 3) the ideal suitability of the stuff to the pedagogical ends of school-dramatists, of whatever faith they may have been. But, again, Masen discerned the piquant turn the familiar matter had received. In Petrarch, as in Scripture, the son returns to a forgiving father; but, in his behavior, Petrarch's youth has been anything but *prodigus*, clinging to his wealth like grim death; while the father, given the opportunity, has become *prodigus* for the greater glory of God, in the manner recommended by St. Ignatius. It will be recalled that Petrarch makes much of the manner in which the father spent the money ("He bought horses most handsomely caparisoned..."), a theme returned to and expanded when the son comes back from Rome. It will be recalled, too, that the father has other sons, as much the victims of their brother's parsimony as the parents have been. Here, again, Masen perceived the chance for fascinating change; for, in Petrarch, the other sons are in utter agreement with their father's behavior. Thus the problem of the parable's disgruntled older son, who so clearly represented good works to the Lutheran mind, and whose presence in the parable so visibly embarrassed Salat in his Catholic treatment, is avoided; Petrarch's (and Masen's) skinflint is eldest of the brood, but little is made of the fact. Whether or not he has "faith," we do not know; but we are aware that — unlike the rest of the family

— he is quite oblivious to the necessity for good works. Masen is not re-telling the biblical parable; but he wants his audience to be reminded of it while watching his play, and to note the resemblances *and* the contrasts.

IV

The drama of the sixteenth century was regularly used to make comment upon large contemporary events, e.g., the Reformation; on occasion — perhaps more frequently than we are aware — it was used to discuss smaller happenings or local situations as well.[28] (We think of Nikolaus Manuel's inclusion of actual figures from pre-Reformation Bern in *Vom Papst und seiner Priesterschaft*, of the depiction of the much-detested Duke Heinrich of Braunschweig-Wolfenbüttel in Naogeorgus' *Incendia*, of the appearance — a little more flattering — of Charles V in Birk's Latin *Susanna*, under the mantle of Nebuchadnezzar). In the seventeenth century, too, we can readily find plays which speak directly, or obliquely, about a specific and recent happening. Everyone knows that Vondel portrayed the legal murder of Jan van Oldenbarnevelt by Maurits of Orange in *Palamedes* (1625), and that Vondel's *Leeuwendaelers* (1647) is a plea for the reunion of the Netherlands; everyone knows of the commentary on contemporary events in the *Friedensspiele* of Rist and others; everyone remembers the horror expressed by Gryphius at the execution of Charles I in *Ermordete Majestät*; and scholarship has lately made us aware that the Jesuit dramatist of the senescent Leopold's court, Johann Baptist Adolph, attempted to make dramatic amends for his order's involvement in Ferenc Rákóczy's escape from his Austrian jailors: *Judae Maccabaei gloriosa in Deum fiducia* (1702) celebrates the triumphs of Judas Maccabeus (Prince Eugene) and the downfall of Nicanor (Rákóczy).[29] The Adolph drama comes on the heels of the operatic plays in which the Jesuit Avancini (outdoing even the Protestant Lohenstein in his devotion) had celebrated the house of Hapsburg on the stage. There are, of course, other plays in the annals of the order about "contemporary" Jesuit vicissitudes that took place at some distance (the Japanese and Ethiopian martyrs, for example); but it would be interesting to discover what plays of the order dealt, however circumspectly, with the order's immediate circumstances in a European locale.[30] (A similar practice was certainly not unknown in the Jesuit lyric: see Sarbievius and Balde). That such plays could make their points by inference, understandable only to the initiate or a specific audience, is to be expected; for, diplomats that they were, the Jesuits would not want to be entrapped in political controversy by a member's dramatic statement; and, since the plays of the order were, usually, a "transportable" or "exportable" article, as good for use at one of the order's various centers of learning as at another, clearly local references would be forbidden as such. On the other hand, there was nothing to prevent a Jesuit drama from being employed for ends of persuasion — indeed, was that not the main purpose of these plays, some of which, such as Bidermann's *Cenodoxus*, could reduce an audience of Bavarian and Austrian noblemen to tears? The persuasion could well be applied with respect not only to eternal but to temporal and local matters, that is, if the dramatist was sufficiently skillful at oblique statement.

In the case of the *Ollaria*, it may be suggested (although it cannot be proved) that Masen, with his attention to the question of the proper use of wealth, and his reversal of the customary roles of *senex* and *juvenis*, has made a comment upon conditions pertaining in the Lower Rhenish province of the order, and particularly, in Cologne, during the first half of the seventeenth century. Although we know little about Masen's life, it is clear that Cologne lay at its center. He was born at Dahlem (near Schleiden) on the old Roman road from Cologne to Trier; he studied at the Gymnasium Tricoronatum in Cologne, and took part there, on 16-18 November 1627, in a performance of a *Stephanus* drama, in which he played four different roles. Two years later, the gifted young man contributed an essay to the volume commemorating a major event in the history of Cologne Jesuits: their entrance into their new and splendid church (later called St. Mariae Himmelfahrt), the building of which had just been completed after eleven years of work. As has been mentioned above, Masen entered the Jesuit order at Trier in the spring of the same year, 1629; on 3 May 1648, he took his solemn vows of profession at Cologne. Where he spent the intervening nineteen years cannot be determined with exactness; F. X. Kraus says that he taught at Cologne until 1640, Scheid speaks (and Duhr copies him) about "14 volle Jahre" spent in pedagogical work at Cologne. But he appears also to have been at Trier for a time (he served as a preacher there in 1641), and to have taught at Emmerich; his connection with Münster, during the Congress, has already been mentioned. From 1654 until 1657 he was at Düsseldorf where the *Palaestra* was completed; the latter part of his life, according to Scheid and Kraus, was spent in Cologne again, where he died. In short: Cologne, and its Jesuit "college", were Masen's earthly home.[31]

The situation of the Jesuits in the Rhenish province was a curious one; Peter Canisius had founded the first German house at Cologne in 1545, and the province developed in a most satisfactory way, with the number of members increasing from 381 in 1601 to 800 in 1626,[32] when it was divided into the Upper and Lower Rhenish provinces. However, the order was confronted with problems of a nature less familiar, if not unknown, in the Upper German and Austrian provinces. The Rhenish province could not draw upon the direct and continued financial support and, as matters would turn out, military protection, of a major European house, as did the Jesuits of the Upper German province (with the Wittelsbachs) and the Austrian province (with the Hapsburgs). The Wittelsbachs, to be sure, were generous donors to the Cologne Jesuits because of familial connections; after the conversion and marriage of Gebhard Truchsess von Waldburg, in that splendid scandal of the 1580's, Ernst of Bavaria had become electoral prince and archbishop of Cologne. Ernst's brother, Duke Wilhelm V of Bavaria — like Ernst, a sometime student of the Jesuits and, on the Bavarian throne, their devoted servant — had given large sums of money to the Jesuit college at Cologne; after Ernst's death in 1612, he was succeeded by his nephew Ferdinand (the son of Wilhelm the Pious) who, together with his elder brother Maximilian I of Bavaria, contributed funds for the building of the great Jesuit church. However, such financial support from the Wittelsbachs was necessarily limited, especially after the beginning of the Thirty Years' War; the numerous delays in the building of the church and the adjoining college (for a fire in 1621 had destroyed both the Jesuits' older spiritual headquarters, the Achatius Church, and the building used for the college) bear witness to the difficulties involved.

It was, after all, a most expensive undertaking; the edifice was to be the largest of Cologne's many churches,[33] save the cathedral itself, and easily the most splendid product of that urge to build which characterizes the order everywhere in the Lower Rhenish province during these years;[34] in his work on the construction of the German Jesuits, Joseph Braun remarked that: "In ihrer Wirkung ist die Kölner Kirche zweifellos die bedeutendste unter den vielen Jesuitenkirchen in Deutschland."[35] At the outset, no cost was spared to secure the services of the best architectural and artistic talents; for the architect of record was Christoph Wamser, who had earlier designed the Jesuit church at Molsheim, the Catholic rival town to Strassburg; the sculptures of the interior were done by, among others, Jeremias Geisselbrunn of Augsburg. To the thinking of the order, it was appropriate that the Society of Jesus should be so splendidly represented by this monument, which filled contemporary observers with wonder.[36]

All the same, the building of the church (and of its smaller companions elsewhere in the province) aroused criticism in the city and beyond. For one thing, the Jesuits were not popular with the inhabitants of Cologne; it has been pointed out that they had no sense for the "Verquickung von Kirchlichem und Weltlichem, wie sie nun einmal die Geschichte und Verfassung der Reichsstadt mit sich brachte",[37] and that their asceticism often found itself in conflict with the "kölnischen Hang zu Geselligkeit," and that the order's "monarchistic" mentality, and its system of command-and-obedience, was scarcely in harmony with the traditionally democratic way of thought of the Cologne citizenry.[38] By the time the exterior church had been completed, it had cost 130,000 Reichsthaler, a sum which should be regarded in the light of the fact that Germany had not yet recovered from the fearful inflation of the "Kipper- und Wipperzeit" of 1621-22, during which, because of the flood of worthless currency, a great many private fortunes had been wiped out. It should be added that Cologne itself was in special economic decline, a process which had begun in the previous century and which was encouraged by the events which (as readers of sixteenth-century

German literature know) darkened the last years of that pleasant Cologne family-chronicler, Hermann von Weinsberg: the "Cologne War" (1582-84) between the supporters of Gebhard Truchsess and those of Ernst of Bavaria, and the spilling over of the revolt in the Netherlands into Cologne's territory; within the city itself, persecution of the Protestants, a persecution in which the Jesuits and their friends played a leading propagandistic role,[39] led eventually, in 1608, to the expulsion of the city's Protestant families — an act which meant, among other things, that a good number of commercial houses went elsewhere. In addition, the city — which never came under attack during the Thirty Years' War, but which lived in constant fear of such an event — had had to put an extraordinary amount of money into its fortifications, and the citizenry was requested to make voluntary contributions of money for the work, a request which drew so wretched a response that the city government threatened to draft able-bodied males for forced labor on the barricades.[40] Cologne, although declining, was still a rich prize; and the war, in fact, contributed to its temporary financial advantage, for the city provided supplies to both sides (an activity of which we get an inkling in the Cologne episodes of *Simplicius Simplicissimus*);[41] but the rigidity of the city, in confessional and guild matters, led directly to the loss of this advantage, and the passage of economic leadership to Frankfurt.[42] Money, in other words, was very much on the mind of Cologne's citizens, and they could well ask themselves why the Jesuits could spend so much of it on a splendid edifice — the Jesuits who were not popular, the Jesuits who had been threatened with expulsion (among those "adverse events" to which Aegidius Gelenius hastily refers before expatiating upon the "Novi Templi descriptio"), the Jesuits who had even run afoul of the Cologne guilds because they imported their workers in good part from the outside. (The order had to appeal to the prince-archbishop for protection against the irate cabinet-makers.)[43]

Masen had been a student of the Jesuits at Cologne during the long years of the Jesuit church's building; that performance of the *Stephanus* play in which he took four parts was given in the church, and in connection with its completion; he was certainly aware of the mood in the town. It would seem likely, then, that with the *Ollaria*, Masen intended a defence of the Jesuits' building program, both in Cologne and elsewhere. The old man of Petrarch's story buys and expands an already spacious house, filling it with fine adornments, and he does it for the greater glory of God; he also sees to it that his other sons are well taken care of; and he gives to the poor. All these elements corresponded not only to the *Spiritual Exercises'* reflections on the proper use of wealth, but they provided the material for a dramatic apology for the order's activity: its church building, its educational endeavors, and its concern with public welfare — a concern which was great, and to which the life of another member of the Lower Rhenish province, Friedrich Spee, bears witness. We do not know, of course, the nature of Masen's audiences, other than those at the Münster Congress; but we may assume that when the *Ollaria* was given at the Tricoronatum in

Cologne, parents of students and the *honoratiores* of the city attended, here as elsewhere. The hint could not have been lost upon them: that the Jesuits had acted in keeping with the will of God. And we may wonder if the play did not make a subsidiary point of local propaganda as well: with its emphasis on the good things of life, it could offer a gentle reminder that the Jesuits were not quite as sternly ascetic as the people of Cologne had thought.[44]

The Petrarch-material could likewise afford the chance for another sort of persuasion, here less in specific favor of the order than of Roman Catholicism in general. The polemical literature of the Jesuits was vast and often cruel; Jakob Gretser was far better known to his contemporaries as a polemicist than as a dramatist (the capacity in which he is read today), and Konrad Vetter has entered general literary history solely on account of his valor at this "ständigen, schärfsten Federkrieg mit den Protestanten";[45] and, in the Northwest, Masen himself was a polemicist of distinction, or notoriety, depending upon the side from which he was viewed. His hope was to see Germany reunited in Roman Catholicism, and his *Meditata concordia protestantium cum catholicis in una confessione fidei ex sancta scriptura descripta* (1661) was discussed at several meetings of the electoral princes, according to Masen's biographer Scheid. The proposal was honored by coming under sharp attack from Protestant quarters.[46] Jesuit drama, on the whole, was not used for the Counter-reformation's directly polemical purposes; here, again, the drama works with hints instead of tirades — hints, for example, in *Cenodoxus* concerning the exaggerations of Neo-Stoicism and late Humanism. The confessional situation in the Northwest was so delicate, and feelings were so raw, that only the slightest pressure from a skillful dramatic finger was needed to excite pro-Catholic and anti-Protestant identifications: to make an audience see the Holy Mother Church herself in the figure of the wise, generous, and cultured old man, and Calvinism, specifically, as the grasping son, who — in particular as Masen expands the unpleasant qualities of Petrarch's figure in his play — is sly, unfeeling, and quite without any sense for the esthetic. In the eyes of a Catholic of the Lower Rhine, and certainly of a Jesuit, the Calvinists were the enemies *par excellence*. They were triumphant, more or less, in the nearby Netherlands, they had been regarded as a source of disturbance, if not worse, in Cologne since the middle of the previous century (the "liberal Catholic" Weinsberg has an instructive anecdote concerning the anxiety Calvinist preachers caused among the city's good citizens); it was believed that Calvinist agents from the Netherlands had instigated the demonstrations against Cologne's city government that took place in 1609, demonstrations in the calming of which, for the rest, members of the Marian Sodality, an organization under the Jesuit aegis, and Peter Johan Rutger, a Jesuit who was currently cathedral-preacher, had a decisive part.[47] Nor was Cologne the only trouble-spot in the (Lower) Rhenish province. The Jesuits at Emmerich were repeatedly called to the aid of Catholics in the Duchy of Kleve, where the events of the long struggle over the Jülich-Kleve succession had placed

Catholics and Calvinists in direct confrontation with one another. (On the eve of the Thirty Years' War, one of the two heirs, Wolfgang Wilhelm of Pfalz-Neuburg, had become a Catholic for his marriage to the sister of Maximilian of Bavaria; while Johann Sigismund of Brandenburg had been converted to the Reformed Church.) Elsewhere, in Siegen, the Jesuit order was expelled in 1632 by the Calvinists, after having made remarkable progress in the work of conversion, supported by the troops of Johann the Younger of Nassau-Siegen, himself a Catholic convert. If, as we have assumed, Masen wrote the *Ollaria* as a young man, then it is not surprising that he put hints into it concerning matters of immediate concern to the order which had educated him and of which he became a member; these were the topics of discussion, and of action, in the milieu in which he grew up. But, as the dramatist fully aware of the customary "universal application" of the Jesuit play, he restricted himself to the giving of signals to the initiate. *Ollaria* could have spoken as an anti-Calvinist document — or a document with anti-Calvinist overtones — to the members of the order itself, familiar as they were with the often repeated story of churches and schoolbuildings supported by Catholic rulers, destroyed or turned to other uses by Calvinist ones.[48]

V

We have just discussed the suggestions the play might have made to the audience of the time; however, they are not the main stuff of the play. Like all Jesuit dramas, *Ollaria* teaches a universal lesson, a lesson that could be grasped, and grasped readily, by viewers quite unfamiliar with the situation in Cologne or in the Lower Rhenish province. The *Ollaria* is a straightforward play, and a play made for acting; it corresponds fully to the program which Masen announces in the introduction to his dramas: that he believes that "plays are more to be acted than to be examined," that he means to appeal more "to the ear of the listener [in the audience] than the eye of the reader"; he will offer "something so moderated that the meaning of the words is to be discerned by the performance of the ears alone, without the laborious investigation of the mind, ... something neither to be investigated with great study nor becoming worthless through extreme rhetoric," although "some people have written tragedies more suitable to the eyes of the reader than the ears of the listener."[49]

In order to show what Masen has done with Petrarch's material, and to tell what message, or messages, he has for the public, a resumé of the *Ollaria* will now be given. It is probable that not very many students of Germany's literature have read the play.

The prologue informs us that the comedy is not a mere web of "theatrical nonsense and Attic fables": "Auctor nobis Petrarcha est, locus Italia." Then Masen calls attention, as we might have expected, to the unusual nature of the story in Petrarch, of the "avarus juvenis et liberalis senex," and tells briefly how the father had attempted to persuade the son to give his money "to God, to the poor, to his family, and to himself." But persuasions were in vain, and so the father took recourse to "honesta fraus"; the son is brought back to the ways of piety, the poor are given succor, and the family home is adorned "cultu nobili." This last deed is done, the prologue says, by the son, his gold gone, his way of life improved; in fact, in the play to follow, it is the father who does these good things, before the son is aware that his money is missing; but we may assume that, once he is transformed at the play's end, the son will continue in the father's path. He will imitate the father, and the members of the audience are expected to learn and do likewise.

> Haec acta quondam, agere nunc rursum juverit,
> Ut quisque ex auro mores formet aureos.

Act One

The first scene is given over to three allegorical figures, Avarice, Deceit, and Wealth (Avaritia, Dolus, Plutus), the former two, in cahoots with one another, chide the third, asking him why, at present, Italy is not devoted to his cause. Wealth puts the blame on the Christians (we may think here of the dispossessed gods in the opening scenes of Bidermann's *Philemon*). Avarice and Deceit advise him that he still has many secret admirers — that, indeed, the world cannot work without him. Following their catalogue of the things (by no means necessarily bad in themselves) wrought by Wealth, he is told, flatteringly, that mankind can become sated with every object of desire, save him: "Omnium rerum aliqua est satietas, praterquam tui." Desiderius, the son of Abundius, is pointed out as a particular devoté of Wealth: look at him and behold a zealous worshipper. All well and good, Wealth retorts, but once men have me, they hide me — a repetition of what Aristophanes' Plutus says in the play of that name (11. 236 ff.), a play which also deals, more cynically than Masen's, with the proper use of money. Hereupon, the allegorical figures leave the stage and do not return; Masen, with his frequently noted desire for a clean-lined "classicism," does not give them speaking roles elsewhere in his oeuvre.[50] But they have served their purpose; Wealth is not essentially evil — indeed, "he" is a necessary component of life. With these few lines we have been made to think of him as something of a powerful booby, who does not know his own strength, who wants somebody to love him.

In scene two, the human action of the play begins. The young man Desiderius (whose name speaks: he is the "yearner" for money) tells of the power which wealth brings — princes themselves, not just small fry, wish the company of a rich man. Desiderius' speech here, as throughout the play, is shot through with ironies of which he is not aware: he boasts of the popularity which wealth brings but, suspicious wretch that he is, wants forever to be alone. He gives wealth a vivid, "living" description (a "spring of bubbling water") but buries it beneath the ground. His servant, Strobilus — "with faithfulness long tried, and bound by generous promises" — is summoned; he bears the name of the honest servant of the bachelor Megadorus in Plautus' *Aulularia*.[51] The language of the conversation between master and man is full of double meanings: the hiding place of the gold is called a tomb, and Desiderius fears that "hunting dogs" will smell the corpse and dig it out of its grave. (In other words, the gold, removed from use by the miser, has died and become putrescent; its owner — we may continue the thought — is in danger of spiritual death as well.[52]) Strobilus promises that he will keep close guard: the exaggeration of his language — he will be as watchful as still another dog, Juno's Argus, as devoted to duty as a hen sitting on golden eggs — is intended to make the spectators laugh, but also to make them think: he is debased by his inclusion in his master's passion. Desiderius then expresses the wish that the inhabitants of his father's house be blind, "caeci," whey they pass by the hiding place; he himself, of course, is the victim of blindness of spirit. (At the end of Act II of *Cenodoxus*, Bidermann has a similar play on *caecitas* in the conversation between the learned professor of Paris and the rustic.)

No scene in *Ollaria* is without its twofold humor; in the back-and-forth between Desiderius and Strobilus, quick laughs have been elicited by the hyperbole of the master's attitude and the hyperbole of the servant's speech: "I shall serve you with all the eyes I have, and with both feet." A slower but deeper amusement is aroused by the instructive and unintentional ironies of both partners. In scene three, where Abundius (the "abundant" man in spiritual and cultural fact) attempts to persuade Desiderius to abandon his passion for wealth, the simpler humor lies in another verbal trick: Abundius indulges in word-plays, puns of a readily comprehensible and, at the same time, sententious sort: "I'd call you a golden boy if you did not cling so tightly to gold," and: "Once upon a time, without gold, the age was golden." A youth of very sharp wits (albeit with no insight into himself), Desiderius fights back adroitly, inquiring whether the industry by which he has acquired money is somehow evil (doesn't father want a hard-working son?), and pointing out, once again, that Queen Money rules the world (hasn't father learned this lesson from experience?). The parry of Abundius is an observation on the fickleness of fortune: experience has taught him that today's Croesus may be tomorrow's Codrus. The opponents are both tenacious: a long dispute ensues, in the course of which, as the speakers grow more breathless, and more annoyed at one another, extended speeches change into stichomythies, and these into antilabes; the young practical man, Desiderius takes the line that it is what a person has, not what he is, that counts; and Abundius, the gray-thatched idealist, makes exhaustive listings of the evils which arise from avarice. In his disposition of roles, Masen does not permit the moralizing Abundius to get an easy victory; indeed, there seems to be no way the old man can breach Desiderius' defence; for Desiderius very rightly observes that "Money is the spirit and blood and sinews of public life."[53] But then, a good stage psychologist, Masen allows Desiderius, zealous and confident, to talk his way out of his strong position; in the heat of his praise of money's virtues, Desiderius cries out that riches are the very stuff of generosity and beneficence (the last of his several unexceptionable statements, and his last speech in the scene); and the audience is reminded that Desiderius, having buried his wealth, cannot put it, and has not put it, to any of the excellent uses he so enthusiastically describes.

Realizing that he has not out-argued his father, and made uncomfortable by the interest the old man has showed in his gold, Desiderius turns to his servant in the first act's finale. Strobilus needs to be made aware of the new danger to the treasure. Taking up the theme of blindness-and-sight again, Desiderius adorns it with carrion imagery: "Would that [Abundius] would be more the old man, less keen-eyed ... by his vigilance, he gets the jump on my own watchfulness everywhere ... [he's the] very picture of a vulture, opening its mouth for the prey."[54] Strobilus tries to soothe his master; he has told Abundius no more about the treasure "than, sleeping, a dormouse [would have told] the ground" — "Non plùs quàm dormiens / Humi glis." (Strobilus and the other servant figure in the *Ollaria* are walking glossaries of the more respectable idioms from Roman comedy, instruments by which Masen teaches the Roman comic language "in moderation," thus achieving a pedagogical end mentioned in both the introduction to the dramas and the dramaturgy itself.) Then Strobilus proposes that the treasure be moved to another cache, while stones, sand, and iron scraps are placed in the present tomb; the father will be allowed to discover the rubbish, and the son, coming up, will cry out that thieves have stolen his treasure. Avarice's best friend is deceit; Desiderius seizes delightedly upon the scheme, and reminds the audience of the corpse-theme once again as he says: "Eruamus auri hoc cadaver. Nondum putruit," continuing with another funereal word-play; "Arenam hac in arena sepeliamus quantocyus." The transfer is quickly carried out, and so the support is prepared for the string of *errores* on which much of the subsequent action of the play is hung — invented misapprehensions, not in the original Petrarchan tale. (And so the illustration was provided for the point about true fable and invented misapprehensions which Masen would make in the *Palaestra* later on [see pp. 33-34 above].)

Act Two

Devoting the first scene to the four brothers of Desiderius, Masen might seem to succumb to an endemic disease of the school drama — the adduction of roles over and beyond dramatic necessity. But, by their conversations, the brothers reveal the extent of the family's poverty, a revelation which Abundius, in his dignity, cannot make. (The mother of the Petrarchan story is not included in the

Ollaria, because of the customary Jesuit avoidance of feminine roles.) The brothers are brave enough to laugh at their indigence, and are meant, of course, to get the audience to laugh with them; Masen lets them begin with talk about their ragged dress. Otto, the brother who elsewhere serves as a spokesman for the group, makes fun of Marinus for "preening himself in his plumes." The plumes are rags, Marinus retorts, adding a comment on the contrast between the family's clothes and its station: "Codri herculè / De stirpe videmur esse, qui censemur nobiles." Remaclus makes a homely joke about the "windows in his clothes," and Claudius contributes a pun both descriptive and up-to-date: "Ex Lapponum / Ego genere videri possim." (The word-play on "Lappi" or "Lappones" and German "Lappen" was gladly made by supporters of the imperial cause in the Thirty Years' War, who liked to apply it to the troops of the Swedish crown, especially the ragged and uncouth Finns.)[55] Otto, we now realize, has opened the passage with a word which can be taken as national paronomasia; he has called Marinus "Germane," "brother" and "German"; following Claudius, he steers the national jibing in another direction: Do not his boorish brothers recognize the latest foreign fashions when they see them?

> O rudes hujus seculi!
> An nescitis eam nunc esse elegantiam Gallicam,
> Vestem habere perlustrum, hinc et inde pendere segmina.

Now, after these sartorial hints concerning the poverty of the German church,[56] and the identity of two of its foes, the Swedes and the French, the scene's humor is concentrated directly upon the family's wretchedness again: the stomach-aches that hunger causes are brought up, and Otto inquires if there is not at least some bran-bread in the pantry, "Nonne panis furfuracei / Quantum satis in armatio?" Claudius' retort, using one of the simple *figurae etymologicae* meant for the audience's amusement, at the same time gives a reminder that the watchers are beholding a variation upon that familiar dramatic topic, the Prodigal Son:

> Si furfuribus
> Pasci tibi volupe sit, ad porcos cum prodigo migres.

The poor starved brothers are, of course, not prodigal; the stingy brother is, in his inverted way; and the father, as it turns out, will rejoice more over the miser-prodigal's conversion than over the aid which Otto, Marinus, Remaclus, and Claudius so gladly give in bringing the conversion about. Having called the parable to mind, Masen gets his plot moving once more; very much his father's son, Otto delivers a *sententia*, decorated with a pun, on keeping up appearances ("Multi ut famam tueantur palàm, occultè fament"), and then tells his brothers that fortune has told him in his sleep how to find that place where Desiderius and Strobilus hang out, and where the treasure is hidden: "Today we shall find out how clever we are."

Scenes two and three are reserved for verbal duels between Abundius and Strobilus, and between Abundius and Desiderius. In both cases, the old man tries to convince his opponent of the error of his ways — to persuade Strobilus that he is wrong in being so devoted to Desiderius, and to persuade Desiderius that he is wrong in putting his faith in Strobilus. And, in both cases, Abundius convinces himself that he has succeeded; he can easily be misled because he does not know that his opponents have moved the treasure. He praises the faithfulness of Strobilus, however misdirected it has been, then promises him a reward if he will tell where the treasure is, then excuses him for his involvement in the matter ("errasti, sed absque malitia"); as Strobilus persists in his silence, Abundius tells him that faithfulness in a bad matter is worse than perfidy ("In re mala fidem praestare, pejus est perfidiá"), and, thinking he has harangued the servant sufficiently, confronts him with a clear choice: the galleys, if he refuses to speak up, a share in the treasure, if he tells: "Si *par*ueris, *pars* auri tua erit merces, elige," Abundius says, punning true to form. As clever as his namesake, Strobilus II in the *Aulularia,* or Terence's Phormio, Strobilus appears to give in; throughout the scene, he has toyed with the old man as skillfully as any Roman slave or parasite, letting the public know early that he has Abundius on the hook: "Vici, senem occupavi." Strobilus has caught him, to be sure; yet the servant, in his fashion, has fallen victim to a delusion more lasting, and more dangerous, than the old man's, since — pleading a loyalty to Desiderius which he, apparently, is about to give up, in order to maintain it in fact — he cannot perceive the ultimate truth of Abundius' arguments.

The same pitting of cleverness with good intentions against cleverness with bad ones is the stuff of the following conversation (II/3) between Abundius and Desiderius. Summoned by his father, Desiderius finds the old man weeping; Abundius will soften Desiderius up by appealing to his filial devotion. Having done so (he thinks), he wipes his eyes and goes straight to the attack with the weapon which (he believes), he has won from Strobilus:

> Quid est cur servo homini
> Aurum concredas? tibi, patri, familiae subtrahas?

Why trust a servant? Blood is thicker than water. Confidently, the father offers to test Strobilus' loyalty while Desiderius is hidden behind a curtain; Desiderius agrees. As he does so, he uses a phrase which predicts the circumstances of his conversion in Act Five; presently, however, it must seem to be only another comical exaggeration of language, or, to the more perceptive minds in the audience, still another expression of the suspiciousness which never leaves Desiderius:

> Volo. Et si vel mutiat
> De auro abs me condito, *reus ero* (italics added).

"All right. And if he even so much as mutters anything about the gold I've hidden, I'll be a culprit." Called in, Strobilus willingly agrees to follow Abundius' plan: that Strobilus and another servant, Messenio, should go to dig up the gold, but in disguise, in case they should meet the young master. Strobilus himself adds a helpful detail; the excavation should take place at night, that

Desiderius may be the more easily fooled. (Behind the curtain, Desiderius utters groans, groans intended as signals to the audience's ears;[57] he has hoped for a while that Strobilus has been at work on the agreed plan to trick Abundius ["Adhuc spero fraudem faciet"], but as Strobilus makes his contributions to Abundius' scheme, Desiderius — gnawed by the suspicion which makes the miser destroy himself — gives way utterly to misapprehension, misapprehension of the opposite sort from that into which Strobilus has led Abundius: Desiderius thinks faithful Strobilus is false, Abundius thinks Strobilus, faithful in fact to Desiderius, is false to the son, faithful to himself. And Strobilus persists in the worst misapprehension of all; putting his faith in the wrong place for the wrong reasons.) After Strobilus leaves, Desiderius expresses his rage at the "false servant" and says he will go after him directly; but Abundius, the good man now infected by the distrust which a single member's avarice brings to the whole family, tells the servant Messenio not to let Desiderius out of his sight: does he fear what his son might do to Strobilus, or that his son will hurry off to move the treasure forthwith? Desiderius says that there is no need for a bodyguard; he will take his father to the treasure — that is, he will take him to the place where the stones and sand are; thus he will outsmart both Abundius and, if his suspicions about Strobilus' perfidy are correct, the servant too. Abundius likewise believes that *he* and his family have triumphed; Strobilus (offstage) that he and his master have won, not knowing that he has fallen under his master's suspicion.

Meanwhile, the brothers (II/4) have found the first location of the gold on their own, following the tip which Fortune gave Otto in his sleep. The four sacks are dug out, without demur from Desiderius; he identifies a large bag of gold (marked A) and a small one (B), a large bag of silver (C) and a small one (D). Filled with joy at his son's sudden willingness to share the treasure ("Commune bonum est, vobis illud ac mihi condidi," Desiderius mouths piously), Abundius proposes a drawing of lots between himself and Desiderius, so that the son will not be wholly deprived of the fruits of his diligence. (A moment before, Abundius has chided energetic Otto for trying to take out the sacks himself; again, Abundius shows the traits of the father of the prodigal son, rejoicing at his bad offspring's presumed conversion, not at his good offspring's enthusiastic righteousness.) In a casket scene less romantic than Shakespeare's, Messenio holds out the sacks one by one behind the backs of the father and son: Desiderius gets a mere C and curses: "Sors adversa fuit. Damnationis haec nota est. Resigno." (Does he speak out of his true miserly nature, momentarily forgetful that he holds a sack of rubbish in his hands, or has he decided to play his role of reformed miser so subtly that he will *pretend* to fall back into his lately "abandoned" miserliness, in order to be the more convincing in his next *replique*?) As Abundius is drawing his first sack, B, Desiderius lets out a far more piercing whoop; this time the audience can be sure he is acting, albeit a part that he was born to play. After "Herculè, Pol, Mecastor, occidi," Desiderius pretends to faint: he has "discovered" the rubbish in the sack. His father and his brothers, as much the good family members as he is the bad one, work hard to bring him back to life; and the "secret" is out: the gold, the revived Desiderius moans, has been stolen. Directly, Desiderius tries to cast suspicion on the brothers who, a moment before, have been so anxious to aid him; then Abundius (who once again has acted as the prodigal son's father, scolding the brothers for taking umbrage at Desiderius' charge) proposes Strobilus as the thief instead, and Desiderius allows himself to be persuaded to agree. Spinning his plot further (since he does not trust Strobilus), he asks his father and brothers to tell Strobilus nothing of what has happened: he will await Strobilus himself. Messenio need not get into his disguise.

Apart from its piling of misapprehension upon misapprehension, the second act has let the audience see characters: good-hearted Abundius, using his wiliness, such as it is, for what he trusts will be his son's reformation, Strobilus, good servant of a bad master, a clever man but not clever enough, and Desiderius himself, who has developed from the smart and greedy youth of the opening to a monster of duplicity: a small-gauge Volpone, ready to sacrifice even his fellow conspirator, as he has abused the sympathies of father and brothers. The last scene (5) of the second act is a soliloquy by Desiderius, giving, as the descriptive title tells us, congratulations to himself for his trickery. I alone, he says, am able to weave so intricate a cloth of tricks: "Servem fratresque fefelli, et quod palmarium est, senem!" He is particularly proud of the last-named victim, "hanc vulpem," because he appreciates one aspect of his father's character — the old man's own trickery in attempting to get the treasure; yet, himself in deepest error, Desiderius cannot grasp his father's reasons for wanting to win: he imputes to him a greed like his own. And that cleverness of his, for which he praises himself at length, has failed him at another point, a failure of which he, this time, is cognizant: he still does not know what Strobilius' intentions are. Was Strobilus in fact going to perform the trick on Abundius which Desiderius, getting ahead of him, himself carried out? Or did Strobilus have more selfish designs? Desiderius will wait, in disguise, until Strobilus arrives for what the servant thinks is his appointment with Messenio, and then his faith will be tested. In human relations as in matters of money, Desiderius is forever desirous of more, ever greedy, without giving of himself; Strobilus is too good a servant to be cast away without proof positive. But Avaritia's boon companion is Dolus, and Desiderius expects everyone else — even the faithful servant — to be as deceitful as he is.

Act Three

The third act is the briefest of the five; but it contains, all the same, a turning point in the exterior action of the play (Desiderius is called away to Rome), and in the interior action (Desiderius becomes convinced at last of his servant's genuine devotion). This conviction will prepare, in its turn, for the salvation of

Desiderius at the conclusion of the last act. As we have beheld the perfidy of Desiderius toward all who surround him in the soliloquy ending Act Two, so we have here, juxtaposed, a second soliloquy (III/1), in which Strobilus tells us of the miseries of his lot, but adds that he is determined to stay faithful to Desiderius. The poor fellow finds himself under claims made by two masters:
> Miserrima est servitus duobus eundem Dominis
> Obsequium debere.

He means both Abundius, who still makes demands of fealty on him, and then Desiderius himself. But in his speech we hear the scriptural basis; "Nemo potest duobus dominis servire: aut enim unum odio habebit et alterum diliget, aut unum sustinebit et alterum contemnet: non potestis Deo servire et mammonae" (Matthew 6: 24). Strobilus has chosen to serve the wrong master, and we may feel a grudging admiration for him in his wrongheadedness; in his *error* of serving the master given up to Mammon instead of God. Yet we of the audience, catching the scriptural echo with our mind's ear, are warned at the same time not to be too sympathetic with Strobilus; for his faithfulness derives in part from his own devotion to Mammon, to the gold which Desiderius has promised him. These questions, of choosing the right master and of his own motivation, are too complex for the superficially clever Strobilus to think about very long; instead, his fertile mind works at a continuation of the plot which he believes had been agreed upon in II/2. When Messenio appears, likewise in disguise, Strobilus will give him the sand-filled pot to carry home to Abundius, and then he will charge his fellow-servant with having stolen the treasure when the worthless contents are discovered: thus, Strobilus and his master Desiderius will be able to enjoy the treasure undisturbed. (His essential naiveté is demonstrated by the fact that he never considers the possibility of Desiderius' double-crossing him, although he has had ample chance to observe Desiderius' madly avaricious nature.) To be sure, Strobilus does not have to carry out his plan, made to his master's advantage and to the murderous disadvantage of an innocent fellow-servant; as Strobilus discovers, the treasure is already gone. Thereupon he sees "Messenio" approaching (it is Desiderius in masquerade), and telling himself once again that he must stay loyal to Desiderius, and that "death is preferable to perfidy" ("Etenim certum mihi fixumque est fidem Desiderio/Tueri integram, et mortem tolerare ante perfidiam"), he puts on his own disguise, as Abundius had ordered, following the father's plan, but for the son's sake. Messenio-Desiderius gives a hiss, to tell Strobilus of his arrival, and the latter, as senior servant, orders "Messenio" to dig the treasure out; informed that the hole in the ground is empty, Strobilus begins to beat "Messenio", taking the money out of his hide, as it were. The beating is a part of his own variation on the plot he and Desiderius had devised: blaming Messenio for the theft, he will convince Abundius that the treasure is gone; simultaneously — and, more important still, to Strobilus' way of thinking — he demonstrates once again his "fidem inviolatam" to Desiderius.

After the beating, Desiderius scampers off to remove his disguise; he sees (it is the first moment of flickering insight he has had) that he cannot complain at his servant for having thrashed him:

> Ut Dii nebulonem hunc verberent!
> Sed frustra insonti irascor. Virtus in illo fuit,
> Et amor, & fides in me. Praemium meretur suum.

Such faith is a treasure not to be thrown away; better to accept the beating without complaint, and not to reveal to Strobilus that he has not enjoyed his master's full trust. While the audience is wondering about the nature of Desiderius' reactions here (does the miser still regard Strobilus only as a useful tool, or is there some hint of a genuine regard for Strobilus' virtue?), it will probably overlook the import of what Strobilus says next; indeed, until it has seen the fifth act, where the play almost turns into a tragedy, it has no cause to perceive anything but Strobiline and comical exaggeration in the servant's words, as he tells his master what has happened, events with which Desiderius is perfectly well acquainted:

> Auro herculè tragoediam lusimus, sed quae denique
> evasit in comoediam.

Laughter is caused by Strobilus' exaggeration, laughter is caused by Strobilus' misapprehension, laughter is caused by Strobilus' story of the beating given "Messenio," so violent "that he won't need a rubdown for eighty-two whole days"; but the laughter at the climax of the scene is turned toward Desiderius, who says wryly, "Misereor miseri" — indeed he does feel sorry, with his back still smarting from the blows, and the audience knows how well he deserves them.

The dialogue between Strobilus and Desiderius is cut short by a *sententia* from Strobilus, underscoring what has gone before, filled, as usual, with ambiguity its speaker does not intend: "Qui aurum petit, hoc saepe praemium / Auferre pro auro meretur." Desiderius has sought gold, and has got "this reward," a shock he did not expect; before the play ends, the shock he gets will be a much ruder one than a beating. But now the messenger appears to call Desiderius to Rome; Desiderius is pleased, since the summons bears out the theories he has earlier announced — that powerful people like the company of people with money. Immediately, though, his suspicious mind returns to its primary fixation: what will become of his treasure in his absence? (Even Desiderius' reaction to the Pope's summons has been infected with suspicion: exactly what is it the Pope wants of him?) Ever aware of his master's anxiety, Strobilus now proposes a second transfer of the treasure: it should be moved back to its original hiding place, where no one will think to look. As the faithful Strobilus goes off to fetch the treasure, Desiderius makes still another of those self-justifying speeches of his in which he shows how little he understands his father's motives, and his own; but which has just enough truth in its charges against the old man *almost* to engage the listener's sympathies: we can understand what Desiderius is driving at. After all, he says, my father deserves to be tricked because he himself resorts so much to trickery. And: he does not think himself a miser, ("Senex / Ille avarum esse se non credit"), yet he employs a miser's thousand tricks to find the gold. And: he calls me Euclio (the old miser of the *Aulularia*), but is careful to look after his own money, and to protect it against theft. Desiderius again falls into unconscious and instructive punning with "qui suo utitur": the miser-son thinks of the verb *utor* in its sense of sheer possession, whereas the father *uses*, enjoys the *use* of his gold, and therein lies the difference between them. Having swayed us for a moment, Desiderius — a true Euclio — has pulled the rug out from under his own argument. Upon Strobilus' return with the treasure, the servant is assigned the task of watching it while Desiderius prepares for his journey; and as the scene ends, Strobilus sings a lament on the watchfulness to which miserliness consigns the miser, or, in the present case, the miser's servant: "like a man condemned to the galleys, like a dog tied to a pole." Discontent Strobilus may be, but he still cannot imagine that he might free himself, by a simple decision, from his servitude. He is no wiser than his master.

Desiderius has come close to ruining his father and brothers by his avarice, and he comes closer still to ruining his servants; Strobilus' catalogue of the watchman's miseries has a continuation in the last scene (3) of the third act, where Davus and Messenio, assigned by the ever generous father to accompany the young "Euclio" (now even the servants give Desiderius the old miser's name) on his Roman trip, list the miseries which await them on the road. Here, more than anywhere else in the play, the language and imagery of the *Aulularia* are drawn upon, language and imagery taken, in bowdlerized form, from the conversation between the steward Strobilus and the cooks Anthrax and Congrio in lines 280-327 of Plautus' play. For example, Plautus says:

>   [*Str.*] ...quin cum it dormitum, follem obstringit ob gulam.
>   [*Anthr.*] Cur?
>   [*Str.*] Ne quid animae forte amittat dormiens.
>   [*Anthr*] Etiamne obturat inferiorem gutturem,
>   ne quid animai forte amittat dormiens?

And Euclio saves not only his breath; he also clings to his used bath-water, his hunger, and his nail-parings; in Masen, we find that Desiderius is so frightened lest some of his hair will get away that he shuns the comb, and that, if a flea drinks some of his blood, he hangs onto the insect, lest he suffer some loss. A close comparison of the two scenes will show how restrained Masen is; but he is still able to make pointed use of the kitchen chatter of his two servants, mindful of their hunger-to-come. Earlier in the play, the talk has been about one employment of the *olla*, as a pot for keeping treasure; now, the *olla* is an instrument, usually empty, for preparing food. If the first pot is full of gold and hidden in the ground, then the second, in the kitchen, will be empty, and quite as useless as its buried sister, a homely summation (from homely lips) of the play's lesson about wealth's proper employment. The act ends as Strobilus calls his colleagues to their duties; and Davus makes the smart observation: "Adhuc stomachus noster vacat": "my stomach is empty [and free from duty] just now."

Act Four

Act Four, Scene One, takes up where the third act left off, with low life and hunger, just as Acts Two and Three are linked by the soliloquies of Desiderius and Strobilus. The episode in which a wealthy man is besieged by a beggar, or beggars, has its scriptural source in the story of Lazarus the beggar and the nameless rich man (Luke 16: 19-31), which ends with the rich man's damnation. In dramatic treatments of the theme in the sixteenth and early seventeenth centuries, Lazarus was often surrounded by other beggars, with distinguishing and sometimes comical characteristics. Macropedius' *Lazarus mendicus* (1544) has a blind and good-natured beggar and a sullen lame one, as well as greedy Molobrus, who is a kind of street-entertainer; Rollenhagen's *Spiel vom reichen Manne und armen Lazaro* (1590) retains these figures, and adds a widow and a pair of poor farmers; in Ayrer's *Tragedia vom reichen Mann und armen Lazaro*, the widow disappears, but the peasants are made more miserable still, "die Ermsten aller Armen." In *Cenodoxus*, Bidermann uses the suppliants for serious comedy: Navegus, the ship-wrecked man, is refused succor by Cenodoxus when the latter is alone, but learns from the clever prisoners-of-war, Exoristus and Ptochus, that Cenodoxus gladly gives alms when friends or acquaintances are there to watch.[58] In Masen's *Ollaria,* the scene takes a slapstick form, but it makes a spiritual point all the same: it provides a demonstration of the injury done by Desiderius to a third group, not his family or his servants (although they come off ill, here, too) but to the poor, whose care the scriptures (and Petrarch's tale and St. Ignatius' *Exercises*) have assigned to the man of means. Desiderius fails to perform the work of charity which is a part, a good part, of Abundius' program for the proper use of wealth; the scene is funny but contains the warning (one of the play's many) that, unless he mend his ways, Desiderius will be denied mercy as finally as Lazarus' rich man was. Two beggars with tag-names, Macer and Lausus (like Macropedius' Bronchus and Typhlus, Rollenhagen's Typhlus and Cholus, Bidermann's Exoristus and Ptochus)[59] appear at the gate of Abundius' house; Strobilus, very much his master's brutal man (here, as in his intended trick on Messenio), threatens them with a beating. Lausus is ready to abandon the assault, for he knows Desiderius: he continues the descriptions of Desiderius' miserliness from III/3. Masen's beggars have their origins in the New Testament's parable and in the preaching plays of Macropedius and his successors, but they have learned to talk (once again) from Plautus' servants and parasites:

                Frustra es, Macer.
Frustra, nam faciliùs vena silicis emollibitur
Hic quam homo, arido oleum speras ex pumice.

As Lausus makes his linguistic crescendo on miserliness, Macer tries the line of ever more exaggerated pleas, imploring Strobilus, and through him Desiderius, to have mercy on an empty stomach:

> Per Jovis pateram,
> Per Bacchi te amphoram, per currum ego Triptolemi
> Et Cereris spicas obtestor, per Neptuni denique
> Pisces, per Silvani vitulos, per boves Herculis,
> Miserere vacui stomachi.

Lausus' despairing insults and Macer's hopeful and learned objurations show a kind of verbal virtuosity meant to appeal to schoolboys; when Desiderius appears, at last, the humor changes from words to actions, and we hope that Masen succeeded in his intention of making his schoolboys (and others) laugh all the more. The young man, behaving like the choleric *senex* of Roman Comedy, like Euclio and Demipho, grows so angry that he begins to throw bread from the expedition's supplies at the beggars; Macer thanks him, and Lausus asks to share the punishment: "Hem, & me petite, nam & ego scelestus fui." Davus and Messenio — in a burlesque repetition of the theme of the servant's loyalty ill-applied — imitate the young master's example, and are caught at it by Desiderius, who has just realized that his anger has led him into wastefulness. Davus says that he was but following Desiderius ("tuo id here / Exemplo fecim?"), Messenio that he and his mate acted out of sheer indignation; but Desiderius, again the unreasonable *senex* in youthful form, tells them that, on the journey, they will be docked the rations they have thrown away. Loyalty to such a master leads again and again to bitter reward.

In the three remaining scenes of the Fourth Act, the unravelling of the knot tied by Desiderius' avarice proceeds rapidly. Ever hopeful of pleasing his father, and ever like the true elder son of the parable of the Prodigal, Otto announces that he has found the treasure; likewise, Abundius — as unresponsive to good Otto as he is responsive to bad Desiderius — grows annoyed at Otto's rambunctious shouting and flatly refuses to believe him. But Otto, whose dream it was that uncovered the initial hiding place of the gold, is right; he has followed a dog to the pit and the pot. (In Act One, Desiderius feared that a dog's keen nose would smell out "the cadaver."[60]) Persuaded at last, Abundius accompanies Otto to the site of burial, and asks the strong-armed youth to help him lift the treasure from its tomb, in a phrase that is clearly a resurrectionist's:

> Agedum, mihi dextram commoda, ut hunc mortuum
> Exsuscitemus denuo.

They open the sacks and find the treasure. Overjoyed, Abundius orders Otto to put a false hoard of sand and stones into the ground; as Otto does his bidding, Abundius reflects on his good fortune ("ego senibus senex fortunatior") in finding wealth in sufficient quantity to do good for the poor and family and friends ("multis...pauperibus, familiae, proximis"), and in being able to take away "the bilge-water of avarice...the material of trickery" ("Avaritiae sentinam...illam fraudium / materiem") from his son. Now he understands the son's whole plot, his "vulpine cunning," and the "fainting spell" ("ut jacuit humi prostratus, ut patrem conterruit"). That the lust for gold could have caused Desiderius to play so falsely with the devotion of his father seems the worst of his crimes to Abundius; yet even now the father intends to use his own cleverness in a last attempt to save his son, for he is moved by compassion, like the forgiving father in the parable. Abundius' instructions to the guileless Otto (who gets a quick course in trickery from his father) are interrupted by the return of Messenio. The servant tells how, on the road to Rome, Desiderius grew increasingly brutal to man and beast alike: Messenio's donkey had collapsed, from overloading and from hunger, and so Desiderius ordered Messenio to take up the donkey's load, although the servant too was weak from short rations. Messenio ran away; his flight gets Abundius' approval. Now, after Abundius, ever kind, has seen to it that Messenio has been refreshed, the servant is given detailed instructions about his next job: he is to go into the city and buy new clothes for the family, new tapestries for the house, new provisions for a party, and, finally, is to invite the poor to the feast. The scene concludes as Abundius plans to abandon his "old ruin" of a house and to purchase a new one; all these things must be done before Desiderius returns — "Verbis non potui, exemplo corrigam."

If the cure of Desiderius is to be attempted by the father, then cure of Strobilus falls to the stay-at-home brothers. Otto, Remaclus, Marinus, and Claudius have decided to dress up as ghosts (the *Mostellaria*'s device: "spirits" guarding a treasure) in order to make Strobilus and Desiderius think that ghosts have been at work, should man and master discover the sand substituted for the gold. Abundius approves the plan, albeit unwillingly; taking up a thought uttered by Strobilus himself in III/2 ("Auro...tragoediam lusimus, sed quae denique evasit in comoediam"), he reverses it: Strobilus remarked then that the "tragedy" of the gold had turned into a comedy, but Abundius fears that things will go the other way: "Videte ne ex comoedia nascatur tragoedia," a fear which is almost realized in the last act.

Abundius' anxiety concerns not Strobilus but Desiderius; Otto has said that their trick will perhaps "improve" Desiderius, and, as ever, Abundius springs directly to his prodigal's defence. But the ill, if it may be called that, and the change befall Strobilus alone. Indeed, he is in a bad way before he meets the ghosts. Continuing his argument from III/1, he tells how hard he has tried to be a faithful servant under all circumstances; but the task of being a watchdog (here he takes up his complaint from III/2)[61] is too much for him: only a surrogate skinflint, he has been worn to a frazzle by the miser's inherent anxiety. Suddenly, he catches sight of the "ghosts" near the pit, and, in his exhausted state, is immediately reduced to abject terror: the shades lift the pot out of the hole, dance around it, whisper incantations to it, and appear to carry it down into the hole again to be buried, as Strobilus imagines, in the very middle of hell. The servant is filled with a loathing for gold, he wishes that the gods would destroy it all, he realizes that his life will last longer, freed from a sentinel's care; and he perceives that his master, to whom he has maintained unswerving loyalty, has himself been pursuing a false goal. It may be an acute piece of psychology on Masen's part that he has his Strobilus see the flaw in Desiderius only after he has been taught a "negative reaction" to gold by the spirits; in other words, his loyalty may have depended, to an extent of which he himself was unaware, on his devotion to the thought that he himself would someday be given a share in the treasure. As the transformed Strobilus chatters on and on, he grows ever more aware of the nature of Desiderius' flaw, his unquenchable thirst for money: the master's son, however noble he may be, has attained a state of servitude "as great as any he may serve" ("Quantam hic serviat servitutem assequitur satis"). The more gold he has, the more he needs: he is a slave to his vice. And whatever he acquires, he buries — again, like a useless cadaver ("ut cadaver inutile"). After a description of the full ground and empty larder such avarice causes (the theme first introduced by Abundius in his opening dispute with Desiderius [I/3], and to be taken up again by Abundius in his final plea to Desiderius [V/5]), Strobilus turns to his own case once more, and to a recognition of his predicament, his servitude to the servant of avarice:

> Taedet servitutis oppidò.
> Qui sola spe tantum vivo, rebus tantum incubo.

Here, it would seem, Masen had a chance to expand the character of Strobilus, making him employ his free will: in an abandonment of Desiderius, at least until his master has realized the nature of his own servitude. Instead, Masen leaves Strobilus in the "base" frame of the servant-parasite of Roman Comedy: in the future, he will believe somewhat more in his stomach, and somewhat less in the promises concealed in the earth.[62] Yet, from his servant's standpoint, Strobilus has expressed the lesson the play teaches again and again — the lesson expressed in the title of Hart's and Kaufman's once familiar play, *You Can't Take It With You*. Strobilus says: "Equidem bonis dum aderunt utar bené." — "I'll make use of good things while they're present." It will be the job of Abundius, in the last act, not only to make Desiderius see how the miser slights himself, as Strobilus has just perceived; he must also teach Desiderius (of nobler stuff than Strobilus is, of course) how gold is meant to be used for the greater glory of God. The conversion of the man prefigures, in its limited way, the conversion of the master.

Act Five

The last act begins as the second had, with the good sons passing in review: there, they were in rags, here they parade before Abundius in their new finery, and each is given a fine-sounding word to say, the plural of the proper name of a handsome youth:

[*Otto*]⁶³ Narcissos aequamus. [*Marin.*] Et Hyacinthos. [*Remacl.*] Et Adonides. [*Claud.*] Et Ganymedes.

Abundius tells them to go out to meet their brother, and the quartet wonders how Desiderius will take the change — Claudius rather ingenuously remarking that Desiderius will rejoice if he knows about it. (Masen allows every character to fall victim to misapprehension at some point in the play). Directly (Scene 2) the brothers set out, and, in an extension of Petrarch's story (where the traveler has difficulty in recognizing his siblings), the brothers have to identify themselves to Desiderius. Upon learning that the family has a new home as well, Desiderius begins to comprehend what has happened; as he sees his father, walking royally, dressed splendidly, he wonders if he is awake or dreaming. Abundius replies: "Euge Desideri, fili mi, tene, hic coràm intuor." The incredulous Desiderius asks again: "Pater es?"; and Abundius says: "Sum verò, nisi à me possideas alium." There are parallelisms in these two scenes with the account of the prodigal son's return: in the detail of the son beheld afar, in the preparations for the feast, and in Desiderius' address to his father; but Masen means to make his audience aware how distant the *Ollaria*'s prodigal still is from repentance: Abundius has readied the feast beforehand, in order that it may be a tool in what he hopes will be his son's conversion; and Desiderius addresses his father in disbelief and selfish fear, not in anxious contrition. Only the *misericordia* of the father, in Scripture and in the play, is identical.⁶⁴ The prodigal son in Luke is happy, evidently: "they began to be merry"; Masen's prodigal grows ever more panic-stricken as he thinks of what has happened: he demands to go to the family's former home. Abundius warns him that the old place is infested with ghosts, but Desiderius fears only for his pot ("Ah quàm ollae metuo, ne quod infortunium viderit!") and rushes off to the haunted house.

When Desiderius inquired after Strobilus, missing at the welcome, Abundius told him that the poor fellow was trying to purify the old home — he wrestles with ghosts and is almost a ghost himself ("cum larvis indies / Luctatur, ac penè ipse larva est"). Desiderius finds Strobilus weeping with terror (V/3), comically afraid lest the ghosts come back again, but simultaneously in the clutches of a fear he, and the audience, must take more seriously: lest the gold itself, the bringer of evil, return ("Vereor, ut ad nos redeat / Aurum"). He is not afraid, it should be noted, of some punishment from his master; other thoughts have pushed this customary anxiety of the Palliata's servant out of his head. Still loyal to his master, (and hoping that Desiderius will begin, at least, to see the light), he accompanies his master to the pit, scared as he is. Desiderius urges him on, saying, with unwitting ambiguity: "Contra Inferos / Hodie pugnandum est: non levi pretio certabimus" — "Battle must be done today against hell's powers — it's no small prize we're striving for," and Strobilus continues the thought: "De *vita* hic agetur" [italics added]. It is, indeed, a question of a battle against hell, and of eternal life, although Strobilus is thinking only of his physical skin. Like some monster, Desiderius' strength grows limitless as he battles for the object of his passion, his gold, and he easily bests his brothers, the ghosts, threatening to kill one of them — his miserliness almost leads him to unintentional fratricide. Otto identifies himself, and Desiderius (whose rage becomes ever more violent, like that of old Euclio in *Aulularia*, upon his discovering that Strobilus II has run off with his gold) turns his wrath at his own Strobilus, whom he accuses of having stolen the treasure. Pulling himself together, now that he knows the ghosts are his master's brothers, Strobilus looks into the pit and observes that "the sacks are all there, in the same place and the same number." But Desiderius, examining the trove more closely, finds that they contain sand and stones, a discovery that drives him to attempt murder on Strobilus, shouting that he will make a sacrifice of him ("mactabo hostiam") to the Styx. Strobilus runs away, calling a curious promise over his shoulder: he will give his master satisfaction. Otto tries to calm his brother by telling him that the gold is safe, in their father's hands; and Desiderius, blurting out another of his double meanings, demands to be taken to his father. ("Is it possible that I shall give my life for the gold?": in fact, Desiderius stands in the greatest danger of losing his spiritual life for the gold's sake.)

Strobilus has decided (V/4) to hang himself, thus to show his master that he has stayed true, and to save his master the trouble of carrying out his recent threat. Marinus tries to save him, but to no avail; at his brother's cries for help, Desiderius approaches: he cuts his servant down, ministers to him, and restores him to life; he is as solicitous of Strobilus' well-being after this real near-death, as Abundius had been of Desiderius after his false fainting spell (II/4). Desiderius has almost killed Otto, now he has come within a hair of causing Strobilus' death (recall his prediction about himself in the oath of II/3: "I shall be a culprit," — "reus ero"); here, at last, he shows signs of compassion — his conversion has begun.[65] However, the arguments Desiderius gives Strobilus for a continued life are still from his old, miser's nature: first, he says that the noose is more becoming to him than to his servant, since he, as the owner of the gold, has felt its loss more keenly; and, second, "adhuc in vita tibi mihique es utilis": Desiderius persists in seing Strobilus as the useful instrument (although he has the good grace to remember that Strobilus can be of some good to himself, "tibi", as well). The good servant passes from the play at this point, having made a last remark, ironic and self-deprecating: "To be sure [I'll be useful] — having lost all my labor and your gold." Strobilus does not see that he has been the instrument of his master's salvation.

Finally (V/5), Abundius can make his plea and succeed with it, however unchanged Desiderius may seem at the scene's beginning. Desiderius hurls charges against his father: Abundius has killed master and servant before their death, Desiderius has expended his labors in vain. He still does not realize that he (and his servant) are more alive now than ever they have been before, nor that Strobilus' lost "opera" (of his final speech) and his own "labores" have now been directed toward noble ends: Strobilus' faithfulness toward his master's salvation, the fruits of his master's industry (and greed) toward a fuller and richer life for himself and his father and his family, and all the poor who are dependent on that family. Abundius meets his son's points one after another, as he had done in the first act; but now the structure of their dispute is no longer stichomythic, a conversational form implying an equality of the speakers: making bi-part replies, in which he first describes the evil and then addresses himself to the good which replaces it, the father has much more to say than does the son. Desiderius claims that he has lost everything; Abundius rejoins that he has also lost the burden of worry; Desiderius counters that he has lost the foundation stone of human friendship, Abundius retorts that he will win friends in heaven, "Nam quidquid impensum pauperibus, hoc Deo fuit"; Desiderius says he has lost his possessions, and Abundius replies that fate could have taken them away at any moment: seek the treasure of virtue instead; Desiderius says that the loss of property causes exquisite pain, Abundius retorts that wounds hurt most when they are healing; Desiderius says he is wretchedly unhappy, Abundius says that the miser lacks much, the poor man little. Upon Desiderius' outcry, "Ah utinam morerer!", Abundius observes that his son has made himself unworthy of life at any event. Thinking a little more clearly after this dash of cold water, Desiderius offers the most penetrating of all his charges: "Why have you spent the money on our family, if money is worthless?" Abundius answers reason with more reason: "Volui te nosque sanos, illo frui" — "I have wanted you and the rest of us to use it as reasonable men." The reply could well be cited by those critics who have seen Masen as a forerunner of the next century's rationalism. Abundius speaks in the spirit of the Horatian ode on miserliness (II/2), addressed to Sallustius Crispus, a foe of gold unless it "shines by temperate use":

> ...inimico lamnae,
> Crispe Sallusti, nisi temperato
> splendeat usu.

However, Masen is still a man of his time and his order, ultimately interested in the salvation of Desiderius, not just in his persuasion to a more reasonable way of life. Abundius will show Desiderius that the treasure has not been wasted, that it is more than "integer"; it is "integerrimus." Otto and Marinus bring in the pot, Otto saying: "Appulimus in portum cum hac navi," and the ship of Desiderius' soul, by an extension of the familiar baroque topos, will soon be in port, too. Abundius advises Desiderius to let the "very full pot and crammed sacks" be buried again, and to make no effort to find out what is in them, gold and silver or sand and stones. "Imagine that it contains gold, and you will have gold; imagine that it contains stones, and it will need no guarding" — it is all one: the lesson taught, one last time, is that it is useless to know the true nature of the buried stuff, because the trove, whatever its nature, is useless when buried.

"What, though, if I dig the treasure up in my old age?" asks Desiderius. Abundius replies that he has been promised neither a long life, nor the certainty that gold is there: someone else may have stolen it in the meantime — if it *was* there in the first place. In the ground, it is no longer yours:

> Quid si alienis id manibus, non patris factum tui?
> Quid si aliis impensum, non tuis tibique?

By these suggestions, Abundius has fully opened Desiderius' spirit: dangling from his rope, Strobilus first shocked his master into remembering his human responsibilities; by cooler argument, Abundius persuades his son — the miser who so badly wanted security — to accept the only security there is: that of faith in the loving kindness of the father in heaven (the father of the parable in Luke), and the only life there is: devotion to one's fellow men on earth. Desiderius makes an outcry, the likes of which we have not heard from him before: "Ah Pater,/ Ita acervasse aes poenitet!" He understands how cruelly his love of money has punished him, how debased he has become through his vice, in what danger he has stood. Abundius rejoices; these are the words he has been waiting for throughout the play, and he predicts that Desiderius will now become a singular figure among the wealthy, rich in spirit as in coin; whatever profit he makes henceforth, he will share with the poor, with himself, and with his family. And Abundius ends (does he look out at the audience as he speaks?) with these words:

> Providet munificis Deus.
> Liberali nihil defuturum est diviti, avaro omnia.

A brief epilogue reiterates the plea for charity: the wise man buries his wealth in the bosom of the poor, "where it flourishes, free from all peril, without care, full of profit, and bearing interest to be deposited in heaven."

NOTES

[1] Curt von Faber du Faur, *German Baroque Literature: A Catalogue of the Collection in the Yale University Library* (New Haven, 1958), p. 256.
[2] Harald Burger, "Jacob Masens 'Rusticus imperans': Zur lateinischen Barockkomödie in Deutschland," *Literaturwissenschaftliches Jahrbuch der Görres-Gesellschaft* [*LJGG*], 8 (1967), 31-56, has given a summary of the mentions (and omissions) of Masen in the histories of baroque literature; to his list may be added the popular presentation by Marian Szyrocki, *Die deutsche Literatur des Barock: Eine Einführung* (Hamburg, 1968), p. 193, where Masen appears only as the author of a dramaturgy.
[3] Burger, "Masens 'Rusticus' "; Burger has also provided a critical edition of the text: *LJGG*, 10 (1969), 53-94.
[4] *Palaestra Eloquentiae Ligatae. Dramatica. Pars III & ultima* (Cologne, 1664), pp. 312-313 [Faber du Faur, 1004]. All quotations from Masen in the present essay are from this text, a new edition, "priori longè correctior," of the first printing of the *Palaestra*, published in 1654-57. (The *Dramatica* were thus first printed in 1657). The two commentaries on the passage have given it interpretations which are at variance with one

another. Paul Bahlmann, "Jesuitendramen der niederrheinischen Ordensprovinz," *Beihefte zum Centralblatt für Bibliothekswesen*, 15 (1896), assumes that only the three mixed plays were given at Münster; on the other hand, Masen's biographer Nikolaus Scheid (*Der Jesuit Jakob Masen, ein Schulmann und Schriftsteller des 17. Jahrhunderts* [Cologne, 1898], p. 41, n. 1), argues that the comedies and the single tragedy were also given during the Congress: "wenn der Vergleich der Stücke untereinander auch in Münster gemacht werden konnte, [müssen] die Lustspiele und die Tragödie ebenfalls dort aufgeführt worden sein."

5 Johannes Müller, *Das Jesuitendrama in den Ländern deutscher Zunge vom Anfang (1555) bis zum Hochbarock (1665)* (Augsburg, 1930), I, 85; Bernhard Duhr, "Christoph Brower und Jacob Masen," in Joseph Klinkenberg, ed., *Das Marzellen-Gymnasium in Köln 1450-1911: Festschrift des Gymnasiums anlässlich seiner Übersiedelung gewidmet von den ehemaligen Schülern* (Cologne, 1911), p. 100, n. 4: "In den Jahresberichten von Münster wird bemerkt, dass dort von 1642-1648 viele Komödien besonders von P. Masen gespielt worden seien." In his *Geschichte der Jesuiten in den Ländern deutscher Zunge in der ersten Hälfte des XVII. Jahrhunderts* (Freiburg i. B., 1913), II/1; 689, n. 1, Duhr repeats the above statement ,and gives more details: a *Philippus Bonus* (i.e., the *Rusticus imperans*) and the *Telesbius* were presented in 1645, and *Androphilus* in 1646; "die Aufführung von 'Barlaam und Josaphat' wurde durch den Regen gestört."

6 Scheid (p. 41) paraphrases thus: "für Härten und Unebenheiten der eigenen Sprache bitte er um Nachsicht: es seien zumeist Jugendarbeiten, an denen sich eine spätere Feile nur schwer anwenden lasse."

7 Cf. F. X. Krauss, "J. M.," *ADB*, XX, 558-59; Scheid, p. 2; Ludwig Koch, "J. M.," *Jesuiten-Lexikon* (Paderborn, 1934), pp. 1178-80.

8 Even in the case of so famous a Jesuit dramatist as Bidermann, the problems of chronology have not been solved; cf. Rolf Tarot's afterword to his edition of the *Ludi Theatrales* (Tübingen, 1967), I, 6*-13*; II, 10*-14*.

9 Anton Dürrwächter, "Das Jesuitendrama und die literarische Forschung am Ende des Jahrhunderts," *Historisch-politische Blätter*, 24 (1899), 289; what Dürrwächter says is a contraction of Scheid's opinion (p. 42). Bernhard Duhr quotes Dürrwächter in the section on Masen in the *Geschichte der Jesuiten*, II/1, 689; Scheid himself, in his "Das lateinische Jesuitendrama im deutschen Sprachgebiet," *LJGG*, 5 (1930), 57-58, repeats verbatim what he had written thirty-two years before: "Das Stück baut sich mit regelmässig steigender Entwicklung und heiterer Lösung im fünften Akte, ganz nach Masens Theorie, sehr einfach auf; die Höhe liegt im dritten Akte, in dem der Diener Strobilus — ein durchtriebener, listiger Bursche — die Probe der von seinem jungen Herrn angezweifelten Treue besteht..."

10 Duhr, *Geschichte der Jesuiten*, II, 1, 689, argues that the dramatic theory itself was finished by 1649, since Masen refers to it in the introduction to the *Nova ars argutiarum*, a theoretical work on the epigram which appeared in that year.

11 Cf. Burger, "Masens 'Rusticus'," 45: "In komplexen Schichtungen... vollzieht sich der Aufbau des Komischen im 'Rusticus imperans'; von der unmittelbar-drastischen, aus urtümlichen Schichten des Menschlichen stammenden Komik der Vitalsphäre über die Komik der Kontrastsituation, die aus dem ständigen Heraus- und Abgleiten aus der moralischen, bzw. gesellschaftlichen Norm entsteht, zur Zeitkritik und zum satirischen Fürstenspiegel."

12 J. B. Trenkle, "Über süddeutsche geistliche Schulkomödien," *Freiburger Diözesan-Archiv: Organ des kirchlich-historischen Wesens,* 2 (1866), 160-163 and 187-188, has given a summary of the third act of this "wohlgetroffenes Zeitbild" (as Scheid called it, p. 51), providing a German translation of the rhymed Latin songs of the original — a sampling of the linguistic and metrical variety which Masen could achieve.

13 Masen mentions the *Bacchi schola eversa* thrice; the "mixed plays" *Josaphatus* and

Telesbius are named four times, *Androphilus* eight, and the tragedy *Mauritius* once; this last-named play was written, as Masen says in the introduction to his dramatic works, only to prove that he could work in the genre: "In tragicis multa, & vetus, & posterior aetas habet lectu dignissima, ut meam hac in re operam desiderare nemo possit. Ne tamen omnino nihil huc symboli contulisse videar, Mauritium Imper. tragico in schemate exhibui" (p. 130).

14 "...ita ut illius antiquitatem hujus puritate ac moderatione castiges: hujus verò remissionem, illius, qua in moribus formandis comitate, pollet: excites: intra tamen urbanitatis limites, quos, dum ingenia vilissimorum hominum consectatur, nonnumquam praeter vectus est. Hoc propositum nobis fuit in *Rustico Imperante* et *Ollaria* nostra."

15 "Poetae erit, ita ad verum rem componere, ut delectationi esse possit. Sic in *Ollaria*, rei veritas in defossa à filio sub terris pecunia (pro qua Pater lapides substituerit) consistit. Accessit prudens monitum patris, tantundem sub terra lapides, quantùm argenti massam praestare. Hanc rem qui suis adjunctis, perplexitatibus, aliisque atque aliis eventibus exposuerit, historiam in Dramate non destruit, sed ornat. Minus fidei assensusque habiturus, nisi ingeniosè fabuletur." Translation by the present writer.

16 (Lyons, 1585), pp. 495-498. Translation by the present writer.

17 The German translation of Masen's Latin retelling of the tale runs as follows (pp. 32-35): "Petrarcha schreibet / daß sich seiner Zeit folgendes zugetragen. Es ware newlicher Zeit ein Reicher mit vielen Gütern wohl versehener Edelmann in Italien / aber viel reicher an Tugenden / als an Baarschaften; der hatte einen Sohn / welcher mit großer Sorg und Fleiß große Reichthumben und Schätze zusammen gebracht hatte (ein wunder Ding) der alte Vatter ware freygebig / der junge Sohn nicht kostfrey. Der alte ermahnete seinen Sohn, er wollte in Zusammenscharung Golts und Silbers der Gottsforcht und seines guten Gerüchts nit vergessen / endlich sein Gut ihme selbst / seinen Eltern / und denen Armen lassen zu Nutz kommen. Es ware aber einem Tauben geprediget / er legte was er erhaschet / in seine Schatzkammer / und was er noch nicht hatte / dem stellete er ernstlich nach. Als er nun etwas weit verreiset ware / bringt der gutherzige Vatter den verborgenen Schatz ans Tag-Liecht / wendet ihme selbigen / seinen Haußgenossen / seiner Haußhaltung / und denen Armen bester / freygebiger maßen zu nutz an / füllet die Geltsäcklein voll Sandt / und Steinen / leget selbige an ihr voriges Orth. Als der Sohn anheim kame und sahe dass seine Brüder / auch seine Eltern ebenmäßig newe Kleyder antrugen / und er sie kaum anerkennete: neben diesem auch das gantze Hauß / und Haußgenossen sehr wohl gezieret sahe / lauffet er erstarrt zu seiner Geltkisten: als er aber alles an seinem Orth / und die Säcke angefüllet / wie er selbige verlassen hatte / gefunden / hat er sein Gemüth etwas in Ruhe gestellet / und sich zu seinen Mitgesellen verfüget: und aber als er unlängst darnach alles / und jedes durchkundiget / und nit mehr als Sand und Steine in seinen Säcken gefunden / ruffet er voll Schmertzens und Tobens eines klagens und wehklagens über das andere. Der Vatter lauffet hinzu / fraget / was Ungleichs ist dir mein lieber Sohn begegnet? Ach / mein Gelt / antwortet er / ach mein Gelt / welches ich mit so vielem wachen / mühe und sorgen zusammen getragen. Ach / wo ist mein Gelt! welches Gelt? sprachs der fromme alte Vatter / ich sihe ja dass alle Säcke voll seynd: Voll / ja voll Sande und Stein / aber kein Gelt ist vorhanden / antwortete der Sohn. Da redete der gute alte gantz unverstöret / was ists / mein Sohn / welcher underscheid ists / ob deine Säcke mit Sandt / oder ob sie mit Gelt angefüllet seyen? du brauchest eines so wenig als das andere / und eines nimbt so viel raums ein als das andere. Bilde dir eyn diss sey Golt / oder gedenckt / als wissestu nit / daß es Steine seyen / so wirds eben gleichen nutzen schaffen. Ich hab es aussgetheilet und verursacht dass die Reichthumben unser seyen / das hastu deinem Vater zu dancken / daß er dich vieler sorgen befreyet / und das gewisse Laster des Geitzs von unserm gantzen Geschlecht durch ein ehr- und lobwürdige That abgewendet. Diss ware warlich ein herzliches Mittel / und Arzney gegen unmäßige Begirlichkeit.

> Ob wohl der Seckel mögt zerreissen /
> So thut der Geitzhals doch mehr heissen.
> Gnug / gnug / und aber gnug
> Hat der / so sagt / ich hab gnug.

Dieser verständige fromme Vatter hat seinem Sohne / gantzem Hauß und Geschlecht nit aufrichtiger Reichthumb zuschieben können / als da er auff solche weiß das Gelt verschwendet hat."

18 Standard studies on the impact of Roman comedy in Germany were provided by Karl von Reinhardstoettner, *Plautus: Spätere Bearbeitungen plautinischer Lustspiele* (Leipzig, 1886), and Otto Francke, *Terenz und die lateinische Schulkomödie in Deutschland* (Weimar, 1877); Masen's *Ollaria* is not mentioned in either of them.

19 See the following surveys: A. Klapp, *"L'avare ancien et moderne tel qu'il a été peint dans la littérature* (Programm des grossherzoglichen Friedrich-Franz-Gymnasiums zu Parchim), (Parchim, 1877); C. Klöpper, "Avare" in *Französisches Real-Lexicon* (Leipzig, 1898), I: 444; and Cornelia Grassi, *L'Avaro nella Comedia: Studio Critico* (Rome, 1900). None is very penetrating, and none explores the German and German-Latin plays on the figure.

20 In another Italian play of the time, *La Sporta* (1543) of Giovambattista Gelli, the plot is much simpler. A hamper full of money is found by the old Ghirigoro de' Macci, as he is clearing out a cottage, and, afraid, "as most old people are," that whoever sees it will try to take it away from him, Ghirigoro hides it in various places. At length, it is discovered by Franzino, the servant of Alamanno Cavicciuli, a young man who has made Ghirogoro's daughter pregnant, and promised to marry her; Alamanno, as it were, gives his bride her dowry in the form of her father's treasure, and the new grandfather happily accepts his fate; his last speech is: "O genero mio buono, buon prò cí faccia, che benedetto sia tu per mille volte. Andiann' a cena a casa a vedere un pò la Fiammetta [his daughter] e quel mio nipotino" (*La Sporta* [Florence, 1602], p. 87).

21 See John MacGillivray, *Life and Works of Pierre Larivey* (Leipzig, 1889), pp. 43-45; and Karl Vitus Meurer, *Lariveys Les esprits als Quelle zu Molières Avare, unter Berücksichtigung der Aulularia des Plautus* (diss. Jena, Koblenz, 1873). An extensive bibliography, "Zum Fortwirken der lateinischen Komödie," can be found in Wolfgang Salzmann, *Molière und die lateinische Komödie* (Heidelberg, 1969), pp. 260-261.

22 This is the King James' translation, and Luther's bible says the same: "Denn Geiz ist eine Wurzel alles Übels." However, the Vulgate says: "Radix enim malorum est cupiditas," which permits the translation of the Confraternity edition: "For covetousness is *the* root of *all* evils" (italics added).

23 See Erik A. Nielsen's interpretation of the plays as "et styke eminent pædagogik, den kan gå sit kristeligt-moralske ærende uden at sætte sin kunstneriske kvalitet over styr" in "Skolen på komedie," *Kritik*, 11 (1967), 25-45.

24 Müller, *Jesuitendrama*, I, 86, also calls attention to the Jesuit Jacob Gretser's use of the miser-motif as a possible "Vorbild" for Masen's play: *Comedia de Timone ex Luciano* (1584). But Timon is not so much a miser as a man who does not know how to handle his sudden good fortune. Was Masen acquainted with the miser-play, *Philargyrus* (printed 1565) of the Swiss Petrus Dasypodius? In its picture of the debasement which avarice causes, it resembles Masen's play.

25 Translation by Joseph Rickaby, *The Spiritual Exercises of St. Ignatius Loyola: Spanish and English* (London, 1923), p. 117. The Latin text runs: "Tertius binarius (tertia classis) vult tollere affectum, sed ita illum vult tollere, ut etiam non tenatur affectione ad rem acquisitam retinendam, vel non retinendam: sed vult solum velle illam, vel nolle, prout Deus Dominus noster ipsi dabit velle, et (prout) personae tali melius videbitur ad servititum et laudem divinae suae Majestatis" (*Exercitia Spiritualia S. Ignatii de Loyola*, meditationibus illustrata... auctore F. X. Weiniger [Mainz, 1883],

p. 131). A recent American paraphrase of the passage runs: "the third kind of man wants to discard his unauthentic bias and is just as ready to observe that the one or the other course of action would be more opportune in the cause of God..." (Lewis Delmage, *The Spiritual Exercises of Saint Ignatius Loyola* [New York, 1968], p. 79).

26 Hermann Joseph Nachtwey, in his *Die Exerzitien des Ignatius von Loyola in den Dramen Jakob Bidermanns S. J.* (diss. Münster, 1937), passes over this point in his discussion of *Jacobus usuarius* (pp. 28-36).

27 Summarized by Hugo Holstein, *Das Drama vom verlorenen Sohn* (Geestemünde, 1880); Hugo Holstein, *Die Reformation im Spiegelbilde der dramatischen Literatur* (Halle, 1886), pp. 146 ff.; Franz Spengler, *Der verlorene Sohn im Drama des 16. Jahrhunderts* (Innsbruck, 1888); and Adolf Schweckendiek, *Bühnengeschichte des verlorenen Sohnes in Deutschland. I. Teil (1527—1627)*. Theatergeschichtliche Forschungen 40 (Leipzig, 1930); a more comprehensive treatment is by J. F. M. Kat, *De Verloren Zoon als letterkundig motief* (Amsterdam, 1952).

28 In her edition of *Das Spiel von den alten und jungen Eidgenossen* (Bern, 1963), Friederike Christ-Kutter has discussed the difficulties of dealing with such allusions (p. 31): "Wir vermuten indessen, daß das Spiel auf Lokalereignisse anspielt, von denen wir heute nichts mehr wissen, die damals aber wesentlich zu geistvoller Unterhaltung beitrugen."

29 See Kurt Adel, *Das Jesuitendrama in Österreich* (Vienna, 1957), pp. 89-90; and Adel, *Das Wiener Jesuitentheater und die europäische Barockdramatik* (Vienna, 1960), pp. 102-103.

30 Claus Zander, "Jesuitentheater und Schuldrama als Spiegel trierischer Geschichte," *Kurtrierisches Jahrbuch*, 1965-66, pp. 64-68, 143-159, has taken a step toward the investigation of these problems.

31 Josef Kuckhoff, *Die Geschichte des Gymnasium Tricoronatum* (Cologne, 1931), pp. 448-453, gives an account of Masen's pedagogical activity at the Cologne Jesuit gymnasium.

32 See Duhr, *Geschichte der Jesuiten*, II/1, 14 ff.

33 Joseph Braun, *Die Kirchenbauten der deutschen Jesuiten* (Freiburg i. B., 1908), I, 64-104; Herbert Rode, *Köln* (Cologne, o. D. [1970?]), p. 58: "St. Mariae Himmelfahrt wurde mit 77 m. Länge (Außenmaße) nach dem Dom die grösste Kölner Kirche..." In his article, "Neue Funde zur Baugeschichte der Kölner Jesuitenkirche," *Stimmen aus Maria Laach*, 76 (1909), I, 282-296, Braun calls the Jesuit church in Cologne "die in jeder Beziehung hervorragendste Kirche, welche das 17. Jahrhundert im Westen Deutschlands entstehen sah..." Here, he gives still more details than in his book about the difficulties of financing the project.

34 Edmund Renard, "Die bildende Kunst" *in Geschichte des Rheinlandes von der ältesten Zeit bis zur Gegenwart* (Bonn, 1922), II, 436-439.

35 Braun, *Die Kirchenbauten*, p. 102.

36 Aaegidius Gelenius, *De admiranda, sacra, et civili magnitudine Coloniae Claudiae Agrippinensis Augustae Ubiorum Urbis* (Cologne, 1645), Book III, which devotes three pages (505-508) to the "Novi Templi descriptio," and Matthäus Merian, *Topographia Archiepiscopatuum Moguntinensis, Trevirensis, et Coloniensis* (1646; facsimile edition, Basel and Kassel, 1961), p. 74, where the relics of St. Ignatius Loyola and St. Francis Xavier, on display in the church, are described.

37 Joseph Klersch, *Volkstum und Volksleben in Köln: Ein Beitrag zur Soziologie der Stadt*, Beiträge zur kölnischen Geschichte, Sprache, Eigenart, 45. (Cologne, 1968), III, 160-161.

38 Klersch, III, 162; Justus Hashagen, "Das Geistesleben im Wandel der Zeiten," in *Geschichte des Rheinlandes*, II, 328.

39 Leonhard Ennen, *Geschichte der Stadt Köln* (Düsseldorf, 1880), V, 357 ff., 380 ff.

40 Bruno Kuske, "Das soziale und wirtschaftliche Leben Westdeutschlands im Dreißigjähri-

gen Krieges," in Kuske, *Köln, der Rhein, und das Reich: Beiträge aus fünf Jahrzehnten wirtschaftsgeschichtlicher Forschung* (Köln-Graz, 1956), p. 196.

41 Book III, Chapter 23-24.

42 Kuske, p. 190.

43 Braun, *Die Kirchenbauten*, p. 91, p. 99; "Neue Funde," p. 295. It should be remembered that, in this works, Braun is concerned to place his order in as good a light as possible.

44 Josef Kuckhoff, "Erstes Jahrhundert des Jesuitenschauspiels am Tricoronatum in Köln," *Jahrbuch des kölnischen Geschichts-Vereins*, 1928, p. 48, lists "Ein Spiel von der Avaritia," performed at the Tricoronatum in November, 1647. In his *Geschichte des...Tricoronatum*, p. 449, Kuckhoff concludes that the play "nichts anderes gewesen sein durfte, als [Masens] unter dem Namen Ollaria bekanntes Drama." Elsewhere (p. 339), Kuckhoff observes that Adam Kasen, director of the Tricoronatum from 1626 to 1653, was particularly anxious to have his school's plays emphasize the Jesuits' "besondere Verbindung" with Cologne and its well-to-do citizens.

45 Duhr, *Geschichte der Jesuiten*, II/2, 391 ff.

46 Scheid, *Der Jesuit Jakob Masen*, pp. 65-66; Duhr, *Geschichte der Jesuiten*, III, 587. Masen likewise wrote directly in defence of his order, and, in *Gretserus reviviscens*, republished a rebuttal which Gretser had made against the claims of the ex-Jesuit Zahorowski concerning the so-called secret edicts of the order.

47 Ennen, *Geschichte der Stadt Köln*, V, 535, and Duhr, II/1, 21-22.

48 Kuckhoff, "Erstes Jahrhundert," pp. 38-40, describes a play, *Colonia Agrippina Pagana*, given at the Tricoronatum in 1635. In it, the empress Agrippina, recently converted, drives the forces of paganism out of the city; they, with considerable anachronism, appeal to Luther and Calvin for aid. Later: "Aufruhr und alle Kriegsnot drohen Agrippina, der Feind rückt gegen die Mauern Kölns. Die Providentia ruft alle Bürger zur Abwehr auf, und der Feind wird zurückgeschlagen. Das alles war ja seit der Schwedengefahr 1632 den Zuschauern noch in lebhafter Erinnerung, und die Darstellung wird den Eindruck nicht gefehlt haben."

49 This emphasis by Masen upon the immediate aural perception of his plays is of major importance, not only because (after Bidermann, whose career as a dramatist was over by the middle 1620's) he offers the strongest Jesuit voice against the increasing dependence of the order's theater upon spectacle, but also because he is an opponent, as well, of rhetoric for its own sake. In other words, as all students of baroque drama know, Avancini in Vienna, Masen's contemporary, presents a concept of the theater in direct contrast to Masen's.

50 Müller (p. 86) calls attention to Masen's knowledge of the work of the "classicistic" French Jesuit dramatist, Nicolas Caussin.

51 The name is also given to the tricky servant ("Strobilus II") of the love-sick Lyconides in the same play; this problem — two servants with the same name in the same play — has been a source of some trouble to Plautus scholars and translators, and has been solved in various ways.

52 In Guglielmus Gnaphaeus' famous prodigal-son play from some hundred years before, *Acolastus*, the prodigal himself — spiritually dead — smells like a corpse, and his scent is caught by the parasite who will prey on him.

53 "Anima Reipublicae / Et sanguis, & nervi pecunia est" (p. 137), a sentiment to which the Cologne *honoratiores* surely would have subscribed.

54 "...utinam ille quidem senex magis, / Aut minus oculatus esset, qui ubique meis excubiis / Suá adeo vigilatiá praestruit...Vulturis instar praedae huic inhiat..." Does Masen want us to think that Desiderius simply wishes his father would be more decrepit? Or is he awakening literary associations on the part of his audience: does Desiderius wish his father would be the traditional "senex avarus" of comedy?

55 Jacob Balde uses the insult in his "Ad aquilam romani imperii" (Odes I: 38):

> Pelle Finlandos age, pelle corvos;
> Ora Stymphali vacuetur Hunnis:
> Milviis ningat lacerisque Lappis
> Fluctuat aer.

In Max Wehrli's translation of Jakob Balde, *Dichtungen* (Cologne and Olten, 1963), p. 25:

> Auf, verjag, verjag nun die Raben Finnlands,
> Von den Hunnen säubre das Land Stymphalien.
> Geiern soll es schnein, von zerfetzten Lappen
> Woge der Luftraum!

See also Benno Müller's note in Jakob Balde, *Carmina Lyrica* (Munich, 1844), *Annotationes*, p. 25.

56 It may be worth noting that the four brothers bear the names of saints somehow "German": Otto of Freising, the author of the world-chronicle, Marinus, "the companion of Saints Virgil and Declanus," according to the "Regensburger Schottenlegende," whose bones were placed in the cloister at Neustift by Otto; Remaclus, whose activity belongs to the Ardennes; and Claudius, one of the so-called "Twenty-one German martyrs," a Goth who fell in love with a Christian girl, was converted by her, and suffered martyrdom with her.

57 It is to be assumed that neither Abundius nor Strobilus hears them; otherwise, the jig would be up.

58 In *Frau Wendelgard*, Nikodemus Frischlin employs the beggar scene to make a different and completely uncharitable observation: that beggars are tricksters, and that masters — certainly, saintly ones like the play's and the legend's Count Ulrich von Buchhorn — are much more inclined to be generous than are their servants, who can see through the beggars' dodges.

59 Skinny and (German dog-Latin) Lousy; Windpipe (Wheezer?) and Blind; Blind and Halt; the Expelled One and Cringer.

60 In the anonymous Latin comedy from the age of Theodosius II, *Querolus*, ed. R. Peiper (Leipzig, 1875), and Gunnar Ranstrand, *Göteborgs Högskolas Arsskrift*, 57:1 (Gothenburg, 1951), the urn with the supposed treasure in fact contains the ashes of the dead miser Euclio, whose money is sought by his peevish son, Querolus.

61 It is possible that both speeches are suggested by the soliloquy of Strobilus II in *Aulularia*, 11. 587 ff. "Hoc est servi facinus frugi, facere quod ego persequor, / ne morae molestiaeque imperium erile habeat sibi...", etc. In an appendix to the *Dramata* ("Appendix Selectorum ex Plauto discursuum, Phrasium & Verborum maxime imitatione dignorum"), Masen adduces the soliloquy's first line (p. 514); the appendix also includes (p. 513) the comical lines on stinginess quoted above (text, p.55) in connection with the conversation between Davus and Messenio (III/3).

62 Masen's ultimate lack of interest in the fate of Strobilus may have its basis not only in Roman comic tradition but in scripture as well; John 8:35: "And the bondservant abideth not in the house forever, but the son abideth forever." It is what happens to the soul of Desiderius that counts.

63 In this scene and the next (V:1-2, Otto is called Goto, becoming Otto again in V:3. These are printer's errors, as is the instance in V:1 where Remaclus briefly becomes Romaclus.

64 The miser's return in *Ollaria* may be contrasted with the counterpart scene in *Karrig Niding*. In the Catholic play, the transformation of poverty into an opulence that disguises the family is carried out with the hope of converting the miser; in the play by the Danish pastor, the same trick is performed with the clear intention of punishing, and destroying, Niding.

65 In Bidermann's *Philemon* (III/1), the actor-musician keeps the despairing Christian Apollonius from hanging himself, and subsequently receives the job of sacrificing to

Jupiter in Apollonius' stead, the role-playing which leads to his conversion and salvation: in I/19 of Grimmelshausen's *Das wunderbarliche Vogelnest*, ed. Rolf Tarot (Tübingen, 1970), p. 125), the musketeer observes a shepherd about to commit an act of bestiality, and cries out to him to stop. The terrified shepherd prepares to hang himself, but the invisible musketeer persuades him of God's infinite mercy — and then thinks to himself: "Wer bist du ... / der du in diesem Sünden Schlamm steckest biß über die Ohren / und wilst andern den Weg zum Himmel weisen; hast du doch nicht einmal an deine eigene Bekehrung gedacht? und bist so kühn andere zu lehren / was du selbst zu deiner Seelen Heyl niemal von Hertzen zu thun unterstanden?"

THE IMPERILED SANCTUARY: TOWARD A PARADIGM OF GOETHE'S CLASSICAL DRAMAS

Theodore Ziolkowski

Most epochs can be more accurately characterized by the questions they ask than by the answers they find. Answers are qualified by the available means of investigation while questions, reflecting the often unconscious obsessions of the period, are restricted only by the limits of the imagination. Our present era would seem to be distinguished by its attempt to perceive, in every area of intellectual endeavor, broad patterns that underlie and unify the discrete phenomena so assiduously collected, catalogued, and analyzed by earlier generations. The shift in emphasis in linguistics from taxonomic classification to transformational-generative theory is paralleled in many disciplines by a move from descriptive analysis toward synthetic understanding. The historian directs his attention from the study of specific insurrections to the theory of revolution; the political scientist and sociologist set up "models" that account for political action and social behavior in different societies. Cultural anthropologists come to grips with the consciousness that produces identical myths in different times and places, while literary scholars turn increasingly from the interpretation of individual texts to the ascertainment of the structures, both formal and thematic, that they share. It is no accident that many of our most imaginative critics in recent years have devoted their energies to defining the "epochal style" that characterizes all the arts of a given period.

These preliminary observations, which any reader can supplement from his own experience, are intended merely to suggest that our attempt to isolate an underlying pattern or paradigm that unites Goethe's classical dramas is not motivated by any conviction that we see better or more acutely than our predecessors. We have simply become accustomed to look at literature and culture in a somewhat different way. Instead of finding, collecting, analyzing, classifying, or interpreting, we grope instinctively for common denominators that characterize the group. Appropriately enough, it might be argued that our age has come full circle to a typically Goethean way of viewing reality. During the years when he wrote his major dramas Goethe himself was obsessed with the phenomenon of the "Urpflanze." In a famous letter incorporated into the *Italienische Reise* (17 April 1787) he insisted that nature must surely include such primal types. "Woran würde ich sonst erkennen, daß dieses oder jenes Gebilde eine Pflanze sei, wenn sie nicht alle nach *einem* Muster gebildet wären."[1] [italics added] (*HA*, XI, 266) And elsewhere (17 May 1787): "Mit diesem Modell und dem Schlüssel dazu kann man alsdann noch Pflanzen ins Unendliche erfinden, die konsequent sein müssen..." (*HA*, XI, 324) The similarity between Goethe and our own epoch is evident not in the answers obtained — modern science has often gone beyond Goethe's findings — but in the way the question is put. For Goethe is concerned less with the discrete phenomena than with the general pattern that unifies them.

If earlier scholarship neglected to follow Goethe's lead, it was due in part to a preoccupation with other pressing problems: notably the hunting for sources and biographical influences that obsessed positivism, the delineation of the intellectual and cultural background that interested *Geistesgeschichte*, and the interpretation of individual texts that dominated the various ergocentric methods of recent decades. Thus Ronald Peacock, in a thoughtful and perceptive volume on Goethe's dramas, still did not feel that the major plays display any "development toward a single typical form."[2] It became possible to appreciate Goethe's suggestion only when our own intellectual climate had prepared us for it.

A second factor was also involved in the failure of scholars to look for common patterns underlying Goethe's classical dramas: the failure to agree that any such category existed. As long as *Iphigenie auf Tauris* and *Torquato Tasso* were taken more or less in isolation as a pair of thematically related works from the same period, their similarities could be explained in various simple ways. It is not necessary to assume the existence of a category in order to account for parallels in two contemporaneous works. But as soon as parallels become evident in a third work conceived almost twenty years later — *Die natürliche Tochter* — it is imperative to set up a more general paradigm to account for the similarities.

Goethe himself plainly thought of the three dramas as a group. In a letter to Cotta (14 June 1805) he specified that *Iphigenie, Tasso,* and *Die natürliche Tochter* be published together in the edition of 1806 — a disposition retained for the ninth volume of the *Ausgabe letzter Hand*. Despite Goethe's own feelings, for a hundred and fifty years *Die natürliche Tochter* was regarded as a source of embarrassment by many of Goethe's most ardent admirers — a work to be ignored or tactfully explained away. In his *Goethe* (1916) Friedrich Gundolf conceded that the work is "technisch das durchstilisierte Ende der Iphigenie-Tasso-Reihe" (p. 474), but maintained that otherwise it is without interest or merit apart from a certain superficial linguistic brilliance. In the second volume of his *Geist der Goethezeit* (1930) H. A. Korff mentioned the play solely to note that it was not worth considering. And as recently as 1959 Peacock omitted the play from his study of the dramas on the grounds that it is no more than "a shadow at the side of Goethe's best work" (p. vii). Virtually the only scholars who concerned themselves with the drama were those who regarded it as a document for Goethe's attitude toward the French Revolution and those who amused themselves with often extravagant attempts to reconstruct the trilogy to which the drama was originally supposed to belong. It was not fashionable to take the play seriously as an aesthetic creation or to think of it in conjunction with the other two major "classical" dramas.

Within the past fifteen years there has been a conspicuous effort to rehabilitate

Die natürliche Tochter. Notably Emil Staiger, Verena Bänninger, and Theo Stammen have argued persuasively that the drama can be read as a work of poetic integrity and inherent merit — that it needs to be justified neither as a "torso" nor simply as a document of Goethe's political views.[3] But all three scholars regard the play as exceptional and substantially different in nature from *Iphigenie* and *Tasso*. While these studies have added considerably to our understanding and appreciation of this specific work, they have contributed little to our apprehension of *Die natürliche Tochter* as representative of Goethe's classical dramas.

Three critics in particular have pointed out that Goethe's own grouping reflects a basic congruence among the three plays. Max Kommerell called them Goethe's "drei klassische Dramen" and noted the presence of a common motif: "das edle Blut im Exil."[4] Hans-Egon Hass suggested that the three plays are unified by their common theme of "Entsagung."[5] And Sigurd Burckhardt even spoke of "Goethe's dramatic trilogy in blank verse" in order to stress his conviction that the common poetic form linking these three dramas signifies a shared attitude toward language and the word.[6]

It is against this background that we undertake to establish a basic pattern or paradigm underlying Goethe's classical dramas. Our epoch has become accustomed to look for such patterns, and literary scholarship has rehabilitated *Die natürliche Tochter*, making it possible to view Goethe's classical dramas in a new configuration. While we shall make use of the similarities of motif, theme, and language noted by other critics, we shall focus our attention primarily on those common elements that contribute to a larger consistent pattern. I can think of no better methodological principle to guide us than the one with which Goethe introduced his "Erster Entwurf einer allgemeinen Einleitung in die vergleichende Anatomie" (1795):

> Die Erfahrung muß uns vorerst die Teile lehren, die allen Tieren gemein sind, und worin diese Teile verschieden sind. Die Idee muß über dem Ganzen walten und auf eine genetische Weise das allgemeine Bild abziehen. Ist ein solcher Typus auch nur zum Versuch aufgestellt, so können wir die bisher gebräuchlichen Vergleichungsarten zur Prüfung desselben sehr wohl benutzen.[7]

I

Let us start with simple facts. *Iphigenie* gets underway when Thoas, King of the Taurians, confronts the priestess of Diana in the sacred grove before the temple. When she again refuses him her hand in marriage, he warns her that the ancient ritual of sacrifice, discontinued since her arrival over ten years earlier, must be reinstated. *Tasso* begins when Alfons, the Duke of Ferrara, seeks out his sister Leonore in the garden of the palace at Belriguardo. Having escorted the ladies to the country, Alfons is on the point of returning to the city, where urgent business requires his presence. *Die natürliche Tochter* opens when the King encounters Eugenie in a dense forest near the estate where she has grown up. It is revealed that Eugenie is the Duke's illegitimate daughter, and the King agrees to acknowledge her as his niece. For the present, however, strict silence must be observed because both Eugenie and the King are threatened by conspiracy.

Let us concede the differences at the outset. *Iphigenie* is taken from Greek myth; *Tasso* is based on an episode from the cultural history of the Italian Renaissance; *Die natürliche Tochter* is the stylized dramatization of a true story lifted from an eighteenth-century *mémoire*. In addition, Goethe has furnished us with often cited catchwords that conveniently sum up the themes of the three works. In *Iphigenie* he sought to present "reine Menschlichkeit," which is personified in the heroine as "ganz verteufelt human." In *Tasso* he exposed the glaring "Disproportion des Talents mit dem Leben." And *Die natürliche Tochter* became a vehicle through which the author hoped to air his thoughts regarding "die französische Revolution und deren Folgen." Yet for all the dissimilarity necessitated by the differences in source, setting, and theme, the basic situation in the three plays reveals a remarkable identity of pattern. In each case the ruler of the land encounters a young woman in an outdoor setting that is uniquely associated with her; even though he has temporarily left behind the civic realm and its problems, the atmosphere is distinctly unsettled by a certain tension and urgency. But let us look more closely.

It has been frequently noted that Goethe's dramas are informed by the concept of the triadic rhythm of history that was widespread in the later eighteenth century. As Kommerell observed, the ballad makes use of three temporal stages: "die Zeit der reinen Ordnung"; "die Zeit der angemaßten Gewalt," and "die Zeit der Wiederherstellung."[8] The proper time of drama, and certainly of the three classical dramas, is the "Zwischenzeit" of disharmony that lies between the primal order of the past and the restored unity of the future.[9] In *Iphigenie* the ancient law of sacrifice — the "alte Sitte" (l. 2045), the "alten grausamen Gebrauch" (l. 122), the "alt Gesetz" (l. 1831) — has been suspended ever since the priestess' arrival in Tauris. The action takes place during the transitional period between that old order and the "neue Sitte" of humanity, which is proclaimed at the end of the play. Similarly, Tasso and the Princess agree that the original Golden Age is gone; the present is an intermediate time in which ideal human relationships — e.g., between poet and hero, or even poet and princess — are impossible; yet both believe that the Golden Age can be restored by kindred spirits who share the same values. *Die natürliche Tochter*, finally, is by its very nature as a study of revolution based on a triadic conception of history. The action occurs during a period of "vermummte Zwietracht" (l. 312) that threatens to shatter the authoritarian unity enforced upon earlier ages. The drama ends with the vision of a future society in which present turmoil will have subsided into a new harmony.[10]

Their role as rulers during periods of historical transition puts Thoas, Alfons, and the King into roughly analogous positions. All three, who represent traditional values (that is, the first stage of the triad), feel menaced in their authority by present developments. Thoas' dilemma stems from the recent death of his son in battle. The people, discontent with the now fatherless ruler, blame Thoas for his son's death because he discontinued the ancient ritual of sacrifice. At the same time, Thoas distrusts the other noblemen, for all of them aspire to see their own sons as his successor.

> Der fröhliche Gehorsam, den ich sonst
> Aus einem jeden Auge blicken sah,
> Ist nun von Sorg' und Unmut still gedämpft.
> Ein jeder sinnt, was künftig werden wird,
> Und folgt dem Kinderlosen, weil er muß. (ll. 239-43)

In *Die natürliche Tochter* the King is even less well suited to deal with the forces of rebellion. A mild and kindly man, he encourages insubordination by his very personality. This weakly scion of a family of heroes has inherited a throne too lofty for his abilities. The King is well aware of the impending revolution:

> O diese Zeit hat fürchterliche Zeichen:
> Das Niedre schwillt, das Hohe senkt sich nieder,
> Als könnte jeder nur am Platz des andern
> Befriedigung verworrner Wünsche finden.... (ll. 361-64)

Like Thoas, he knows that the noblemen surrounding him have split into factions. It is ultimately in response to these pressures — he presumably accedes to the demands of the younger party behind the Duke's son — that he revokes his promise to Eugenie.

Even though Alfons is not threatened by the same sort of imminent rebellion as Thoas and the King, he still lives in a state of tension and suppressed anxiety. Ferrara is not in open hostility with Florence, yet envy and suspicion keep Alfons and the Medici at odds. Antonio assures the Duke that his mission to Rome was successful, yet Alfons cannot relax: he worries that hindrances of some sort will still block their success. He has just arrived in Belriguardo, yet he must rush back to the city that same evening in order to finish his business:

> Entschlüsse
> Sind nun zu fassen, Briefe viel zu schreiben:
> Das alles nötigt mich zur Stadt zurück. (ll. 350-52)

These tensions are aggravated by a sense of insufficiency when Alfons compares himself with his ancestors. To sustain the reputation of Ferrara as a bastion of the arts, he supports a court poet: yet it is clear that, epigone that he is, he regards Tasso as no more than his chattel. (Like Thoas and the King, he is also contemptuous of his people as a group.) Thus all three rulers suffer under the strains of societies in a state of turmoil and transition.

II

A more elaborate complex of characteristics typifies the heroine whom the ruler encounters in the landscape. First, they are all related to the ruler. Leonore is Alfons' sister; Eugenie is the king's niece; and Iphigenia, though not a blood relation, repeatedly calls Thoas "mein zweiter Vater" (l. 1641, l. 2004, l. 2156), thereby articulating the essential relationship between them. Iphigenia's insistence on this kinship points to a second similarity: the inherently virginal nature of the three women. As the priestess of Diana, Iphigenia freely acknowledges the goddess' exclusive claim upon her.

> So ruf' ich alle Götter und vor allen
> Dianen, die entschlossne Göttin, an,
> Die ihren Schutz der Priesterin gewiß
> Und Jungfrau einer Jungfrau gern gewährt. (ll. 197-200)
> ....
> Hat nicht die Göttin, die mich rettete,
> Allein das Recht auf mein geweihtes Leben? (ll. 438-39)

Similarly Princess Leonore, when Tasso voices his fear that she may accept the hand of a suitor and leave their happy group, assures him that she has no lust for marriage:

> Hier bin ich gern, und gerne mag ich bleiben.
> Noch weiß ich kein Verhältnis, das mich lockte.... (ll. 1060-61)

And Eugenie, who agrees to wed the Magistrate in order to save herself from exile to the dreaded islands, does so only under the condition that the marriage not be consummated.

> Vermagst du zu versprechen, mich als Bruder
> Mit reiner Neigung zu empfangen? (ll. 2887-88)

This last passage suggests still another relationship that distinguishes the virgin: her position vis-à-vis the hero is sororal.[11] Iphigenia is Orestes' natural sister; Eugenie insists that she and the Magistrate must live together as brother and sister. And although the same image does not occur in *Tasso*, it is clear that Leonore is satisfied with a sisterly affection for the poet, while Tasso brings troubles upon himself when he seeks to transgress that limit.

Perhaps the most salient attribute of all three virgins is the fact that they have been purified, almost apotheosized, through a symbolic death. Iphigenia was saved from the sacrificial altar at Aulis by Diana:

> Sie wollte nicht mein Blut und hüllte rettend
> In eine Wolke mich; in diesem Tempel
> Erkannte ich mich zuerst vom Tode wieder. (ll. 427-29)

Leonore had just recovered from a long and critical illness when Tasso first arrived at Ferrara:

> Mit breiten Flügeln schwebte mir das Bild
> Des Todes vor den Augen, deckte mir
> Die Aussicht, in die immer neue Welt. (ll. 853-55)

And this experience of death, to which she refers several times, effectively shaped her personality.[12] Likewise, Eugenie is twice saved from death. At the beginning she barely survives the fall from her horse:

> So hob ich mich vor kurzem aus der Nacht
> Des Todes an des Tages Licht herauf. (ll. 1876-77)

And her banishment is repeatedly designated metaphorically as a form of death that has removed her from all previous earthly attachments:

> Sie ist dahin für alle, sie verschwindet
> Ins Nichts der Asche. Jeder kehret schnell
> Den Blick zum Leben und vergißt, im Taumel
> Der treibenden Begierden, daß auch sie
> Im Reihen der Lebendigen geschwebt. (ll. 1183-87)

This spiritual purification through a symbolic death helps to account for another quality of the virgins: they are all prima donnas of renunciation. The fact that they eschew marriage and conventional social relationship is secondary to the fact that they advocate patience in the achievement of the Golden Age of the future. They alone understand that the historical cycle cannot be accelerated. In one of her prayer-like monologues Iphigenia says that only the gods know when to pluck the golden fruits of heaven:

> Und wehe dem, der, ungeduldig, sie
> Ertrotzend, saure Speise sich zum Tod
> Genießt. (ll. 1112-14)

Similarly, the Princess warns Tasso that the Golden Age cannot be won by impatient striving, but only through *Sittlichkeit*. Eugenie is warned by the King (ll. 461 ff.) and by the Governess (ll. 893 ff.) that her safety and happiness can be attained only through renunciation. And that is the lesson she has learned when she gives her hand in marriage to the Magistrate:

> Vermagst du, hohen Muts
> Entsagung der Entsagenden zu weihen? (ll. 2887-88)

She wants to be preserved, as an "unblemished talisman," for the day when she will once again be needed by her father, her monarch, and her country.

The purification through death and renunciation accounts, no doubt, for the vaguely prophetic powers of the virgins. Since they have liberated themselves from the turmoil of the present, they can look into the future with greater perceptiveness than the rulers, who are hard pressed by temporal circumstances. Iphigenia alone is concerned with what lies beyond the immediate fate of Orestes and Pylades: she looks both to the end of the curse that has weighed upon the Tantalides for generations and the end of the cruel practice of sacrifice that has barbarized Tauris. The Princess is awakened by events at Belriguardo to forebodings of future strife:

>Nun überfällt in trüber Gegenwart
>Der Zukunft Schrecken heimlich meine Brust. (ll. 1878-79)

By the same token, when Eugenie has recovered from her symbolic death by exile and when she has made up her mind to renounce temporal claims, her thoughts turn away from the present to the future of her nation:

>Vom eignen Elend leitet man mich ab,
>Und fremden Jammer prophezeit man mir.
>Doch wär' es fremd, was deinem Vaterland
>Begegnen soll? Dies fällt mit neuer Schwere
>Mir auf die Brust! Zum gegenwärt'gen Übel
>Soll ich der Zukunft Geistesbürden tragen? (ll. 2815-20)

It is this insight that produces her decision to preserve herself for the future that will require her.

The assurance and selflessness that characterizes these virgins contributes to their restorative powers. Iphigenia's presence heals Orestes of his afflictions just as the Princess' calming nature restores Tasso:

>Wie den Bezauberten von Rausch und Wahn
>Der Gottheit Nähe leicht und willig heilt,
>So war auch ich von aller Phantasie,
>Von jeder Sucht, von jedem falschen Triebe
>Mit *einem* Blick in deinen Blick geheilt. (ll. 876-80)

And Eugenie's decision is motivated by the conviction that she will be able to aid her country in a time of distress.

The virgins are so wholly purged of selfish motives that they are able to entrust themselves to the impulses of their hearts. This emotional certainty represents a vivid contrast to the calculating *Realpolitik* that motivates the rulers. When Thoas tries to come to terms with very significant political pressures from his people, Iphigenia implores him not to cogitate:

>Bedenke nicht; gewähre, wie du's fühlst. (l. 1992)

When Pylades urges her to follow the dictates of reason, she replies:

>Ich untersuche nicht, ich fühle nur. (l. 1650)

Her faith in her own feeling is inspired by an almost Rilkean conviction that the gods choose the pure heart as their vehicle:

>Sie reden nur durch unser Herz zu uns. (l. 494)

Similarly, in the midst of the turmoil produced by Tasso's quarrel with Antonio the Princess reflects that all human confusion arises merely because, in our rationality, we neglect the simple dictates of our hearts:[13]

> Ach daß wir doch, dem reinen stillen Wink
> Des Herzens nachzugehn, so sehr verlernen!
> Ganz leise spricht ein Gott in unsrer Brust,
> Ganz leise, ganz vernehmlich, zeigt uns an,
> Was zu ergreifen ist und was zu fliehn. (ll. 1670-74)

And Eugenie is moved by the genuine impulses of her heart when she assures the Magistrate that it is not fear that makes her accept his hand in marriage:

> Ein edleres Gefühl — laß mich's verbergen! —
> Hält mich am Vaterland, an dir zurück. (ll. 2885-86)

The appropriate common denominator for Iphigenia, Leonore, and Eugenie might be the term "sacral virgin." Purified and rendered clairvoyant by the experience of death and renunciation, they follow the dictates of their hearts in an effort to heal those who have been seared by present turmoil and in order to preserve in their own persons those timeless values that are in danger of being submerged by the wave of political unrest threatening the world outside.

III

The sacral virgins are introduced as the *genii loci* of the landscapes with which the plays open. As the priestess of Diana, Iphigenia is at home in the sacred grove. Leonore remarks that she has a special love for Belriguardo because she spent the happiest days of her youth there. The King first meets Eugenie in the forest surrounding the hidden estate where she has grown up (And at the end of the play she arranges with the Magistrate to return to a similar solitude.)

For all the differences among them, the grove of Diana, the Arcadian garden, and the secluded forest can be subsumed under the neutral heading of a sanctuary.[14] Iphigenia specifically refers to the grove as a "Schutzort" (l. 440), and it affords Orestes sanctuary from the pursuing Erinnyes of his mind:

> Sie dürfen mit den ehrnen frechen Füßen
> Des heil'gen Waldes Boden nicht betreten.... (ll. 1129-30)

Similarly, Belriguardo has acquired powers of sanctuary through the time-honored tradition of majesty. After Tasso has drawn his sword in the palace, Antonio reminds the Duke that Belriguardo is a "Heiligtum," whose very walls are built upon the principle of security (ll. 1505-09). Eugenie's father resolves to reify the metaphor by creating a true sanctuary on the site of the encounter between the King and his daughter:

> Hier soll kein Schuß,
> Solang' ich lebe, fallen, hier kein Vogel
> Von seinem Zweig, kein Wild in seinem Busch
> Geschreckt, verwundet, hingeschmettert werden. (ll. 524-27)

The sanctuary is the place where the sacral virgin is able to maintain intact the pure being that she embodies. As such, it is specifically called a place of preservation. Orestes reminds Iphigenia that she has been spared by the goddess who

> Bewahrte dich in einer heil'gen Stille
> Zum Segen deines Bruders und der Deinen. (ll. 2131-32)

Eugenie has likewise been preserved in the "secret temple" of her childhood:

> Gar manchen Schatz bewahrt von Jugend auf
> Ein edles, gutes Herz und bildet ihn
> Nur immer schöner, liebenswürd'ger aus
> Zur holden Gottheit des geheimen Tempels.... (ll. 702-05)

When she resolves to marry, it is in order to obtain once again a sanctuary of preservation for herself:

> Im Verborgnen
> Verwahr' er mich, als reinen Talisman. (ll. 2852-53)

And Belriguardo, as the sanctuary where the Princess spent the happiest hours of her youth, is the appropriate spot to preserve *Sittlichkeit*, that inner certainty of being that alone can one day bring about the true renewal of the Golden Age on earth.

As the place where pure being is preserved, the sanctuary reveres the priority of the pure word: notably prayer and poetry. The grove of Diana, as the home of truth, inspires Orestes to his outburst: "zwischen uns sei Wahrheit" (ll. 1081-82). Sigurd Burckhardt has observed with a certain poetic accuracy that in *Iphigenie* the world of the sanctuary even has its own language — the hymnic rhythms of the priestess' prayers, which differ sharply from the blank verse of human communication.[15] The representative of the political world, Pylades, is unable to comprehend this reverence for the word:

> Man sieht, du bist nicht an Verlust gewohnt,
> Da du, dem großen Übel zu entgehen,
> Ein falsches Wort nicht einmal opfern willst. (ll. 1674-76)

Belriguardo, where Tasso completes his epic, also honors the pure word of poetry above the human word of political action: to Antonio's chagrin it is the poet who has won the wreath, not the statesman. As E. M. Wilkinson has demonstrated, the entire play can be read as a glorification of the poetic word.[16] Eugenie, finally, is punished precisely because she disenfranchises the pure word of the sanctuary when she fails to keep her promise of secrecy to the King and her father.[17]

By its very nature the sanctuary tends to be absolute and hermetic: cut off from the world, it is the home of absolute freedom of thought, absolute truth, absolute virtue. For this reason the sanctuary is regularly contrasted with the world outside, where its values do not always obtain.[18] When Iphigenia lectures Pylades on virtue and truth, he reminds her that the absolutes she has preserved in the temple are not always possible in life:

> So hast du dich im Tempel wohl bewahrt;
> Das Leben lehrt uns, weniger mit uns
> Und andern strenge sein.... (ll. 1653-55)

When Tasso makes up his mind to leave Belriguardo, Antonio warns him that he will encounter a wholly different kind of life outside: "Schmerz, / Verwirrung, Trübsinn harrt in Rom auf dich. ..." (ll. 2734-35). And when Eugenie eagerly anticipates her new life at court, the Governess cautions her:

> Aus stillem Kreise trittst du nun heraus
> In weite Räume, wo dich Sorgendrang,
> Vielfach geknüpfte Netze, Tod vielleicht
> Von meuchelmörderischer Hand erwartet. (ll. 1122-25)[19]

It belongs to the irony of the dilemma that representatives of the sanctuary and representatives of the political world, accustomed as they are to different languages, often talk at cross purposes. This accounts for the phenomenon of "fruitless speaking" that Burckhardt noted.[20] Since in effect two languages, based on two different ethical systems, are being spoken, the figures often talk past one another uncomprehendingly: Iphigenia vis-à-vis Thoas and Pylades; the Princess vis-à-vis Leonore Sanvitale as well as Tasso vis-à-vis Antonio; and Eugenie vis-à-vis virtually all the other figures of her drama.

If we pause at this point to recapitulate, we can formulate the following paradigm that underlies the three classical dramas. *In a Sanctuary, untouched by the movement of history that threatens the Ruler of the temporal realm, a Sacral Virgin preserves pure and timeless being.* (Each of the principal — that is, capitalized — terms, as we have seen, involves a consistent set of secondary characteristics.) We can now go on to see that the action of the plays amounts in each case to a modification of this basic paradigm.

IV

As long as the outside world and the sanctuary remain separate and independent, there can be no action or dramatic conflict. The ruler may be affected by the historical forces of transition, but the integrity of the sanctuary is not violated; this has been the case at Tauris, Belriguardo, and Eugenie's secluded estate for a number of years prior to the time of the dramatic action. The sanctuary and the temporal realm are normally brought into contact by a fortuitous circumstance — the capture of Orestes and Pylades, the arrival of Antonio from Rome, Eugenie's fall from her horse. This initial accident, however, is merely the occasion for the action, not its deep-lying cause. The dramatic action is generated by a threat to the sanctuary, and it is in the nature of the threat that the differences between the plays emerge.

The most obvious case arises when the sacral virgin is herself tempted to violate the principles of the sanctuary: this produces the action of *Iphigenie*. When Orestes and Pylades arrive at Tauris, Iphigenia nearly forsakes the tenets of the sanctuary in order to save her brother. After her talk with Arkas she realizes that such hasty action would simply make a bad situation worse:

>   Meinen Bruder
> Ergriff das Herz mit einziger Gewalt:
> Ich horchte nur auf seines Freundes Rat;
> Nur sie zu retten, drang die Seele vorwärts.
> ....
>
>   Nun hat die Stimme
> Des treuen Manns mich wieder aufgeweckt,
> Daß ich auch Menschen hier verlasse, mich
> Erinnert. Doppelt wird mir der Betrug
> Verhaßt. (ll. 1516-26)

If we disregard the secondary Orestes-plot, the basic dramatic conflict stems from Iphigenia's predicament: her initial temptation to violate the absolute principles of truth and humanity and her subsequent decision to force the world to accommodate itself to the principles of the sanctuary.

A second possibility arises when a woman destined to become a sacral virgin is tempted to go astray: this produces the plot of *Die natürliche Tochter*. At the outset Eugenie is a sacral virgin in every respect but one: she has not learned to tame her boldness and worldly ambition. She is repeatedly characterized by such words as *kühn* (l. 151), *überkühn* (l. 589), *tollkühn* (l. 1357) or *verwegen* (l. 1165) and by her insistence upon *unbedingte Freiheit* (l. 1369). Her rash behavior precipitates the action. Her father had planned to wait for a more auspicious moment for her first public appearance. But Eugenie's excessive daring, which causes her fall from the horse, brings about a premature meeting with the King, at which she elicits from him the hasty promise to introduce her at court. This same audacity makes her alleged death plausible when she is kidnapped and sent into exile: it is rumored — and believed by all who know her — that she again fell from her mount and was dragged to death. In the second part of the play (Acts IV and V) her ambition at first prevents her from accepting her destiny with equanimity. Instead, she approaches various people in the harbor city — the Magistrate, the Governor, the Abbess — and vainly implores their aid against the mighty powers that hound her. Only when she renounces her claim to personal happiness and resolves to live for the future of her country does she become a true sacral virgin and return, once again, to a new sanctuary. The variation that we find in this play amounts to the *Lehrjahre* of a sacral virgin.

The situation in *Tasso* is more complex because the plot of the sacral virgin has become secondary. To be sure, the Princess is tempted by her affection for the poet: as a result, the paradigm of the imperiled sanctuary is suggested in the secondary plot. But the paradigm remains valid and indispensable even in the principal Tasso-plot. In this case, namely, the sanctuary is endangered by an inhabitant who, becoming impatient, is unwilling to abide by its laws and twice offends them. By drawing his sword Tasso breaks the rule of inviolability; and by attempting to embrace the Princess he implicitly threatens the sisterly chasteness of the sacral virgin. The point is this: Tasso's drama is possible only within such a framework as that provided by the basic paradigm. In the outside world neither of his transgressions would amount to a violation, and there would be no real dilemma. Antonio might kill him in a duel; the Princess might slap his face or succumb to his blandishments. But there would be no dramatic conflict. Tasso, in short, is a creature of the sanctuary, and his story is possible only against its background.

In all three cases, finally, the threat to the sanctuary is abetted by a Tempter, who represents the voice of worldly reason that seeks to corrupt the pure voice of the heart. Pylades almost induces Iphigenia to resort to deception, arguing that her absolute faith in truth and humanity is valid only within the confines of the sanctuary while subtlety, craft, and reason must prevail in the world outside. Leonore Sanvitale, for reasons of personal aggrandizement, succeeds in persuading both the Princess and Tasso that it would be desirable for the poet to leave Belriguardo for the time being. It is perfectly conceivable that without her intercession the final misunderstanding would not have taken place and that the tragedy might have been averted. And the Governess appeals to Eugenie with increasingly outspoken arguments to marry in order to save herself from destruction.

We are now in a position to add the second stage to the dramatic paradigm. *The Sanctuary is imperiled when the Sacral Virgin is tempted by circumstances to violate its absolute principles in order to achieve temporal goals. But despite the efforts of Tempters the Sacral Virgin reaffirms the values of the Sanctuary and resolves to preserve them for a future that she envisions beyond the present historical turmoil.* Iphigenia, in the most optimistic of the plays, actually seems to inaugurate the "neue Sitte" by converting the temporal realm into a sanctuary of absolute truth and humanity. The Princess, forced to leave the sanctuary desecrated by Tasso's impetuosity, embodies its values in her own being with the aim of re-establishing a sanctuary of preservation elsewhere. And Eugenie, though she abandoned her original sanctuary, creates a second one into which she withdraws to await the future that will emerge from the present revolution. All three dramas, in short, depict an essentially ethical ideal that is reified in the image of the sanctuary. Within the framework of our paradigm the meaning and dramatic function of the various figures can be defined largely with respect to this ideological focal point: the Imperiled Sanctuary.

V

Up to this point we have used the neutral term "paradigm" to designate the underlying pattern of Goethe's classical dramas. This was done intentionally in order to avoid contaminating our very specific topic with associations that inevitably cling to such general concepts as structure, myth, or archetype. Without belaboring the point, I suggest that the paradigm primarily reflects the situation that Goethe encountered when he arrived in Weimar. It is commonly recognized that the figures of Iphigenia and the Princess owe much to the impact of Charlotte von Stein[21] while Orestes and Tasso certainly share aspects of Goethe's own personality. The vision of the Sanctuary can be seen in part as an idealization of the court at Weimar while the turmoil of the temporal realm mirrors its actuality. It is not necessary to resort to archetypal myth in order to explain the presence of the paradigm in the three classical dramas.

At the same time, it is clear that the paradigm of the Imperiled Sanctuary bears a distinct resemblance to the more universal myth of the Fall from Paradise. For this reason we find Biblical allusions in the two dramas in which they are plausible. In the pre-Christian setting of *Iphigenie* such references would be out of place even though the mythic analogy is still present (sanctuary, innocence, temptation). But in the other two works, although the sanctuary is now wholly secularized, it is repeatedly called "holy" and "paradise." In his argument with Antonio, Tasso acknowledges the sanctity of the sanctuary in the instant before he violates it by drawing his sword, thereby compounding his offense by his consciousness of his deed:

> Kein Heiligtum heißt uns den Schimpf ertragen.
> Du lästerst, du entweihest diesen Ort.
> . . . .
> Dein Geist verunreint dieses Paradies. . . . (ll. 1386-90)

Indeed, the whole description of the Arcadian setting with which the play opens can be read, on another level, as the depiction of a primal paradise: "Ja, es umgibt uns eine neue Welt!" (l. 28), Leonore exclaims. Similarly, the unspoiled seclusion in which Eugenie grows up is repeatedly called a "paradise" with the conventional attribute of innocence. After the King has agreed to accept Eugenie into court, her father laments:

> Ach! soll ich nun nicht mehr ins Paradies,
> Das dich umgab, am Abend wiederkehren,
> Zu deiner Unschuld heil'gem Vorgefühl
> Mich von der Welt gedrängter Posse retten! (ll. 471-74)

At the spot where Eugenie has been acknowledged by the King he intends to create a sanctuary that will make the astonished traveler believe that he has stumbled "into Paradise" (ll. 623-24). And Eugenie, with the retrospective knowledge of consciousness, realizes belatedly what a paradise she has forsaken:

> Ach, alles um mich her, es war so reich,
> So voll und rein, und was der Mensch bedarf,
> Es schien zur Lust, zum Überfluß gegeben.
> Und wem verdankt' ich solch ein Paradies? (ll. 1947-50)

In *Die natürliche Tochter* Goethe's genius for translating metaphor into symbolic action renders the fall from paradise by means of an actual fall: Eugenie's first appearance is occasioned by her plunge from her horse and from a cliff. This "fall," repeatedly designated as such (both "Sturz" and "Fall"), is only the symptom, not the cause of her removal from her childhood innocence and paradise. Goethe has provided psychological motivation: her failure to observe the oath of silence exacted by the King and her father. That very evening she betrays their confidence by trying on the garments and jewelry that her father has laid aside for the occasion. When she later recalls how she succumbed to that temptation, she translates her fall into Biblical images:

> O, so ist's wahr, was uns der Völker Sagen
> Unglaublichs überliefern! Jenes Apfels
> Leichtsinnig augenblicklicher Genuß
> Hat aller Welt unendlich Weh verschuldet. (ll. 1920—23)

To make the analogy absolutely clear, the whole episode of Eugenie's "fall" is paralleled in condensed form in the case of the Secular Priest, who recalls how he was tempted by the malevolent Steward to forsake his "paradise of restricted joys" in exchange for the questionable rewards of the political world. (ll. 1200-17).

In *Tasso* the Fall is not reified, but the poet of *La Gerusalemme Liberata* refers on several occasions to his exclusion from Belriguardo as a "fall." In the monologue following his interview with Leonore Sanvitale, Tasso combines the image of the Fall with another image in which the Tempter assumes the traditional Biblical guise:

> Ich war begünstigt, und sie schmiegte sich
> So zart — an den Beglückten. Nun ich falle,
> Sie wendet mir den Rücken wie das Glück.
> Nun kommt sie als ein Werkzeug meines Feindes,
> Sie schleicht heran und zischt mit glatter Zunge,
> Die kleine Schlange, zauberische Töne. (ll. 2505-10)

Both Tasso and Eugenie, then, plainly think of their destinies in terms of the Biblical Fall from Paradise. As clear as these parallels are, the Biblical motif is secondary to the basic paradigm outlined earlier. To put it most simply: Goethe did not set out to dramatize a postfiguration of the myth of the Fall. Instead, he adduced Biblical imagery, where appropriate, to illustrate and lend vividness to his own vision of the Imperiled Sanctuary.

This paradigmatic approach to Goethe's three classical dramas should not be misconstrued as an attempt to interpret the plays. We have virtually ignored such central aspects as the Orestes-plot and the Tasso-Antonio action in an effort to isolate the common elements that constitute the paradigm. But the paradigm does not conflict with various interpretations of the individual plays that have been cited. And it provides us with an additional objective means of establishing parallels between the plays of the "dramatic trilogy in blank verse" and of distinguishing them, as a category, from works with which they may share other characteristics (e.g., *Egmont* and *Faust*). In addition, the paradigm provides a useful tool for further interpretation: we can inquire, namely, in what ways Goethe had to modify the basic paradigm to suit the exigencies of the individual dramas. If the paradigm is valid, it helps to explain why Goethe chose certain subjects for his classical dramas while discarding others (e.g., the *Tell* legend): he felt instinctively that they corresponded to the pattern of his own being and experience. Modifying his own statement on metamorphosis in nature, we might conclude: "Mit diesem Modell und dem Schlüssel dazu kann man alsdann noch Dramen ins Unendliche erfinden, die konsequent sein müssen."

NOTES

[1] Goethe's work are cited according to the text of the *Hamburger Ausgabe* [*HA*] in 14 vols.: *Goethes Werke*, ed. Erich Trunz (Hamburg: Wegner, 1948 ff.).
[2] Ronald Peacock, *Goethe's Major Plays* (Manchester: University Press, 1959), p. 144.
[3] Emil Staiger, *Goethe* (Zürich und Freiburg im Breisgau: Atlantis, 1956), II, 366-402; Verena Bänninger, *Goethes Natürliche Tochter: Bühnenstil und Gehalt* (Zürich und Freiburg im Breisgau: Atlantis, 1957); Theo Stammen, *Goethe und die Französische Revolution: Eine Interpretation der 'Natürlichen Tochter'* (München: C. H. Beck, 1966).
[4] Max Kommerell, "Goethes Ballade vom vertriebenen Grafen," *Neue Rundschau*, 47 (1936), 1209-19; here p. 1211.
[5] Hans-Egon Hass, "Die natürliche Tochter," *Das deutsche Drama vom Barock bis zur Gegenwart: Interpretationen*, ed. Benno von Wiese (Düsseldorf: August Bagel, 1962), I, 215-47; here p. 245.
[6] Sigurd Burckhardt, "*Die natürliche Tochter*: Goethe's *Iphigenie in Aulis?*" *Germanisch-Romanische Monatsschrift*, 10 (1960), 12-34; rpt. in Burckhardt's *The Drama of Language: Essays on Goethe and Kleist* (Baltimore and London: The Johns Hopkins Press, 1970), 66-93; here p. 66.
[7] *Hamburger Ausgabe*, XIII, 172.
[8] Kommerell, "Goethes Ballade," p. 1209.
[9] Kommerell's idea has been developed by Josef Kunz in his commentary to *Tasso* and *Die natürliche Tochter* in vol. V of the *Hamburger Ausgabe* (esp. pp. 445 ff. and p. 483).
[10] In another article I have argued that it is essentially this focus on a future ideal that distinguishes Goethe's dramas from the tragedies of Schiller, which operate within a framework of present order. See "An Ontology of Anxiety in the Dramas of Schiller, Goethe, and Kleist," *Lebendige Form: Festschrift für Heinrich E. K. Henel*, ed. Jeffrey L. Sammons and Ernst Schürer (München: Wilhelm Fink, 1970), pp. 121-45.
[11] Oskar Seidlin, "Goethes Iphigenie — 'verteufelt human'?" *Modern Language Quarterly*, 10 (1949), 307 ff.; rpt. in Seidlin's *Von Goethe zu Thomas Mann: Zwölf Versuche* (Göttingen: Vandenhoeck & Ruprecht, 1963), p. 12, underscores this quality when

he writes that "Iphigenie ist nicht *eines* Menschen Schwester, sondern die Schwester des Menschen."

12 Wolfdietrich Rasch, *Goethes 'Torquato Tasso': Die Tragödie des Dichters* (Stuttgart: Metzler, 1954), p. 149, suggests that the Princess' illness left her with "eine Dämpfung des Anteils am Leben," which "kennzeichnet ihr Wesen."

13 Rasch, p. 80, argues that the Princess' *Sittlichkeit* is not a moral imperative but "die Sicherheit des inneren Gefühls, die gleichsam als Erbe der Goldenen Zeit in wenigen Einzelnen, zumal in den 'edlen Frauen' noch lebt."

14 My interpretation of the sanctuary does not conflict with the exhaustive analysis of landscape and garden offered by Gerhard Neumann, *Konfigurationen: Studien zu Goethes 'Torquato Tasso'* (München: Wilhelm Fink, 1965), pp. 18-33, 67-79. But I disagree with Stammen, *Goethe*, pp. 18 ff., who maintains that the forest setting in *Die natürliche Tochter* is colored by sinister images and who makes much of the (in my opinion mistaken) fact that the King and Duke are lost in the wilderness. Actually, the Duke knows precisely where they are since it is his own estate.

15 Sigurd Burckhardt, "The voice of truth and humanity': Goethe's *Iphigenie*," *Monatshefte*, 48 (1956), 49-71; rpt. *The Drama of Language*, pp. 43 ff.

16 E. M. Wilkinson, "Torquato Tasso," *Das deutsche Drama*, ed. Benno von Wiese, I, 193-194.

17 See Burckhardt's piece on *Die natürliche Tochter*, *The Drama of Language*, p. 81.

18 This distinction has been frequently noted in all three plays. Bänninger, *Goethes Natürliche Tochter*, p. 45, contrasts the "Welt der Humanität" and "Welt der Politik" in the drama; Arthur Henkel, "Iphigenie auf Tauris," *Das deutsche Drama*, ed. Benno von Wiese, I, 174-75, speaks of the realm of "Herz" and the world of "Vernunft"; and so forth.

19 In both *Tasso* and *Die natürliche Tochter* the image of the "ring" or "circle" is used frequently to characterize the enclosed sanctuary while, especially in the later play, the image of the "net" or "maze" exemplifies the world of political reality. In *Tasso* the image is reified in the wreath placed on the poet's head.

20 In his piece on *Die natürliche Tochter*, *The Drama of Language*, p. 168, n. 12.

21 Notably Barker Fairley, *A Study of Goethe* (1947; rpt. London: Oxford University Press, 1961), discusses *Iphigenie* and *Tasso* as "the two Charlotte dramas."

CAVEAT FOR FAUST CRITICS

Harold Jantz

An early difficulty that a reader can have with Goethe's *Faust* is similar to the one that the dear lady of anecdote had with Shakespeare's plays: they were just too full of quotations. So many people know so many particulars about *Faust* (various of these not even in Goethe's version) that they tend to see them in isolation, to detach them from their context, and even to give them meanings that disrupt the intent of the whole. In some instances no great harm is done by a popular misinterpretation, in others the consequences are graver. First a relatively innocent though typical example.

Floating about independently in the aerial regions of the *geflügelte Worte* is that proud tribute to a great city:

> Mein Leipzig lob' ich mir!
> Es ist ein klein Paris, und bildet seine Leute.

This is usually accompanied by the claim that Goethe said it. He did not, of course. The person who said it was drunken Frosch in Auerbachs Keller. If one looks at the other statements Frosch made just before and after this wingèd one and then considers the influence that Leipzig had on his *Bildung*, one will at least have to wonder whether the attitude of the author himself was not ironic.

In our time most critics would realize this, of course. So far so good, but critical understanding seems to be less advanced with regard to another well known particular. Near the end of the preceding scene, the last study scene, Faust asks Mephistopheles:

> Wohin soll es nun gehn?

and is answered (ll. 2051-54):

> Wohin es dir gefällt.
> Wir sehn die kleine, dann die große Welt.
> Mit welcher Freude, welchem Nutzen
> Wirst du den Cursum durchschmarutzen!

What has happened is that the interpretations have considered only the first line and a half of the answer, outside the context of the next two lines, and a critical consensus has been reached that Mephistopheles is here outlining the future course of the drama: from the "small world" of the Gretchen drama to the "great world" of the imperial court and Faust's realm. But can we possibly

89

see it this way in the larger context of the decidedly scurrilous "durchschmarutzen"? What Mephisto's real intent was here, I indicated in my "Patterns and Structures in *Faust*" (*MLN*, 83 [1968], 375-77). But there is another even more striking instance of Mephisto's perversion of these terms; we shall examine it a bit later, in full context.

Here, indeed, we have a typical example of one of the chief failings in *Faust* criticism: the disregard of contextuality. When, as in the above two instances, the interpretation out of context is combined with the mouthpiece principle (i.e., it is Goethe himself who is talking throughout and *Faust* is not really a drama), then the critic can proceed confidently to the third basic approach for misunderstanding *Faust*.

This third approach originates in an atavistic affection for the primitive simplicity of the old folk book in which Mephistopheles was plainly an agent of Hell who was leased out to Faust on a contractual basis. By contrast, the sophisticated ambiguities of this character in the Goethean drama are disquieting, to the point of creating grave confusion, as at that critical point where complex psychological processes cause the notion of a pact to be dropped and a wager to be put in its place. The original sin of resimplification was committed long ago by the directors and actors of the stage play who simply disregarded the text's very clear and specific directions as to how Mephisto is to clothe and behave himself. They dress him instead in sinister lines and colors, with peaked skull cap and diagonal eyebrows, and send him slinking and hissing about until that high point of involuntary humor is reached in the scene where Gretchen quizzes Faust about his religion. She confides to him that somehow, she does not know why, this companion of his gives her the shudders. Faust in admiring astonishment at her remarkable intuition replies (l. 3494):

> Du ahnungsvoller Engel du!

Here one is at the theatre and has in the preceding scenes observed the typical stage Mephistopheles in at least semi-diabolic make-up and costume rant and leer in all-too-obvious diabolic postures. How can one possibly credit Gretchen with any higher intuitive powers in having sensed his sinister nature? Indeed it would take a rather feeble-minded girl not to get the point of the actor's blatant hellishness. And, of course, Goethe never intended to present Gretchen as feeble-minded or Faust as overcome with astonishment to find even this small ray of intelligence in her.

Now the most alarming aspect of this patent absurdity is not simply that one never hears a single member of a German audience laugh or even snicker at this point, one never even hears of a single drama critic writing in protest against this perversion of the drama's intent. It does not even seem to be known that Goethe himself had carefully coached the great Carl La Roche in a quite different realization of the role of Mephistopheles or that there exists a detailed report on the elegant understatement with which this actor achieved his subtle and sophisticated characterization. When we reflect that there is not a single living German who has ever seen even an approximation of the Mephistopheles that Goethe intended, can we be too surprised at the wall of critical misunderstanding that has arisen between the reader and the work? All that remains is the Director's resigned cynicism (ll. 99-100):

> Gebt Ihr ein Stück, so gebt es gleich in Stücken!
> Solch ein Ragout, es muß Euch glücken...

So much then by way of preliminary examples. To be sure, they do not do justice to the present state of *Faust* criticism. Indeed they would be gravely unfair if they were intended as such. And yet, they are not unfair to a still prevailing critical consensus. Only a small though growing minority is consciously aware of the dubious nature of the Leipzig eulogy. All the commentaries continue to be naive about Mephistopheles' "kleine" and "große Welt." No audience is yet ridiculing the misfit stage Mephistopheles or demanding a more authentic one. The main point, however, is that these are not mere isolated particulars, these are actually brief, obvious examples of what is variously continuing to happen in *Faust* criticism, even though in a more subtle, sometimes far more subtle manner. In order to have access to these more subtle cases, let us first state the prime fallacies in a more generalized form. They are:

1. The assumption that Goethe uses the various characters in *Faust* as mouthpieces for the expression of his own opinions or intentions — this in disregard of the principle of multiple points of view that prevails throughout the drama.

2. The assumption that Mephistopheles especially serves as such a vehicle of the poet's attitudes and purposes — this in disregard of that character's notorious twisting and perverting of the facts and phenomena and of the particular tone and choice of words that accompany such twistings.

3. The assumption that a passage or a scene can be interpreted in isolation or with reference only to such scenes and passages that lend support to the desired interpretation — this in disregard of Goethe's own announced principle of contextuality, of "wiederholte Spiegelung," that brings a passage or scene, in itself obscure or ambiguous, to reasonable clarity and singleness of meaning.

4. The assumption that the *idea* of a scene or passage is the main thing and that everything else is relatively negligible: the tonal and verbal signs, the connotations, the frame of reference, the exact sequence, and such specific details as the stage directions and typographical dispositions — all this in disregard of Goethe's repeated remarks that the *Faust* is not a philosophical but a symbolic drama and that proper access to it can come only through the poetic and pictorial imagination.

To return to the small and the great world, I pointed out on a earlier occasion that whenever Mephistopheles uses the terms, either in their German form or in their Greek form as "microcosm" and "macrocosm," or in some oblique, allusive form, he reacts to them with peculiar animosity and uses all the resources of his wit and sarcasm to debase them or make them appear ludicrous. For the *Faust*, as for the centuries before it, the one valid meaning of *microcosm* is *man*. This concept of man as a microcosm, with its implications of creativity and human dignity, being so offensive to Mephistopheles (cf., e.g., ll. 284-5, 1347, 1789-92, 1801-2), arouses him to a perversion of the terms (anticipating modern usage). The perversion of the terms, at the departure, is the prelude to the perversion of the microcosm itself in the next two scenes, where he is master of ceremonies. It is an old compositional habit of Goethe's in poem, novel, or drama, to suggest casually at the end of a stanza, chapter, or scene, what the theme or subject of the next unit is going to be. He does so here: in the next scene we behold the degenerated "microcosms" that have been drowned in the drink of "Auerbachs Keller," and then in the following scene, the "Hexenküche," we behold the parodistic microcosms of the talking monkeys who verbalize quite free of any brain control, with rhyme taking the place of reason and free association that of responsible con-sequence.

But there is another instance of Mephisto's use of the "kleine" and "große Welt" that has led the critics astray, especially those who have found great depths of meaning in it. Again there is the prime fallacy and its associated fallacies that Mephisto is serving as a mouthpiece to convey Goethe's philosophical reflections or dramatic intentions, that he is playing no tricks, and that the passage can be interpreted outside its related context and environment. It comes at that point in the "Walpurgisnacht" where Mephistopheles diverts Faust from the mainstream of devotees, who are surging up to the great scene of Satanic worship, over to some interesting "side shows" along the way, with Faust objecting because he wants to press onward in order to explore the mystery of iniquity (ll. 4030-47):

> *Faust* Du Geist des Widerspruchs! Nur zu! du magst mich führen.
> Ich denke doch, das war recht klug gemacht:
> Zum Brocken wandeln wir in der Walpurgisnacht,
> Um uns beliebig nun hieselbst zu isolieren.
>
> *Mephistopheles* Da sieh nur, welche bunten Flammen!
> Es ist ein muntrer Klub beisammen.
> Im Kleinen ist man nicht allein.
>
> *Faust* Doch droben möcht' ich lieber sein!
> Schon seh' ich Glut und Wirbelrauch.
> Dort strömt die Menge zu dem Bösen;
> Da muß sich manches Rätsel lösen.
>
> *Mephistopheles* Doch manches Rätsel knüpft sich auch.
> Laß du die große Welt nur sausen,
> Wir wollen hier im Stillen hausen.
> Es ist doch lange hergebracht,

> Daß in der großen Welt man kleine Welten macht.
> Da seh' ich junge Hexchen nackt und bloß,
> Und alte, die sich klug verhüllen.

When Mephisto dampens the ardor of Faust's quest after the mystery of iniquity, where "many a riddle must be solved," with his wry remark that many a riddle is also made, his chief intent is not the innocently pedagogical one of making sure that Faust sees the metaphysical implications. His chief intent is diversionary: it would go gravely counter to his purpose and interest if Faust were to turn the Walpurgis expedition into a quest to fathom this mystery, and so he does the best he can to discourage him from such a course. His purpose and interest were exactly what he had outlined in an earlier monologue, to lead Faust through "flache Unbedeutenheit" (1861); and these separate tableaus on the Blocksberg are just such shallow inconsequentialities. How badly he miscalculated, here and in the last study scene, has not been clearly recognized.

As for the quip itself, on the old custom of making small worlds in the large world, it should be clear enough that the tone of voice, the context, and the speaker quite preclude such pseudo-profundities as a few of the critics have tried to read into it. I have no wish to indulge in personal censure, so I shall merely quote from one unnamed English critic, adding only that I could have quoted from a German critic just as well:

> Through exploration of the expansion and development of this one cell, the word *world*, we gain intimate knowledge of the movement and growth of the whole vast organism — so that when we light again on Mephisto's words,
>
> > It's something that has long been done
> > To fashion little worlds within the bigger one. (ll. 4044-4045)
>
> it strikes us with new resonance and is pregnant with our experience of all the "worlds" we have encountered whether in the poetry or the dramatic action.

The usual, more sober explication of the lines, that in the large world of society and affairs the continuing formation of cliques is an old tradition, is satisfactory enough within this limited setting. But if we keep the larger contexts and perspectives in mind, we need to note: 1) that Mephisto everywhere else uses the term and concept of microcosm maliciously, 2) that frequently, almost at every good opportunity, he likes to twist a remark or a situation into an obscenity, and 3) that his very next lines are not only obscene but are also the prelude to the most obscene episode in the whole of *Faust* (ll. 4124-43). In the jesting talk of Goethe's day, and since, "Kinder machen" was a common euphemism for the sexual act, often with the implications of illegitimacy. Such considerations must lead us at least to consider the possibility that what Mephisto is implying here is that the typical goings-on of the great world of high society have through the ages resulted in the production of microcosmic little bastards.

However, there is no compelling need to accept this explication if the reader finds the standard one more comfortable. He should merely beware of approaching such passages with an innocence that is more becoming to a Gretchen than a critic. Elsewhere too where obscenities occur, the poet often takes care to veil them in such a way that an explicator of good will can convey a more harmless meaning to a genteel audience.

To turn to more serious and important matters, our new insights into the diversionary tactics, the devious twistings and misdirections of the old rascal bring us face to face with one of the most frequently recurring problems in the detailed criticism of *Faust*. It is a well-grounded and generally accepted critical observation that Mephistopheles does occasionally tell the truth, that his statements can at times be relied on. To be sure, these occasions are rarer than is generally assumed and impressively numerous critical blunders continue to result from an all too trusting reliance upon the comments and interpretations he makes at various points throughout the drama. Then too there is the complication that he may occasionally tell the truth not from motives of pure candor but in order to obfuscate a confused situation still more, that he may occasionally utter a cynical truth simply to prick the bubble of Faust's or another's self-conceit or overexaltation, or that he may make a quip just for the fun of it, not failing occasionally even to laugh at himself. How then can we distinguish the times when he is being reliable from the times when he is leading us by the nose?

First of all, from the larger context, of course. When he describes himself to Faust as "der Geist, der stets verneint," and so forth (ll. 1338 ff.), this turns out to be in close agreement with what the Lord had said about him and disagrees with the Lord's statements in the "Prolog" in no particular except in the appropriately negative, anti-creative bias. When he describes the realm of the Mothers, his report is found to be in general agreement with Faust's upon return, and beyond that, in the larger context, with the whole continuum of the feminine creative throughout the drama. It would seem then that when Mephistopheles is speaking on the laws of his function and place in the spirit world, its conditions and relations, he is under higher obligation to speak the truth. Likewise, when Faust's demands exceed Mephisto's capabilities and when he needs the assistance of spirit worlds and forces beyond his own, he must be straightforward and truthful, albeit with the added ingredient of his usual negative slant or slur. On all other occasions: let the reader and critic beware. He has set more traps and caught more victims in them than has ever been realized.

But there is a second way in which we can tell, one that can best be used in combination with the first for the purpose of attaining still greater reliability of judgment. This second way is based upon a careful sensitive listening to the language level, to the tone and diction of Mephistopheles' statements. Even by itself alone this approach can lead to generally reliable results, as Kurt May has demonstrated in his *Faust II. Teil in der Sprachform gedeutet*. His observation of the elevated and serious tone that prevails in Mephisto's speeches in the Mothers' scene ("Finstere Galerie") and his description of quite different tones in his speeches elsewhere are for the most part right, and we can on their basis make reasonably good judgments on the intent and on the degree of reliability of Mephisto's statements at a particular point.

This is equally the case in Part One. If we look at the diction of Mephisto's self-description in the "Studierzimmer," we find a careful, dignified choice of words with none of the scurrilities of phrase or implication he indulges in so frequently elsewhere. On the other hand, when his statement about seeing the small and the great world occurs in combination with the inelegant "munching through this course," then let the critic beware: the old rascal is up to no good, he is setting yet another trap for the simply trusting. All the more so, when he is reflecting on the sex life of the upper classes in the "Walpurgisnacht," and immediately appends remarks on the dress and undress of witches, then an elevated intellectual vision is hardly the critical instrument to deal with the situation.

The "Walpurgisnacht" can lead us to another observation, small in itself, but grave in its implications for critical method. Years ago, in an article on "The Function of the 'Walpurgis Night's Dream' in the Faust Drama" (*Monatshefte*, 44 [1952], 397-408), I indicated incidentally that this scene, called an "Intermezzo" by Goethe, can artistically be an intermezzo only between Part One and Part Two of the drama. The carrying over of themes, motifs, and actors from the framework of the scene to the first scene of Part Two would appear to confirm this observation. And when we find the motifs of the enclosed satiric review in the "Dream" reappear in Part Two, the political satire conspicuously in Acts One and Four, then the transitional function of the playlet seems obvious. However, objections to such an interpretation could well rest upon the fact that between this intermezzo and the beginning of Part Two there are the three scenes that conclude the Gretchen tragedy and Part One. This playlet would thus seem to be in the wrong place for an interlude. At the time I offered only as much of the internal evidence as seemed necessary since my interest was concentrated more on other important structural matters: just why artistic considerations called for elves on the Brocken at this point, and especially why artistic considerations forbade the carrying out of the "Walpurgisnacht" to its conclusion in the Satanic rites, even as they forbade the carrying out of a Persephone scene in Part Two.

Before final judgment can be made, this interlude, this "Intermezzo," will have to be seen in the context of the several other interludes in the drama and of Goethe's technique of the interlude. I take up this formal device, among others, in my forthcoming book, *The Form of Faust*. For our present purposes, however, further confirmatory evidence from the text itself will suffice — not the text as the modern editors present it to us, but the text as Goethe originally intended and presented it. Modern editorial practice in *Faust* confronts us with a sad paradox: though every slightest verbal shift of *e* and apostrophe, of *m* and *n* is solemnly weighed, there is a bland disregard of the scene headings and even the scene divisions, without any thought that these may have been of artistic significance for the author. The verbal intellectual bias has again obscured the artistic, the visual, the spatial factors. In Part Two editorial interference has at several points resulted in a serious disturbance of the intended scenic balance, and at one point it has even, as we shall see, imposed an embarrassing error of judgment and an anachorism on the Goethean text.

Here, for Part One, it would be well for every critic to take in hand the first complete edition (Tübingen: Cotta, 1808), and carefully examine its typographical disposition. There are separate title pages (so-called half-titles), with following blank pages, for each of the three preliminary parts, the "Zueignung," the "Vorspiel auf dem Theater," and the "Prolog im Himmel." Then follows another such for "Der Tragödie Erster Theil." Then come the separate scenes, each of them, from the first Faust monologue onward, with only a title heading and stage directions in small type. Each new scene begins on a new page, but there are no blank pages in order to have a new scene begin on a right-hand page. This continues to be the case through the "Walpurgisnacht," which has its title heading in the usual small type. But then, after the end of this scene, there comes a blank left-hand page, then facing it a special title page, inscribed in large type:

Walpurgisnachtstraum

oder

Oberons und Titanias goldne Hochzeit.

Intermezzo.

The verso of this is blank again, and then only, on a right-hand page, does there follow the text of the interlude. The ensuing last three scenes have simple title headings once more, in small type. Goethe's final edition of Part One (in the *Ausgabe letzter Hand*), despite its greater typographic economy, does not save space at the expense of such a disposition but carefully preserves the half-titles and blank versos of the first edition.

The purely intellectual critic may feel that he can disregard this visual disposition and formal arrangement. However, the critic who is interested in *Faust* as a work of art must face the facts and phenomena: the first three preludial parts have separate title pages; the only other scene of Part One that is brought into visual correlation with them is the "Walpurgisnachtstraum." Once the facts are faced, the question "why" must be asked, and if there is any reasonable answer beyond the one I suggest, namely that this scene is a bridge to Part Two, it has not yet been made. In my forthcoming book I do suggest that there is another, supplementary reason for this title page. But at this point I can safely leave it to the reader to judge whether the traditional disregard can be justified, merely observing that for Goethe the external formal aspects were never dissociated from the intrinsic ones.

Acts Two and Three of Part Two have suffered most from editorial intervention and misunderstanding. The results are less grave in Act Three, the Helena drama. The first scene is designated in the usual way: "Vor dem Palaste des Menelas zu Sparta," so is the second scene, "Innerer Burghof" — but only in the modern editions. In the original editions there is no typographical demarcation for either the second or the third scene. There are only directions in parentheses, just like the other stage directions in this act or elsewhere in the drama. Thus again the ideological bias of the modern editors, disregarding the importance of the poet's pictorial imaginative intent, has falsified the text by supplying misleadingly clear and definite scene divisions that are not present in Goethe's original text. The poet, for special artistic purposes, wanted no sharp divisions in this act but rather a magical almost imperceptible blending over, as the nature of the transition through the mist between the palace of Menelaos and the inner courtyard of Faust's castle plainly shows. Goethe's letters at the time of the completion of the Helena act indicate such an intent of unity, and when it was published separately in 1827 in volume four of the *Ausgabe letzter Hand*, the disposition was no different from that of the completed first edition.

Another kind of ambiguity in scene shift occurs variously, for one in the first scene of Act Four, "Hochgebirg": as we reach the last sixth of it, not so much a change as a shift of scene is suggested when the stage directions tell us about Faust and Mephistopheles (after l. 10296): "Sie steigen über das Mittelgebirg herüber und beschauen die Anordnung des Heeres im Tal...."

The modern editions have not tampered with this *Wanderszene* by changing stage directions into scene divisions and thus creating an unauthorized and unintended new scene. But in the case of another shifting or wandering scene they have intervened in a way that has impaired the understanding of the poet's intent. This hapless editorial intervention occurs in Act Two, in the "Klassische Walpurgisnacht." In the first place, there is no authority for inserting a scene division, "Am oberen Peneios," between lines 7079 and 7080. There is also no need for it. If the modern editors had merely consulted an atlas of antiquity, they would have realized that the initial scenic indication, "Pharsalische Felder" (before l. 7005), places the whole scene at the headwaters of the Peneios. The second unwarranted insertion, "Am untern Peneios" (between ll. 7248 and 7249), relegating the real title, "Peneios umgeben von Gewässern und Nymphen," to a stage direction, is an actual falsification of the poet's intent and saddles him with a painful blunder that he himself would never have committed. Quite obviously, he would know that a river god in ancient art and imagination is always represented as being at the source, not near the mouth. Here the god is even surrounded by the tributary "Gewässer." Thus the scene, in its beginning, is certainly at the upper, not the lower Peneios. And it is with appropriate symbolism at the source that Faust has his vision of Leda and the swan. Soon thereafter, however, when he has mounted Chiron, he is borne swiftly through the night to the lower reaches of the Peneios, to the foot of Mount Olympus, where, at the battle field of Pydna, as Chiron explains allusively, King Perseus of Macedon was defeated by Aemelius Paulus (in a battle array, incidentally, closely anticipating that of Act Four). Only when one understands the whole continuity, will one be saved from drawing false inferences from the next, genuine designation of scene (between ll. 7494 and 7495), "Am obern Peneios" originally in the manuscript, then changed to "Am obern Peneios wie zuvor" and so first printed. The action in the one scene has simply wandered downstream and in the next scene is back again at the headwaters where the seismic events take place and Mephisto at last finds kindred spirits at the edge of chaos. There is one further arbitrary editorial intervention in this act, and altogether it should be apparent by now that if Goethe had any intent toward a harmonic disposition of scenes (and he certainly did), then it is effectively obscured in the modern texts.

Nevertheless, the modern editors have contributed far less than Mephistopheles toward confusing the issues. His tricky, twisty running commentary on the course of events has led to more errors of interpretation than any other cause. It is one small aspect of Goethe's poetic genius that he was able to create a fictitious rascal, charlatan, deceiver who was able to hoodwink some of the best critical minds that fell under his spell. It is another aspect, however, that the poet, the literary artist, has not participated in the deception; quite the opposite: he has dealt fairly all along with the alert (or forewarned) reader and furnished him, within the text itself, with the means for seeing through the flimflam of this old confidence man.

Let us examine a specific instance in the last study scene. After Faust's great curse (ll. 1583-1606), the chorus of spirits sings a dirge to the beautiful world he has destroyed and calls upon him to reconstruct it more splendidly (ll. 1607-26). Thereupon Mephistopheles at once adds (ll. 1627-34):

> Dies sind die Kleinen
> Von den Meinen.
> Höre, wie zu Lust und Taten
> Altklug sie raten!
> In die Welt weit,
> Aus der Einsamkeit,
> Wo Sinnen und Säfte stocken,
> Wollen sie dich locken.

Then he continues in a "sincere," "sympathetic" tone to adjure Faust to abandon his self-consuming introspection and plunge into the active life of the world. It is hardly to be believed, yet true, that critics have seriously debated whether the spirits of this chorus are truly Mephisto's minions; a few have even rendered a verdict in the affirmative. If one merely compares what he claimed they said with what they actually said, one will observe an almost total discrepancy. It so happens that this is probably Mephisto's clumsiest and least convincing effort at "covering up," at diverting the attention from what had really been said. The chorus had summoned Faust from his zero point of nihilism to a new life of creativity, and creativity is for Mephistopheles just the most maddening factor in God's universe, as he indicates from the "Prolog" onward, with his baldest anti-creative statement coming in the preceding scene (ll. 1337-44). In brief, the spirits, far from being his minions, had here intervened (in mountebank parlance they had "queered his pitch"). He was disconcerted, thrown off balance, and in his moment of panic improvised an "interpretation" so implausible that it should never have deceived anybody, and then furthermore felt compelled quickly to cover up this makeshift again in his "hearty," "man-to-man" exhortation to Faust to surmount his grief. Once it is pointed out, his shiftiness here is quite obvious.

Through the whole scene Mephisto never quite recovers from the nasty surprise of the spirit chorus and this early he commits the blunder that he repeats several more times in the course of the scene, the second and third time crucially, for the blunder results in his losing the chance of attaining a firm quid-pro-quo compact with Faust and forces him to agree to Faust's counter-proposal of an open-ended wager (winner take all, loser lose all). At this point critical confusion will readily give way to clarity if one carefully observes what happens in the order in which it happens, and also observes why there was a sudden shift from an expected compact to an unexpected wager. The first time Mephisto makes the blunder, he quickly covers over (ll. 1637-40):

> Die schlechteste Gesellschaft läßt dich fühlen,
> Daß du ein Mensch mit Menschen bist.
> Doch so ist's nicht gemeint,
> Dich unter das Pack zu stoßen.

Then comes the discussion of the terms of the originally intended compact. With Faust recklessly disregarding the future consequences, Mephisto sees victory at hand and to clinch the bargain, holds out delightful prospects for Faust (ll. 1671-74):

> In diesem Sinne kannst du's wagen.
> Verbinde dich; du sollst, in diesen Tagen,
> Mit Freuden meine Künste sehn,
> Ich gebe dir, was noch kein Mensch gesehn.

Ironically, however, these words turn out not to be the final inducement to persuade Faust to agree to a compact, they turn out to be Mephisto's major blunder, a badly miscalculated case of "overselling," an insult to Faust's intelligence, as the latter's indignant reply at once makes clear (ll. 1675-77):

> Was willst du armer Teufel geben?
> Ward eines Menschen Geist, in seinem hohen Streben,
> Von deinesgleichen je gefaßt?

This state of indignation arouses Faust first to his bitter paradoxical listing of self-destructive values and then, after Mephisto stupidly repeats his blunder (ll. 1690-91) to his counter offer of a wager, which Mephisto must accept in place of a compact. Even after the paper containing the terms of the wager is signed, Mephisto's blind spot in his view of man causes him to persist in his blunder (ll. 1760-64) and this time elicits from an irritated Faust his opposing statement of purpose for the life he plans to lead (ll. 1765-75). Even this is not the end of Mephisto's stupidity: his wrong estimate of Faust's wish and intent echoes on to the scurrility of "den Cursum durchschmarutzen" and the futile introduction to the "schlechteste Gesellschaft" assembled in "Auerbachs Keller."

To return to the spirits, clearly they are not Mephisto's minions or they would not be so sorrowful at destruction and so fervently advocating a course of creativity. Equally clearly they are not purely benignant spirits, for in the previous scene they wickedly relish Mephisto's dilemma but also good-naturedly and coöperatively sing Faust to sleep — do so in a song of high imagination and noble beauty far beyond the range of Mephisto and his kind. A merely ideological approach is likely to be insensitive to the poetic aspects and not to realize that it is disregarding just what is essential. An intellectual analysis, helpless before the tangle of contradictions, can do no better than speak abstractly of neutral spirits, as though these little fellows could ever be insipidly neutral. Actually, any child (or any Irishman) with some inner understanding of folklore can come more closely and quickly to insight into the poet's intent: these are the little people about whom the common people are so well informed: benignant, tricky, whimsical, capricious, good-natured, malicious elves, gnomes, fairies, *Heinzelmännchen*. One trait of theirs recurs repeatedly in legend and fairy tale: their sorrow and dismay at any kind of destructiveness. Exemplifying this are the various and wide-spread legends that their song of lament can be heard in the air shortly before a great disaster such as the destruction of a town. In the one study scene the spirits were gaily capricious and melodiously poetic, in the other deeply concerned.

In brief, some of the knottiest problems in *Faust* will find their ready solution if one does not overintellectualize, if, for instance, one is willing to take these spirits folkloristically instead of metaphysically. Furthermore, if Mephisto's weak improvisation about the spirits has had some power of persuasion, how much greater a power of deception must emanate from his better planned and more subtle twists and turns. *Caveat criticus.* If only two precautionary measures are taken against him, the danger of misdirection will largely be removed. The first precaution is to view any attractive or "convincing" statement of his in its larger context. The second precaution is to listen with a sensitive ear to the tone of voice, the choice of words in each statement of his. Cool comparative analysis and alert ear will preserve us even from his most cunning traps.

Despite the greater care of recent years in examining the precise content of the text of *Faust*, there are still to this day a number of further instances where the exact wording and sequence of a scene have not been accurately observed. One such can be found in the standard interpretation of the scene of Faust's burial, the "Grablegung," which I reexamined for an essay in the Detlev Schumann Festschrift entitled "Goethe's Last Jest in *Faust*."

It would be possible to multiply the examples of misinterpretations that result from dubious critical criteria and assumptions or from inaccurate observation. But there is no need to do so. The selection here offered will suffice to alert the reader and critic to the chief dangers awaiting him in the interpretations of particulars in the work. There are the dangers from the autobiographical or "mouthpiece" approach, to be countered by the observation of the principle of multiple points of view that prevails in the drama, and by a wariness against accepting any one point of view, worst of all Mephisto's. There are the dangers from the fragmentist approach, to be countered by the careful regard for the full contextuality and mutually illuminating relationships. There are the dangers from the ideological approach, to be countered by the clear observation of the images and configurations. A centrally artistic approach will take its perspectives from the larger poetic traditions here pertinent, will carefully examine the particular themes and sequences, will give due regard to the principle of contextuality, and, not least of all, will listen with sensitive ear to the special voice and sustaining tone that so frequently, even usually, indicate attitude and intention.

ONCE MORE *AMPHITRYON*: LINES 1564-1568

Donald H. Crosby

> Wenn du, der Gott, mich jetzt umschlungen hieltest
> Und jetzo sich Amphitryon mir zeigte,
> Ja — dann so traurig würd ich sein, und wünschen,
> Daß er der Gott mir wäre, und daß du
> Amphitryon mir bliebst, wie du es bist. (ll. 1564-1568)[1]

The lines quoted above will be familiar to students of Kleist's tragicomedy *Amphitryon*. They contain Alkmene's answer to the last of a series of questions put to her by Jupiter, the divine *poseur* who has assumed the guise of her lawful husband. The trust of Jupiter's questioning had already become apparent twenty lines earlier, when he returned to a tack taken (unsuccessfully) in the first act of the drama: his attempt to insinuate a distinction between the lover and the husband, i.e., between himself and Amphitryon. For the sake of clarity this key passage in the second act bears quoting in its entirety:

Jupiter: Wenn ich nun dieser Gott dir wär —?
Alkmene: Wenn du
— Wie ist mir denn? Wenn du mir dieser Gott wärst
— — Ich weiß nicht, soll ich vor dir niederfallen,
Soll ich es nicht? Bist dus mir? Bist dus mir?
Jupiter: Entscheide du. Amphitryon bin ich.
Alkmene: Amphitryon —
Jupiter: Amphitryon, dir ja.
Doch wenn ich, frag ich, dieser Gott dir wäre,
Dir liebend vom Olymp herabgestiegen,
Wie würdest du dich dann zu fassen wissen?
Alkmene: Wenn du mir, Liebster, dieser Gott wärst — ja,
So wüßt ich nicht, wo mir Amphitryon wäre,
So würd ich folgen dir, wohin du gehst,
Und wärs auch, wie Euridike, zum Orkus.
Jupiter: Wenn du nicht wüßtest, wo Amphitryon wäre.
Doch wie, wenn sich Amphitryon jetzt zeigte?
Alkmene: Wenn sich Amphitryon mir — ach, du quälst mich.
Wie kann sich auch Amphitryon mir zeigen,
Da ich Amphitryon in Armen halte?
Jupiter: Und dennoch könntst du leicht den Gott in Armen halten,
Im Wahn, es sei Amphitryon.

> Warum soll dein Gefühl dich überraschen?
> Wenn ich, der Gott, dich hier umschlungen hielte,
> Und jetzo dein Amphitryon sich zeigte,
> Wie würd dein Herz sich wohl erklären?
> *Alkmene:* Wenn du, der Gott, mich hier umschlungen hieltest
> Und jetzo sich Amphitryon mir zeigte,
> Ja — dann so traurig würd ich sein, und wünschen,
> Daß er der Gott mir wäre, und daß du
> Amphitryon mir bliebst, wie du es bist. (ll. 1540-1568)

The final four lines demanding our attention here would seem to be straightforward enough both in their literal meaning and in their implication: Alkmene confesses that, faced with a choice between the god posing as Amphitryon and her lawful husband, she would wish that her *husband* were the god ("Daß er der Gott mir wäre"), so that she could remain in the embrace of the "other" Amphitryon, the divine impostor. Alkmene's choice here is a *Wunschbild* in the most literal sense of the word, one which prefigures the actual choice she makes in the final act of the play, when she rejects her husband and identifies the imposter as the "real" Amphitryon.

Surprisingly, these lines have evoked almost as much diversity of opinion as Alkmene's final sigh, the ambivalent *Ach* which closes the play. E. L. Stahl sees in this passage "the veritable seduction of Alkmene," but contends, paradoxically, that it represents "Jupiter's most signal defeat."[2] Walter Silz supports this view and adds the cautionary observation that "the fact that Jupiter has lost does not mean that Alkmene has won."[3] The late Peter Szondi professed to see no choice at all in Alkmene's answer: "Sie entscheidet sich also weder für Amphitryon noch für Jupiter, sondern gegen beide, die nur in ihrer Vorstellung existieren, und für jenen, der ihr gegenwärtig ist. Und diesen Jupiter-Amphitryon, der nicht der Gott ist, sondern der göttliche Mensch, der Mensch in der Göttlichkeit seines Gefühles, bezeichnet sie im dritten Akt vor dem Volk Thebens als den wirklichen Amphitryon und den wirklichen als den Betrüger."[4] Helmut Arntzen concedes the factive reality of Alkmene's choice, but then adds the interpretation: "Alkmene liebt weder den realen Menschen Amphitryon noch glaubt sie dem Gott, zu dem sie betet, sie bekennt sich zu ihrem Idol."[5] Most recently, Wolfgang Wittkowski, writing in the 1968 *Festgabe* of the Heinrich-von-Kleist-Gesellschaft (*Kleist und Frankreich*), advances the interpretation that Alkmene simply wishes that the two might exchange places, but without prejudice to the husband: "in jenem angenommenen Fall wünscht sie, beide möchten ihre Rolle oder ihre Plätze tauschen, so daß ihr der Gott vom Leibe bliebe und der Gatte sie im Arme hielte, wie er es tut."[6] Typical of the tender-hearted school of *Amphitryon*-criticism which finds it embarrassing to take Alkmene at her word, this reading flies in the face of the text, which specifically states that Alkmene would prefer to remain in the embrace of the god while keeping the *Gatte* at arm's length. Wittkowski does admit that Alkmene's theoretical choice anticipates the final scene of the play, but goes on to insist that Alkmene rejects the god and forces him to confess his "endgültige Niederlage."[7]

Writing cheek-by-jowl with Wittkowski in the same *Festgabe*, Lawrence Ryan contradicts the former critic's interpretation and offers a rather tentative one of his own: "Zwischen dem Amphitryon gewordenen Gott und dem Gott gewordenen Amphitryon entscheidet sie eigentlich nicht, sie wünscht sich die Einigkeit beider. Damit entscheidet sie sich *in einem gewissen Sinne* [italics mine] für Jupiter und gegen Amphitryon, der vor dem Tor steht und auf sein lächerliches Menschenrecht [sic] pocht." Ryan concludes by exculpating both Alkmene and Jupiter: "... ihrem Manne wird sie damit keineswegs untreu, Jupiter will sie auch nicht zur Untreue überreden."[8] This charitable assessment of Jupiter's motives is unfortunately not reconciled with Kleist's retention (from his source) of both the frivolously prolonged love night (ll. 110-118) and the god's insistence on the distinction between the lover and the husband (ll. 443-500). Also, in ascribing a pedagogical purpose to Jupiter's visit, ("Der Gott [möchte] ihr zu einem tieferen Verständnis der Liebe verhelfen...")[9], Ryan follows in the footsteps of an earlier commentator, Hans-Georg Gadamer, who concluded that Jupiter wanted to "teach" Alkmene to respect "das untrügliche Gefühl":

> Der innere Sinn dieses Gesprächs scheint mir darin zu bestehen, daß der Gott Alkmene lehren will, das untrügliche Gefühl, das in ihr ist, nicht zu verleugnen, und daß sie, wenn sie an sich selbst zweifelt, auch an der Göttlichkeit des Göttlichen zweifelt, und umgekehrt, daß wenn sie zu ihrem eignen Gefühl steht, sie den Gott in seiner wahren Göttlichkeit sein und erscheinen lässt... Indem sie nicht mehr zwischen dem Gatten und dem Geliebten unterscheidet, gibt sie beiden, dem Gatten und dem Gott, ihr Sein. Der Gott ist der Gott des innersten Gefühls. Es ist nur konsequent, daß Alkmenes Verwirrung von nun an behoben ist [sic!] und nicht mehr wiederkehrt.[10]

This is indeed one of the more puzzling interpretations of the key scene of Act II, for if Alkmene is in fact cured of her confusion — as Gadamer insists — how is one to explain her aberrant behavior (her choice of the "wrong" Amphitryon; her cursing of her husband; her near-fatal collapse) in Act III? If Alkmene is not *verwirrt* in the closing scene of the play, one might be hard-pressed to identify any Kleistian hero (or heroine) to whom this condition might be ascribed. These examples could be multiplied, but since the main lines of argumentation among recent Kleist scholars are limned by the above statements one may perhaps dispense with additional quotations. The arguments — they are by no means mutually exclusive — may be summarized as follows: 1) the passage marks Jupiter's defeat in his quest for Alkmene's love; 2) Alkmene's feelings do not betray her and she chooses her husband after all, since Jupiter is still wearing the mask of Amphitryon; 3) Alkmene chooses neither her husband nor the god, but rather a mystical composite.

To deal with these arguments in turn: it is difficult to see how the passage marks a "defeat" for Jupiter, since Alkmene's words convey admissions Jupiter has sought to elicit from the very beginning of the drama: the factive distinction between the lover and the husband and the superiority of the former over the latter. Previously, every attempt Jupiter had made in order to draw this admission from Alkmene had been rebuffed. In his first appearance (Act I, scene 4) he had pressed Alkmene to reveal "Ob den Gemahl du heut, dem du verlobt bist,/ Ob den Geliebten du empfangen hast?" (ll. 456-457), without receiving much more than the ego-gratifying compliment that the lover in the husband had excelled himself (ll. 487-489), and that the past love-night had seemed shorter than previous ones (ll. 506-507). Yet in Alkmene's consciousness lover and husband were still one, "...da die Götter eines und das andere/In dir mir einigten..." (ll. 490-491). As if to compensate for this rebuff, Jupiter uses his supernatural power to alter the initial in the diadem of Labdakus from "A" to "J", hoping through this sleight-of-hand to impress upon Alkmene the distinction he had failed to insinuate in the earlier scene. He succeeds only to the extent that Alkmene recoils in shame from the thought that she has embraced an impostor and thus vitiated her marriage vows. Jupiter, forced into playing his trump card, now confesses that "Zeus selbst, der Donnergott, hat dich besucht" (l. 1336). From this point onward Alkmene is cognizant of the fact that "ein anderer" had visited her, but her piety towards "Der Götter ew'ger, und der Menschen, Vater" allows her to accept, without stain to her virtue, the signal "honor" bestowed upon her. Yet at this juncture of the plot her feelings toward Jupiter (her deity, not the god-lover before her) betray nothing more than reverence, an inference which is borne out by her admission in lines 1538-1540: "Läßt man die Wahl mir — die Wahl, so bliebe meine Ehrfurcht ihm,/Und meine Liebe dir, Amphitryon." Hence if one is to speak of Jupiter's "defeats" (as do Stahl, Silz, and Wittkowski), one must seek them earlier in the play, in any case before the climactic lines 1564-1568 of Act II.

Jupiter's putative omniscience fails him more than once, as for example in his abject confession:

>   *Er* war
> Der Hintergangene, mein Abgott! *Ihn*
> Hat seine böse Kunst, nicht dich getäuscht,
> Nicht dein unfehlbares Gefühl! Wenn er
> In seinem Arm dich wähnte, lagst du an
> Amphitryons geliebter Brust, wenn er
> Von Küssen träumte, drücktest du die Lippe
> Auf des Amphitryons geliebten Mund.
> O einen Stachel trägt er, glaub es mir,
> Den aus dem liebeglühnden Busen ihm
> Die ganze Götterkunst nicht reißen kann. (ll. 1287-1297)

In other words: in his "liebeglühnden Busen" Jupiter had yearned to be loved in his own person, not as a surrogate husband whose form he had usurped. That the god cannot "be" Amphitryon, but rather retains his divine identity is made clear through this confession; it is a distinction which becomes vital for the later course of the drama. Here the god has lost only a battle, however, not the war, and in the space of a few lines he marshalls another argument for the divine visitation: Jupiter is a jealous god who wanted to "punish" Alkmene for having venerated her husband:

> Wer ists, dem du an seinem Altar betest?
> Ist ers dir wohl, der über Wolken ist?
> Kann dein befangner Sinn ihn wohl erfassen?
> Kann dein Gefühl, an seinem Nest gewöhnt,
> Zu solchem Fluge wohl die Schwingen wagen?
> Ists nicht Amphitryon, der Geliebte stets,
> Vor welchem du im Staube liegst? (ll. 1447-1453)

For all its theological trappings, this argument marks still another attempt, on Jupiter's part, to draw a distinction between the god-lover and the husband. Here again he fails, for although Alkmene penitently vows to think of Jupiter, rather than of her husband, during her morning devotions, she all but vitiates the vow by adding ingenuously that afterwards she will "forget" Jupiter:

> Gut, gut, du sollst mit mir zufrieden sein.
> Es soll in jeder ersten Morgenstunde
> Auch kein Gedanke fürder an dich denken:
> Jedoch nachher vergeß ich Jupiter. (ll. 1486-1489)

Jupiter's most crushing *Niederlage* — to use Wittkowski's term — comes, however, a few lines later, after the god's smug prediction of Alkmene's reaction to an unmasked Jupiter, i.e., to the god revealed in all his divine aspects:

> Du sahst noch sein unsterblich Antlitz nicht,
> Alkmene. Ach, es wird das Herz vor ihm
> In tausendfacher Seligkeit dir aufgehn.
> Was du ihm fühlen wirst, wird Glut dir dünken,
> Und Eis, was du Amphitryon empfindest.
> Ja, wenn er deine Seele jetzt berührte,
> Und zum Olymp nun scheidend wiederkehrt,
> So wirst du das Unglaubliche erfahren,
> Und weinen, daß du ihm nicht folgen darfst. (ll. 1497-1505)

These are strange lines, largely neglected by commentators of the drama, although they prefigure precisely Alkmene's reaction in the final scene of the play, where she indeed saves her "Glut" for the god and reacts "icily" to her husband. For all their prescience, though, the lines evoke another crushing blow to Jupiter's ego; for Alkmene's answer contradicts the strangely fallible god:

> Nein, nein, das glaube nicht, Amphitryon.
> Und könnt ich einen Tag zurücke leben,

> Und mich vor allen Göttern und Heroen
> In meine Klause riegelfest verschließen,
> So willigt ich —
> ....
> So willigt ich von ganzem Herzen ein. (ll. 1506-1511)

Jupiter's wounded vanity expresses itself in an "aside," which, as Walter Silz remarks, "[smacks] of the 'curses!' of many a foiled villain:"[11]

> Verflucht der Wahn, der mich hierher gelockt! (l. 1512)

Alkmene's rebuff seems to mark a signal defeat for Jupiter — paradoxically enough, since he has just made a prediction which will be borne out by the events of the final act — but it is a defeat only in an *abstract* sense. What Alkmene is really saying is that the *idea* of being loved by Jupiter does not appeal to her; if possible she would just as soon be spared the honor. This rebuke to Jupiter's pride forces the god into an appeal to pity. Taking his cue from Molière's love-struck Olympian, who is not above comic-opera posturing,[12] Jupiter beseeches Alkmene for her favor:

> Du wolltest ihm, mein frommes Kind,
> Sein ungeheures Dasein nicht versüßen?
> Ihm deine Brust verweigern, wenn sein Haupt,
> Das weltenordnende, sie sucht,
> Auf seinen Flaumen auszuruhen? Ach Alkmene!
> Auch der Olymp ist öde ohne Liebe.
> ....
>
> Wärst du vom Schicksal nun bestimmt
> So vieler Millionen Wesen Dank,
> Ihm seine ganze Fordrung an die Schöpfung
> In einem einzgen Lächeln auszuzahlen,
> Würdst du dich ihm wohl — ach! ich kanns nicht denken,
> Laß michs nicht denken — laß —   (ll. 1514 f.; 1528 ff.)

This undignified appeal evokes nothing more in Alkmene than pious resignation:

> Fern sei von mir,
> Der Götter großem Ratschluß mich zu sträuben,
> Ward ich so heilgem Amte auserkoren.
> Er, der mich schuf, er walte über mich.
> Doch —   (ll. 1533-1537)

The avowal culminates in the distinction, mentioned earlier, between the *Ehrfurcht* she would grant to the god and the *Liebe* she would prefer to reserve for "you, Amphitryon."

Up to this point, it is possible to speak of Jupiter's "defeats," but one must recognize that the god has been rejected only on an abstract level, i.e., that Alkmene has stubbornly resisted the *idea* of loving Jupiter more than — or even as much as — she loves her husband. But the purity of Alkmene's feelings, the absolute quality of her love — qualities made abundantly clear in this extended *Verhörszene* — cannot becloud the fact that her "innerstes Gefühl" has misled her, and that her "Goldwaage der Empfindungen" has failed to warn her that she has been embracing an impostor. Because he senses this discrepancy, the love-struck god forces her (in lines 1564-1568) to make a theoretical choice; *Ehrfurcht* is not enough for the father of the Gods, who wants to be loved in his own person: "*Er* will geliebt sein, nicht ihr Wahn von ihm" (l. 1522). The confession Jupiter elicits from Alkmene provides just that gratification he has so relentlessly pursued. Faced with the choice between the *two* Amphitryons, one the divine impostor holding her in his arms, the other the lawful husband, Alkmene would "wish" that her husband, approaching upon the scene, were the god (to whom she owes *Ehrfurcht*), so that she could remain in the embrace of the counterfeit husband, the impostor whom she would then "wish" to be Amphitryon.

Defenders of Alkmene are reluctant to concede that so exemplary a woman could willingly — even in a subjunctive *Wunschbild* — commit an act of infidelity. They argue, in effect, that Alkmene chooses the god "...Im Wahn, er sei Amphitryon." They thereby overlook the fact that Jupiter has already dealt with this contingency ("Und dennoch könntest du leicht den Gott im Arme halten...") and has insisted upon an unequivocal choice between himself and her husband. Just as in the final act, Alkmene is here forced to choose between two distinct personalities. By rejecting her husband — as she clearly does — she violates the very marital laws which are so sacred to her. The severity of this judgment is not lessened by Alkmene's self-reassuring concluding lines: "...und daß du / Amphitryon mir bliebst, wie du es bist." (ll. 1567 f.)

Jupiter's question, it must be remembered, is a hypothetical one ("Doch wenn ich...dieser Gott dir wäre"); hence Alkmene has no reason to doubt that she is, at this moment, embracing her husband. Her fidelity becomes tainted, however, when she admits that, under the circumstances posited by Jupiter, she would turn her back on her husband, so that "...you [the god] would remain my Amphitryon, just as you are."

Measured against textual evidence, Alkmene's theoretical choice in lines 1564-1568 cannot possibly mark Jupiter as the "loser," for it grants him the triumph he has so greedily sought: the conquest of the beautiful mortal in spirit as well as in body. How else is one to explain the jubilant, narcissistic tone of Jupiter's reaction, a reaction so spontaneous that the putatively omniscient god himself seems surprised by Alkmene's choice?[13]

>Mein süßes, angebetetes Geschöpf!
>In dem so selig ich mich, selig preise!
>So urgemäß dem göttlichen Gedanken,
>In Form und Maß, und Sait und Klang,
>Wie's meiner Hand Aeonen nicht entschlüpfte! (ll. 1569-1573)

These are scarcely the words of a rejected suitor. And yet only in the context of Jupiter's search for requited love could Alkmene's infidelity qualify her as being "so urgemäß dem göttlichen Gedanken, / Wie's meiner Hand Aeonen nicht entschlüpfte." One would expect that conjugal *fidelity*, rather than its breach, would be closer to the "göttlicher Gedanke!" The ecstatic tone of Jupiter's response stands in contradiction to Lawrence Ryan's assertion that the god was not intent on inducing Alkmene to commit adultery; were this in fact the case, her answer should have evoked despair rather than jubilation. For surely the answer of a truly virtuous woman under such circumstances would be couched in terms such as the following: "If you, the god, were holding me in your arms, and suddenly my Amphitryon were to appear, then I would be so sad, *but I would turn away from you in remorse and shame and return to his side.*" Such an avowal, rather than the patent confession of an adulterous wish, would elicit praise from an orthodox ethical god; that it does not reflects negatively on Kleist's *Gottesbegriff*.

As for the argument that Alkmene's feelings do not lead her astray, because her choice reinforces rather than betrays her fidelity to her husband (Gadamer and Ryan; see also H. A. Korff[14] and Benno von Wiese[15]): it is difficult to see how this reasoning can be confirmed by textual evidence. To be sure, not even the sternest moralist could fault Alkmene for having given herself to Jupiter the night before, since the god's supernatural powers had beclouded her judgment:

> Ich hätte für sein Bild ihn halten können,
> Für sein Gemälde, sieh, von Künstlerhand,
> Dem Leben treu, ins Göttliche verzeichnet.
> . . . .
> Er wars, Amphitryon, der Göttersohn! (ll. 1189 ff.)

The choice between *two* Amphitryons is an entirely different matter, as the final scene makes clear. To excuse Alkmene's choice on the grounds that Jupiter is merely Amphitryon in higher potency is to fall back on the god's own pseudo-pantheistic arguments, although these arguments fail to convince Alkmene (lines 1257 ff.) and (as Silz and Wittkowski have pointed out[16]) defy logical analysis. If Jupiter were indeed all things ("Die Kadmusburg und Griechenland, etc." [l. 2298]), as he grandly claims, he would have had no need to purloin Amphitryon's identity in the first place.[17] Such an argumentation, furthermore, ignores the tragic duality which pervades much of Kleist's work: the discrepancy between illusion and reality, between *Sein und Schein*. It would have been strange indeed had Kleist, writing in 1806 in the wake of his own tragic disillusionments, sought to resolve a tragic dilemma with facile pantheistic rationalizations.

It also makes no sense to insist (as do Szondi and others) that Alkmene, in her wish-projection, does not really make a choice, since the god-lover at that moment "is" Amphitryon; such an argument is inconsistent with the play's conclusion, during which both "Amphitryons" appear side-by-side. This climactic scene represents the intensification of II/5, since it brings the factual realization of what in the earlier scene had merely been a hypothetical construction. Once again, as in lines 1564-1568, Alkmene is misled by the irresistible charisma of the god and betrayed by her *innerstes Gefühl*. Figuratively speaking she is still in the embrace of the god, as she was in fact at the end of II/5. As her lawful husband draws near she turns away from him, but the actual confrontation provokes cold fury rather than the "sadness" of verse 1566:

>Du Ungeheuer! Mir scheußlicher,
>Als es geschwollen in Morästen nistet!
>Was tat ich dir, daß du mir nahen mußtest,
>Von einer Höllennacht bedeckt,
>Dein Gift mir auf den Fittich hinzugeifern?
>Was mehr, als daß ich, o du Böser, dir
>Still, wie ein Maienwurm, ins Auge glänzte?
>Jetzt erst, was für ein Wahn mich täuscht', erblick ich.
>Der Sonne heller Lichtglanz war mir nötig,
>Solch einen feilen Bau gemeiner Knechte,
>Vom Prachtwuchs dieser königlichen Glieder,
>Den Farren von dem Hirsch zu unterscheiden? (ll. 2240-2251)

The intensity of Alkmene's attack on her husband — Silz rightly compares it with Penthesilea's attack on Achilles — marks a tragic insight on Kleist's part: the crushing realization that the *Urphänomen* of conjugal love can be traduced; that the most sacred bonds of human feeling can be rent asunder. Surely the beautiful lines spoken by Amphitryon just before his wife's savage outburst may be read as Kleist's own conception of the mystery of conjugal love. How typical for this poet that his projection of the *unio mystica* goes beyond the bounds of language. Words are inadequate to express this holiest of mysteries, and hence eyes, ears, and *das innerste Gefühl* become the translators of love:

>Dir wäre dieser Busen unbekannt,
>Von dem so oft dein Ohr dir lauschend sagte,
>Wie viele Schläge liebend er dir klopft?
>Du solltest diese Töne nicht erkennen,
>Die du so oft, noch ehe sie laut geworden,
>Mit Blicken schon mir von der Lippe stahlst? (ll. 2215-2220)

For a poet who cherished an idealized conception of love, especially of conjugal love, the tragic insight into the fallibility of conjugal affection must have sounded depths registered only by his Kant- and *Guiskard*-crises. It is an especially bitter irony that Alkmene, one of Kleist's most exalted *Frauengestalten*, is both the victim and the vehicle of this fallibility. Given Kleist's empathy with his female characters,[18] his feelings toward Alkmene might well have been anticipated by those of Valentin towards Gretchen:

>Als du dich sprachst der Ehre los,
>Gabst mir den schwersten Herzenstoß.

Interpretations of Alkmene's final "Ach" have been numerous and contradictory[19]; but it is surely in the light of lines 1564-1568 (plus lines 2240-2262, comprising her verbal assault on Amphitryon) that her wordless sigh must be understood. It is an expression of anguish wrung from her by the convergence of two tragic realizations: that she has broken the sacred bond of matrimony; and that her god-lover has left her forever. The god's prediction: "So wirst du das Unglaubliche erfahren, / Und weinen, daß du ihm nicht folgen darfst" (ll. 1504-1505), is here made manifest.[20]

And yet: the fact that Alkmene has lost (to modify Walter Silz's comment) does not mean that Jupiter has won. For Alkmene's verbal flaying of the man she regards as her violator, though directed at her husband, actually strikes — a fine touch of irony! — the Father of the Gods himself. To whom else, after all, do lines 2242-2246, quoted above, apply?[21]

In *Die Familie Schroffenstein* God had merely been a "Rätsel" (ll. 1213 f.); and in a letter of August, 1806, Kleist had written: "Es kann kein böser Geist sein, der an der Spitze der Welt steht; es ist ein bloß unbegriffener." In *Amphitryon*, however, the epithets "Teufel...Ungeheuer...Böser" — mark the nadir of Kleist's disillusionment with orthodox deism. One is reminded perforce of the devastating conclusion of *Das Erdbeben in Chili*, where a brutal lynch mob, inflamed by a prelate "im Tempel Jesu," commits murderous outrages in His name; and of the gloomy end of *Der Findling*, where God's grace is rejected so that a condemned man can pursue his revenge in hell.

Finally, one must question whether there are any clearly defined winners or losers, saints or sinners to be descried by the time the final curtain has fallen on Kleist's tragicomedy. To this extent *Amphitryon* looks forward to the poet's final drama, *Der Prinz von Homburg*, where guilt and innocence, right and wrong, even life and death are values hidden behind a scrim of ambivalence. In the earlier play Jupiter savors his moment of triumph, as we have seen, but ultimately he must depart forever from his mortal beloved and return to the barrenness of his Olympian existence. Amphitryon, for his part, has "faced up" to the god in the final scene, has had his identity restored before his fellow citizens, and can console himself with the forthcoming birth of "his" son Hercules. But he must live with the knowledge that he has been bested, in a humiliating public confrontation, in a contest for his wife's affection; that their marital bed has been violated; and that his wife has been impregnated by an impostor (albeit a divine one). As for Alkmene: by becoming one of the loves of Jupiter she has acquired instant immortality, so to speak, and additional fame will accrue to her after the birth of the demi-god Hercules. Her near-fatal faint ("doch laß sie ruhn, wenn sie dir bleiben soll"), however, punctuated by her anguished "Ach," supplies mute but eloquent testimony to the price that has been extracted from her: loss of virtue, loss of conjugal happiness, loss of that precious harmony of self which for Kleist's characters is the last existential bastion in a world of uncertain values. More than any other play of Kleist's, *Amphitryon* exemplifies the pessimistic dictum from the celebrated *Marionettentheater* essay: "Doch das Paradies ist verriegelt und der Cherub hinter uns; wir müssen die Reise um die Welt machen, und sehen, ob es vielleicht von hinten irgendwo wieder offen ist."

NOTES

1 Quotations are taken from the following text: Heinrich von Kleist, *Sämtliche Werke und Briefe*. Ed. Helmut Sembdner. 2nd ed. (München, 1961), I, 321-428.
2 E. L. Stahl, *Heinrich von Kleist's Dramas* (Oxford, 1948), p. 65.
3 Walter Silz, *Heinrich von Kleist. Studies in his Works and Literary Character* (Philadephia, 1961), p. 51.
4 Peter Szondi, *Satz und Gegensatz* (Frankfurt, 1964), p. 56.
5 Helmut Arntzen, *Die ernste Komödie* (München, 1968), p. 235.
6 Wolfgang Wittkowski, "Der neue Prometheus," *Kleist und Frankreich*, ed. W. Müller-Seidel (Berlin, 1969), p. 50.
7 *Ibid.*, p. 50.
8 Lawrence Ryan, "*Amphitryon*, doch ein Lustspielstoff!" *Kleist und Frankreich* (Berlin, 1969), p. 95.
9 *Ibid.*, p. 88.
10 Hans-Georg Gadamer, "Der Gott des innersten Gefühls," *Die neue Rundschau*, 72 (1961), 347.
11 Silz, *Kleist*, p. 62.
12 E.g., in Act II, scene 6, where Jupiter poses a patently fraudulent suicide (!) threat.
13 For a divergent reading, see Gadamer, "Gott," 347: "Nun findet Jupiter sie 'urgemäß dem göttlichen Gedanken' — offenbar deshalb, weil sie Amphitryon nicht mehr, weil er Amphitryon, das heißt ihr Gatte ist, liebt, sondern weil sie den wählt, den sie liebt und als gegenwärtig in ihrem Gefühle hält. Damit erfüllt sie das Maß des göttlichen Gedankens."
14 H. A. Korff, *Geist der Goethezeit*, IV. 2nd ed. (Leipzig, 1955), 60: "Nicht Verwirrung, sondern Sicherheit des Gefühls trotz aller scheinbaren Verwirrung: das ist in Wahrheit das Grundthema."
15 Benno von Weise, *Die deutsche Tragödie von Lessing bis Hebbel*. 4th ed. (Hamburg, 1958), p. 304: "Alkmene bleibt... unverwirrt, sich selbst treu."
16 Silz, *Kleist*, p. 63; Wittkowski, "Prometheus," 44-47.
17 The French author Jean Giraudoux comes to grips with this very problem in his *Amphitryon 38*. In Act III scene 4 his Jupiter explains "entre hommes" that he loves *both* Amphitryon and Alkmene and views himself as a divine "Dritter im Bunde:" "Je n'aime pas seulement Alcmène, car alors je me serais arrangé pour être son amant sans te consulter. J'aime votre couple. J'aime, au début des ères humaines, ces deux grands et beaux corps sculptés à l'avant de l'humanité comme des proues. C'est en ami que je m'installe entre vous deux."
18 Witness his identification with Penthesilea ("Sie ist nun tot!"), as recorded by his friend Pfuel. See *Heinrich von Kleists Lebensspuren*. Rev. ed., ed. Helmut Sembdner. dtv Gesamtausgabe, VIII (München, 1969), 140.
19 For a brief but well-reasoned discussion of the final "Ach" see Werner Milch, "Das zwiefache 'Ach' der Alkmene," *Kleine Schriften zur Literatur und Geistesgeschichte*, ed. Gerhard Burkhardt (Heidelberg, Darmstadt, 1957), pp. 156-159.

20 For a poet's projection of what might befall Alkmene beyond the final curtain, one may turn again to Jean Giraudoux. With what might be described as Gallic coolness his Alcmène outlines her future to her husband as follows: "Envisages-tu la vie avec cette épouse qui n'aura plus de respect d'elle-même, déshonorée, fût-ce par trop d'honneur, et flétrie par l'immortalité? Envisages-tu que toujours un tiers nom soit sur nos lèvres, indicible, donnant un goût de fiel à nos repas, à nos baisers? Moi pas." (*Amphitryon 38*, Act III, scene 3).

21 Wittkowski, "Prometheus," 42 ff., demonstrates this convincingly.

KLEIST'S *KÄTHCHEN* AND THE MONOMYTH

Robert M. Browning

That Kleist's *Käthchen von Heilbronn* is essentially a dramatized fairy tale or myth has long been recognized.[1] The main purpose of the following remarks is to show to what an astounding degree this is indeed true and to point out some of the possible implications. Being neither a psychoanalyst nor an anthropologist, but merely a student of German literature, I have relied on the authority of Joseph Campbell in his study *The Hero With a Thousand Faces* as the principal source of my information on the structure of myth.[2]

He who ventures into the field of myth interpretation treads on uncertain ground — indeed he might be said to enter a quagmire. "There is no final system for the interpretation of myths," Campbell writes (p. 381), "and there never will be any such thing." Mythology is a Proteus. But in outlining the basic structure of myth, Campbell (p. 30) provides us with a thread through the labyrinth:

> The standard path of the mythological adventure of the hero, is a magnification of the formula represented in the rites of passage: *separation — initiation — return*: which might be named the nuclear unit of the monomyth. A hero ventures forth from the world of common day into a region of supernatural wonder: fabulous forces are there encountered and a decisive victory is won: the hero comes back from this mysterious adventure with the power to bestow boons on his fellow man.

The basic scheme of myth is one that was bound to appeal to the romantic imagination: the triad is the prototypical form of romantic thought from Novalis, Hölderlin and Hegel through Wagner. Such a bare outline, however, the mere "nuclear unit" itself, will hardly serve our purpose. Campbell provides more. In the fourth chapter (pp. 24 ff.) he gives the "keys" to the mythological round, i.e., the salient points of the adventure that every mythological hero undergoes, though each does not undergo all, since some are mutually exclusive and others may be suppressed, or modified to suit local conditions. Archaic traits, for instance, are generally eliminated or subdued. I reproduce Campbell's diagram (p. 245) reduced to those features that seem particularly relevant for *Käthchen*. Of the following "keys" the absolutely essential ones are: 1) the call to adventure, 2) the threshold crossing with attendant struggle, dismemberment, crucifixion or the like, 3) tests, 4) sacred marriage and attainment of elixir, 5) return and boon.

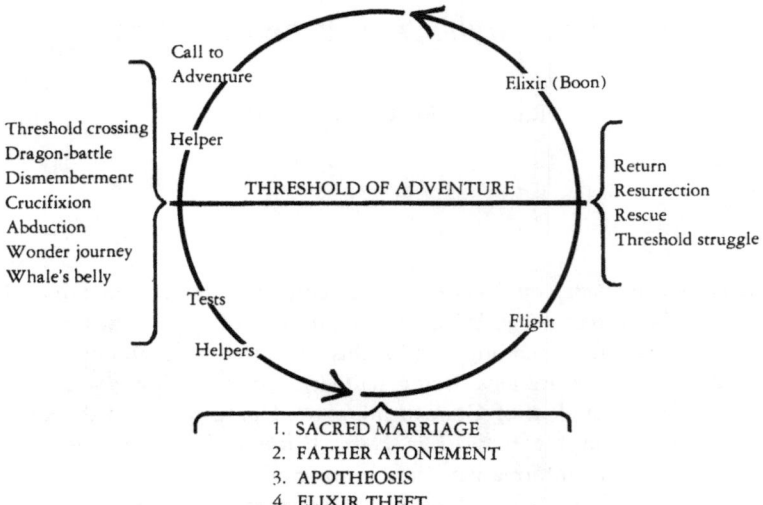

Mere inspection of the diagram will immediately make apparent to anyone familiar with Kleist's play its obvious correspondence with the basic plot of the mythological adventure. In *Käthchen*, as in almost any specific example we might take, certain features are masked, displaced, or suppressed, and some are modified to fit the local landscape. On the whole, however, the scheme of the monomyth is preserved in astounding purity. The course of the mythological adventure is perfectly summarized in line 72 of the poem that introduces the second part of *Heinrich von Ofterdingen*:

Die Welt wird Traum, der Traum wird Welt ...

And this is exactly what happens in *Käthchen*.

Kleist's play is a particularly fascinating example of dramatized myth (or fairy tale, if one will) because it contains two heroes, Käthchen and Strahl, one of whom accepts the call to adventure and one of whom refuses it. The call, which "rings up the curtain ... on a mystery of transfiguration" (Campbell, p. 51), comes to both in the New Year's Eve dream. The helper is naturally the cherub, about whom, as is the rule with such summoners, be they beasts or angels, there is "an atmosphere of irresistible fascination" (Campbell, p. 55). Käthchen accepts the call without the slightest question and lives henceforth in that somnambulistic state characteristic of those who have have placed their lives in the service of a higher power — she is "acting under orders." The Prince of Homburg acts in exactly the same fashion.

Strahl and Käthchen are the primal pair, the two created originally one, the androgynous Adam, now living — since the Fall — in separation. Käthchen is the vessel of healing (Heilbronn=Bronn des Heils) and is identified with a locality. When she appeared in the streets of the town "so lief es flüsternd von allen

Fenstern herab: das ist das Käthchen von Heilbronn; das Käthchen von Heilbronn, ihr Herren, als ob der Himmel von Schwaben sie erzeugt, und von seinem Kuß geschwängert, die Stadt, die unter ihm liegt, sie geboren hätte" (I/1, 76 ff.).[3] She is worshipped (there is no other word) as a local deity and dispenser of blessing. The call comes to her because the blessing which she represents is to be universalized, no longer restricted to the narrow burgher world of which she is at the beginning the supreme representative. Strahl, as his name eloquently indicates and as the imagery insists (see, e.g., I/1, 154 f.; 229 ff.; I/2, 398 f.; 442 f.), is the heavenly principle. Through the marriage of heaven and earth the world is to receive a high boon. This is the divine plan — not Kleist's, the myth's — which is to be effectuated by the (re-)union of the primal pair, Käthchen and Strahl.

The call, the first stage of the mythological round, "signifies that destiny has summoned the hero and transferred his spiritual center of gravity from within the pale of society to a zone unknown" (Campbell, p. 58). This is obviously what happens to Käthchen. It does not happen to Strahl, who continues to lead his everyday life, because he refuses the call. His refusal takes the form of a fixation on "the Emperor's daughter," that is, he aligns himself with social prejudice, pride of ancestry and so on. Thus he cannot pass the barrier into the unknown. If he could, there would be no play. The action concerns his salvation. The refuser of the call, Campbell tells us (p. 59), "loses the power of significant affirmative action and becomes a victim to be saved." Which is Strahl's situation precisely. The agent of his perdition is Kunigunde, the anti-Käthchen, the "false bride," and the other "Emperor's daughter."

One of the most "archaic" traits in the play is the manner in which Käthchen crosses the first threshold. The threshold is normally guarded by custodians of the known world objectified as demons, monsters, enchantresses, which are reflections of drives considered dangerous to the society in which the hero lives (Campbell, p. 79, gives as examples of such drives incestuous libido and patricidal destrudo). With these the hero must wrestle until they bless him. In our play we find no such monsters (though Theobald, playing the mythic father role, regards Strahl as one); the trait is suppressed or made unnecessary by the character of the heroine; but another such "key," equally archaic, is present, namely, that of dismemberment (cf. Campbell, pp. 92 f.). When Strahl leaves Theobald's workshop, "schmeißt sich das Mädchen...dreißig Fuß hoch... auf das Pflaster der Straße nieder...Und bricht sich beide Lenden..." (I/1, 188 ff.). This is threshold crossing with a vengeance. Käthchen has now entered the other world, she is in the belly of the whale, the realm from which she will be reborn at Easter (!): "Zu Ostern, übers Jahr, wirst du mich heuern" (IV/2, 2082). Passage of the threshold is a form of self-annihilation, which is the meaning of dismemberment. (The rite of baptism makes use of the same imagery, as do all initiatory rites.)

Now comes the wonder-journey and the road of trials. This aspect of the mythological round is well developed in *Käthchen*, as it is in most myths. "Once having traversed the threshold, the hero moves in a dream landscape of curiously fluid, ambiguous forms, where he must survive a succession of trials" (Campbell, p. 97). But the hero (or heroine) is covertly aided by "secret agents of the supernatural helper." Gottschalk, as his name tells us ("Knecht Gottes"), is such a helper, albeit an unwitting one, and of course the cherub himself steps in during the "Feuerprobe." But Käthchen's principal helper is, in true Kleistian fashion, her perfect trust. Her trials are many. The merely physical ones she undergoes with dreamlike ease, but the cross-examination by the "Feme" and by Strahl tries her soul. "Ihr versucht mich" (I/2, 374), she tells her judges and faints when she must keep her promise to return to her father and follow Strahl no longer (I/2, following 646). (The faint means, in Kleist's sign language, that two authorities, both absolute, are in conflict.) In Kleist's work there is an important "double take": every trial that tries Käthchen also tries Strahl, though he does not realize it. This becomes fully evident in the supreme test, the "Feuerprobe," which stands in the middle of the play. Here even his eyes, blinded by his fixation on the "Emperor's daughter," begin to be opened to the true nature of Kunigunde.

But the "Feuerprobe" is not the turning point or scene of final insight. This comes, quite in accord with the basic structural principles of the monomyth, in the adventure of "The Lady of the House of Sleep" (Brynhild and Sleeping Beauty are two well known examples), that is, in the scene with Käthchen asleep beneath the elder bush.

> The ultimate adventure, when all barriers and ogres have been overcome, is commonly represented as a mystical marriage (*hieròs gámos*) of the triumphant hero-soul with the Queen Goddess of the World. This is the crisis at the nadir, the zenith, or at the uttermost edge of the earth, at the central point of the cosmos, in the tabernacle of the temple, or within the darkness of the deepest chamber of the heart. (Campbell, p. 109)

It is in the scene beneath the elder bush (IV/2-3) that "der Traum wird Welt," "Welt" having up to now been "Traum." "Woman, in the picture language of mythology, represents the totality of what can be known. The hero is the one who comes to know" (Campbell, p. 116). She lures him on step by step, guides him, finally causes him to burst his fetters. (This is the meaning for Strahl, the refuser of the call, of the tests that Käthchen undergoes.) "And if he can match her import, the two, the knower and the known, will be released from every limitation" (ibid.). The Lady of the House of Sleep "is the paragon of all paragons of beauty, the reply to all desire, the bliss-bestowing goal of every hero's earthly and unearthly quest. She is mother, sister, mistress, bride," Campbell tells us (pp. 110 f.). When Strahl comes to know Käthchen, his search is at an end, the boon won. All that remains is to recross the threshold and bestow the boon on mankind. Käthchen herself is the "elixir," as her name (Heilbronn) says — through her marriage with Strahl, through the union of heaven and earth, mankind is to receive untold benefits.

Strahl recognizes that Käthchen is the elixir long before he learns that she is also the Emperor's daughter of their double dream. At the end of the monologue which opens Act II he says:

> Nein, nein, nein! Zum Weibe, wenn ich sie gleich liebe, begehr ich sie nicht; eurem [der Ahnherren] stolzen Reigen will ich mich anschließen...Dich aber, Winfried, der ihn führt,...dich frag ich, ob die Mutter meines Geschlechts war, wie diese [Käthchen]...hättest du *sie* an die stählerne Brust gedrückt, du hättest ein Geschlecht von Königen erzeugt, und Wetter vom Strahl hieße jedes Gebot auf Erden!

On the motif of the Emperor's daughter the whole action hinges. It is the "second order" given to Strahl and keeps him from obeying the first, that is, from accepting Käthchen. The Prince of Homburg's actions are the mirror image of Strahl's: the Prince acts according to the command of the dream and ignores the second command concerning the order of battle. Like Käthchen, he crosses the threshold at the first opportunity.

The ultimate adventure, the mystical marriage with the Goddess, takes place, we recall, "at the nadir, the zenith, or at the uttermost edge of the earth, at the central point of the cosmos, in the tabernacle of the temple, or within the deepest chamber of the heart." In *Käthchen* it takes place in at least two of these localities, namely in the heart and at the central point of the cosmos, that is, at the World Navel or Immovable Spot, around which the world revolves. The accuracy with which Kleist's sign language reflects this ancient motif is a strong argument for the doctrine of archetypes. In speaking of the World Navel or Immovable Spot, Campbell says (p. 41):

> Beneath this spot is the earth-supporting head of the cosmic serpent, ...symbolical of the waters of the abyss, which are divine life-giving energy..., the world-generative aspect of immortal being. The tree of life, i.e., the universe itself, grows from this point. It is rooted in supporting darkness; the golden sun bird perches on its peak; a spring, the inexhaustible well, bubbles at its foot....the hero himself as the incarnation of God is himself the navel of the world, the umbilical point through which energies of eternity break into time.

The world navel may of course be anywhere — it is any place of the "breakthrough into abundance" (p. 43). Kleist places it outside the walls of Strahl's castle

> ....am zerfallnen Mauernring
> Wo in süßduftenden Holunderbüschen
> Ein Zeisig zwitschernd sich das Nest gebaut. (I/2, 594-96)

The weighty metaphysical symbolism of the Immovable Spot of the Buddha legend is naturally transformed in Kleist into the lighter, homelier imagery of the fairy tale, but all the essential features are preserved: the tree of life, the golden sun bird, perhaps even the well, for "An den Zweigen sieht man ein Hemdchen und ein Paar Strümpfe usw. zum Trocknen aufgehängt" (stage direction to IV/2). The *Zeisig* or siskin, a bird the size of a sparrow with a round black head and greenish golden breast, makes an excellent "sun bird." More important is the *Holunderstrauch* (elder), as one soon discovers upon perusing the article "Holunder" in *Handwörterbuch des deutschen Aberglaubens*.

The elder plays a great role in folk medicine and folklore. "Vor dem Holunder muß man den Hut abnehmen," say the peasants. It is a "Glücksbaum" and a "Lebensbaum." It must not be cut down; if one harms it, harm will come to one. Beneath the elder live the "Unterirdische" (cf. Campbell: "Beneath this spot is the earth-supporting head of the cosmic serpent...") and dwarves seek its shade, attracted by the fragrance. It has a clear connection with two important motifs in our play: branches of the plant cut on New Year's Eve, if bent into a wreath and hung up in the house, protect against the outbreak of fire. Furthermore, the elder wards off witches and aids in their detection — she who sleeps beneath the elder recognizes the witch Kunigunde. It also, as we and Kleist know from folk songs, plays a role in popular eroticism: "Rosenstock, *Holderblüh*, Wenn ich mein Liebchen sieh..." In *Penthesilea* the heroine tells Prothoe: "Entfleuch, daß er [Prothoe's Greek captive] dir nicht verloren gehe, / Aus dem Geräusch der Schlacht mit ihm, *bergt euch / In Hecken von süß duftendem Holunder*..." (5, 824 ff.; my italics). Here she, the "Lüsterne," can immediately celebrate the feast of love. Because it is so hard to kill, the elder also figures as a "Todesbaum," that is, as a plant that promises life beyond the grave, and is often planted in cemeteries, buried with the corpse and so on. It is more than clear that Kleist does not associate Käthchen with this magical plant by accident.[4]

In our play we also find father atonement (double!) and apotheosis (Käthchen *is* the Emperor's daughter), while the elixir theft is incorporated in the "Gottesurteil," by means of which Strahl "steals" Käthchen from her father(s). The flight motif does not appear, but there is a "threshold struggle" at the point of return. For Strahl, this is also incorporated in the sacred ordeal, the duel with Theobald; for Käthchen it appears in the form of what one might regard as a typical example of Kleistian "cruelty," namely, in Strahl's deception of Käthchen up to the last moment as to the true identity of the bride (also motivated, to be sure, as vengeance on Kunigunde). For Käthchen, this is the final test. As for the boon, now begins the time when a "race of kings" is to be procreated and "every command on earth" to bear the name of Wetter vom Strahl, which is surely not too much to expect from the union of heaven and earth. "Der Himmel segne das hohe Brautpaar," the herald cries (V/13, 2650 ff.), "und schütte das ganze Füllhorn des Glücks, das in den Wolken schwebt, über ihre teuren Häupter aus!" We may be sure that this comes to pass.

The structural correspondence between *Käthchen* and the "monomyth" is so complete that one might think Kleist had written it with a modern handbook on mythology at his elbow. No satisfactory "source" of the work has ever been discovered, though one always hears about Schubert's *Nachtseite der Naturwissenschaften* (somnambulism), Bürger's translation of the English ballad "Childe Waters" (Strahl's harsh treatment of Käthchen), Goethe's *Götz* (Adelheid into Kunigunde), and Wieland's tales, especially "Die Entzauberung" (as source of the "sympathy" motif). But all this is really beside the point — Kleist was writing as we all dream: in archetypes. It may be amusing to reconstruct an "Urkäthchen" called "Kunigunde von Thurneck" and puzzle over Tieck's alleged cryptic utterance about the scene the poet rewrote because it "[spielte] das ganze Stück gewissermaßen in das Gebiet des Märchens oder Zaubers hinüber,"[5] but at bottom this is merely sterile rationalistic speculation: "Nach innen geht der geheimnisvolle Weg."

Since Kleist himself calls attention to the mirror-image similarity between *Käthchen* and *Penthesilea*, we cannot leave the former without saying a word about the latter. "Denn wer das Käthchen liebt," Kleist wrote to Collin under date of 8 December 1808, "dem kann die Penthesilea nicht ganz unbegreiflich sein, sie gehören ja wie das + und — der Algebra zusammen, und sind ein und dasselbe Wesen, nur unter entgegengesetzten Beziehungen gedacht."[6]

But *Penthesilea*, despite its mythical air and ancient costume, does not follow the pattern of the monomyth. At most, we can call it an *aborted* myth. A tragic myth is a contradiction in terms. Myth deals with the reintegration of the personality, not with its disintegration. Its mode is comedy. Myths end with weddings, not with cannibalism. Nonetheless, *Penthesilea* begins mythically and contains a number of standard mythological features.

The play begins, like *Käthchen*, with the heroine's *crossing the threshold of adventure*. Odysseus describes it to us and to his fellow Greeks (1, 57 ff.):

> Wir finden sie, die Heldin Skythiens,
> Achill und ich — in kriegerischer Feier
> An ihrer Jungfraun Spitze aufgepflanzt,
> ....
> Gedankenvoll, auf einen Augenblick,
> Sieht sie in unsre Schar, von Ausdruck leer,
> Als ob in Stein gehaun wir vor ihr stünden;
> ....
> Bis jetzt ihr Aug auf den Peliden trifft:
> Und Glut ihr plötzlich, bis zum Hals hinab,
> Das Antlitz färbt,....

The *call to adventure* is described in Scene 15, 2137 ff. On her deathbed Otrere tells her daughter (emphasis added):

> ...."geh, mein süßes Kind, Mars ruft dich!
> *Du wirst den Peleïden dir bekränzen:*
> Werd eine Mutter, stolz und froh, wie ich —"

And Penthesilea leads the campaign against the walls of Troy: "...Mars weniger, / Dem großen Gott, der mich dahin gerufen, / Als der Otrere Schatten, zu gefallen" (15, 2167 ff.). The *boon* is envisioned in Achilles' words (15, 2230 ff.):

> Du sollst den Gott der Erde mir gebären!
> Prometheus soll von seinem Sitz erstehn,
> Und dem Geschlecht der Welt verkündigen:
> Hier ward ein Mensch, so hab ich ihn gewollt!

In short, Penthesilea and Achilles are another primal pair whose union would bring the world untold blessing.

The play becomes a tragedy because the mythological round cannot be completed. Penthesilea is defeated by the threshold guardians, objectified especially in the High Priestess, the personification of the Amazon state and its taboos. The turning point comes at the end of Scene 19, where Penthesilea recognizes her guilt in the eyes of her own society. She then recrosses the threshold back into the bosom of this society without having obtained the boon. The placing of the mutilated corpse at the feet of the High Priestess in the final scene is clear proof that she considers herself the executrix of the will of society and her deed an act of penance. Thus the play becomes a tragedy of the disoriented personality: Penthesilea is spewed out of the belly of the whale before she can cross to the other side of the sea of subconscious being.

In such terms might one interpret the tragedy from the standpoint of the monomyth. From a somewhat different point of view one could well consider it a tragedy of Hebbelian stamp: a new step in the world process is to be taken and the one destined to accomplish this step must perish — the old order demands a sacrifice before the new can triumph. Penthesilea, whose conception of the nature of love makes her a mystery to both Greeks and Amazons, must perish for the new order. The crown of nettles (24, 2705), the crash of the golden bow (24, 2769 ff.), the strewing of the ashes of Tanaïs, the *Urmutter* of the Amazons, to the wind (24, 3009) are gestic language showing the end of an age and an order. But the marriage of this primal pair can take place only in the realm of a psychic Beyond (24, 3035 f.):

> Sie stirbt!
> Sie folgt ihm, in der Tat!
> Wohl ihr!
> Denn hier war ihres fernern Bleibens nicht.

NOTES

[1] Cf., e.g., Erich Schmidt, ed., *Heinrich von Kleists Werke* (Leipzig, Wien: Bibliographisches Institut, [1904-1905]), II, 177: "Die märchenhafte Stimmung des Ganzen..."; Heinrich Meyer-Benfey, *Kleists Leben und Werke* (Göttingen 1911), p. 251: "Wir

befinden uns... in einer Welt des Wunderbaren — sagen wir gleich: des *Märchenhaften*" (M.-B. interprets the play as a variation on the fairy tale of the true and the false bride); Friedrich Braig, *Heinrich von Kleist* (München 1925), p. 290: "Das 'Käthchen von Heilbronn' ist ein liebliches Märchen von der göttlichen Führung zweier urbildlich füreinander bestimmter Menschen..."; Ernest Ludwig Stahl, *Heinrich von Kleist's Dramas* (Oxford 1948), pp. 92 ff., compares *Käthchen* "with dramatized fairy stories and tales in the 'Gothic' manner..." It is perhaps worthy of note that Friedrich Koch, *Heinrich von Kleist: Bewußtsein und Wirklichkeit* (Stuttgart 1958), pp. 182 f., denies that *Käthchen* is a "Märchen." If I understand him, however, it is because he considers the play a myth, a finer distinction than is necessary in this case. Other examples could doubtless be adduced, but these will suffice to show a strong tendency in the criticism of this drama. No account that I have found points out the precise mythical structure of the play.

2 All references in the text are as to the following edition: Joseph Campbell, *The Hero with a Thousand Faces* (New York: Meridian Books, 1956). According to Campbell (p. 30, n. 35), the term "monomyth" was originated by James Joyce in *Finnegan's Wake*.

3 Kleist's text is cited according to *Sämtliche Werke und Briefe*, 5th ed. Ed. H. Sembdner, (Darmstadt, 1970).

4 In "Der goldne Topf" E. T. A. Hoffmann also locates the world navel, the place of "breakthrough into abundance," under an elder. After his first adventure with the "Äpfelweib," Anselmus finds "ein freundliches Ruheplätzchen" "unter einem Holunderbaum" on the banks of the Elbe. Here the chthonic powers, the gold-green (!) snakes, manifest themselves to him and he is called to adventure.

5 Friedrich Röbbeling, *Kleists K. v. H.* (Halle, 1913), 109 ff., points out the many inconsistencies in Tieck's words (as reported by Eduard von Bülow). Perhaps most convincing is the note, p. 110, remarking on the un-Kleistian ring of the verse Tieck supposedly found so beautiful: "Da quillt es wieder unterm Stein hervor." (What scene, one wonders, could have rendered *Käthchen* more "märchenhaft" than it already is!)

Nonetheless, there is, I think, at least one firm textual indication that Kunigunde was once conceived as a nixie, namely, IV/1, in which Käthchen refuses to wade the stream, though it is only a "Forellenbach" and though she has perfect confidence in Gottschalk. As it stands, it is motivated — ridiculously enough — by Käthchen's excessive modesty ("Nun, bei Leibe, schürzen nicht!"). Kunigunde is a shapeshifter, an archaic trait rationalized in the play as expertness with cosmetics. She is definitely connected with the elements: we first meet her in the midst of a violent storm (II/4 ff.) and in IV/4 we see her "von Kopf zu Fuß in einen *feuerfarbnen* Schleier verhüllt," which almost looks as though the poet were over-compensating for having once conceived her as a nixie.

6 Heinrich von Kleist, *Sämtliche Werke und Briefe*, ed. H. Sembdner. I, 934. After completing this contribution, my attention was called to the article by Valentine C. Hubbs, "The Plus and Minus of Penthesilea and Käthchen," *Seminar*, 6 (October 1970), 187-94, which interprets, and very convincingly, the two heroines as "the positive and negative aspects of the feminine archetype" (p. 194). Hubbs, though he points out various mythological aspects of the two plays, is not primarily interested in the overall pattern, which it has been my aim to clarify.

A READING OF FRANZ GRILLPARZER'S *SAPPHO*

George Reinhardt

As Childe Harold sailed by the base of the Leucadian promontory, his heart glowed with the memory of the tragic fate of the poetess who had leapt from it into the Ionian Sea:

> Dark Sappho! could not Verse immortal save
> That breast imbued with such immortal fire?
> Could she not live who life eternal gave?
> If life eternal may await the lyre,
> That only Heaven to which Earth's children may aspire.[1]

A few years after the publication of Byron's poem, another young romantic, the Austrian dramatist Franz Grillparzer, fell under Sappho's spell. In the space of a few summer weeks in July, 1817, he produced his second major drama, entitled *Sappho*, ostensibly to demonstrate that he was as adept in the classical style of Weimar — "plowing with Goethe's calf" in his words — as at creating a crowd-pleasing fate tragedy like his recent success, *Die Ahnfrau*.[2]

"Dark," Lord Byron's epithet for Sappho, is doubly appropriate for Grillparzer's poetess-heroine. The conflicting elements of her character do not readily submit to rational analysis, as the discordant state of academic criticism of the play proves. Her emotions too are dark. The instability of her heart assumes a dimension of morbidity as she modulates abruptly between resolution and enervation, love and loathing, the hauteur of a creative *grande dame* and the lethal jealousy of a woman scorned.

With the boldness of youth Grillparzer presents the spectators and readers of his play with a portrait of the artist varying widely from conventional nineteenth-century academic icons of Parnassus.[3] Instead of transforming the dross of experience into poetry, Sappho neglects her art for love. Instead of attempting to regain her lost lover through a display of superior intellect and magnanimity, she races towards her defenseless rival with dagger drawn and later dispatches her arbitrarily into exile, though the girl is guilty of no crime but love. Only at the very end of the play does Sappho's soul attain a perilous equilibrium. After blessing those who have spitefully used her, she seeks reconciliation with the gods through self-immolation.

Aesthetic moralizers prone to exalt "Art" above "Life" equate Sappho's characterization of herself as a traitor to her art with Grillparzer's personal conviction about the poet's fate:

> Wen Götter sich zum Eigentum erlesen,
> Geselle sich zu Erdenbürgern nicht;
> Der Menschen und der Überird'schen Los,
> Es mischt sich nimmer in demselben Becher.
> Von beiden Welten Eine mußt du wählen,
> Hast du gewählt, dann ist kein Rücktritt mehr! (*HKA*, I/1, ll. 948-953)

The religion of art forbids its hierophants to allow themselves to be sullied by life. Sappho's "immersion in Life and her betrayal of Art have been such that the return to a life dedicated to Art is no longer possible. If she is to salvage what remains of her individuality, she must renounce life itself. Her suicide is a flight to a region where the temptations of life can no longer touch her."[4] Sappho, in short, is the quintessential artist whose kingdom is not of this world.

Such is the minority viewpoint. Aware that the moral judgments of the final scene do not follow necessarily from what precedes and loath to establish their interpretations on so fragile a base, many critics emphasize the disagreeable, though not quite tragic plight of a jealous — some add: aging — woman who is coincidentally an artist.[5] The analyses of this school appeal most frequently to two almost unimpeachable authorities: the author himself and Professor August Sauer, the first editor of the *Kritische Ausgabe*. Grillparzer introduced the following disparaging remark about "artist dramas" into the portion of his autobiography describing the creation of *Sappho*:

> Ich war nämlich immer ein Feind der Künstler-Dramen. Künstler sind gewohnt, die Leidenschaft als einen Stoff zu behandeln. Dadurch wird auch die wirkliche Liebe für sie mehr eine Sache der Imagination als der tiefen Empfindung. Ich aber wollte Sappho einer wahren Leidenschaft und nicht einer Verirrung der Phantasie zum Opfer werden lassen! (*SW*, IV, 84)

Grillparzer also conceded that he had not been entirely successful in investing Sappho's character with an aura of poetry.[6] Small wonder in the face of such an admission that Sauer asserts in his introduction:

> Zum Künstlerdrama wurde das Werk erst allmählich ausgestaltet. Das Künstlerische ist das sekundäre, wie auch Grillparzer später zu Foglar sagte (19. Februar 1844, Gespräche Nr. 814): 'Was man meiner Sappho zum Vorwurf machte, ist vielmehr ein Vorzug des Stückes — daß ich nämlich mehr das liebende Weib als ihr poetisches Element hervorhob.' (*HKA*, I/1, lxxxiv)

Much evidence for an interpretation discounting Sappho's poetic mission can be found in the text of the play. At the moment only three examples will be cited. Reinhold Backmann is disturbed by Grillparzer's apparent failure to let Sappho "find herself again" at the beginning of the final act. He realizes that the credibility of her ultimate change of heart is seriously weakened because she is guided more by the suggestions of someone else, her former lover Phaon, than by the promptings of her own conscience.[7] George Wells has recently observed that Sappho condemns herself as a traitor to her art not in the fifth act, as might be expected if this were the standard by which Grillparzer wished her to be judged, but in the third act. "In what follows she certainly does not act on this conviction that she has kinship with the gods and not with man."[8] Measured by the standards of psychological verisimilitude, Sappho's suicide has appeared to many to be as pathetic as it seemed to Ludwig Börne in 1820: "Kleiner noch als im Leben zeigt sich Sappho sterbend. Sie versöhnt mit ihrer Schwäche nicht, sie entzieht sie nur dem Vorwurfe. Der Bogen zeigt nicht seine Kraft; er bricht und zeigt seine Gebrechlichkeit."[9]

The case would seem to be closed: Sappho is far more a woman overcome by love and jealousy than she is a poetess. Authors, however, often contradict themselves when speaking of their works. Grillparzer also insisted that the probability of the catastrophe depended upon Sappho's being a poetess and designated the irrevocable conflict between art and life, "die natürliche Scheidewand, die zwischen beiden [i.e., art and life] befestigt ist," as a fundamental theme of his play.[10] There is also the question of the final scene: is Sappho merely deluding herself and those around her, or has Grillparzer, as mutable as his heroine, created a flawed play, lacking the coherence of great art?

Only by reading Sappho at two levels — the psychological and the archetypal — can the dilemma posed by the final scene be resolved. On the one hand, Sappho offers a psychological study of characters who to a greater or lesser extent evince a sustained willingness to deceive themselves. They manipulate their prejudices in order to create as flattering as possible images of themselves. The relationship between Sappho and Phaon is also a struggle between the sexes for dominance. In it Sappho bears the dual burden of being older and wiser than her lover. On the other hand, the content of the original Sappho's poetry and the preservation of her awesome reputation from antiquity to the present endow her with mythic grandeur wholly consonant with the lofty sense of mission which finally overwhelms and transfigures Grillparzer's heroine. Those who — following Grillparzer in a moment of humility — maintain that he has not given his Sappho the profile of a poet fail to indicate how he could have done so further, and they cannot explain why he should include in his play a translation of the original Sappho's "Hymn to Aphrodite" as well as a visionary panegyric concerning her immortal fame. She is for Grillparzer, as she was for antiquity, the tenth Muse.

Reason can explore the depths of Sappho's ravaged psyche. Empathy alone, aroused and assisted by the skill of a great actress, can fully appreciate Grillparzer's tragic vision of the artist as both more and less than the average mortal. By accepting the dual nature of Sappho, the passionate woman who is also an archetypal Muse, one can reconcile otherwise discordant elements of her character: the will to destroy and the will to produce, wrath and love, and the capacity to arouse both pity and awe. The following reading broaches the possibility of such an interpretational synthesis.

The opening scene of *Sappho* is brief and agitated, strikingly different from the tone of restrained grief of Iphigenie's initial soliloquy. Cymbals, flutes, and distant acclamation herald the approach of the heroine. Rhamnes, the venerable retainer who first taught Sappho music and poetry, sets her handmaidens, among them the adolescent Melitta, scurrying to hail their mistress' triumphant return from the poetry contest at Olympia. A moment later, perhaps dismayed because their elation does not match his own, he sends them back to their domestic tasks. Against such a background Grillparzer swiftly and skillfully establishes an atmosphere of psychological tension arising from two conflicting views of Sappho: as a public figure, the chief cultural adornment of Lesbos, and as a private personality, a woman enraptured by love.

Rhamnes identifies with his mistress and former pupil to so great a degree that her victory at the poetry contest in Olympia has become for him a personal triumph. His eagerness to enhance her reputation induces him to try, in vain, to commandeer the emotions of others. "Ihr solltet wissen, daß euch Freude Pflicht" (35), he tells Melitta with the arrogance of the petty bureaucrat towards an underling. By contrast Melitta responds to Sappho's advent as one woman interested in another. Her impetuous reply to Rhamnes' question: "Seht ihr den Kranz?" betokens affection and curiosity: "Ich sehe Sappho nur! / Wir wollen ihr entgegen!" (23-24). Her enthusiasm is quickly deflected towards Sappho's companion, Phaon, whose godlike youth fascinates her more than Sappho's costly garb. Once Grillparzer has juxtaposed Rhamnes' blind adoration for his protégée with Melitta's inconstant response to a woman to whom she owes so much, he is ready to present his heroine.

In depicting Sappho's entrance Grillparzer reveals a keen awareness of the interplay between the charismatic personality and its followers. The people of Lesbos, led by Rhamnes, wish to bask in the glory reflected upon them by their preeminent native daughter. She is for them "die Hohe" (59), "die Herrliche" (62, 100). Sappho disappoints no one. In contrast to Phaon in his plain dress, she appears "köstlich gekleidet, auf einem mit weißen Pferden bespannten Wagen, eine goldene Leier in der Hand, auf dem Haupte den Siegeskranz" (stage direction after verse 43). Her opening "bescheidene Rede," as one of the bystanders calls it (60), shrewdly combines self-praise — she speaks of "des Vollbringens Wahnsinn-glühnde Lust" (50) — and *captatio benevolentiae* (45-46).[11] Though her excessively flattering introduction of Phaon — "Von den Besten stammet er" 72 ff.) — induces a mild protest from its object, Sappho soars on the wings of her rhetoric till she identifies the divine will with her own:

> Ich liebe ihn, auf ihn fiel meine Wahl.
> Er war *bestimmt* in seiner Gaben Fülle, [italics mine]
> Mich von der Dichtkunst wolkennahen Gipfeln
> In dieses Lebens heitre Blüten-täler
> Mit sanft bezwingender Gewalt herabzuziehn. (88-92)

The single harsh note in a paean of mutual admiration rings out when Sappho complains that her poetry in the past has evoked her people's respect and veneration but not their love (98). When shouts of "Preis" and "Heil" (100) validate the legitimacy of this complaint, Sappho, ever the "Gebieterin," terminates the scene by inviting all to festivities in her honor which she later, patronizingly, belittles as a fulfillment of her social obligations towards a group whose only pleasure is wine (731).

Alone with Phaon, Sappho woos him by recounting her wretched past. Mercantile imagery at the outset indirectly reveals their "love" as a precarious foundation for the life of humble bucolic domesticity Sappho envisions. Sappho thinks of life as a "Wechseltausch" (109) in which she hopes her lover will not feel "übervorteilt" (112). She appeals to his sympathy by recounting the loss of her parents and siblings and lamenting the perfidious nature of love and friendship. (Critics who see Life and Art as incomptatible have ignored Sappho's admission that, long before her encounter with Phaon, she had experienced "der — Liebe Täuschungen," with no concomitant loss of poetic gifts.) To her urging — a veiled threat — that he try to approximate her own limitless capacity for emotion, Phaon can only reply like one of the recently departed throng: "Erhabne Frau!" (130). The pattern for the relationship has been set. Each will try to confirm his own illusory vision of their mutual attraction by imposing it upon the other.

Sappho's half-plaintive, half-imperious rejection of Phaon's tribute to her sublimity: "Nicht so! / Sagt dir dein Herz denn keinen süßern Namen?" (130-31) falls on uncomprehending ears.[12] Phaon either can or will not respond to her anxious attempt to evoke tenderness instead of tribute: "Du schmückest mich von deinem eignen Reichtum, / Weh, nähmst du das Geliehne je zurück!" (202-203; another commercial image). Phaon is too modest to take seriously her praise of him as warrior, orator, poet, and friend-in-need (74 ff.). He is also too inexperienced to grasp what "Hellas' erste Frau" craves from "Hellas' letzten Jüngling" (255-56). Overwhelmed by his reception and bemused by Sappho's talk of Life versus Art, Phaon concludes that he is in the thrall of a sorceress, a "holde Zauberin" (278). Taking his cue from the imagery with which the scene began, he protests that he will never be able to repay Sappho for her kindness.

How greatly this word, "Güte" (299), would have wounded Sappho if she had been listening to Phaon! At first she interprets his fervor as flattery — "Du schmeichelst süß, doch, Lieber, schmeichelst du" (144) — because she *will* not understand that his adoration of her "hohes Götterbild" does not extend beyond the public to the private sphere. Gradually she yields to his rapturous eloquence and to her determination to see things not as they are but as she would have them. As once before (85), she stifles her subconscious realization that Phaon does not love her by appealing to destiny: "Dem Schicksal tust du unrecht und dir selbst!" (257). Her art now seems a mere sterile enterprise which leaves her begging in front of "des Lebens Überfluß!" (277). Her love is, after all, the decree of fate.[13]

So that her youthfully feminine but unrealstic vision of a love idyll which knows "keine Sättigung / Nur des Genußes ewig gleiche Lust" (290-91) may be legitimized through public acceptance, Sappho summons her servants and *commands* them to respect Phaon as their master. The omens for her wanton self-deception are unfortunately not auspicious. Both Rhamnes' bewildered but quickly stifled protest (302) and Phaon's groping towards insight and clarity (317) indicate that Sappho's dream scenario may be unrealizable.

In the ensuing scene with Melitta, Sappho continues to believe that she can mold reality. By drawing Melitta's attention to Phaon she is either taunting her servant with her conquest or incapable of conceiving that an adolescent girl is a potential rival. She reveals the magnitude of her need for approbation and reassurance concerning Phaon by seeking to elevate her slave to the position of confidante: "Freundin" (349) and "traute Schwester" (361). Like a spoiled child eager to have its way, Sappho is even willing to promise to reform her character: "Oh, ich will gut noch werden, fromm und gut!" (364). No longer will she torment Melitta with her quick temper and biting tongue (359 ff.).

Melitta's reaction to Sappho's friendly overtures parallels that of Phaon. Unlike the Melitta of the first scene, she now sees Sappho's garland but not Sappho. She has no desire to exchange confidences with a woman who will always remain for her "die Gebieterin" (393). (Grillparzer learned the wariness of the underling in his own experiences with nobility.) As Sappho gradually and grudgingly admits to herself that the past cannot be recovered, that a wide chasm separates her from Phaon,[14] and that fame is no substitute for love, Melitta consoles her with evasive platitudes: How could Phaon help but be happy in Sappho's presence? (369). How many thousands have striven in vain to win the garland that Sappho has voluntarily removed from her brow (411-412)!

"Von Tausenden gesucht und nicht errungen!" Sappho numbs her sense of loss and frustration by twice repeating Melitta's expression of respect for her lofty reputation (413-15). This is the first but not the last time that Sappho will take the cue for her conduct from the voice of conventionality. In her eyes the garland ceases to seem "die frevle Zier" (58). Placing it on her forehead again, she resolves to salvage her self-respect by equating the riches of her fame with Phaon's vital abundance: "Wohl mir, Ich bin so arm nicht. Seinem Reichtum / Kann gleichen Reichtum ich entgegensetzen" (419-420).

The fear that the springtide of her life is past is silenced by the consideration that she has as much to offer Phaon as he to her. Far from being merely "eine historisierende Intarsie,"[15] the "Hymn to Aphrodite" which concludes the opening act documents both Sappho's poetic accomplishment and her determination to gain Phaon's love. Its final stanzas celebrate her victory over an obstinate lover:

> Flieht er dich jetzt, bald wird er dir folgen;
> Verschmäht er Geschenke, er gibt sie noch selbst;
> Liebt er dich nicht, gar bald wird er lieben,
> Folgsam gehorchend jeglichem Wink. (448-451)

Only the gesture of fatigue with which she leans her head back as the curtain falls betrays a lack of confidence in her ability to carry the field.

The full impact of Sappho's soliloquy can only be appreciated in the theatre. The "Hymn to Aphrodite" is read in a few minutes; as sole warrant of Sappho's poetic genius, however, it requires forceful, skilled declamation in order to convince the audience of Sappho's stature. The Swedish poet Atterbom described his response to a performance of *Sappho* with the original cast as follows:

> Der Kulminationspunkt ihrer (i.e., Sophie Schröder's) Deklamation war eine Hymne an Aphrodite. ... Diese Hymne rezitierte sie mit einer an Gesang grenzenden Aussprache.... Du kannst es glauben, wir vermeinten wahrhaftig Sphärenklänge zu vernehmen, und nicht bloß *ich* weinte, der ich stets ein leicht zu rührendes Heimchen war, sondern auch mein riesenhafter Herzensbruder Rückert war rein außer sich vor glückseligem Schmerz.[16]

The tears of Atterbom and his companion may be taken as a partial measure of Grillparzer's success in imparting to his heroine — at least for many of his own generation — the radiance of a demi-goddess as well as the pathos of unrequited love. They justify his insistence, against the advice of such a competent theatre professional as Adolf Müllner, upon introducing *Sappho* with so apparently static a first act.

The opening scenes of Act II belong to Phaon and Melitta. At the outset Phaon wavers between repudiating and defending his love for Sappho. Disappointment enables him to acknowledge that his love flourished more when her actual presence did not curb his imaginative flights (487 ff.). As his thoughts stray homewards to the parents to whom he, normally a dutiful son, has neglected to write, he recalls their puritanical disapprobation of female musicians.[17] Torn between convention and pride at his new conquest, he tries to banish confusion with shopworn rhetoric: even his father will some day have to concede that Sappho embodies "Der Frauen Zier, die Krone des Geschlechts!" (505). His chivalric notion of love culminates in a desire to defend his beloved against all detractors (506 ff.) — an ironic foreshadowing of his rescue of Melitta from Sappho. But his quandary persists. At Melitta's approach he flees to a grotto, the archetypical symbol of the Self in pursuit of itself.[18]

Phaon is actually fleeing his true goal. Melitta's presence soon draws him from the path of introspection to the entrance of the grotto where he stands listening to her plaintive soliloquy. Both he and she are sufficiently naive to diagnose the symptoms of awakening love as homesickness. Inevitably they are drawn to each other by the principle of "gleich und gleich gesellt sich gern."[19] Their love's symbol is a solitary rose which — another irony — Sappho's handmaidens overlooked while weaving garlands for Aphrodite's festival. The prelapsarian innocence of their feelings toward each other is guaranteed by a memory: Melitta recalls that in her lost eastern homeland she had been caressed — and with paternal approval — by a man "so schön und hold / Mit braunem Haar und Aug," a man like Phaon (642-43)!

What reaction can the lovers expect from "die Gebieterin," Sappho? Because they require her cooperation, they do not consider the possibility of a change of Sappho's heart. To Phaon she still appears "gut und milde" (621). Melitta confirms his opinion, though with qualifications: "Doch wenn auch heftig manchmal, rasch und bitter, / Doch gut ist Sappho, wahrlich, lieb und gut" (671-72). Frost invades Eden when Sappho arrives just in time to witness the new lovers' embrace. In an effort to win Phaon as a woman rather than as a poetess she has again divested herself of her garland and her lyre. Too late. By dismissing Melitta peremptorily she retracts the offering of sisterly affection made in Act I. She now behaves as an anxious matron concerned for the welfare of a lovable but neither bright nor talented child whose impressionable heart must be shielded from unscrupulous swains. Melitta must remain in bondage until her education is finished. Like many a worthy predecessor among the best women of Mytilene, she too will some day shine as "Sapphos Werk" (751).

Sappho's conduct here is as puzzling as her drawing Melitta's attention to Phaon in Act I. She undermines her own position. Can she truly expect to arouse Phaon's love by assuming a maternal, even matronly role — "Wir wollen / Ein andermal noch diesen Punkt besprechen!" (779-80) — and thereby drawing attention to the difference in maturity between them? What does she think will be his response to her imputation of lecherous motives to him vis-à-vis Melitta? Phaon makes his attitude of injured bewilderment painfully clear with distracted monosyllables, sarcasm ("Recht schön! Recht schön!"), and, finally, dismissal (787). Both then retire, separately, in pursuit of their true selves. Sappho enters the grotto and Phaon falls asleep.

In the third act the gap between Sappho and Phaon widens. Although he is asleep on the grass, Sappho for a time does not see him. Intent upon maintaining her self-respect, she refuses to confront the truth of her loss. At first she contemplates suicide to rid herself of the intolerable image of her humiliation (795-99). There are other less desperate expedients. Like many a Grillparzer character, Sappho banishes an unpleasant reality from her mind by denying its existence (803-04). She contrasts her capacity for deep emotion, an echo of the "Unermeßlichkeit" of verse 126, with Phaon's, in fact, with fundamental masculine shallowness (811 ff.). She would rather all men be fickle — and thus beyond the range of her love — than surrender Phaon to Melitta.

Her rationalizing is checked by her discovery of her sleeping lover. Overwhelmed by his presence, she hastily convinces herself that he is an exception among men. From "der liebliche Verräter" (843) he becomes a pure temple, besmirched only by her unjustified accusations (851). Phaon awakens at her kiss and dispels her illusion with one word: "Melitta." Phaon's buoyant spirit and his recounting of a dream in which Sappho became Melitta — "der Lorbeerkranz, er war mit eins verschwunden" (914, a foreshadowing of 2039 and, perhaps, an echo of Goethe's Egmont after his vision of victory) — make further self-deception on Sappho's part impossible. Not only has Sappho been bested in love; she has been humiliated by a servant. Against this background of lost love and hurt pride her public personality reasserts itself. She at whose feet kings have sat, the jewel of Hellas (940; cf. 1830), now concludes that the gods have punished her defection:

> Wen Götter sich zum Eigentum erlesen,
> Geselle sich zu Erdenbürgern nicht. (948-49)

Her art and her fame render her immortal at the cost of her own mortality: "Den Lebendigen gehörst du nimmer an!" (957). In the light of what follows, it seems strange that some critics have utilized Sappho's self-aggrandizing speech, clearly a form of sour grapes, as an interpretive key. Her words are but another proof of her determination to view herself in as favorable a light as possible.

Instead of returning in humility to Aganippe's fount, the logical course of action if she believed her own words, Sappho sets out to humble her victorious rival. She belittles Melitta as "ein albern Kind / Mit blöden Mienen" (966) with but a child's playfulness and fear of punishment (here again, a veiled threat).[20] Eucharis' praise of Melitta's beauty brings quickly suppressed tears (of rage?) to Sappho's eyes (1012). In the fourth scene Sappho for an instant understands that her pride is the slave of her unrequited love. At Melitta's appearance (scene 5), however, near-paranoid jealousy seizes her. Like King Ottokar in *König Ottokars Glück und Ende* and Rustan in *Der Traum ein Leben,* Sappho elects to consider herself the victim of a treasonable deception because she cannot have what she most wants. Melitta, as a serpent whose every word is false (1021, 1035, 1094, 1122), is now endowed with an intelligence previously denied her — "Du bist so blöde nicht!" (1091) — in order to render this conspiracy theory plausible. Sappho's appeal to her "sister" Melitta's gratitude for past favors (1048-58), a transparent form of emotional blackmail, changes at the sight of the roses on Melitta's breast and the blushes on her cheeks to enraged denunciation, bullying, and outright assault. If Melitta will not give up the rose, the symbol of Phaon's love, Sappho will coerce her.

Phaon rescues Melitta and Sappho gradually sinks into a daze. Her injured pride reasserts itself long enough to reject Melitta's claim of responsibility for having provoked the incident: "Weh mir, bedürft' ich jemals deiner Großmut!" (1131, foreshadowing 1954). It cannot withstand Phaon's unambiguous defense of innocence and condemnation of arrogance in women. For him the "holde Zauberin" (278) stands unmasked as a Circe (1174).[21] As Phaon leads Melitta away, Sappho is left behind, alone, with arms outstretched towards her departing lover. Her fading voice utters no word but his name.

Sappho's imploring call: "Phaon" and, later, the question she imagines putting to him: "Was hab' ich dir getan,/Daß du mich tötest!" (1530-31) repudiate the argument that Phaon is too insignificant to be a cause of her death.[22] He seems so to some commentators but not to Sappho; otherwise she could resume her poetic career after dismissing the Phaon episode as a bagatelle. She realizes, however, that she has reached her life's turning point. Repudiation of her love is out of the question, though she will never again be able to convince herself that the man still addressed at the beginning of the act as "Geliebter!" (851) reciprocates her devotion. Somehow she must steer a course between the extreme options open to her: magnanimous acquiescence in the manner of Hofmannsthal's Marschallin, or a Medea-like elimination of her feminine rival as an act of vengeance upon her former lover. As Act IV progresses, Sappho's anger waxes until it assumes the dimensions of Medea's fury. In the fifth act her self-respect, a sense of responsibility to her art, and a concern for her future fame (one might even say: her super-ego) curb her rage sufficiently to effect at least a seeming metamorphosis of Medea into Marschallin.

Night has fallen between the third and fourth acts. The pathetic fallacy is here operative: Sappho's loneliness and despair find their natural counterpart in the moonlit landscape. To the conventional association of night with death and surcease from care Sappho adds a note of romantic egoism. Not only does she wonder how she can continue to exist; she expects the world to have tumbled down in tribute to her cosmic grief (1189-91). Her thoughts revert to the themes of ingratitude and treachery. She delivers a rhetorical set piece whose pathetic tone (*vorgestellter Genitiv*, personified abstractions, drastic images from the Schillerean abyss) points up the hollowness of her attempt to justify the deportation of Melitta on the basis of Phaon's hypothetical ingratitude.[23] Comprehending that "des Innern düstre Geister wachen auf" (1220), Sappho prays to the gods — her first invocation of them — for self-control. But the association of serpents and hydras with Phaon proves irresistible. Her sense of outrage gains the upper hand when she remembers how she would have immortalized his name in poetry, just as she has transformed slaves into good citizens (751). Casting self-restraint aside, she reverts to face-saving self-delusion. She decides the gods wish her to restore the moral order violated by Phaon and Melitta. Her plan is to send Melitta to Chios, far from the treacherous Phaon. Since Melitta is her "Werk" (1244, later 1872), she is free to destroy her at will. "Von euch [i.e., the gods] kam der Gedanke" (1233); "Unsterbliche, habt Dank für diesen Wink" (1242). With such sophistry she legitimizes her scheme to separate the lovers.[24]

For a second Sappho's intelligence grasps the futility of her plan. What is to prevent Phaon's love from following Melitta? (1249). Though her reason accepts the conclusion that she can never again possess Phaon's heart, she refuses to forget their mutually shared past except for the last few painful hours. With her poet's imagination she conjures up a masochistic vision. If she torments herself enough, perhaps he will relent! She banishes herself to a cliff by the seacoast in cloudy climes where thorns flourish among the sterile rocks.[25] Here she will make a cult of Phaon's love (1262). Her past too is refurbished. She forgets the disappointments and emotional deprivation of her youth, as recounted in Act I (cf. 120 ff. with 1275), and turns the waters of Aganippe into a Fountain of Youth:

> Was meinem Lied ich gab, gab es mir wieder,
> Und ew'ge Jugend grünte mir ums Haupt. (1279-80)

Phaon's first encounter with her, formerly described as mute and bashful homage to her genius (249-254), is now imaged in terms of plunder, almost of rape: "Mit frechen Händen / Reißt er den goldnen Schleier mir herab" (1281-82).

The archetypical situation symbolized by the presence of Aphrodite's altar upon the stage throughout the play will soon be partially clarified. As later in *Des Meeres und der Liebe Wellen*, the mature authorities seek to part the young male lover from his adolescent consort. Both Sappho and Hero's uncle-priest interpret this act of separation as a divine decree. Virginity must be placed beyond the pale of ardor. Sappho even employs the verb "atone" in connection with the future she desires for Melitta, who must "mit der Liebesqual der Liebe Frevel büßen" (1240). To Rhamnes, Sappho entrusts the task of transmitting Melitta to her father's (!) "Gastfreund" on the isle of Chios. He accepts the commission unquestioningly. Rhamnes now becomes a dual father figure: to Sappho — as her first teacher and chief herald of her reputation; to Melitta, who addresses him as "Vater" (1414) and whom he calls "Mädchen" and "Kind" until she defies him (1357, 1362, 1370; in line 1454 she is Phaon's "Mädchen").

In the ensuing variation on the Oedipal contest the mother is aligned against the son and the prize is Melitta. For Phaon, to rescue his beloved from Rhamnes and from Medusa-Sappho (1428) is to complete the rite of passage by proving himself a man. She is for him "dies Himmelsabbild" (1397), "die Reine" (1450), and "das reine Haupt der Unschuld" (1601). He foresees a life with her of primal bliss in harmony with nature and with the older generation (1459-61), a Rousseauean vision in miniature. Only once does he reveal his insecurity when he implies that Sappho's hold on Melitta may be so strong that she will have to be abducted: "Komm mit! und folgst du nicht, bei allen Göttern / Auf diesen Händen trag' ich dich von hinnen" (1464-65).

Rhamnes, the father figure, is old and weak, impotent even before he is threatened with the (phallic?) dagger Phaon has wrested from Sappho: "Was ich gewollt, ich kann es nicht vollführen" (1399). The impression of weakness is reenforced by the forms of address: while Rhamnes repeatedly calls Phaon "Herr," the latter dismisses him patronizingly as "Sklave!" and "du allzu fert'ger Diener fremder Bosheit" (1388-90). In the earliest manuscript version of *Sappho* Phaon actually captures Rhamnes and shackles him to a column before fleeing from Lesbos (*HKA*, I/17, 200).

Phaon's capacity for self-delusion matches that of Sappho. He too considers himself a victim of malice, as well as a favorite of the gods. Both are convinced, for opposite reasons, that the trip to Chios is divinely inspired. (Phaon: "Amphitrite ist der Liebe hold" [1469]). Phaon, however, believes the gods want him to accompany Melitta.

The similarity between the frenzied states of mind of the two protagonists is underscored by a number of stylistic subtleties: by the parallel wording and position in the blank verse of the statements of inspiration (Sappho's "Ihr lebet, ja! — Von euch kam der Gedanke" [1233] and Phaon's "Ich nehm' es an! Von euch kömmt's gute Götter!" [1419]); by the employment of the same derogatory adjective (Sappho dubs Phaon "der Rauhe" [1281], and he condemns her island as "dies feindlich-rauhe Land" [1427]); and by their use of the same Schiller-inspired rhetoric.

The opening of the fifth act is paradoxical. At the moment of her victory Sappho becomes weak, communicating only in monosyllables and with gestures. Before the last scene she utters less than one hundred words. (The situation will be reversed at the end when despair limits Phaon to brief outcries and desperate imperatives.) Apparently triumphant — the fleeing lovers have been brought to bay — Sappho hesitates to exercise her legal rights. As in the third scene of the fourth act, she again avoids confrontation, this time by falling "hingegossen" before Aphrodite's altar (stage direction after 1649). When Phaon calls her to account, she feebly insists on the justice of her cause. When he compels her to look at him, she shudders. Spurning Melitta's offer to abide by her decision, even if it involves the sacrifice of Phaon, she withholds her blessing from the lovers. Her anguished protestation: "Hinab in Meeresgrund die goldne Leier, / Wird ihr Besitz um solchen Preis erkauft!" (1731-32), the fixed look in her eyes, and her cold gesture of disdain upon withdrawal (stage direction after 1784) hold little promise of imminent reconciliation.

At the moment of his humiliating capture Phaon seems to gain strength. Sappho's servants are unable to restrain him. Selfrighteously indignant, he taunts Sappho because she remains silent: "So stumm? der Dicht'rin süße Lippe stumm?" (1661). He betrays no awareness of her inner torment, which he mistakes for rage (1663) and, a little later, for pride (1794). Repeatedly he condemns her magic powers (1617, 1644, 1665) and attributes base traits to her which are not hers: greed and a cold heart. She is a viper, unworthy of the lyre, unfaithful to her poet's mission (1685). His is an idealization of the artist, whose melody is the product of purest inspiration, "der reinsten Kräfte Kind" (1690) — a naive outlook expressed in traditional botanical imagery (1689) on a par with his dream of a pastoral existence shared with Melitta.

Phaon next tries flattery. Sappho's passion, he explains, is but the result of an evil spell: "Wer hat dich denn mit Zauberschlag verwandelt?" (1702). If she will only sanction his union with Melitta, her divinity will be restored:

> Mit Höhern, Sappho, halte du Gemeinschaft,
> Man steigt nicht ungestraft vom Göttermahle
> Herunter in den Kreis der Sterblichen. (1726-28)

When Sappho still does not cooperate, Phaon insults her further — he has already told her he prefers to remember her as he had pictured her before they met (1716 ff.) — with a retrospective analysis of the emotions he had mistaken for love. With the brutal candour of youth he praises Melitta to Sappho, only to be outraged when Sappho orders Melitta to go. Between the threat of violence (1765-66) and the expression of contempt for Sappho (1811)[26] Phaon sets the stage for Sappho's apotheosis by urging her to accept the inevitable consequences of her poet's nature:

> Den Menschen Liebe und den Göttern Ehrfurcht,
> Gib uns was unser, und nimm hin was dein!
> Bedenke was du tust, und wer du bist! (1782-84)

In such a highly charged context and from such a desperate source the sentiment originates which Sappho will pronounce only a moment before her death (2025).

Phaon protests too forcefully. As the act progresses, a reversal of sympathy takes place. In his arrogance and insensibility Phaon dwindles in stature, becoming at the last an object of scorn to all who mourn for Sappho. Even though his escape has failed and his and Melitta's position among strangers is precarious (1805), he will attain his aim and capture the bride. His victory, however, will be Pyrrhic, the result of Sappho's resignation rather than of masculine prowess and bought at the price of total alienation from his fellows, including even Melitta, who lies in a faint as the curtain falls.

Grillparzer entrusts to Sappho's servants the arrangement of Sappho's apotheosis, both a tribute to her poetic immortality and a vengeful act against Phaon and Melitta. In the words of the *Landmann*, Sappho is their liege lady, "nicht weil sie gebeut, weil wir ihr dienen" (1642). Even Melitta pleads with Sappho like a disobedient child to its mother (1760) and insists that she cannot continue to live if Sappho, her moral exemplar, disapproves of her actions (1788-91).

Phaon is now cast in the viper's role he assigned to Sappho (1820). Returning to the financial imagery of Act I, Rhamnes contrasts the wealth (1822) of Hellas' jewel (1818, 1830), whose immortal name glows in diamond letters in the firmament (1836), with Phaon's insignificance and poverty of spirit. As a father berates a son for not appreciating his parents' efforts sufficiently, Rhamnes explains to Phaon that his pride is solely the result of Sappho's former favor (1831) and the nobility of her loving heart (1858). In his enthusiasm Rhamnes even ascribes Phaon's love for Melitta to Sappho's success in transmitting to her slave a touch of her own *maternal spirit* (1870-72; italics mine to indicate the Oedipal element). He caps his tirade with an improbably prescient denunciation: Phaon, the murderer of Sappho and the enemy of beauty and of the gods

11

(1878-81), will live homeless and outlawed for the remainder of his days. Rhamnes' acrimonious words and his eagerness to make Melitta quake at the recognition of her wrongdoing — "*Die* Rache wenigstens vermisse Sappho nicht!" (1854) — manifest his fundamental motive: the vengeance of the father upon the son who has usurped the love both of the wife-mother, Sappho, and of the daughter, Melitta.

Rhamnes foretells Sappho's death but does nothing to dissuade her from suicide. The conclusion of his speech marks the point in the play at which mythology becomes more important than psychology. In the final scenes the ritual will be consummated by which Sappho is restored to the gods. The maid Eucharis' report describes the initial phase of her transfiguration.

Eucharis tells how, after forsaking the lovers, Sappho rose above mortal concerns by ascending to an altar on a cliff overlooking the sea. Here she cast her flowers, gold, and jewels — mementoes of an almost-dead past — into the loud waters. Motionless, "im Kreis von Marmorbildern, fast als ihresgleichen" (1907), she assumed the still grandeur of a statue or icon. From her lips awe-inspiring words resounded: *not* Sappho's words (1923) but those of an incarnate Muse. Eucharis' narrative glows with pentecostal ecstasy: when the breeze from the sea set the strings of Sappho's abandoned lyre singing, Sappho trembled, "wie von Berührung einer höhern Macht" and hastened to her "Freundin an der Wand" (1925). Before Eucharis' dazzled gaze — "Denn wie ein Blitzstrahl flirrte mich's vorüber" (1929) — the miraculous transformation begins. Pressing the golden lyre to her bosom, her brow wreathed with Olympian laurels and her shoulders covered by regal scarlet (a recapitulation of the opening act), Sappho descends from the high steps of the altar and from the cliff to take leave of the living. Only her "lebend toter Blick" links her incipient radiance (1940-46) with the woman whose heart was stricken by Phaon's inability to love her.

Solemn and composed, Sappho exposes her unforgiving heart through scornful words. She brushes Melitta's anguished plea for pardon aside by misrepresenting it as an act of superfluous generosity (1953-54). Forbidding Phaon to touch her, she repays his insults with the patently false claim that he did not hold ("fassen") her heart. The emotion that prevents her from speaking further, however, belies her sedate comparison of their past relationship to the brief encounter of two travelling companions (1965-71). Phaon and Melitta are put in their place in such summary fashion that the punitive, self-pitying overtones of Sappho's last farewell should be audible to all: "Die tote Mutter schickt dir diesen Kuß!" (2020). That they are not is a tribute to Grillparzer's dramatic ingenuity.

Sappho cannot show mercy to the lovers until she has overcome her feminine frailty. Before the altar of Aphrodite she communes with the gods, "den Meinen" (1979). Grateful for their gifts — her emotions, intellect, creative power, and enduring fame — she acknowledges her willingness to pay the requisite price:

> Ihr habt der Dichterin vergönnt zu nippen
> An dieses Lebens süß umkränzten Kelch,
> Zu nippen nur, zu trinken nicht. (1995-97)

Since her creative mission has been completed (2001), her sole desire is to die at the height of her powers (2005-06). Thus she may avoid becoming an object of ridicule to the fool who imagines himself wise (2010; the circumlocution barely conceals her rancor towards Phaon). The victory and fulfillment she boasts of are not quite yet hers. A little later she prays: "Laßt mich vollenden, so wie ich begonnen"; and "Gebt mir den Sieg, erlasset mir den Kampf" (2012, 2015). Her rhapsodic aria ends as the sun rises and the flames leap high on the altar.

The gods grant Sappho's prayer. Before the adoring eyes of her retinue (and, presumably, of the audience) she becomes a goddess. "Verklärt ist all ihr Wesen, / Glanz der Unsterblichen umleuchtet sie!" (2023-24). Her apotheosis is accomplished when she pays the last debt of her life by bestowing her blessing on Phaon and Melitta. Freed from jealousy, Sappho now consecrates her existence to an abstract deity of love (2022). With her leap into the primal element, "des Meeres heil'gen Fluten," (2037), she detaches herself from mortality to assume her rightful place among the immortals.

Why can't Sappho return to life and go on creating? Why must she die? Various explanations based on psychological analysis have been proposed. The most obvious suggests that, because she cannot live without Phaon, her suicide represents a drastic form of renunciation of love.[27] Sappho's grief at the loss of Phaon (1530-31) and her plea that she may not be mocked in her weakness and torment of soul (2008-15) may be adduced as evidence. Though valid psychologically, this hypothesis reduces the final blessing to an elaborate charade.

Other suggestions also circle around the idea of weakness: Sappho fears growing old and the loss of her creative powers; she seeks to punish those she leaves behind for her humiliation; she realizes that she will not always be able to control her passionate nature, and that she would be an unworthy ambassador of the gods if she went on living.

The problem of Sappho's age has provoked much disagreement.[28] The role was created by Sophie Schröder, a thirty-seven year old star noted for her liaisons with younger men, including Grillparzer's friend Moritz Daffinger, and for her lack of beauty. Her assumption of the role sufficed to imprint the image of an aging bluestocking upon Grillparzer's heroine.[29] The *Schadenfreude* felt by a portion of the public at Sappho's death gave rise to such parodies as the comic melodrama *Seppherl* in which the young tailor Phanzel discovers the counterfeit nature of his beloved Seppherl's teeth, hair, and glass eye.[30] The text provides some, but scant support for the hypothesis that Sappho is much older than her lover: Sappho's history of failure in love (119-20, 381-82), the "Kluft" which separates her from Phaon (394), the presence of her protégées among Mytilene's "beste Bürgerinnen" (749-51), and — ambiguously — the desire to die "in voller Kraft, in ihres Daseins Blüte" (2005).

Grillparzer imagined Sappho to be twenty-five or twenty-six.[31] To make this plausible, he established the maternal relationship between Sappho and Melitta thirteen years before the beginning of the play when Sappho was "selber noch ein kindlich Wesen" (1054). Though he accepted Madame Schröder for the play's debut, he rejected the notion of entrusting the role to "ältere oder reizlose Frauen" as contrary to his intentions.[32] The currents of *Torschlußpanik* and Kierkegaardian ennui some modern commentators have detected in *Sappho* cannot be considered primary causes of her death.[33] Grillparzer presents not aging, but a gap in age between lover and beloved; not *taedium vitae*, but a deliberate anesthetizing of emotion.

Though not explicit, Sappho's desire for retaliation against the lovers she leaves behind is implied.[34] By identifying Grillparzer with Phaon a psychoanalytically oriented critic can read the final scene both as wish-fulfillment and self-inflicted punishment: the mother who attempted to monopolize the affections of her young lover is compelled to acquiesce in his union with her almost-daughter, Melitta, and withdraw from life.[35] Retribution comes swiftly. When confronted by Sappho's suicide, Melitta swoons and Phaon can only cry: "Weh mir! Unmöglich, nein!" (2038; cf. 1893 and 1896). (Grillparzer actually contemplated introducing the corpse of Sappho upon the stage.)[36] However legitimate this intellectualized insight may be, it too disregards the most effective dramatic moment of the last scene: Sappho's prayer to her gods.

Sappho does not fear that she may compromise by her passionate nature the gods whose envoy she considers herself.[37] The flames on Aphrodite's altar blaze the goddess' endorsement of her claim that her life has accorded with divine decree:

> Vollendet hab' ich, was ihr mir geboten,
> Darum versagt mir nicht den letzten Lohn! (2001-02)

Her sole acknowledgement of indebtedness is directed towards the living: her blessing of Phaon and Melitta is in payment of "die letzte Schuld des Lebens" (2027). There is otherwise no confession of obligation or guilt on Sappho's part to substantiate the thesis that passion demands atonement because the votaries of art must restrict themselves to the domain of pure contemplation, the sanctuary of the *vita contemplativa*.[38]

Quite the contrary. Sappho dies as she lived. Among the gifts of the gods she numbers "ein Herz, zu fühlen" (1985). As she exalted Aphrodite in her existence and in her poetry, she dedicates her suicide to the goddess of love: "Nun hin, dort an der Liebesgöttin Altar / Erfülle sich der Liebe dunkles Los!" (2021-22) By her death she strives to vindicate her passionate past, affirming love as the dual source of her life and of her art. By her art she gains life eternal.

The ear of the attentive reader hears the sound of the surf — the loud sea

(1910) — throughout the play.³⁹ It symbolizes the archetypal realm to which Sappho is related as poet and as woman.⁴⁰ Surrogate mother, educatrix, woman in love, she can be solicitous and arrogant, wise and foolish, strong and weak, time's slave and eternity's ward. Above all, she creates. Her passionate heart is the wellspring of her poetry.

Here there is no moral imperative. The gods have not decreed to the poet: "Thou shalt remain in the shrine of art, on life's periphery!" He cannot live aloof if he would fulfill his creative mission. Grillparzer was keenly aware of the relationship between his own violent nature and his genius: "Ich habe heftige Leidenschaften, ... und gewiß das muß ein Mensch besitzen, der nur eingermaßen Anspruch auf den Namen eines Dichters machen will."⁴¹ During the year of the composition of *Sappho* he made the following diary entry concerning Shakespeare: "Ich glaube, daß das Genie nichts geben kann, als was es in sich selbst gefunden, und daß es nie eine Leidenschaft oder Gesinnung schildern wird, als die er selbst, als Mensch, in seinem eigenen Busen trägt."⁴²

The Muse exacts a harsh penalty: her own must come to know the "malheur d'être poète" (Grillparzer's own phrase).⁴³ Because Sappho is a genius her love will not be reciprocated. Lost in veneration, the common herd does not sense the warmth of the hard, gemlike flame. It can but shout: "Heil, Sappho, Heil!" (8). The poet is a marked man, doomed to isolation and denied human companionship. In the rarefied atmosphere of the lonely heights nothing alleviates the pain of his involuntary exile except the promise of immortality, the awareness of having sown "Saat für die Ewigkeit" (1991).

Grillparzer's contemporaries grasped his sombre message immediately. After reading *Sappho* in Italian, Lord Byron confided to his diary: "The man has done a great thing in writing that play. And *who is he?* I know him not; but *ages will.*"⁴⁴ Another romantic aristocrat, Graf von Platen, found in Sappho a kindred spirit whose "triste destinée" he would probably not escape.⁴⁵ Among Grillparzer's many Viennese admirers his friend Caroline Pichler was dismayed by the idea, "daß die Kunst ihre Jünger nicht glücklich mache."⁴⁶ Limiting its application to the author's individual case, she concluded that, though many artists lead happy lives, her friend was not among their number.

How could he have been? It took an almost reckless courage for Grillparzer to pursue a dramatist's career in the Vienna of Metternich. Lacking connections and money, exposed to the vagaries of censorship and the patronage system, he was trapped between the contrary claims of poetic ambition and the necessity to support a family consisting of a hypochondriacal mother and several spendthrift younger brothers. His slender means eliminated the possibility of marriage. Despite its success, *Die Ahnfrau* had reaped more critical animosity than financial reward. Such constricting circumstances often put him in a mood to mourn "des Dichters blendend, trauriges Geschick," a recurrent theme in the poems of this period.⁴⁷

In "An Ovid" (1812) Grillparzer finds in the Roman poet's exile an analogue of his own fate. Ovid was punished for lèse-majesté while he is but an innocent victim of "des Schicksals allgewaltige Eisenhand" (*SW*, I, 72). The Byronic tone resounds in his lament for having lost the opportunity to sin and in his entertainment of the thought of suicide. In the storm-tossed sea of his life there is no consolation but the assurance of a poet's immortal fame. The fatalism of "An Ovid" also marks "Der Bann" and "Abschied von Gastein" (both 1818). The poet in "Der Bann" had no control over his faculties when he turned his back on love: "Hab' ich im Wahnsinn widerstrebt" (*SW*, I, 109). Now he must live "vogelfrei," condemned to misunderstanding, disillusionment, and loneliness. (Grillparzer here reverses Rhamnes' judgment upon Phaon in line 1882: Phaon is "vogelfrei" because he chose love above poetry. One is damned either way.) "Abschied von Gastein" likens the poet's gifts to the flaming glory of a tree struck by lightning, the beauty of a pearl produced by the oyster's pain, and the splendor of a waterfall dashing itself against rocks. What the poet makes delights others but brings him nothing but torment. As in *Sappho,* his misery does not betoken a defective character but is inherent in his calling.[48]

A dramatist looks at life from more than one vantage point. The poet's destiny did not always appear bleak and passive to Grillparzer. In "Die tragische Muse" (1819), written shortly before the completion of *Das goldene Vließ*, he presents the conflict between the promise of eternal fame and the yearning to come down "zu den Meinen" from the cliffs jutting into the clouds (the "Gipfel" image again). The garland now seems worth the sacrifice to the poet who follows the Muse higher onto uncharted paths.[49] In "Zu Mozarts Feier" (1842) life and art are intertwined, not antipodal:

> Er [i.e., Mozart] aber klomm so hoch, als Leben reicht,
> Und stieg so tief, als Leben blüht und duftet,
> Und so ward ihm der ewig frische Kranz,
> Den die Natur ihm wand und mit ihm teilet.[50]

"Alles wirkliche gehorcht dem Maß" (*SW*, I, 285). The synthesis has been effected by Mozart's infallible sense of balance.

Mozart succeeded where Sappho failed. Grillparzer too did not leap off a cliff. Even before his imagination was fired by Sappho's history, he understood the need for restraint. The same diary entry which locates the passions of the *dramatis personae* in the heart of their creator distinguishes carefully between potentiality and realization. Emotion must be tempered by the moral sense and by reason.

> Also sollte Shakespeare ein Mörder, Dieb, Lügner, Verräther, Undankbarer, Wahnsinniger gewesen seyn, weil er sie so meisterlich schildert? Ja! Das heißt, er mußte zu dem allen Anlage in sich haben, obschon die vorherrschende Vernunft, das moralische Gefühl nichts davon zum Ausbruch kommen ließ. (*HKA*, II/7, 101)

In *Sappho* the poetess does not admit this distinction between life and art. She is what she writes. Grillparzer's awareness of the moral "Gefühl" expresses itself solely in his striving for harmonious form.

Sappho has a "classical" surface. The unities are observed, the number of characters limited, the diction to a great extent modeled on Goethe's *Iphigenie*. At the end the rising sum illumines the stage. The surface, however, is deceptive, a thin crust over lava.[51] The mood of the piece is plaintive and dark in accordance with Grillparzer's admitted propensity to satisfy his "elegische Natur" by lamenting before an audience. "Vom Augenblick an, da es mir kein Vergnügen mehr macht, vor dem Publikum zu klagen, macht es mir auch keine Freude, für dasselbe zu dichten" (*HKA*, II/8, 291). A "spätverirrter Fremdling" (1199) like his heroine, Grillparzer too sends the sound of his weeping through the night. Into his Sappho he projects his own pent-up violence, frustrated sexuality, doubts about his fame, contempt for mediocrity, and longing for an idyllic (not a bourgeois!) existence. As Goethe did in writing *Werther*, Grillparzer simultaneously indulges and exorcises his craving for self-annihilation. *Sappho* is also akin to *Werther* in its fusion of analytic detachment with intense sympathy for the sufferings of a sensitive spirit.

Narcissistic masterpieces like *Werther* and *Sappho* seldom evoke a neutral reaction. Tender souls quiver before the mirror image of their own torment. Admirers of balance and reason aim barbs of ridicule and parody. Valid subjectively, such extreme responses are unfair to the poet. To follow the youthful genius on his explorations in the cavern of the human psyche the reader must have developed a certain amount of night vision; to appreciate the magnitude of the accomplishment when form is imposed upon emotional chaos he must have an eye for proportion and nuance. The romantic imagination reveals its full splendor only to those equipped with bifocals of empathy and analysis.

NOTES

1 "Childe Harold's Pilgrimage," Canto II, xxxix, *The Works of Lord Byron*, ed. Ernest Hartley Coleridge (London: J. Murray, 1922), *Poetry*, II, 125.
2 Franz Grillparzer, "Selbstbiographie," in *Sämtliche Werke*, ed. Peter Frank and Karl Pörnbacher (München: Hanser, 1960-65), IV, 148. Henceforth abbreviated *SW*, this edition will be quoted, because of its accessibility, except when it does not include items found in the *Historisch-kritische Ausgabe* [*HKA*] of August Sauer and Reinhold Backmann (Wien: Schroll, 1909-1948). The text of *Sappho* will be quoted according to *HKA*, I/1.
3 O. E. Lessing's "Sappho-Probleme," *Euphorion*, 10 (1903), 592-611, e.g., registers the disgruntlement of those who seek in Grillparzer the precisely defined antitheses of a Schiller.
4 Franz Grillparzer, *Sappho*, ed. Keith Spaulding (London: Macmillan, 1965), p. xvii.
5 In his discussion of the "necessity" of Sappho's suicide Ludolf von Wedel-Parlow tallies

five negative — his own makes six — and four positive votes among his critical predecessors. See "Der junge Grillparzer," *Euphorion*, 30 (1929), p. 506, n. 31. Among more recent commentators Berndt Breitenbruch concludes: "Die Dichterin verschwindet völlig hinter dem liebenden und eifersüchtigen Weib. Nur als solches ist sie schließlich noch existent. In der letzten Szene verdirbt Grillparzer freilich alles, indem er Sappho dann doch wieder zu 'sich selbst', d. i. zur Dichterin zurückfinden läßt." See *Ethik und Ethos bei Grillparzer*. Quellen und Forschungen zur Sprach- und Kulturgeschichte der germanischen Völker, N. F. 18 (Berlin: De Gruyter, 1965), p. 142.

[6] Letter to Adolf Müllner, March, 1818, *SW*, IV, 743.

[7] Reinhold Backmann, "Zur Entstehungsgeschichte der 'Sappho'," in *Grillparzer-Studien*, ed. Oskar Katann (Wien: Gerlach und Wiedling, 1924), pp. 116-17.

[8] George A. Wells, *The Plays of Grillparzer* (London: Pergamon, 1969), p. 40.

[9] Ludwig Börne, "Sappho. Trauerspiel von Grillparzer," in "Dramaturgische Blätter" 59, *Sämtliche Schriften*, ed. Inge and Peter Rippmann (Düsseldorf: Melzer, 1964), I, 428-29.

[10] Letter to Adolf Müllner, March, 1818, *SW*, IV, 743.

[11] Werner Vordtriede's interpretation of this speech exaggerates: "stärkste Verurteilung der Kunst" and "Sehnsucht nach den 'Wonnen der Gewöhnlichkeit'" are phrases too strong for Sappho's playing the gracious lady. Vordtriede mistakes the "Demutsformel" for a confession. See "Grillparzers Beitrag zum Poetischen Nihilismus," *Trivium*, 9 (1951), 108. Sappho does feel attracted to the common lot but she does not condemn her art. In fact, she intends to glorify domesticity, "häuslich stillen Freuden," with song (96-97).

[12] The motif of Sappho's loftiness is further developed as Phaon addresses her as "hoch" (145, 155, 246). In Grillparzer's imagery in this and other plays the "Gipfel" (e.g., 90) is associated with elevation, isolation, art, worship, and dominion. See the dissertation of Harald A. Reger, *Das Sprachbild in Grillparzers Dramen* (Bonn: Bouvier, 1968), p. 125; p. 266.

[13] Like the characters in *Blanka von Kastilien* and *Die Ahnfrau*, Sappho adjusts her conception of fate to fit the circumstances. In *Grillparzer e i suoi drammi*, (Milano e Napoli: Ricciardi, 1958), p. 60, Leonello Vincenti categorizes *Sappho* as a fate drama.

[14] Is the "Kluft / Die zwischen ihm (Phaon) und mir (Sappho) verschlingend gähnt" (394-95) Sappho's art or the difference in age between the partners? On art: Herbert Seidler, "Das sprachliche Bild in Goethes 'Iphigenie' und Grillparzers 'Sappho'," *Germanistische Abhandlungen*, ed. Karl Kurt Klein und Eugen Thurnher. Innsbrucker Beiträge zur Kulturwissenschaft, 6 (Innsbruck, 1959), 173; reprinted in H. Seidler, *Studien zu Grillparzer und Stifter* (Wien: Böhlau, 1970); on age: Adolf D. Klarmann, "Psychological Motivation in Grillparzer's 'Sappho'," *Monatshefte*, 40 (1948), 275. The readings are not mutually exclusive.

[15] The phrase is from Gerhart Baumann, *Franz Grillparzer. Sein Werk und das österreichische Wesen* (Freiburg/Wien: Herder, 1954), p. 52.

[16] Norbert Fürst quotes Atterbom's reaction in his *Grillparzer auf der Bühne* (Wien und München: Manutius, 1958), p. 41.

[17] In Grillparzer's works fathers generally distrust artists. The following note, made on the *same* day Grillparzer was inspired to write *Sappho* (29 June 1817), demonstrates the primacy of this tendency to appraise conduct by paternal standards: "3 Akt Er [i.e., Phaon] erinnert sich seiner Eltern, die er verlassen. Begriff seines Vaters von den Dichtern und von Sappho insbesondere." *HKA*, I/17, 174. Phaon partially shared his father's prejudice. Analyzing the emotions he felt upon first meeting Sappho, he says: "Du warst — zu *niedrig* glaubte dich mein Zorn, / Zu *hoch* nennt die Besinnung dich — für meine Liebe" (1740-41; Grillparzer's italics). Cf. Wolfgang Paulsen's emphasis upon the frequent juxtaposition in Grillparzer's early works of zither and

18. lute players (rootless artists or morally ambivalent characters such as Zawisch in *König Ottokars Glück und Ende*) with "protobürgerliche Menschen" in Paulsen's "Der gute Bürger Jakob. Zur Satire in Grillparzers 'Armem Spielmann'," *Colloquia Germanica* (1968), 289.
18. On caves as "symbols of the self-in-hiding" see Morse Peckham's *Beyond the Tragic Vision* (New York: Braziller,, 1962), p. 111.
19. Grillparzer's phrase: *SW*, IV, 973.
20. Grillparzer was acutely aware of the virago's contempt for softly feminine women. Cf. Queen Gertrude's dismissal of Erny as "dieses Wesen, / Kaum schön, von schwachem Geist und dürftgen Gaben, / Halb töricht und halb stumpf," *Ein treuer Diener seines Herrn* (1084-86). Critics who cite Sappho's comparison of Melitta's affection to a snail (761 ff.) as an example of Grillparzer's stylistic immaturity overlook the obvious: Sappho wishes to disparage Melitta while seeming to praise her. See, e.g., W. E. Yates, *Grillparzer. A Critical Introduction* (Cambridge, Eng.: Cambridge University Press, 1972), pp. 70-71.
21. André Tibal *Études sur Grillparzer* (Paris: Berger-Levrault, 1914), p. 143, compares Phaon's praise of silence in a woman to Rhamnes' "Der Mann mag das Geliebte laut begrüßen, / Geschäftig für sein Wohl liebt still das *Weib*." (38-39). Tibal's Grillparzer, "un petit bourgeois...antiféministe" (p. 149), must condemn Sappho because, though a mere woman, she aspires towards Parnassus. Are Phaon and Rhamnes really to be considered Grillparzer's spokesmen? The Circe motif is more than a minor detail. It serves to integrate psychology and myth. Phaon's shifting attitude toward Sappho's "black" and "white" sorcery contributes to his characterization. It also leads to the mythic realm where the Muse is invariably endowed with the magic power anthropologists designate as *mana*. For a discussion of *mana* in relation to poetic inspiration see Herbert Read, "The Poet and his Muse," *Eranos-Jahrbuch*, 31 (1962), 217-248 (especially 235 ff.).
22. Wells, p. 45; Spaulding, p. xix: "robust but mediocre."
23. Does this rhetorical set piece, with its echoes of Schiller and *King Lear* (I/4), characterize Sappho as a woman deluding herself with desperate words? Or is it a sign of Grillparzer's stylistic dependence upon past models? As early as *Sappho*, Reger, p. 305, detects a concern for what the naturalists called *Rhythmus der Persönlichkeit*; but Baumann, p. 32, writes scornfully: "Die Schwäche des Ganzen tritt in der Sprache zutage; denn so wenig Grillparzer sich selber besitzt, so wenig ist er einer wahrhaft eigenen Sprache mächtig."
24. Hebbel's *Judith* offers a noteworthy parallel. At the beginning of Act III, Judith convinces herself that God's will coincides with hers: "Nur Ein Gedanke kam mir, nur Einer, mit dem ich spielte und der immer wiederkehrt; doch, der kam nicht von Dir. Oder kam er von Dir? — (Sie springt auf.) Er kam von Dir!" Friedrich Hebbel, *Sämtliche Werke, Historisch-kritische Ausgabe*, ed. Richard M. Werner (Berlin: Behr, 1904), I/1, 26.
25. Existence on an island no longer represents "eine höhere, reinere Lebensform," as it did in the imagery of the eighteenth century. See Bernhard Blume's "Die Insel als Symbol in der deutschen Literatur," *Monatshefte*, 41 (1949), 244-45. Blume could have included this passage from *Sappho* among the early examples, along with Chamisso's "Salas y Gomez," of a barren isle of disenchantment and exile. There is a certain irony here, since Sappho is already on the island of Lesbos. Horst Brunner's commentary on "Salas y Gomez" in *Die poetische Insel. Inseln und Inselvorstellungen in der deutschen Literatur*. Germanistische Abhandlungen, 21 (Stuttgart: Metzler, 1967), p. 200, is here relevant: "In Chamissos Insel aber wird die Überzeugung deutlich, daß die Natur dem Menschen feindlich und er außerhalb der menschlichen Gesellschaft verloren sei." Professor Siegfried Mews drew my attention to Brunner's study.
26. The full force of the word "verachten" has been overlooked in the critical literature.

Cf. Otto von Meran's violent reaction to Erny's contempt in *Ein treuer Diener seines Herrn*, (898-900; 1274-77).

27 "Und so erscheint auch ihr tragisches Ende logisch nur als Folge der eben dargestellten Liebestragödie," is the conclusion of August Ehrhard, *Franz Grillparzer. Sein Leben und seine Werke* (München: Beck, 1910), p. 79.

28 Emil Reich argues persuasively for a Sappho in her twenties. See *Grillparzers dramatisches Werk* (Wien: Saturn, 1938), p. 55. In "Grillparzer's 'Sappho'," *German Studies Presented to Professor H. G. Fiedler*, M. V. O. (Oxford: Clarendon, 1938), p. 475, Douglas Yates insists that Sappho is an older woman who has taken advantage of Phaon's innocence. Yates's argument is chiefly biographical, beginning with the incorrect assumption that Grillparzer wrote with Madame Schröder in mind. (He did not; see *HKA*, I/17, 142, item 13.) Basing his speculation on the Viennese *mores* of 1818, Heinz Politzer in *Franz Grillparzer oder Das abgründige Biedermeier* (Wien / München / Zürich: Fritz Molden, 1972), p. 92, prefers a riper Sappho of thirty-one. Politzer suggests that in verse 1054 ("selber noch ein kindlich Wesen") Sappho is striving to diminish the span of years between herself and Phaon.

29 Auguste von Littrow-Bischoff, *Aus dem persönlichen Verkehr mit Franz Grillparzer* (Wien: Rosner, 1873), p. 103.

30 *Seppherl* is summarized in Margret Dietrich, *Jupiter in Wien* (Graz / Wien / Köln: Böhlau, 1967), pp. 46-47.

31 Littrow-Bischoff, p. 103. Grillparzer was himself twenty-six when he wrote *Sappho*.

32 *Ibid.*, p. 103.

33 In his direction of a Viennese staging of *Sappho* in 1955, J. Glücksmann aimed, "den Begriff der Torschlußpanik zu verwerten." Quoted by Fürst, p. 54. (One need not have passed thirty to experience moments of *Torschlußpanik*.) The *taedium vitae* diagnosis is Gerhard Fricke's in "Wesen und Wandel des Tragischen bei Grillparzer," *Studien und Interpretationen* (Frankfurt a. M.: H. F. Menck, 1956), p. 272.

34 Douglas Yates, p. 488, deplores Sappho's patronizing manner: "her atonement takes the form almost of condescending forgiveness." In "Geschichte, 'Geist' und Grillparzer," *Weimarer Beiträge*, 7 (1961), Claus Träger indicts her even more forcefully: "Sappho will sich im Namen der Kunst an einem Leben rächen, das sich ihr versagt. Sie will zerstören, worum sie sich betrogen fühlt, die Liebe Phaons zu Melitta."

35 Though subtly concealed, the mother-sister-bride motif which Wolfgang Paulsen explored in *Die Ahnfrau. Zu Grillparzers früher Dramatik* (Tübingen: Niemeyer, 1962), pp. 33-34, is also present in *Sappho*. The variant readings (*HKA*, I/17, 207) preserve a spontaneous original version in which the mother role has greater prominence. See, e.g., verses 1774 and 1791/2 (Melitta: "Hat sie doch stets als Mutter mich geliebt! / Phaon: "Stieß sie als *Mutter* grausam dich zurück / Und zückte sie den Dolch nach dir als *Mutter*?" [Grillparzer's italics]). At the end of the first version, Melitta, crying "theure, holde Mutter," collapsed on Sappho's corpse.

36 *HKA*, I/17, 211. This ending divests Sappho's death of any aura of myth. Instead of sinking into the primal sea, she plummets to the rocks at the base of the cliff: "Ihr Haupt zerschmettert an dem schroffen Fels!"

37 Wells, p. 45. Wells's argument is actually close to the line of reasoning he rejects: that the artist soils himself in life.

38 Ilse Münch, *Die Tragik in Drama und Persönlichkeit Franz Grillparzers* (Berlin: Junker und Dünnhaupt, 1931), p. 33.

39 For examples of sea imagery from *Sappho* and *Des Meeres und der Liebe Wellen* consult Hans Gmür, *Dramatische und theatralische Stilelmente in Grillparzers Dramen* (Winterthur: P. G. Keller, 1956), pp. 85-86.

40 An account of the many guises of the Mother-Beloved-Muse is found in "The Images of Woman," Chapter IV of Maud Bodkin's *Archetypal Patterns in Poetry* (London: Oxford University Press, 1934). The destructive aspect of Bodkin's composite image

fascinates Robert Mühlher in "Göttin Kunst," *Jahrbuch der Grillparzer-Gesellschaft* [JGG], 3. Folge, 2 (1956). Mühlher identifies Grillparzer's Muse with the Angel of Death and postulates acute guilt feelings concerning his treatment of his mother — similar to those of Stephen Daedalus in *Ulysses* — in the young playwright.

[41] *HKA*, II/7, 18 (Tagebuch, 1808).
[42] *Ibid.*, p. 101.
[43] Letter to Adolf Müllner, March, 1818, in *SW*, IV, 742.
[44] *The Works of Lord Byron, Letters and Journals*, V, 171.
[45] Graf August von Platen, *Die Tagebücher*, ed. G. V. Laubmann and L. v. Scheffler (Stuttgart: Cotta, 1900), II, 274. Platen's juvenilia include a *Heroide*, "Sappho an Phaon" (1812). "Ewig Phaon hingegeben," Sappho prepares for suicide by rejecting Apollo in favor of her scornful lover. See Platen, *Sämtliche Werke*, ed. Max Koch and Erich Petzet (Leipzig: Max Hesse, n. d.), IV, 160. Not all fellow poets were so enamoured of Grillparzer's heroine. Lenau called her "eine widerliche sinnliche Vettel." Quoted in *"Ach wärst du mein...!" Lenaus Liebesroman*, ed. Eduard Castle (Leipzig: Hesse und Becker, n. d.), p. 209.
[46] See August Sauer, "Grillparzers Gespräche und die Charakteristiken seiner Persönlichkeit durch die Zeitgenossen," JGG, N. F., 1 (1941), p. 3.
[47] Grillparzer in reference to *Sappho*: *HKA*, I/17, 157, item 245. Grillparzer employs the same phrase in the later (1833) poem "Jugenderinnerungen im Grünen," *SW*, I, 228.
[48] *SW*, I, 98.
[49] *SW*, I, 123.
[50] *SW*, I, 284. Chiefly on the basis of this tribute to Mozart, Urs Helmensdorfer designates Grillparzer's view of art as "lebensfreundlich" and warns against one-sided interpretations of *Sappho* permeated by romantic despair. See "Zu Grillparzers Kunstbegriff" in *Grillparzers Bühnenkunst* (Bern: Francke, 1960), pp. 17-20. Like some commentators on *Der arme Spielmann*, Helmensdorfer overlooks the careful distinction Grillparzer drew between music and literature.
[51] The "classical" style has had its admirers and detractors. See note 10, p. 502, of Wedel-Parlow's essay. Most recently, Roy C. Cowen has attempted to demonstrate that *Sappho* literally illustrates the "erworbene Ruhe" of both Sappho and Grillparzer: in "Zur Struktur von Grillparzers 'Sappho'," *Grillparzer-Forum Forchtenstein. Vorträge. Forschungen. Berichte. 1968* (Heidelberg: Stiehm, 1969), p. 71.

Since I completed my essay several interpretations of *Sappho* have appeared: Joachim Müller, "Figur und Aktion in Grillparzers 'Sappho'-Drama," *Grillparzer Forum Forchtenstein. 1970* (Heidelberg: Stiehm, 1971), pp. 7-43; Michael Ossar, "Die Künstlergestalt in Goethes *Tasso* und Grillparzers *Sappho*," *The German Quarterly*, 45 (1972), 645-61; Christa Suttner Baker, "Structure and Imagery in Grillparzer's *Sappho*," *Germanic Review*, 48 (1973), 44-55. Ossar emphasizes the differences between Goethe's and Grillparzer's artists. Baker's examination of the "intricately woven fabric of metaphors and similes" challenges Roy Cowen's essay. Müller's sensitive analysis anticipates many of the points I make concerning the characters' motives and their craving for illusion. The tensions resulting from self-deception form the major theme of Norbert Griesmayer's thoughtful chapter on *Sappho* in *Das Bild des Partners in Grillparzers Dramen*. Wiener Studien zur deutschen Literatur, 3 (Wien/Stuttgart: Wilhelm Braumüller, 1972), pp. 95-133.

REALMS OF ACTION IN GRILLPARZER'S *EIN BRUDERZWIST IN HABSBURG*

Hugo Schmidt

In trying to come to terms with Grillparzer's *Ein Bruderzwist in Habsburg*, the reader will experience the frustrating sensation that T. S. Eliot formulated so well in his line "That is not what I meant at all." He ponders, tries to see through the veils that obscure the essence of the play. An insight may be about to take shape, but in formulating it, he sees that he is missing his mark. He conveys something, finally, that may be true, vaguely, but not entirely germane. What he was trying to get at remains behind the veil. The play is elusive, and its impact is in its atmosphere, in an area that defies penetration by our interpretative tools.

The action, as a whole, is not difficult to follow. It takes place on a realistic level, and the plot can be paraphrased with ease. True, a paraphrase can never convey the *Gehalt* of a literary work; but here it seems to do less than nothing. For example, would it not impart a more essential aspect of the play to mention that Lukrezia always appears as if out of a dream and almost inexplicably, than to give a precise summary of the peace talks in the second act? Or would a description of Rudolf's gestures not come closer to the *Gehalt* of the play than a limning of his views on unrest and revolution?

Critics have claimed that Grillparzer's play is not stage-worthy, that it is a "Gedankendrama,"[1] and that it begins to make sense only after it is comprehended in terms of history and philosophy.[2] The historical and philosophical content is easy to perceive; it is one of the outermost layers of Grillparzer's artistic fabric. Like other historical playwrights, he has taken certain liberties with the actual events, has telescoped time, and has created characters that may have little in common with their historical models. On the philosophical and sociological level, Grillparzer has given voice, through Rudolf, to his conservative views to a degree that is surprising for one who fought frustrating battles against the censorship of an absolutistic era and complained bitterly about the stultifying effect the monarchic system had on the arts. A good comprehension of the intellectual background of the play and its historical content, important though it is, will barely scratch the surface.

The character of Rudolf leads more deeply into the complexities. Obviously, he is not the historical Rudolf. But most critics are willing to forgive Grillparzer his transgressions against history. What is considered a more serious matter is the inconsistency of the character as drawn by the playwright himself. In some scenes, Rudolf's paranoia shows pathological dimensions, in others, he is kind and reveals a sense of humor. He appears to be an apostle of peace and yet is eager to continue the war in Hungary. He is patient and humane in some instances — for example, when he expresses his horror at Ferdinand's ruthless expulsion of the Protestants — and unreasonable in others, for instance, when refusing to listen to a defense of Field Marshall Rußworm. His threat against Don Cäsar to have him executed if he continues to speak out for Rußworm is inconceivable. On the one hand, he has a deep understanding for matters of the heart — he is horrified by Ferdinand's decision to break with the woman he loves and marry an unloved one for political reasons — on the other, he chastizes Don Cäsar for wooing Lukrezia. Most striking of all, he refuses to permit that medical aid be given to his son, whom he loves deeply, thus causing his death.[3]

Such instances are part of a larger, more general tendency in the play. Grillparzer did not seem overly concerned with a tight, logical structure, a close nexus between the events, or even a careful delineation of cause and effect. Criticizing him on these counts merely reveals a wrong premise on the part of the critic: that Grillparzer, since his creative period followed that of German Classicism, should be measured against Goethe and Schiller and their dramatic technique, which was usually flawless indeed with regard to the details mentioned above. But we know that Grillparzer's art was not indebted primarily to Weimar Classicism; he was not a poor, but at best an unwilling pupil, and probably no pupil at all, of Schiller and Goethe. Commenting, in his diaries, on the historical tragedy — a favorite quotation in recent Grillparzer scholarship — the playwright concedes that there can be no question of the dramatist's need to show cause and effect, but he continues: "Aber wie in der Natur sich höchst selten Ursache und Wirkung wechselseitig ganz decken, so ist, in der Behandlung eine gewisse Inkongruenz beider durchblicken zu lassen, vielleicht die höchste Aufgabe, die ein Dichter sich stellen kann."[4]

"Eine gewisse Inkongruenz": Perhaps a heritage from Baroque drama, passed on to Grillparzer via the Viennese popular theater, it can be traced in the theater tradition in which Grillparzer has his place. Hofmannsthal shows it, for example in *Der Schwierige*, with its somewhat inconsistent portrayal of Hans Karl's character, and the very inconsistent one of Count Hechingen, whose role fluctuates between the comic and the serious. It can be seen in plays that are rooted more directly in the tradition of the Viennese popular theater, above all in Raimund's works, and to a lesser degree in Nestroy's. There the dramatic possibilities of the individual scene, its theatricality, are as important as the progress of the action as a whole. If the playwright wants to make a specific point, or a joke, he will do it, through one of his characters, even though this may cause the character to abandon his role for a moment. Brecht, always eager to acknowledge his indebtedness to Nestroy, has further emphasized these traits and placed them prominently in the development of modern drama.

In the passage quoted above, Grillparzer singled out historical plays as vehicles to show a "certain incongruence." In his own historical plays, as has often been observed, Grillparzer tends to treat the motifs of power and worldly splendor in a negative fashion. For example, Ottokar's rise is shown in one act, in sequences that have an unreal, dreamlike quality and depict the hero as proud and callous, while his defeat is treated at great length and with a detailed presentation of his growing humanity. The affairs of the world, its power struggles and intrigues, were motifs that Grillparzer used in order to show lack of human substance. In the quoted passage, he did not clarify, either abstractly or through examples, what exactly he had in mind when speaking of incongruence, but it is possible to see in it also the mutual exclusion of external success and human substance, as it prevails in his plays. In *König Ottokars Glück und Ende*, the development of Ottokar as a human being runs contrary to his political fate, to the rise and fall of his power. In *Ein Bruderzwist in Habsburg*, there is no such obvious juxtaposition. And yet, there is a distinct polarity in the play: The action fluctuates between scenes depicting power struggles and court intrigues on the one hand, and scenes presenting the most intimate manifestations of the individual psyche and of human interaction on the other. At least one critic has spoken of the "inner action" of the play.[5] The external and the internal levels of action are not as clearly discernible as in *Ottokar*; they are interwoven in a more subtle fashion, and the difficulty in coming to terms with the play may well be explained by the high degree of subtlety in which the close, private sphere is contraposed to the grandiose, political.

Grillparzer's Rudolf epitomizes the private, intimate sphere. To be sure, he knows the public sphere and is aware of what he owes it. After he bestows his own private order of the Knights of Peace upon Duke Julius, he is obliged to face the Bohemian estates. Preparing to receive them, he asks for his sword and when Julius — no servant is nearby — brings him the sword as well as the imperial robe, Rudolf is uncertain at first: "Ihr bringt den Mantel auch?" but continues, "Habt Ihr doch recht / Die Welt verlangt den Schein. Wir Beide nur / Wir tragen innerhalb des Kleids den Orden."[6] What is essential and important to him is the private, secretly worn order. It is worn inside, close to the heart. Robe and sword are insignia of a realm from which he has withdrawn spiritually. He exhibits them unwillingly. In the last moment, he decides against wearing the sword and asks Julius to put it down somewhere.

Scenes from which Rudolf is absent, scenes of force, political ambition, and intrigue, are fraught with confusion and futility. The peace negotiations in the second act may be cited as the foremost example. The very fact that there are four archdukes present introduces an element of confusion. It may be true that Grillparzer complained about the oversupply of archdukes in the plot[7]; but he could have made use of the historical playwright's most basic prerogative: to eliminate characters from the plot, for the sake of clarity and expediency. He chose not to. The nature of their debate during the conference further confuses the issue and may be taken as an indication that Grillparzer in effect strove for a measure of entanglement in this scene. The actions of the various participants in the debate are motivated in a distorted way. Klesel speaks out for peace; this may be considered a proper goal for a man of the cloth to pursue, until it becomes evident that he plans to use the conclusion of the peace as an act of revolt against the emperor, and as a crucial step in enhancing Mathias' power. Mathias, Klesel's tool, ought to echo his mentor's views. However, Mathias has lost a battle, once again, and is eager to continue the war in order to have an opportunity for making up the defeat and regaining his personal honor. He is blind to the fact that he will hardly manage a victory with the number of his men cut in half after he had previously been defeated with the forces still intact. Klesel, first upset by Mathias' refusal to speak out for peace, quickly discerns the advantageous side of the situation: If Mathias does not agree with Klesel, for once, the other archdukes will not suspect any foul play on their part and will be less reluctant to go along with Klesel's plans. "Bleibt, Herr, bei eurer Weigrung," he encourages Mathias before Max, Ferdinand, and Leopold enter, "Vielleicht reift unsern Anschlag grade dies" (212). The conference, conducted according to parliamentary procedures, begins in a fashion familiar to all veterans of township, council or faculty meetings: A few words about the table are exchanged — Max is glad that the table cloth is green and not red or blue — one participant is asked to take minutes, another states that he would rather stand than sit because he likes to stand and because he won't sit until he knows what the meeting is all about. Then there is a brief, jocular exchange about Leopold's recent love adventure, and Klesel is asked not to put this into the minutes.

The actual conference, from Max's admonition "zur Sache" to the adjournment, is long by the standards of stage technique: two hundred and forty lines. It is a tour-de-force in the art of conniving and brainwashing. At the beginning of the meeting, none of the archdukes is in favor of concluding the peace; at the end, only Leopold refuses to agree to the treaty. Klesel, the non-voting member of the assembly, masterminds their change of hearts without their noticing it. Some details in the dialog border on the comic. Max chides Mathias for wanting to save face as a commander by continuing the war with his decimated troops. Therefore, Max is against continuing the war. Klesel inquires eagerly, "So seid ihr für den Frieden?" Max: "Ich? Bewahr!" Klesel: "Doch spracht entgegen ihr dem Krieg." Max: "Ei, laßt mich!" (219). The last phrase, which would have to be rendered as "Leave me alone (with your silly logic)," bespeaks the hopeless muddle of the situation. Soon Max and Ferdinand commit themselves to a vote for peace. Mathias states that he might as well join them since he is being outvoted. Leopold reminds him that there would be two of them since he, Leopold, will vote against the treaty. Mathias' remarkable reply is: "Gerade deshalb Frieden auch" (223). Whereas Max's "Laßt mich" at least acknowledged his inability to respond logically, Mathias' answer openly mocks the principle of meaningful discussion.

This bit of parliamentary confusion is set between two scenes that provide a fitting frame. The conference is preceded by a scene in the imperial camp that introduces the motif of confusion on a physical level: A standard bearer relates how the imperial army, caught between two Turkish columns, found itself in such a state of chaos that imperial soldiers pursued and killed other imperial soldiers.[8] There was no leadership during the battle. The troops are close to rebelling. The scene is further complicated by the appearance of a Protestant delegation. A captain comments that he would send them packing if he were the archduke (Mathias); a colonel replies that it was the archduke who had invited them. When the same captain accuses Protestant soldiers of having committed treason by starting the rout during the battle, one soldier contradicts him, saying that it makes no differences, in combat, which religion a soldier favors: "Im Lager hier sind alle Tapfern Brüder" (200).

The motif of fraternal relationships, oddly twisted, is followed through at some length. In the conference scene, two sets of brothers conspire against another brother, the emperor. In the scene just discussed, soldiers are reported to have killed their brothers inadvertently, while members of conflicting religions consider themselves brothers. In the scene following the peace conference, an attempt by Don Cäsar to abduct Lukrezia is thwarted by the appearance of two of the archdukes and their entourages. As in the scene preceding the conference, there occurs the motif of enemy action within one war party. The soldiers hired to perform the abduction flee, and Archduke Leopold comments: "Nicht Türken sinds, des eignen Lagers Auswurf, / Zu Brudermord gezückt das feige Schwert" (235). The only member of the band captured turns out to be the emperor's son.

These scenes comprise the second act, one of the two acts from which Rudolf is absent altogether. The act encompasses a series of incidents that pertain to the world of intrigue, power, and warfare. Nothing is accomplished throughout the act, except that a dubious peace treaty has been concluded, against the emperor's wishes, and that Mathias has been appointed to act in place of the emperor should the latter refuse to ratify the treaty. Both steps leave everyone uneasy, except Klesel, the arbitrator. Leopold comments, "Ihr werdet sehen was ihr angerichtet" (224); and "Wir haben keinen guten Kampf gekämpft" (231). Uncertainty and confusion determine the act, combined with demagoguery and collusion. It illustrates both the dramatic principles that have been outlined above as characteristic of Grillparzer's art: a certain incongruence of cause and effect, and the futility and inscrutability of the affairs of the world. The act does not have the qualities of a *Lesedrama*. It is extremely stageworthy, and the fact that the action is indecisive and confusing is not a weakness but its most salient feature.

One scene in the third act presents a confrontation between the external world with its strifes, and the internal realm, exemplified in the figure of the emperor. The Bohemian estates, newly encouraged by the unrest in the capitol and by the

153

rumor that Archduke Mathias is approaching with armed forces, demand that the emperor sign an agreement granting religious freedom, the "Letter of Majesty." Their arguments are transparent and their demands have the sound of blackmail. Rudolf, fully aware of the nature of their maneuver, responds by speaking to them of love, respect, and belief, and by admonishing them not to question God's wisdom. His words are genuine, simple, direct, and they are poetic. Nevertheless, it is apparent that Rudolf is not reaching them. There is no communication between him and the delegation. He is aware of the falseness of their arguments, but refrains from challenging them. They in turn do not hear what he has to say to them. Their reply, after the close of Rudolf's exhortations, is a renewed request for his approval of their demands. They have talked past each other, each within his own frame of reference. Rudolf signs their document, in disdain, impatient with them, and discouraged. They honor him with an exclamation, "Mit Gut und Blut für unsern Herrn und Kaiser!" (266). Minutes later, they will cheer Mathias as their new champion.

The end of the third act brings to a climax the juxtaposition of the occurences in the physical and the spiritual world. Mathias, in a splendid procession, enters Prague. Bells ring, music is played, and banners are waved. Mathias is shown riding past on a horse, towering over the crowd. The people rush toward him and cheer "Vivat Mathias! Hoch des Landes Recht!" (277). This takes place upstage. Downstage, Duke Julius has tried in vain to persuade Archduke Leopold not to take up arms against Mathias. As Mathias proceeds, Julius turns aside with a gesture of grief. The realms of action are aligned in a striking tableau that concludes the act: Mathias in his glory, the image of a quickly passing worldly triumph; and Julius in his grief, knowing and understanding, the image of introspection, awareness, and integrity.

The play ends with a variation of this scene. Rudolf is dead and Mathias is emperor. Now that he has reached his goal, he is guilt-ridden at his brother's death and wishes he were dead and Rudolf alive. Yet he cannot take his eyes off the imperial insignia that have been brought to him: "Wie ein Magnet ziehts mir die Augen hin / Und täuscht mit Formen, die nicht sind, ich weiß" (337). The people cheer and want to see their new emperor. Reluctantly, Mathias shows himself on the balcony. Again, the shout "Vivat Mathias!" is heard. Back on stage, Mathias kneels and speaks the liturgical formula "Mea culpa, mea culpa, / Mea maxima culpa" (337). The play ends with the shouts of "Vivat Mathias" continuing from the street, and Mathias, on his knees, covering his face with both hands. Like the third act, the fifth closes on a tableau that signifies the deceitfulness and duplicity of power.

Little has been made in criticism of the scene of Lukrezia's death at the hands of Don Cäsar in the fourth act. It does not seem to have any function, in the structure of the play, other than to add to the crimes of the perpetrator and precipitate his downfall. Lukrezia remains a pale, undefined figure to her end. One could view her death as one of Grillparzer's self-contained scenes that are not closely integrated into the action. However, if the deceitfulness and illusoriness of worldly things is indeed one theme of the play, the scene assumes a subtle significance. Don Cäsar, up to this point nothing more than a rash good-for-nothing, is shown in a new light. He approaches Lukrezia for one more time, but only in search for truth. In a concrete sense, he wants to know who and what Lukrezia really is. "Laßt mich erkennen euch, nur deshalb kam ich; / Zu wissen was ihr seid, nicht was ihr scheint" (282). Lukrezia, vague and shadowy throughout the play, is an embodiment of the evasive element that prevails in the action. Don Cäsar's wish to discover her true self seems plausible to the reader; moreover, the motif of the quest for recognition is pertinent in a play that presents an action veiled in the dusk of futility and doubt. Don Cäsar gains stature in this scene. He reveals himself as a person with substantial thoughts and feelings by asking questions that are only asked by minds that have pondered problems concerning the very nature of existence. But his wish to know Lukrezia remains unfulfilled, as does his larger quest for truth. He fails in trying to penetrate the veil that covers the essence of things:

> Und Recht und Unrecht, Wesen, Wirklichkeit,
> Das ganze Spiel der buntbewegten Welt,
> Liegt eingehüllt in des Gehirnes Räumen,
> Das sie erzeugt und aufhebt wie es will.
> Ich plagte mich mit wirren Glaubenszweifeln,
> Ich pochte forschend an des Fremden Tür,
> Gelesen hab' ich und gehört, verglichen,
> Und fand sie Beide haltlos, Beide leer.
> Vertilgt die Bilder solchen Schattenspiels,
> Blieb nur das Licht zurück, des Gauklers Lampe,
> Das sie als Wesen an die Wände malt,
> Als einz'ge Leidenschaft der Wunsch: zu wissen. (282)

The truth that Cäsar seeks is present in the play, although he would not recognize it as an answer to his questions. Rudolf embodies truth. He is the still center around which the fleeting matter of the action revolves. This is shown, in part, through his language. Herbert Seidler has demonstrated that Grillparzer's use of *Prunkreden* lends a certain rhythm to his plays. Scenes of action alternate with reflective pauses in which the essence of the action is crystallized in extended speeches resembling monologues. Such passages show a markedly elevated language and poetic refinement.[9] *Ein Bruderzwist* contains several of these *Prunkreden*, all of them spoken by Rudolf. In fact, a good portion of Rudolf's role consists of *Prunkreden*. According to Seidler's count, two are in the first act (ll. 320-346; 391-439), three in the third act (ll. 1233-1276; 1460-1471; 1533-1669), and two in the fourth (ll. 2239-2269; 2286-2428). Altogether, 436 of Rudolf's lines are are spoken in *Prunkreden*. This leaves 427 lines of his role for dialog other than *Prunkreden*, — slightly less than half. In the fourth act, the last in which Rudolf appears, the proportion is 172 lines of *Prunkreden* versus 18 lines of dialog.

These numbers alone testify to the pivotal significance of Rudolf's role. To some extent, these speeches serve to define Rudolf's philosophical outlook. The contraposition of the *vita activa* and the *vita contemplativa*, shown through the action surrounding Rudolf and his own meditative inaction, has been widely discussed in criticism. However, a concentration on the emperor's philosophical and political views neglects the unique features of this character and reduces the play to a contest of intellectual dispositions. In examining the *Prunkreden*, attention must be paid both to their philosophical significance and to their poetic impact. Rudolf's last speech exemplifies Grillparzer's intent to remove his hero to a realm beyond that of the political intrigues he was supposed to cope with and chose to ignore. It is a realm that comes alive in poetry only. In his meditations, Rudolf's thoughts involuntarily converge on religious subjects. The recollection of Christmas takes him back to his childhood, and forward to the threshold of the hereafter. He asks: "Ist hier Musik?" and Julius replies, "Wir hören nichts, o Herr" (305). Only Rudolf hears the music of a realm he is about to enter, and his departure from one world into another is realized convincingly by the poet:

> Mein Geist verirrt sich in die Jugendzeit.
> Als ich aus Spanien kam, wo ich erzogen,
> Und man nun meldete, daß Deutschlands Küste
> Sich nebelgleich am Horizonte zeige,
> Da lief ich aufs Verdeck und offner Arme
> Rief ich: mein Vaterland! Mein teures Vaterland!
> — So dünkt mich nun ein Land in dem ein Vater —
> Am Rand der Ewigkeit emporzutauchen.
> — Ist es denn dunkel hier? — Dort seh' ich Licht
> Und flügelgleich umgibt es meinen Leib.
> — Aus Spanien komm' ich, aus gar harter Zucht,
> Und eile dir entgegen, — nicht mehr deutsches,
> Nein himmlisch Vaterland. — Willst du? — Ich will! (308)

Here Grillparzer employs the symbol of the voyage, a traditional literary topos, but his poetic power elevates the scene into the realm of the religious and sublime.

Despite Rudolf's saintly death, it is wrong to see in him nothing but a martyr to his age; a man who could not and would not cope with reality; who triumphed, in the end, through his wisdom, kindness, and religious bearing. There are the harsh realities of his occasional ruthlessness and injustice, his whims and pathological capriciousness. Grillparzer did not attempt to pit an unblemished hero against the wicked world. The inner conflict he depicted, as a playwright and poet, is one of atmosphere: the duality between an external action running its futile course in a vague, unfathomable way, and a personage drawn closely and intimately. This duality is at the root of our difficulties in coming to terms with the play, but it is also the source of its strong poetic impact.

Warmth and closeness are created partially through Grillparzer's language. The nature and the characteristics of the playwright's language have long occupied critics. It is unlike Goethe's and Schiller's, unlike Kleist's, unlike Hebbel's. In *Ein Bruderzwist* there is no willful pose in Grillparzer's diction; it runs smoothly, softly, and apparently without effort. A good actor would never choose to recite Grillparzer's lines bombastically and at the top of his voice. They require a gentle approach, and they are most effective when spoken with great understanding and feeling. Even the *Prunkreden* are not meant to be declaimed; they simply require greater insight and penetration. The directness of Grillparzer's language is its most prominent characteristic. Some of Rudolph's questions ring with a sense of closeness and familiarity that immediately establishes a link not only between him and the person addressed, but also between him and the reader or spectator. His last words, "Willst du? — Ich will!" (308), are a foremost example of this stylistic quality. The same is true of the inquiry "Ist hier Musik?" (305), and of Rudolf's reply to Ferdinand's proud statement that he has expelled from his territory all Protestants: "Mit Weib und Kind? Die Nächte sind schon kühl" (190). When Don Cäsar states aggressively that only the Lord is judge in matters of religious belief, Rudolf replies: "Ja Gott und du. Ihr Beide, nicht wahr?" (179). The simplicity and candor of these lines is matched by their poetic impact. Occasionally, Grillparzer uses phrases that are almost quaint. Upon realizing that the man he had not recognized was Ferdinand, Rudolf says "All gut!" (182). Rudolf's chamberlain, Rumpf, carries the quaintness of the language a step further. His is a mixture of officialese and a nearly comic, stenographic, private idiom that imitates the emperor's predilection for elliptic remarks. Rumpf's position in the play is never made quite clear. He is a high-ranking official and chargé-d'affaires at court, but he also seems to serve as a private secretary and, in a scene where the emperor cannot find his robe and calls for Rumpf, as a valet. Rumpf shows traces of the comic person of the Viennese popular theater, traces that are subtly evident in his language. He uses phrases such as "Huldreichst guten Morgen" (168), "hochgnädige Geduld" (168), "Geht nicht" (167), "Guter Gott!" (177, 178), "Du liebe Zeit!" (170), and the comic Austrian interjection "Je" (167, twice).[10] Rumpf is Rudolf's semi-comic foil and counterpart.[11]

Grillparzer's language may have the ring of quaintness even in scenes that do not deal with Rudolf's sequestered world. For example, in the conference scene in the second act, Max invites the other archdukes to sit down at the table with the phrases "Geht sitzen" (214) and "Komm sitzen" (215). In the same scene, Mathias, at a loss for a reply, urges Klesel to answer, formulating his request in a strikingly direct phrase: "Sagt etwas, Klesel!" (216). Shakespeare was a master at such subtle nuances in the dialog, but no author of tragedy in the German language before Grillparzer conveyed such a degree of immediacy with the use of such simple words.

It has been shown that Grillparzer at times chose to forego the use of words altogether in favor of the gesture.¹² In *Ein Bruderzwist*, one of the *Prunkreden* fades away in mumbled sentence fragments and eventually in silence:

> ([Rudolf] Immer leiser sprechend)
> Wenn nun der Herr die Uhr rückt seiner Zeit,
> Die Ewigkeit in jedem Glockenschlag
> Für die das Oben und das Unten gleich
> Ins Brautgemach — des Weltbaus Kräfte eilen
> — Gebunden — in der Strahlen Konjunktur —
> Und der Malefikus — das böse Trachten —
> (Er verstummt allmählich. Sein Haupt sinkt auf die
> Brust. Pause.) (187)

Originally, Grillparzer had planned to complete the passage with its syntax intact and without an indication of Rudolf's voice dying away.¹³ The abandonment of the spoken word in favor of the gesture is significant. The gesture, when subtly used, can convey delicate nuances of meaning. In the present play, Grillparzer used gestures to a great extent. Especially those assigned to Rudolf are capable of creating an atmosphere of poignancy. Rudolf is both awesome as a ruler and engaging as a person — a unique combination in a tragic character. On the one hand, he is infirm and helpless; when in a rage against Don Cäsar, he becomes feeble and has to be helped by his guards. He walks on a cane, or supported by Rumpf. On the other hand, Grillparzer gave him the curious agility that is at times peculiar to very old people.

Rudolf shows a certain lack of inhibitions in his gestures. For example, he reacts with an odd, almost childish gesture when reminded of Leopold's unsuccessful attempt to occupy the city: "Der Kaiser droht heftig mit dem Finger in die Ferne" (295). There are several scenes in the play where Rudolf contributes his share to the dialog with gestures only. There is, above all, his entrance in the first act, and the scene at the well in the fourth. On stage, these passages invariably fall flat and give rise to unwanted laughter, unless they are played with great taste and discernment. His gestures not only lend a fascination to the emperor, but also bring him close to the reader and spectator on a human, emotional level. They express more than mere reactions to what he sees and hears; Rudolf communicates through gestures, and at times he gets across fairly complex messages. For example, he criticizes the poor workmanship in one part of a painting without even stepping up to it, and rejects the painting (172). The people about him have learned to understand his silent language. When he looks at two persons engaged in conversation, Rumpf informs them that the emperor wishes to know what is being discussed (296). Rudolf wags his finger threateningly, and Julius knows that he means Leopold (295). When the emperor shows an interest in the key to Don Cäsar's prison, Julius seems to suspect what his intentions are (297).¹⁴ He can be insistent in his sign language: When he extends his hand to greet Duke Julius and Julius wants to kiss it, Rudolf withdraws his hand, then extends it again, whereupon Julius takes hold of

Rudolf's hand with both of his (293). Grillparzer is able to convey much of his characters' inner qualities through their gestures. They are direct and truthful emanations of their innermost feelings. When giving Leopold permission to bring troops to his aid, Rudolf transmits this instruction through a gesture while off-stage — the ultimate in subtlety: The door of his private chamber opens to admit Leopold. In the first act, Rudolf hears of the arrival of young Leopold and, overjoyed, demands to see him. Leopold is summoned; he enters when the emperor and his court have lined up, about to proceed to the chapel, and he is taken aback at the sight of the formal arrangement. The Spanish court ceremonial which rules in the imperial castle in Prague is a new experience to the straightforward young man from the Austrian provinces. Rudolf, somewhat curtly, asks him to take his place in the procession, and Ferdinand beckons him to his side. Leopold's spirits must be dampened — he had reason to expect a warmer welcome from the emperor. Rudolf senses this and corrects the situation:

> (Der Zug setzt sich in Bewegung, die beiden Erzherzoge unmittelbar vor dem Kaiser. Nach einigen Schritten tippt Letzterer Erzherzog Leopold auf die Schulter. Dieser wendet sich um und küßt ihm lebhaft die Hand. Der Kaiser winkt ihm liebreich drohend Stillschweigen zu und sie gehen weiter. Die übrigen folgen paarweise.)
> Der Vorhang fällt. (193)

The emperor himself takes a quick and secret liberty against the court ceremonial in order to transmit a personal message.

A delicately conveyed, emotional gesture such as this is part of the innermost realm of action in Grillparzer's play. The contrast between this and the realm of the futile, circuitous external action is not primarily one of humanity versus callousness. Rather, it is a contrast between the close and the distant, the inward and the outward, between matter pertaining to the privacy of the heart and matter pertaining to the wordly ambitions of the will and the intellect. Even when Rudolf performs the gesture of dropping the key into the well and in effect executes his son, Grillparzer shows that the dominant emotion prevailing within him during that moment is not cruelty but consuming pain. It is an awesome deed, yet not one performed callously.[15]

The play is open-ended and grants a view into the chaotic times that lie ahead. The external realm is beginning to reign supreme. This prospect is essential to the tragic qualities of the play, as much so as the death of Rudolf and the moral defeat of Mathias. The appearance of young Colonel Wallenstein at the end of the play and his prophecy concerning the duration of the imminent war are often branded by critics as poor in taste. Certainly Wallenstein cuts an offensive figure. Even ruthless Ferdinand is repelled by his overefficiency. Significantly, it is Wallenstein who reports the approach of the emissaries who have come to announce Rudolf's death, and he is the only one to remain untouched by this news. Wallenstein appears as the epitome of the futile ambition that the world has fallen victim to. His figure is odious in the sense that he incorporates all the negative elements of the play. The introduction of a new character in the last scene is not a weakness in the structure of the play comparable to the appearance of Count Bruchsal in Lessing's *Minna von Barnhelm*. Grillparzer's dramatic art is a match for such a challenge: Wallenstein, who will not outlive the war that he is so eager to engage in, unwittingly points to the absurdity of his own ambition.

It is in the figure of Wallenstein, in fact, that the theme of the "vanity of the world," apparent throughout the play, is given its last and strongest embodiment. Led on by Wallenstein, almost everyone on stage cheers the outbreak of the war, and the people in the street cheer the new emperor. But the memory of Rudolf permeates the scene: The imperial insignia are on stage, and Mathias performs his final gesture of repentance.

NOTES

[1] Urs Helmensdorfer, "Ein Bruderzwist in Habsburg," *Grillparzers Bühnenkunst* (Bern: Francke, 1960), p. 99.

[2] *Ibid.*, p. 72.

[3] Heinz Politzer, in "Grillparzers 'Bruderzwist' — ein Vater-Sohn-Konflikt in Habsburg." *Festschrift für Bernhard Blume* (Göttingen: Vandenhoeck, 1967), pp. 173-194, has thrown a sharp light on the father-son relationship in the play.

[4] Franz Grillparzer, *Sämtliche Werke, Historisch-kritische Gesamtausgabe*, ed. A. Sauer. II/8 (Vienna: Gerlach, 1916), 176-177.

[5] Kare Langvik-Johannessen, " 'Ein Bruderzwist in Habsburg.' Versuch einer Offenlegung der inneren Handlung." *Grillparzer-Forum Forchtenstein* (Heidelberg: Lothar Stiehm), III (1967), 34-42; IV (1968), 43-57. Langvik-Johannessen's foremost concern is the investigation of a psychological basis underlying the action.

[6] *Historisch-kritische Gesamtausgabe*, I/6 (Vienna: Scholl, 1927), 259. Future references to this volume will appear by page numbers in the text.

[7] Franz Grillparzer, *Gespräche und Charakteristiken seiner Persönlichkeit durch die Zeitgenossen*, ed. A. Sauer 6 vols. (Vienna: Literarischer Verein, 1904-1916), III, 340.

[8] The scene is repeated during the retreat of Leopold's forces from Prague. Cf. 289-290.

[9] Herbert Seidler, "Prunkreden in Grillparzers Dramen." *Studien zu Grillparzer und Stifter* (Vienna etc.: Böhlau, 1970), pp. 85-117. [First published in 1964 in *Sitzungsberichte der Österreichischen Akademie der Wissenschaften, philosophisch-historische Klasse*, 244/4].

[10] Significantly, "je" occurs many times in Grillparzer's comedy, *Weh dem der lügt*.

[11] Rumpf is related to a number of servant figures in the Austrian theater tradition, notably to Anton in Hofmannsthal's *Der Turm*, a play that shares a number of themes and motifs with *Ein Bruderzwist*, such as the prophecy of danger to the ruler through a member of his family, the father-son conflict, the contraposition of corruptness versus purity, and certain inconsistencies in the characterization.

[12] E.g., Peter von Matt, *Der Grundriß von Grillparzers Bühnenkunst* (Zürich: Atlantis, 1965), pp. 136 ff.

[13] Matt, p. 138.

[14] Cf. Politzer, "Bruderzwist," p. 179.

[15] One possible interpretation of the scene at the well that — to my knowledge —

has not been suggested before would be to see in Rudolf's dropping the key an act of mercy. Since the thwarted abduction of Lukrezia, Don Cäsar has been trying desperately to end his life, first in battle, without succeeding, and now by directly attempting suicide. Could it be that by dropping the key the emperor goes along with his son's intentions and wants to spare him the ignominy of a trial and certain public execution? It is possible to see in Rudolf's words: "Er ist gerichtet, / Von mir, von seinem Kaiser, seinem — / Herrn!" (297), an assertion that only he, as Don Cäsar's father, should judge him, and a final act of fatherly protection. Seen in this light, the scene is considerably less horrid than, e.g., the killing of Emilia Galotti at her father's hands.

KONZENTRIERTER NESTROY:
ZU DER KOMÖDIE *FRÜHERE VERHÄLTNISSE*[1]

Franz H. Mautner

Frühere Verhältnisse ist das vorletzte der etwa achzig Stücke Johann Nestroys. Es hatte seine Premiere in seinem Todesjahr, 1862. Er war vierzig Jahre lang Schauspieler gewesen, sechs Jahre (1854 bis 1860) zugleich Theaterdirektor.

Diese Posse in einem Akt ist konzentrierter Nestroy: Nestroyisch durch ihre Themen, Charaktere, Sprache und den Witz. Sie ist aufs Straffste komponiert: spannend und überreich an Witz zugleich, läßt sie dauernd auf die Satire horchen, die hinter den komischen Situationen verborgen ist. Ihr ganzes Personal besteht aus zwei Männern — einem Holzhändler und seinem Hausknecht — und zwei Frauen — der Gattin des Händlers und ihrer Köchin.

"'s Fataltste bei die früheren Verhältnisse is, daß sie oft später aufkommen tun", ist der mit prachtvollem Witz durchgeführte Grundgedanke der Handlung. Als dauernd vorhandene Furcht und als Vorgang treibt er das Geschehen weiter. Die beiden textlichen Leitmotive des Einakters — und sie sind mehr als bloß textlich — sind "aus gutem Haus" und "So gibt's viel gute Mensch'n, aber grundschlechte Leut'." Das erste steckt voll sozialpsychologischer Satire, das zweite — auch Refrain des Auftrittsliedes Muffls, der Nestroy-Rolle — voll sozialethischer. Es taucht nicht weniger als sechsmal auf, meist in der abkürzenden, nur leicht variierten Form: "O, es gibt schlechte Leut'," aber mit emphatischen Zusätzen: "b'sonders unter die Weibsleut'" (6. Szene), "b'sonders unter die g'wesenen Hausknecht'" (desgleichen), "besonders unter die abgedankten Theaterprinzessinnen" (8. Szene), "besonders unter die Holzhandlerinnen, die früher beim Theater waren" (12. Szene), und dem grimmig entschlossenen "Mir disputieren s' auf der Welt keine Professorstochter mehr auf" (15. Szene).

Dabei sind die Leut' in dieser Posse gar nicht so "grundschlecht"; mehr komisch, und moralisch etwas angestochen, unter dem Druck der Verhältnisse, "früherer" und gegenwärtiger: Der reich gewordene Holzhändler Scheitermann verbirgt vor seiner snobistischen Gattin "aus gutem Haus" — sie ist eine Professorstochter — seine niedrige Herkunft. Auf der Suche nach einem Hausknecht stößt er auf Muffl, einen zugrunde gegangenen "Materialhändler", bei dem er selbst einst Hausknecht war. Muffl, der auch von kleinen Unredlichkeiten weiß, die Scheitermann in seinem Dienst begangen hat — "Du hast nie etwas Anständig's g'stohlen, du warst nie kriminalfähig..., du warst ein sanfter Dieb, aber mit der Zeit macht es auch was aus" —, zwingt ihn durch die (einem mit Schiller vertrauten Theaterpublikum höchst amüsant klingende) Drohung, ihr früheres Verhältnis zu verraten — "ich erzähle der Residenz eine Geschichte, wie man Holzhandler wird" (6. Szene) —, nun ihn in seine Dienste zu nehmen, und bringt so den Parvenu erpresserisch in Abhängigkeit von ihm. (Der sprachliche Spiegel des früheren Verhältnisses: der Prinzipal wird von seinem Hausknecht, seinem früheren Chef, dauernd geduzt, der jetzige Hausknecht aber von seinem Herrn gesiezt.)

Peppi, früher Köchin bei Frau Scheitermann, hat während eines Intermezzos als Schauspielerin Muffl kennengelernt und kehrt nun in ihr "früheres Verhältnis" zu Frau Scheitermann zurück, denn: "So hat in Liebe und in Geld / Getäuscht mich die Theaterwelt!" An ihrem alten und seinem neuen Dienstplatz begegnen sich die beiden Deklassierten, mit erstaunlichen Folgen für die Seelenruhe des Ehepaars Scheitermann. Peppi hat es

> leider nie zu einer guten Bühne bringen können. Eine gute Bühne ist nämlich die, wo in jeder Loge ein Millionär und auf jedem Fauteuil ein Kapitalist [=Rentier] sitzt; da hat man doch Hoffnung, die sich dann und wann zur Möglichkeit, manchmal sogar bis zur Aussicht steigert (3. Szene).

Nestroy hat also in dieser kleinen Komödie sein altes Lieblingsthema, Parvenutum, wieder aufgenommen, verknüpft mit dem seiner reiferen Jahre, Satire auf das Theaterwesen, besonders auf das kommerzialisierte Theater, das Ganze gegen den Hintergrund gesellschaftlich und wirtschaftlich labil gewordener Zustände der nachrevolutionären Zeit sowie der zeitlosen Wurmstichigkeit des ambitionierten Bürgers und umspielt von Sprachkunst, Witz und Parodie.

Der Kern der sozialpsychologischen Komödie — die Wirkung des verschwiegenen gesellschaftlichen Mißverhältnisses — ist dank Nestroys psychologischer Analysierkunst Sprachgestalt geworden im Monolog des Herrn Scheitermann über seine Gattin:

> Prächtige Frau, saubere [=hübsche] Frau, junge Frau, superbe Frau — aber mir g'schieht doch leichter, wann s' aus'n Zimmer geht. Nicht etwan, als ob ich keine Inklination zu ihr hätt", o nein! Konträr! Sie hat nur einen für mich schrecklichen Fehler — sie is aus ein' guten Haus. Das scheniert mich, das beengt mich, ich stich ab gegen sie,

mit dem sprachlich wunderbar bildhaften Schlußsatz:

> O, es ist immer etwas Unangenehmes, wenn man mehr in der Niedrigkeit is und man muß immer emporblicken zu der Stufe, auf der die Frau steht. Es tut ei'm moralisch das G'nack weh. (3. Szene).

Am Ende des Monologs ist der Kummer so überzeugend geworden, daß man seine Komik beinahe vergißt: "Jetzt werd ich mich anziehn und unterwegs ein Glas Wein trinken — da vergiß ich's noch am leichtesten, daß ich a Frau aus ein' guten Haus hab'."

So wie hier schildert Nestroy in seinen Werken immer wieder mit Vorliebe und Virtuosität "die komisch-qualvollen Situationen, in die der dumme, der lügenhafte, der schlechte Mensch, der von unlauterem Ehrgeiz Besessene kommen kann."²

An sprachlicher Kunst in der Charakterisierung eines Milieus und einer Situation kommt Muffls Auftrittsmonolog der Darstellung dieser Kümmernis beinahe gleich. Nach dem kommerzialisierten Theater kommt hier auch die kommerzialisierte Wissenschaft an die Reihe. Er hat eine Kur machen müssen und ist in ein kleines Bad gereist, ein

> neuentdecktes, das heißt, sie haben erst ein' Doktor entdeckt, der ihnen durch chemische Analyse hat entdecken müssen, daß der Kubikmeter von ihrem G'schwabetz dritthalb Gran Jod-Kali, ein neunundzwanzigstel Hektoliter kohlensaures Natron und vierdreiachtel Milligramm Schwefel-Sublimat enthalt't, folglich allen übrigen Bädern vorzuziehen ist, bei welchen durch mineralischen Hydro-Pepsin das Kalzinierungs-Ferment mehr oder minder neutralisiert und dadurch offenbar die Heilkraft um sieben dreisechzehntel Prozent, bei Unterleibskrankheiten sogar um neun elfachtzehntel Prozent, vermindert wird. — Wer daran zweifelt, dem bleibt es unbenommen, seine eigenen Untersuchungen zu machen. [Knieriems Astralfeuer-Monolog aus *Lumpazivagabundus* ist wieder da, Parodie des wissenschaftlichen Jargons, aber angewendet auf einen dem Publikum vertrauten Gegenstand und gewürzt durch dessen Prostitution an geschäftliche Interessen.] Da bin ich hin und war wirklich überrascht; es war zwar alles schlecht, aber teuer wie in die berühmtesten Badeorte. Auch für Unterhaltung war gesorgt; 's Theater war klein, die Künstler gar nicht, das heißt, es waren keine eigentlichen Künstler, nur so Spieler, daß der Abend auf dramatisch hin wird und daß man etwas deprimiert und mit geringeren Anforderungen ins Gasthaus kommt — *da stoßt auf einmal eine verspätete Sternin erster Größe' zur Trupp' als glanzpunktischer Umundauf der ambulanten Entreprise.*³

Dieser Satz kann als Beispiel dienen für Nestroys sprachbewußten, humoristisch erhellenden Gebrauch verblaßter Wörter und Wendungen: Das Klischee 'Stern' (*Star*) für eine 'hervorragende' Schauspielerin ist aus der Erstarrung erlöst durch den im ursprünglichen Bild bleibenden und zugleich Bewunderung ausdrückenden astronomischen Zusatz 'erster Größe.' Die sprachwidrige Femininbildung, ein Lieblingsscherz Nestroys (vgl. unten 'Wurmin'), erhält eine über das Sprach-Komische hinausreichende Funktion, indem das durch 'erster Größe' zur astronomischen Metapher wiederweckte Klischee 'Stern' weiblich und dadurch völlig lebendig geworden, nun im vollen Glanz der Anschauung, der Wirklichkeit und ihres Reizes erstrahlt. Und dies führt weiter dazu, daß auch das von einem andern Klischee, 'Glanzpunkt', neu geformte Adjektiv 'glanzpunktisch' etwas vom alten Glanz des Hauptwortes wiedergewinnt und die Sternin zu einem wahren 'Umundauf' wird. Von solchen Zauberkünsten wimmelt es in Nestroys Werk. — Die Erzählung geht weiter:

> Gleich nach ihrer ersten Vorstellung hab' ich mir kühn den Weg zu ihr gebahnt; es war nicht leicht, schon wegen ihren Künsterstolz, sie hat sich noch viel mehr eingebildet, als wirklich dran war — wie s' schon sind bei die kleinen Theater, bei die großen is das anders! — ... Sie hat mir früher schon Avancen gemacht, denn kokett war sie — wie s' schon sind bei die kleinen Theater, bei die großen is das anders! — Wir waren Verliebte, nach mehreren Tagen Verlobte — aber ohne Erfolg; denn es sind bald drauf sehr reiche Ausländer ins Bad 'kommen, ich glaub', Russen und Engländer, jeder ein gelernter Krösus, und da is sie mir — wie s' schon sind bei die kleinen Theater, bei die großen is das anders! — da is sie mir untreu gewor'dn.

Aus Desperation ist Muffl ganz verkommen und kennt nun das "bittere Gefühl, wenn man oft so hungrig is, daß man vor Durst nicht weiß, wo man die Nacht schlafen soll!"

Sein enges Verhältnis mit der früheren Schauspielerin Peppi macht die Invasion einer gestelzten Theatersprache in den Dialog wie sie sich sonst mehr in Nestroys parodistischen Stücken breit macht, assoziativ angemessen. Ein Irrtum läßt Muffl bei ihrem Wiedersehen glauben, Peppi sei Frau Scheitermann geworden:

> Ich dem niedrigen Dunkel der häuslichen Knechtschaft verfallen, du die stolze Gattin eines vor dir im Staub kriechenden Holzhandlers — o Weib! Ich wollte, ich hätte dich nie geboren! (*Sich korrigierend*) Gesehen, hab' ich sagen wollen (8. Szene).

und drohend ruft er ihr nach, wohl vertraut mit deutscher Literatur und gewandt in Nestroyschen Stilbrüchen:

> Törichte Wurmin, die ich mit etliche mehrsilbige Worte vernichten kann! Die früheren Verhältnisse deines Gatten, dein früheres Verhältnis mit mir, das alles ist so despektierlich, daß ihr zittern müßt vor mir wie Espenläube! O, ich will euch ein furchtbarer Hausknecht sein (9. Szene).

Nicht nur mit den *Räubern, Kabale und Liebe* und der Josephs-Legende, auch mit der österreichischen Amtsterminologie ist er vertraut, und er beruhigt Scheitermann darüber, daß dessen vermeintliche Gattin Muffl die Locken gestreichelt:

> Mein Benehmen war reine Kopie des Aegyptischen Joseph, wie der zu seiner pharaonischbureaukratischen Verführerin gesagt hat: "Ich verwerfe dich, ein deutscher Jüngling!" Du mußt mir einen Mantel kaufen, damit er im Wiederholungsfall als Beweis meiner Unschuld in ihren Händen bleibt (12. Szene).

Der groteske Stil geht hier infolge des von Muffl und Scheitermann geteilten Irrtums in groteske Handlung über und in die absurdeste Situation: Da Muffl Szenen hindurch geglaubt hat, das Dienstmädchen sei Frau Scheitermann, erklärt er Herrn Scheitermann, der seine ahnungslose Frau wegen ihres vermeinten "Treubruchs" anfährt, sie sei gar nicht dessen Frau. Kurz, Ionesco ist nahe, auch sein dialogischer Witz des dem Sprecher unbewußten Doppelsinns und des Nachdrucks auf dem irrelevanten Wort:

> *Muffl* ... Was du bist, das bin ich auch, du Lump du!
> *Scheitermann (erbost).* Das verbitt' ich mir ——! Sie entwickeln eine Grobheit — —
> *Muffl.* Erst entwickeln? Meine Grobheit datiert sich schon lang her (6. Szene).

Dieser scheinbar bloß für sich bestehende Witz aber bezieht sich auf eine konkrete Situation des Stücks, auf die Zeit, da Muffl Scheitermanns Herr war. Ebenso ist seine folgende Reflexion — mit ihrem schönen Bild von der Sordine auf den in einer verblaßten Metapher unerwartet Anschauung werdenden Geigen — zugleich ein Urteil über die gesllschaftlich-moralisch-psychologische Grundkonstellation der Posse. Damit nicht genug, ist sie Ausdruck des von Nestroy so oft verkündeten Mißtrauens gegen das tölpische Schicksal:

> So reich, so dumm und doch so verheiratet! Der hätt' ein degoutantes Glück gehabt, aber die Heirat is das Sordindel auf die Geigen, von denen der Himmel vollhängt. Wär er nicht so reich, hätt' sie ihn nicht geheirat't; wär er nicht so dumm, hätt er sie nicht geheirat't; so aber is beides der Fall, er hat Reichtum und Dummheit gesät, hat also müssen eine sekkante Gattin ernten. So schafft man sich selber sein Haus-Nemesiserl zur Privat-Marterei und arbeitet so der großen Nemesis in die Händ', daß sie nicht ganz den Kredit der Gerechtigkeit verliert.

Auch ein scheinbar albernes Wortspielmißverständnis zeigt verdeckte Triebe an, die des amoureusen Pantoffelhelden. Scheitermann ist ausgeschickt worden, ein neues Dienstmädchen zu suchen, und hat eines gefunden. Seine Frau Josephine ist ihm aber zuvorgekommen:

> *Josephine (auf Peppi zeigend).* Hier steht die neue.
> *Scheitermann.* Meine is aber auch nicht alt (11. Szene).

Frau Scheitermann dagegen gibt, ihrem intellektuellen Wesen gemäß, eine Nestroyisch abstrakte mathematisch formulierte Umschreibung ihrer Eifersucht: "Ich habe eine [=ein Stubenmädchen] fortgeschickt, die mir in dem Grade mißfiel, als sie meinem Mann zu sehr gefiel" (4. Szene).

Auch das alte Stilmittel des komisch hyperbolischen Vergleichs ist bei Nestroy mild sarkastisch gefärbt, über seine Funktion als Vergleich hinauszielend in eine ganz andere Richtung: "Gegen meine Verschwiegenheit kann man ein Grab eine Kaffeeg'sellschaft nennen" (13. Szene). Er macht sich über scheinbar wertungsfreien, aber sozial implizierenden Sprachgebrauch halb explizite Gedanken und läßt den als "Individuum" bezeichneten Muffl "beleidigt" sagen, "Individuum? Keine Schimpfworte"! (17. Szene), hat aber seinen unzerstörbaren Spaß auch am kindlichsten Klangspiel. Josephine ruft aus: "O, mein Vater Professor" [in Anlehnung an "Pater Confessor"] (1. Szene), und Muffl versichert Scheitermann, daß dessen eben eintretende Gattin gar nicht "sie" sei: "Aber du, du irrst di, du! Dö? Dö da, die is ja gar nit dö!" (17. Szene). Selbst in diesen Spaß am bloßen Lautbild schlüpft also schließlich doch noch jener Witz des logisch Paradoxen und psychologisch Absurden hinein: "Besorgt" erklärt Muffl Scheitermann: "Aber, Johann, du phantasierst dir ja das Restl Verstand aus'n Kopf! Dös is ja gar nicht deine Frau."

Die Sprache ist nicht absurder und nicht verspielter als das Geschehen. Am witzigsten ist der Schluß. Frau Scheitermann, vor der ihr Gatte das Stück hindurch wegen ihrer intellektuell-gesellschaftlichen Hochnäsigkeit seine "früheren Verhältnisse" so desperat zu verbergen gesucht hat, hat von ihnen immer gewußt, ihr Wissen aber verborgen: Die Geldheirat war ihr wichtiger als ihr Dünkel — reizvolle Nahrung für den Sozialhistoriker der zweiten Hälfte des neunzehnten Jahrhunderts und im Einklang mit der in Nestroys Werk immer wieder auftauchenden These vom Supremat des Geldes im menschlichen Denken. Und noch eine zweite seiner unwandelbaren Ueberzeugungen setzt dieses bald heiterresignierte, bald burleske Spiel in Handlung um, formuliert in einer Notiz aus Nestroys Nachlaß, die er dann nochmals in einem Gedicht verwendete: "Täuschung ist die feine, aber starke Kette, die durch alle Glieder der Gesellschaft sich zieht; bettrügen oder betrogen werden, das ist die Wahl, und wer glaubt, es gibt ein drittes, betrügt sich selbst."

Das schließt nicht aus, daß man betrügen und zugleich betrogen werden kann, wie Scheitermann in unserem Stück.

ANMERKUNGEN

[1] Der hier veröffentliche Text beruht auf einem Abschnitt meines demnächst im Lothar Stiehm Verlag, Heidelberg, erscheinenden Buches über Nestroy. Die Zitate im Text entstammen der von mir edierten Ausgabe: Johann Nestroy, *Komödien* (Frankfurt am Main: Insel Verlag, 1970), III, 479-508. Grundlage des Textes für *Frühere Verhältnisse* ist: Johann Nestroy, *Gesammelte Werke. Ausgabe in sechs Bänden,* Hg. von Otto Rommel (Wien: A. Schroll, 1948-1949), VI, 447-481.

[2] Lorle Schinnerer-Kamler in einer Premièrenchronik, *Burgtheater-Almanach 1966/67* (Wien, 1966).

[3] Kursiv-Auszeichnung von uns.

DER UNBEHAUSTE MENSCH IM DRAMA GEORG BÜCHNERS

André von Gronicka

Das tragisch kurze Leben des genialen Dichters Georg Büchner fällt in eine wirre Zeit der Übergänge und Umwälzungen, in "diese halbe, irrgewordene Zeit," wie sie Georg Herwegh in seinem "Andenken an Georg Büchner," dieser Trauerode auf den Frühverstorbenen so treffend kennzeichnet:

> Doch hätt er uns ein Leitstern sollen sein
> In dieser halben, irr gewordnen Zeit,
> In dieser Zeit so wetterschwül und bang...[1]

Es war eine Zeit des Provisorischwerdens aller Verhältnisse, von der Alfred de Musset, Büchners französischer Zeitgenosse und viel bewundertes Vorbild, in seiner *Confession d'un Enfant du Siècle* eine so scharfsichtige Diagnose aufstellt. Er führt die Krankheit seiner Generation auf zwei Ursachen zurück: "Toute la maladie du siècle présent vient de deux causes; le peuple qui a passé par '93 et par 1814 porte au coeur deux blessures: Tout ce qui était n'est plus; tout ce qui sera n'est pas encore. Ne cherchez pas ailleurs le secret de nos maux." Und dann entwirft Musset das Gleichnis des unbehausten Menschen:

> Voilà un homme dont la maison tombe en ruine; il l'a démolie pour en bâtir une autre. Les décombres gisent sur son champ, et il attend des pierres nouvelles pour son edifice nouveau. Au moment où le voilà prêt a tailler ses moellons et à faire son ciment, la pioche en main, les bras retroussés, on vient lui dire que les pierres manquent et lui conseiller de reblanchir les vieilles pour en tirer parti. Que voulez-vous qu'il fasse, lui qui ne veut point de ruines pour faire un nid à sa couvée? La carrière est pourtant profonde, les instruments trop faibles pour en tirer les pierres. Attendez, lui dit-on, on les tirera peu à peu; espérez, travaillez, avancez, reculez. Que ne lui dit-on pas? Et pendant ce temps-là cet homme, n'ayant plus sa vieille maison et pas encore sa maison nouvelle, ne sait comment se défendre de la pluie, ni comment préparer son repas du soir, ni où travailler, ni où reposer, ni où vivre, ni où mourir."[2]

Das ist die tragische Lebenslage der Generation Mussets und Büchners, die sich im Werke Büchners spiegelt, am grellsten und eindrucksvollsten in seinen Dramen. Nach schwerer Enttäuschung in politischer Tätigkeit, verraten von den hessischen Bauern, für deren Befreiung aus drückendem Frohndienst er kämpfte, im Anblick der Sinnlosigkeit der "großen" Geschichte der Menschheit, bekennt sich der junge Büchner zu einem illusionlosen Determinismus. Es entgleitet ihm jede Zielsetzung im tätigen Leben. Er fühlt sich

> zernichtet unter dem gräßlichen Fatalismus der Geschichte. Ich finde in der Menschennatur eine entsetzliche Gleichheit, in den menschlichen Verhältnissen eine unabwendbare Gewalt, allen und keinem verliehen. Der einzelne nur Schaum auf der Welle, die Größe ein bloßer Zufall, die Herrschaft des Genies ein Puppenspiel, ein lächerliches Ringen gegen ein ehernes Gesetz, es zu erkennen das Höchste, es zu beherrschen unmöglich.[3]

In präkerster Lebenslage als politisch Verfolgter, in trost- und hoffnungsloser Stimmung schreibt Büchner, nach eigener Aussage, sein Meisterdrama *Dantons Tod* in knappen fünf Wochen. Es wird ein Drama von objektivster Sachlichkeit, zugleich ein klarer Spiegel der eignen Situation als der verfolgte unbehauste Mensch in wirrer Zeit. Es spiegelt sich in diesem Werk Büchners Haß auf die Mächte der Tyrannei, aber auch der tiefe Pessimismus, der Fatalismus des Enttäuschten, die fieberhafte Angst vor drohender Katastrophe. Es ist als dächte Büchner an sich selbst, wenn er seinen Danton die große Rede vor dem Revolutionstribunal halten läßt, an seine eigne Verteidigungsrede, die er im Falle seiner Verhaftung seinen Richtern entgegenschleudern wollte, — hoffnungslos, enttäuscht und lebensmüde und doch groß und mannhaft:

> "Was liegt mir an euch und eurem Urteil? Das Nichts wird bald mein Asyl sein; — das Leben ist mir zur Last, man mag mir es entreißen, ich sehne mich danach es abzuschütteln... Sie haben die Hände an mein ganzes Leben gelegt, so mag es sich denn aufrichten und ihnen entgegentreten; unter dem Gewicht jeder meiner Handlungen werde ich sie begraben. — Ich bin nicht stolz darauf. Das Schicksal führt uns den Arm, aber nur gewaltige Naturen sind seine Organe." (S. 58)

Das ist die Stimme Büchners, des Hellsichtigen, Lebensüberdrüssigen und doch auch wieder des Stolzen im Wissen um seinen geistigen Rang.

Der historische Stoff dieses Dramas, aus der Geschichte der Französischen Revolution gegriffen, wird von Büchner zu einem Kunstwerk geformt, das fern ist aller Verherrlichung dieses epochemachenden Ereignisses. Bezeichnenderweise wählt Büchner die dunkelsten Wochen der Revolution, da sie zum Saturn wird, der seine eignen Kinder frißt. (S. 27) Es ist ein Bild grausamer, allgemeiner Gebundenheit an die Materie, und das historische Fatum. Des Menschen geistige Freiheit ist als Lug und Trug durchschaut. Eine erbarmungslose Gewalt regiert, die jeden in ihren Bann zwingt und die mit menschlichen Mitteln weder zu ergründen noch zu beherrschen ist.

Büchner hat das deterministische Gleichnis von der Marionette geprägt, um die schicksalhafte Gebundenheit alles menschlichen Tuns and Trachtens zu versinnbildlichen: "Puppen sind wir, von unbekannten Gewalten am Draht gezogen; nichts, nichts wir selbst!" (S. 45) Und doch wird von Büchner diese Gebundenheit des Menschen an die erdrückende Allgewalt des Schicksals in den tragischen Gestalten dieses Dramas, vor allem in der Gestalt Dantons, nicht ohne heroisches Pathos, einen Anflug von Erhabenheit gestaltet. Dantons verzweifelter Kampf auf verlorenem Posten entbehrt nicht der Größe, wird mit Energie und Geist geführt, zeigt noch einmal den genialen Machtmenschen in seiner charismatischen Wirkung auf seine Gegner und das wetterwendische Volk. Der dem Schicksal hilflos ausgelieferte Mensch, — "Schaum auf der Welle" (S. 374) des Lebens — bleibt sich hier noch seiner Menschenwürde bewußt. Gewiß, es wäre abwegig hier vom Schillerschen Schicksal zu sprechen, "welches den Menschen erhebt, indem es den Menschen zermalmt." Doch fehlt Büchners Danton nicht die stolze Gebärde, wenn auch der wissende Mensch nicht mehr stolz ist auf sie: "Ich werde mit Mut zu sterben wissen," (S. 43) und: "Was liegt mir an euch und eurem Urteil? ... Das Schicksal führt uns die Arme, aber nur gewaltige Naturen sind seine Organe." (S. 27) Büchners Danton ist eine solche "gewaltige Natur." In welch anderer Gestalt wird der unbehauste Mensch erscheinen in Büchners letztem Drama als der dumpfe, schutz- und wehrlose, der gedemütigte und enterbte Woyzeck.

Büchner beginnt seine dichterische Deutung des historischen Danton mit dessen *Ent*politisierung. Er zeigt warum dieser Kraftmensch von der Revolution, die er selbst heraufbeschwören half, verschlungen wird. Er zeigt wie Dantons *humanitas* den *homo politicus* in ihm schachmatt setzt. Dantons Herz ist nicht steinern, sein Geist nicht beschränkt, sein Gefühl nicht kalt genug, um das durchzuhalten, womit sich sein Widerpart, der konsequente Ideologe Robespierre brüstet, den Terror im Namen der sozial-politischen Utopie. Büchners Danton betritt seine Bühne im Augenblick, da sein Glaube an die reinigende, befreiende Wirkung der radikalen Aktion von Grund auf zerstört ist durch die Erkenntnis, daß die Menschheit im metaphysischen Sinne stets *unfrei* sein wird, durch keine noch so radikale erfolgreiche Tat vom Leiden am Leben, am Menschenlos, erlöst werden kann. Sein fühlendes Herz empfindet, sein skeptisch-wacher Geist erkennt, daß das politische Spiel den Einsatz von zahllosen Menschenleben nicht lohnt. Er ist des Tötens müde: "Ich will lieber guillotiniert werden als guillotinieren lassen. Ich hab es satt; wozu sollen wir Menschen miteinander kämpfen? Wir sollten uns nebeneinander setzen und Ruhe haben." (S. 35) Seinem scharfen Blick hat sich das politische Drama als eine blutrünstige Tragi-Komödie entpuppt, mit einem Text, "worin jedes Komma ein Säbelhieb und jeder Punkt ein abgeschlagener Kopf ist." (S. 63)

> *Mercier*: Blickt um euch, das alles habt ihr gesprochen; es ist eine mimische Übersetzung eurer Worte. Diese Elenden, ihre Henker und die Guillotine sind eure lebendig gewordenen Reden. Ihr bautet eure Systeme, wie Bajazet seine Pyramiden, aus Menschenköpfen.
>
> *Danton*: Du hast recht — man arbeitet heutzutag alles in Menschenfleisch. Das ist der Fluch unserer Zeit. (S. 56-57)

So hat sich für Danton die Welt der Politik, in der er einst beheimatet war und seine große Rolle spielte, in eine feindliche verwandelt, die ihn in ihrem menschenvernichtenden Widersinn namenlos anekelt und abstößt. Nie wieder kann sie Heimat für ihn sein, nie wieder wird er sie betreten, um sich begeistert für seine politischen Ideale einzusetzen und in selbstgerechtem Kampf sich mit seinen Widersachern zu messen. Denn diese Widersacher, ein Robespierre, ein St. Juste, sind in seinen sehenden Augen zu elenden Narren und blutigen Henkern geworden, die ihre Systeme, wie Bajazet seine Pyramide, aus Menschenköpfen bauen.

In der Auseinandersetzung zwischen Danton und Robespierre identifiziert sich Büchner weitgehend mit Danton. Er entlarvt des Ideologen Tugend als eine Form der Heuchelei und des Selbstbetrugs. Mit seinem Danton hält Büchner es für viel aufrichtiger und tugendhafter, offen einzugestehen, daß ein jeder Mensch seiner Natur gemäß handelt, ein jeder nach seiner Façon seinem Glücke und seinem Genuße nachjagt, daß ein jeder Mensch im Grunde seines Wesens ein Epikuräer ist: "Es gibt nur Epikuräer," läßt Büchner seinen Danton behaupten, "und zwar grobe und feine, Christus war der feinste; das ist der einzige Unterschied, den ich zwischen den Menschen herausbringen kann. Jeder handelt seiner Natur gemäß, d. h. er tut, was ihm wohltut." (S. 29, 53) Diese desillusionierende Einsicht Dantons in das Wesen des Menschen ist Büchners eigne. Es ist sein Weg über den sensualistischen Hedonismus zu einem alles nivellierenden Relativismus, in dem sich alle idealistischen Lebenswerte endgültig verflüchtigen, alle hochfliegenden Zielsetzungen der Menschheit aufgehoben sind. Das Leben zeigt sich in seinem wahren Wesen als eine Tragi-Komödie, die uns zu einem tragischgestimmten Gelächter über die Sinnlosigkeit des Menschendaseins auf dieser wackligen und blutigen Bühne reizt.

Büchners Blick bohrt tiefer, seine Erfahrung reicht weit über das sozial-politische Weltbild hinaus. Nicht nur diese Lebenssphäre löst sich ihm in eine blutige Groteske auf. Sein Blick dringt in Tiefen, wo das Leben-an-sich in seiner ganzen Vielfalt problematisch wird, sich aus Heimat in eine entsetzliche, quälende Fremde verwandelt. Dantons große Sehnsucht ist nach der Ruhe des Nichts, seine größte Enttäuschung, daß er diese Ruhe nie wird erreichen können, denn — er weiß es — selbst der Tod wird dem Lebensmüden, dem des Seins Überdrüssigen keine Erlösung bieten: "Da ist keine Hoffnung im Tod; er ist nur eine einfachere, das Leben eine verwickeltere, organisiertere Fäulnis, das ist der ganze Unterschied!" (S. 67) Danton verflucht den unumstößlichen Satz: "Etwas kann nicht zu nichts werden!" denn dieser Satz bedeutet für ihn ewige Daseinsqual: "Und ich bin etwas, das ist der Jammer!" (S. 66) Abgründiger kann die Enttäuschung am Leben, der Widerwille gegen alles Sein nicht erlebt, konsequenter nicht gestaltet werden. Dieser Mensch ist kein Ausgestoßener aus dem Leben; er ist der Unbehauste nach Willen und Entschluß, der seine einzige wahre Heimat im *Nichts* erkennt.

Für Büchner sinken die hergebrachten ethischen wie die ästhetischen Werte dahin. Für ihn gibt es keine Helden mehr und keine Bösewichter, nur noch

Narren, die ihre Narrheit hinter ewig wechselnden Masken verbergen. An seine Eltern schreibt Büchner: "Man nennt mich einen Spötter. Es ist wahr, ich lache oft; aber ich lache nicht darüber, *wie* jemand ein Mensch, sondern nur darüber, *daß* er ein Mensch ist, wofür er ohnehin nichts kann, und lache dabei über mich selbst, der ich sein Schicksal teile." (S. 377-378, vgl. auch S. 39) Es ist dieses Lachen, das wir in Büchners Lustspiel *Leonce und Lena* zu hören glauben.

In diesem Lustspiel führt uns Büchner die Welt als Narrenspiegel und Puppenspiel vor. All diese Menschen, dieser Prinz Leonce, diese Prinzessin Lena, der König und seine Minister, all ihr Tun und Treiben in ihrem winzigen Ländchen, alles hat etwas Automatenhaftes an sich, führt die Scheinexistenz eines Marionettentheaters. Lebendiges Sein scheint in diesen Gestalten zu mechanischer Gestik, zu fingierter Sentimentalität, zu Wortwitz und Wortschwall entartet. Leonces Bemerkung zu Valerio: "Mensch, du bist nichts als ein schlechtes Wortspiel," (S. 126) bezieht sich wohl nicht allein auf den Angesprochenen, sondern, im Geiste dieses Lustspiels, auf den Menschen schlechthin. Das auffallende Vorherrschen des Wortspiels soll darauf hinweisen, daß dem Dichter das Menschenleben zu einem Wortspiel und -witz geworden, wie die ganze Natur zur stilisierten Attrappe. Valerio bezeichnet treffend diese Spiel- und Scheinwelt und sich und andere darin als Spielkarten:

> Die Sonne sieht aus wie ein Wirtshausschild, und die feurigen Wolken darüber wie die Aufschrift 'Wirtshaus zur goldenen Sonne.' Die Erde und das Wasser da unten sind wie ein Tisch, auf dem Wein verschüttet ist, und wir liegen darauf wie Spielkarten, mit denen Gott und der Teufel aus Langeweile eine Partie machen, und Ihr seid ein Kartenkönig, und ich bin ein Kartenbube, es fehlt nur noch eine Dame, eine schöne Dame, mit einem großen Lebkuchenherzen auf der Brust und einer mächtigen Tulpe, worin die lange Nase sentimental versinkt." (S. 134)

Im Büchnerschen Lachen schwingt ein Ton der Ironie, ja des Sarkasmus mit. Dies ist Büchners Art phantasievoll subtile Rache zu üben an einer Welt, die ihn zutiefst enttäuscht und verletzt hat. Es ist eine Rache, die übergoldet ist von launigem Humor, die aber ausbricht in grotesk-bitterer Satire, wie etwa in der Szene vor dem Schlosse König Peters:

> *Landrat*: Lieber Herr Schulmeister, wie halten sich Eure Leute?
>
> *Schulmeister*: Sie halten sich so gut in ihren Leiden, daß sie sich schon seit geraumer Zeit aneinander halten. Sie gießen brav Spiritus in sich, sonst könnten sie sich in der Hitze unmöglich so lange halten...
>
> *Landrat*: Und, Schulmeister, Ihr steht vor die Nüchternheit!
>
> *Schulmeister*: Versteht sich, denn ich kann vor Nüchternheit kaum noch stehen.

Landrat: Gebt acht, Leute, im Programm steht: 'Sämtliche Untertanen werden von freien Stücken reinlich gekleidet, wohlgenährt und mit zufriedenen Gesichtern sich längst der Landstraße aufstellen.' Macht uns keine Schande.

Schulmeister: Seid standhaft! Kratzt euch nicht hinter den Ohren und schneuzt euch die Nasen nicht, solang das hohe Paar vorbeifährt und zeigt die gehörige Rührung, oder es werden rührende Mittel gebraucht werden... Könnt ihr noch eure Lektion? He? Vi!

Die Bauern: Vi!

Schulmeister: Vat!

Die Bauern: Vat!

Schulmeister: Vivat!

Die Bauern: Vivat!

Schulmeister: So, Herr Landrat! Sie sehen, wie die Intelligenz im Steigen ist. Bedenken Sie, es ist Latein!... (S. 139-140)

Der beißende Humor, der absurde Witz dieser Szene entspringt der bitteren Erfahrung des Politikers Büchner mit der bodenlosen Dummheit des Volkes, der hessischen Bauern, mit der bornierten Spießigkeit und Unterwürfigkeit der Intelligenzler, mit der Verlogenheit und Hohlheit der Hofwelt. Doch ginge man fehl, wollte man in diesem Lustspiel lediglich eine Gesellschaftssatire sehen. Es sind nicht das Versagen der Bauern, die Entartung des Bürgers und des Adels, die den Dichter vor allem zu seinem Schaffen reizen; es ist nicht die Fehlleistung dieses oder jenes Standes, dieser oder jener typischen Figur, die Büchner uns zur Erbauung und Belustigung in seinem Lustspiel vorsetzt, wie es etwa Lessing in seinen Jugendkomödien, dem *Freigeist* oder dem *Jungen Gelehrten* oder dann, als Meister der Charakterisierungskunst, in seinem Tellheim und dessen übertriebenem Ehrgefühl getan. Büchners Lachen, seine Komödie entspringt seinem Wissen um die Narretei und Nichtigkeit des Lebens in seinem ganzen Umfang. In Büchners Wirklichkeit gibt es keine befreiende Lustspiellösung mehr, wie sie Lessing noch in seiner vernünftig-sinnvollen Welt, aus der sein Meisterlustspiel *Minna von Barnhelm* hervorwächst, uns geben konnte. In Büchners Welt kann nur noch die Illusion des Märchens seinen Menschen-Marionetten die Erlösung aus der grotesken Sinn- und Gehaltlosigkeit ihres Scheindaseins bringen, nur ein Wunschtraum von Liebe und Glück ihnen den *Schein* einer Rettung vorspiegeln. Und so flüchtet sich die Komödie Büchners in die Unwirklichkeit des Märchens.

Das Büchnersche Lustspiel erinnert uns an die Märchenkomödien Tiecks, an dessen *Prinz Zerbino* oder seine *Verkehrte Welt*. Doch wird bei näherer Betrachtung klar, daß die Romantik im Büchnerschen Stück der Ironie des Dichters wenn nicht zum Opfer fällt, so doch als Spielball ausgeliefert wird: Nachtbegeisterung und Liebestod, die idealistische Philosophie und Friedrich Schlegels gefeierter Müßiggang, Italiensehnsucht und Märchenidylle, romantische Blumensymbolik und die romantische Sprache in all ihren Stileigenheiten, mit all diesem und mit mehr treibt der Dichter sein geistreich persiflierendes Spiel. Die romantische Welt verliert ihren Eigenwert, wird weitgehend zur Parodie ihrer selbst.

Der geistsprühenden Grazie und Ironie des Büchnerschen Lustspiels ist ein Grundton lebensmüder Melancholie und todessüchtiger Trauer beigemischt, wie sie die jungen Romantiker noch nicht kannten, ein Ton, der charakteristisch wurde für die Spätromantiker, die Dichter des Weltschmerzes, Byron und Leopardi, de Musset und Heine und Lenau. Aber selbst diese Stimmung wird von Büchner ironisch aufgelockert, wenn auch nicht völlig aufgelöst. Kaum hat sich der Prinz Leonce, "vor sich hinträumend" über den langen, allzu langen Lebensweg beklagt — "O, jeder Weg ist lang. Das Picken der Totenuhr in unserer Brust ist langsam, und jeder Tropfen Blut mißt seine Zeit, und unser Leben ist ein schleichend Fieber. Für müde Füße ist jeder Weg zu lang...", — da läßt ihn Büchner auch schon seine Melancholie ironisch kommentieren: "Ich hab es, glaub ich ganz melancholisch gesagt. Gott sei Dank, daß ich anfange, mit der Melancholie niederzukommen!" (S. 134-135)

Einzig die Prinzessin Lena umgibt echt romantischer Geist, hauchzart, bis aufs letzte entmaterialisiert und sublimiert. "Eben in der Gestaltung jener Prinzessinwelt aus Klang, Licht und Traum," findet Hans Mayer "die besondere Romantik Büchners."[4] Auch ist es die Prinzessin, und sie allein, in der die abendliche Schwermut und lebensmüde Melancholie ungebrochen ausschwingen: "Und müden Augen jedes Licht zu scharf, und müden Lippen jeder Hauch zu schwer, *lächelnd*: und müden Ohren jedes Wort zu viel." (S. 135) Ihr muß man glauben, wenn sie den Tod als den "seligsten Traum" (S. 137) begrüßt, denn hier spricht Büchners eigne Todessehnsucht ohne ironischen Akzent. Diese Stimmung wird ihren Wiederhall finden in dem Wiener Impressionismus und der Neuromantik. Doch antizipiert das Büchnersche Spiel weit modernere Stimmungen und Stilkunst. Manche Szene seiner Komödie, wie etwa die vor dem Palast des Königs Peter nimmt genialisch die Bühnentechnik des "absurden" Theaters vorweg, dessen Groteskerien ja ebenfalls dem Schwund des Lebenssinnes und -wertes entspringen. Martin Esslin bezeichnet "die Fremdheit des Menschen in der Welt, die Entfremdung zwischen Welt und Mensch,"[5] als *die* existenzielle Grundlage des absurden Theaters.

Ganz wie seine Tragödien, ist auch das Büchnersche Lustspiel Ausdruck seines Leidens am Leben, an dessen Sinnlosigkeit. Der Schritt von seiner Komödie zurück zur Tragödie, zu seinem *Woyzeck* ist kein gewaltsamer Sprung. Der existenzielle Ursprung der Dichtung bleibt unverändert.[6] Nur daß im *Woyzeck* das Leiden am Leben seine ergreifendste, weil völlig unverhüllte Sprache spricht in einer grotesk verzerrten Kleinbürger- und Spießerwelt, ebenso fern dem Phantasiereich des Märchens wie der Bühne des "großen" Weltgeschehens. An Stelle Dantons, der in all seiner Ernüchterung und Enttäuschung dennoch als gewaltige Erscheinung vor uns stand, tritt hier die gehetzte, erniedrigte Kreatur, der unbehauste

Mensch in seinem maßlosen Elend. Und Woyzecks Gegner sind nicht die mächtigen Gestalten der Geschichte, kein Robespierre, kein St. Just; es sind Untermenschen, sadistische Quälgeister, — der Hauptmann, der Doktor, der Tambourmajor, — die in ihrer Veranntheit oder Borniertheit, in ihrer Menschenverachtung, jeder auf seine infame Weise, den ihnen hilflos Ausgelieferten als ein bloßes Versuchsobjekt mißbrauchen und malträtieren.

In der Darstellung dieser Gestalten läßt der Dichter seinem Spott und seinem Haß freien Lauf. Er weiß sich berechtigt zu dieser Darstellungsweise: "Der Haß ist so gut erlaubt als die Liebe, und ich hege ihn im vollsten Maße gegen die, welche verachten... Hochmut gegen Hochmut, Spott gegen Spott." (S. 378) Dieser Büchnersche Spott und Haß ergießen sich über die Verächter und Schänder des Menschen und treiben ihre Gestaltung weit über allen Realismus hinaus zur bitter-bösen Karikatur und Groteske, wie wir sie in der Kunst des Expressionismus bei Paul Kornfeld etwa oder auf dem "absurden" Theater wiederfinden.

Doch auch in diesem Werke bleibt Büchner keineswegs in sozialer Anklage befangen. Auch hier gestaltet er die ewige Beschaffenheit des Menschendaseins in seiner unabwendbaren Tragik. Büchner zeichnet seinen Woyzeck mit einer an Dostoevski gemahnenden Empathie in das Leiden des Unbehausten, mit einer tiefen Liebe für die vom Leben Enterbten: "Man muß die Menschheit lieben," läßt Büchner seinen Lenz erklären, "man muß sie lieben, um in das eigentümliche Wesen eines jeden einzudringen; es darf einem keiner zu gering, keiner zu häßlich sein. Erst dann kann man sie verstehen." (S. 95) So liebt und versteht Büchner den geringen, häßlichen Woyzeck, sieht hinab in die volksmythischen Schichten seiner Natur, erkennt die existenzielle Angst Woyzecks vor dem Unfaßbaren, dem Unheimlich-Drohenden des Lebens:

> *Woyzeck:* Es geht hinter mir, unter mir. *Stampft auf den Boden:* Hohl, hörst du? alles hohl da unten! Die Freimaurer!
> *Andres:* Ich fürcht mich.
> *Woyzeck:* 's ist so kurios still. Man möcht den Atem halten. — Andres!
> *Andres:* Was?
> *Woyzeck:* Red was! *Starrt in die Gegend.* Andres! wie hell! Über der Stadt is alles Glut! Ein Feuer fährt um den Himmel und ein Getös herunter wie Posaunen. Wie's heraufzieht! — Fort! Sieh nicht hinter dich! *Reißt ihn ins Gebüsch.*
> *Andres nach einer Pause:* Woyzeck, hörst du's noch?
> *Woyzeck:* Still, alles still, als wär die Welt tot. (S. 153)

Diese Urangst vor dem geheimnisvollen *Etwas* raubt Woyzeck alle Sicherheit, steigert sein Gefühl der Hilflosigkeit ins Unerträgliche. In seiner Einsamkeit und Hilflosigkeit in dieser feindlichen, dunkeldrohenden Welt wird die Treulosigkeit Mariens für ihn zu einem entsetzlichen Geschehen, das ihn in Wahnsinn und in den Mord treibt an dem einzigen Menschen, der für ihn die letzte bergende

Gemeinschaft war. Woyzecks Mord der Marie ist nicht nur die Ermordung eines Menschen, es ist Woyzecks Rache am Leben, es ist Mord des Lebens selbst, das dem Woyzeck die Treue gebrochen und ihn hinausgestoßen hatte in unerträgliche Einsamkeit. Was dem armen Woyzeck geschieht, das steigert Büchner zu einer Parabel des ausgesetzten, des unbehausten Menschen in dem schaurigen Märchen der Großmutter:

> Es war einmal ein arm Kind und hatt kein Vater und keine Mutter, war alles tot, und war niemand mehr auf der Welt. Alles tot, und es is hingangen und hat gesucht Tag und Nacht. Und weil auf der Erde niemand war, wollt's in Himmel gehn, und der Mond guckt es so freundlich an; und wie es endlich zum Mond kam, war's ein Stück faul Holz. Und da is es zur Sonn gangen, und wie es zur Sonn kam, war's ein verwelkt Sonneblum. Und wie's zu den Sternen kam, waren's kleine goldne Mücken, die waren angesteckt, wie der Neuntöter sie auf die Schlehen steckt. Und wie es wieder auf die Erde wollt, war die Erde ein umgestürzter Hafen. Und es war ganz allein. Und da hat sich's hingesetzt und geweint, und da sitzt es noch und ist ganz allein. (S. 271-272)

Hier ist der Tiefpunkt der Büchnerschen Disillusionierung, seines Nihilismus erreicht. Selbst die Märchenwelt bietet keine Erlösung mehr, verkehrt sich in ihr tragisches Gegenteil, in ein Anti-märchen. Kosmisch-allumfassende Enttäuschung und ewige Einsamkeit, das ist das unentrinnbare Schicksal des unbehausten Menschen im Drama Büchners.

ANMERKUNGEN

[1] Georg Herwegh, *Der Freiheit eine Gasse*, ed. Bruno Kaiser (Berlin: Verlag Volk und Welt, 1948), S. 124.
[2] Alfred de Musset, *Oeuvres Complètes de Alfred de Musset* (Paris, Charpentier, 1866), S. 25.
[3] Georg Büchner, *Werke und Briefe. Gesamtausgabe*, ed. Fritz Bergemann. 8th ed. Wiesbaden: Inselverlag, 1958), S. 374. Auf diese Ausgabe beziehen sich die Seitenangaben im Text.
[4] Hans Mayer, *Georg Büchner und seine Zeit* (Berlin: Verlag Volk und Welt [1947]), S. 309.
[5] Esslin, *Sinn oder Unsinn? Das Groteske im modernen Drama*. Fünf Essays von Martin Esslin [u. a.]. (Basel, Stuttgart: Basilius Presse, 1962), S. 106. In diesem Zusammenhang stellt Esslin (S. 102) einen starken Einfluß Büchners auf die frühen Stücke Arthur Adamovs, eines Hauptvertreters des absurden Theaters, fest: "Adamovs frühe Stücke, die deutlich den Einfluß von Strindberg und Büchner zeigen (Adamov übersetzte *Dantons Tod* ...) kreisen um ein Grundthema: Die Sinnlosigkeit des menschlichen Strebens."
[6] Klaus Völker, "Das Phänomen des Grotesken im neueren deutschen Drama," *Sinn oder Unsinn?* [s. Anm. 5], S. 14: "Das Lustspiel [*Leonce und Lena*] bleibt nicht nur

Literatursatire, das Ende dieser Komödie ist ebenso chaotisch wie *Woyzeck* und *Dantons Tod*. Die im Automatismus erstarrte Welt wird nicht durch die Liebe überwunden, die Liebe ist bereits ein weiterer Mechanismus."

THE INTEGRATION OF FICTIONAL PATTERNS IN HEBBEL'S DRAMATIC STRUCTURES

Otto W. Johnston

Perhaps no other dramatist in German literary history has been examined from such a biased perspective as Friedrich Hebbel.[1] Two themes dominate in the authoritative studies of his dramatic works. Scholars either pose the question of how theory relates to practice[2] or they search for the "Weltanschauung."[3] One of the most influential studies of Hebbel's thought was done in 1938 by Klaus Ziegler, who attempted to explicate the dramas without reference to the theoretical comments of the author.[4] In his zeal to eschew the "theoretician," Ziegler presented Hebbel as a great nineteenth-century philosopher. In his concluding remarks, for example, the critic claimed: "Wenn Hebbel alle weltanschaulichen Hauptströmungen des 19. Jahrhunderts in sich zusammenfaßt, so fassen sich in ihm natürlich auch all die unendlich vielen und weiten Spannungen, Widersprüche und Gegensätze dieser Weltanschauung zusammen."[5] But what is actually being said here concerning the dramatic artist? The exaggerated emphasis on the metaphysical and intellectual problems in the plays has become a chief characteristic of Hebbel research since Ziegler's analysis.[6] In fact, Hebbel's dramatic technique and artistic creativity are discussed only peripherally. From time to time an isolated voice protests such one-sided interpretations,[7] yet no one has succeeded in diverting the attention of Hebbel scholars from the "aesthetician" and "philosopher."

Two factors in particular account for this: first, tracing the history of ideas has assumed a dominant role in German literary scholarship; second, Hebbel's great tragedies lend themselves readily to metaphysical speculation. Until very recently the poet's diary was utilized to justify many an abstract hypothesis[8] since it was believed that its entries comprised a treasure chest of systematic speculation. Hebbel's journals were put on a par with his plays and made the object of independent research. But investigations of these notebooks yielded unexpected results: Peter Michelsen discovered "eine verwirrende Mannigfaltigkeit verschiedenartigster Weltanschauungsansätze in den Tagebüchern" and concluded: "Die Unvereinbarkeit, in der die verschiedenen Positionen sich nebeneinander als gleichberechtigt darbieten, ist nicht aufhebbar."[9] Another investigator, Joachim Müller, refused to accept the entries as "Dokumente eines... weltanschaulichen Gefüges." Despite his discoveries, Müller did not refrain from the shadowy metaphysical vocabulary of earlier Hebbel scholars. With reference to his position in 1955,[10] in a later essay entitled: "Zur Struktur und Funktion von Hebbels Tagebüchern," he reiterates his conclusion: "Ich stehe nach wie vor zu meinem

Vorschlag, Hebbel einen Gestaltdenker zu nennen, der im Gegensatz zum Systemdenker sein Weltbild weniger im Begriff als im Bild und Symbol ausspricht" (*HNS*, p. 109). In short, Hebbel is not a philosopher because he has constructed no philosophical system. What Müller fails to realize is that a "Gestaltdenker" who expresses his conceptual framework in "image" and "symbol" is a *poet* whose creations may be scrutinized in terms of structure rather than concepts.

Where can one find a structural analysis of this "Gestaltdenker"? Which scholars have added to the metaphysical foundations by exploring the basic charasteristics of Hebbel's dramas? The ground work has been done by a few critics whose studies of Hebbel's style are rarely noted today. In 1911 Heinrich Dieters pointed out "das schroffe Nebeneinander von verschiedenen Stilen bei Hebbel."[11] A. M. Wagner examined the monologue, dialogue and the imagery of the dramatist.[12] In 1940 Marga Bührig discussed "den monologischen Dialog" and perceived a technique she termed "das Bewußtmachen unbewußter Regungen."[13] Unfortunately, these analyses lacked direction; they presented no fundamental thesis, substituting "observation" for "interpretation." As a result, Hebbel's "theory" became the *terminus a quo* and the critic fell victim to the intentional fallacy.

By contrast, today's scholar is more interested in the basic concepts of genre; hence in Hebbel research the preoccupation with the "Krise der Weltanschauung" should have yielded by now to structural analysis and to the questions of problems facing the artist. Yet even the so-called "werkimmanente Interpretationen" have not discussed structural characteristics and compositional methodology. The vast majority of "interpreters" have scrutinized Hebbel's plays almost exclusively in terms of their ideas.[14] The format of these studies is becoming less grandiose; the scope has narrowed, but the same questions are asked, the same theories tested. To be sure, the metaphysical approach has made genuine contributions to the understanding of a complex artistic genius, but literature is not simply a depository for the history of ideas. For this reason we turn here to a consideration of the dramatic structure of Hebbel's creations.

In his essay: "Die Struktur der reduzierten Individuation bei Friedrich Hebbel" (*H-Jb.*, 1968), Dieter Gerth observed that Hebbel's dramatic world gives the impression of "merkwürdige Gleichförmigkeit" (p. 9). Despite his accurate formulation, Gerth was not completely successful in explaining the reason for this uniformity. He overlooked the fact that Hebbel's drama consists essentially of three structure-producing units: challenge, mystery and dream. Considerable variation is possible as these units interlock to determine the course of the plot. The most important of these is the *challenge* which frequently manifests itself as a *trial*. In almost every Hebbel tragedy or comedy a central character challenges either (a) supernatural power(s) or his fellow man to give him a sign, confirming or denying the desirability of a planned course of action. The hero demands an omen from his god or he puts his fellow man to the test. If the desired sign fails to appear, this too is often understood as an answer; whether a particular character participates in or refrains from some venture can depend upon the absence of an omen. A variation of the motif occurs when the protagonist himself is put to the test: he must be condemned or exonerated at the conclusion of some ordeal.

As a rule the challenge and trial turn out to be major efforts of the unenlightened at solving a *mystery*. To Hebbel's protagonist both the gods and his fellow man are strangers. Desiring some insight into their true nature, he devises each test in the hope that he will be able to reach some ultimately valid conclusions. But his presuppositions and intuition invariably prove to be deceptions. At the completion of the ordeal he has not solved the riddle. The recurring attempts to penetrate the inscrutable mystery occur at the beginning, in the middle and near the conclusion of almost every Hebbel drama. The riddle motivates the characters and assures coherence in the tragedies and comedies.

Just as the individual "trials" and "challenges" help a main character confirm or reject particular notions, the *dream* provides the starting point for personal action. During the nocturnal vision the course of future events is shown *in nuce*. In many instances the central figure imagines that the actions he carried out in a given dream will provide the key to the mystery he is faced with in the conscious world. Things do not always turn out as he imagined they would; ironic twists occur frequently and often the character does not see that the dream somehow reflected his own fate. For the most part, however, the essential happenings of the past are co-ordinated and the future foreshadowed in dreams. *Trial*, *mystery*, and *dream* are thus the key structural elements in Hebbel's dramatic technique, recurring repeatedly at significant points in each play. It is noteworthy, moreover, that the great dramatist first came upon these thematic units while working in the *epic* genre; as will be shown later, he first utilized them in his prose fiction and subsequently recast them for use on the stage. By integrating these fictional patterns into the tectonic structure of the German classical theater, he added a new dimension to the dramatic form. For this reason, his "Novellen" represent an important and very much neglected phase of his literary career.

The function of these three components may be demonstrated in connection with every drama. The first tragedy, *Judith* (1841), presents a problem since it was not constructed symmetrically as were the later plays. The three components can be distinguished, but they do not appear in central positions. It may be argued, however, that Hebbel was greatly dissatisfied with this "Jugendwerk" and intended in later life to revise it.[15] In his *Nachlaß* fifteen handwritten notes from the years 1849-1851 were attached to a printed *Judith* manuscript.[16] If one incorporates these changes into the text, the systematic organization of the structural units becomes discernible.

The symmetrical integration of these components, which would have been emphasized in the remodeling of *Judith*, became more important to Hebbel during the creation of his second tragedy, *Genoveva* (1843). In addition, trial and mystery are developed along certain lines which are particularly significant in terms of later application. In the course of the drama a complete secularization of these motifs takes place: the situation, determining the confrontation between man and God (as reflected in *Judith*), is gradually transferred to interpersonal relationships. In later plays Hebbel employed the motifs primarily in their secularized form. For this reason we shall examine *Genoveva* more closely. Even if it is not one of his best tragedies, it demonstrates clearly — often in the unsophisticated assimilation of the motifs — the underlying scheme of Hebbel's dramatic artistry.

The motif of the *challenge* emerges most clearly in *Genoveva*. After Golo has heard the farewell conversation between Siegfried and Genoveva, he regards his lord as unworthy of Genoveva's love. Golo alone shall have her favors! Recognizing full well the sinful implications of his resolution, Golo decides to undergo a trial by ordeal which shall determine the course of action: God shall settle whether he may claim Genoveva or not. A group of jackdaws have made their nest in a high tower of the castle, and disturb the sleep of the entire retinue with their ceaseless chatter. Golo climbs the tower in order to drive them away. During this dangerous venture, he calls upon God not to protect him, but to cast him into the abyss:

> .... Du aber Gott, beschirm mich nicht!
> Ich fürcht' mich selbst, drum wend' ich mich an Dich!
> Brech' ich nicht Hals und Bein zu dieser Stund',
> So leg' ich's aus: ich soll ein Schurke sein. (W. I, 107)

When Golo returns unscathed from the would-be trial, he believes he is justified in his evil pursuit. He feels he has placed himself before the highest court, now the villain in him may ripen (W. I, 110). A supernatural sign would have to appear before he will give up his plan. He thinks that he can force a physical solution to his emotional dilemma. Since no sign appears, he considers his resolve, which runs counter to his duty, as a proper course of action.

What has actually taken place here in the metaphysical context? There are sharply divergent opinions on this question. Klaus Ziegler claimed that this episode proves his "nihilism theory"; accordingly, Golo has constructed here "ein Ethos der Sündhaftigkeit" (p. 51). Basing his interpretation on Ziegler's findings, Benno von Wiese has placed the tragedy in the final phase of his study which postulates a literary development beginning with "Theodizee" and ending with "Nihilismus" (pp. 581-589). Modifying Ziegler's contention, Wilhelm Emrich maintains that various features of the composition illustrate Hebbel's anticipation and containment of nihilism.[17] Attacking Ziegler, Wolfgang Witkowski recently refuted his argument point by point (*HNS*, pp. 185-207). Despite numerous efforts[18] to reconstruct the "underlying thought" in this connection, the trial — at least as far as Golo is concerned — does not derive from any systematic "Weltanschauung"; he challenges the supreme magistrate "im Vorgefühl des Ungeheuersten" (W. I, 110). Golo's action is predicated upon premonition, intuition, emotion and pathos, not on any rational system.[19]

Genoveva also sees a divine omen in Golo's successful completion of the undertaking. It is the challenge itself she regards as sacrilege:

> Wenn Gott den Frevelmut des Jünglings schützt,
> So ist's ein Zeichen, daß er schon den Tag
> Im Auge hat, wo er des Mannes bedarf. (W. I, 119)

She does not recognize that the "Turmprobe" has decided her fate as well as Golo's. She declares with some confidence: "Leicht habt Ihr mich, Gott habt Ihr schwer gekränkt" (W. I, 117). What takes place here in the context of the silent relationship between God and the individual is transferred gradually to the relationships between characters. Having failed to elicit a response from God, Golo seeks to tempt Genoveva: "Da ich vor Gottes Thron / Nicht treten kann, so wend' ich mich an Euch" (W. I, 155). When she finally rejects his advances, he challenges her in another way: if she will but hand him a goblet containing poisoned wine, he will give her a letter in which he has confessed to perpetrating a deception; this confession will free her child and exonerate Genoveva. Yet even here the heroine refuses the challenge, exclaiming only: "Führ mich nicht in Versuchung, Herr mein Gott!" (W. I, 243). She passes the test when she pours the wine onto the floor.

Although Golo commits an outrageous crime against Genoveva, she is not the only person he puts to the test. As a child he once broke loose from his nurse and jumped in the Rhine, calling out to her: "Bin ich wirklich Dir so wert / Wie Du mir sagst, so zeig's!" (W. I, 119). Here too he attempted to bring about a physical solution to an emotional problem. He exerts himself repeatedly in an effort to transpose premonitions and desires into a physical context. The unfortunate entanglements, the feelings of guilt and the tragic conclusion are produced by those characters who carry out intuitively perceived, instinctual desires. Moreover, the test-motif is reflected even in the smallest details. Margaretha gives impetus to the temptation of Genoveva with the following words: "Doch versucht sie erst / Und seht, ob sie's verdient. Das tut Gott selbst" (W. I, 167). As in the first act, Golo — completely disoriented by his evil intention — challenges fate once again in the fourth act: he throws himself upon the antlers of a wounded, charging stag (W. I, 193). The initial action, the middle and the conclusion of the play are symmetrically balanced by the fifth act when Hans and Balthasar imagine that they have received a sign from heaven. Hans, who is about to execute the innocent Genoveva, stops abruptly: "Die Sonne blickt die Erde zornig an / Als sähe sie, was sie nicht sehen mag." At this point, Balthasar exclaims: "Schwarzrot! So lang ich das seh', mord' ich nicht!" (W. I, 252). The supreme power has given an omen; man desists from his plan of action. In the final scenes Balthasar puts Golo to the test: "Ich prüf' ihn. / Bring' ich's heraus, so nutz' ich's, wie ich kann" (W. I, 264). What he discovers at the completion of this test, gradually clears up the mystery. Balthasar's premonition proves correct; characteristically for Hebbel, his new knowledge brings him not only the solution he sought, but death as well.

At central points in the *Genoveva* tragedy the main characters are confronted by a mystery. They are successful in ascertaining only pieces of the concealed puzzle. Genoveva misjudges Golo from the outset and is unable to guard against him because she does not understand herself. In the first act she says: "Als ein Geheimnis, kaum mir selbst bekannt, / Durch's Leben tragen, wollte ich mein Herz!" (W. I, 95). Her essential character remains a total mystery to Golo, who is overwhelmed by his own desire. He is unable to control his "love" because of its mysterious nature: "Dir widerstehen, heißt den Kampf mit Gott / Und mit dem Weltgeheimnis einzugeh'n" (W. I, 99). In front of her picture he wants to become a painter and lose himself: "in's Geheimnis ew'ger Schönheit" (W. I, 159). Concealment of this kind produces the challenge and test. Even Siegfried sees himself before a dark mystery: the serious indictment against his wife is incomprehensible to him. Desperate to establish certainty of any kind, he employs a crystal ball, claiming: "Der schweigende Kristall, vor dem ich nicht erröten darf, soll mir's vertrauen" (W. I, 210). Hence it can be shown that all the main characters stand before a riddle — Genoveva in the first act, Golo in the third, Siegfried in the fourth. In the concluding act the mystery motif is varied in a number of ways: the secondary characters reveal aspects of their lives they have tried to keep secret. Hans and Balthasar relate confidential matters in the first scene. Through the letter of confession Golo betrays his secret. In the sixth scene the pattern of concealment takes on its original religious connotation: when Klaus kills Hans, Genoveva indicates that God in his infinite mercy has given a mysterious sign; she asks, therefore: "Ewiger Gott, bist Du's?" (W. I, 259). Golo assures himself at the end of the play that he will never understand the eternal mysteries. He comes to the following conclusion: "Gott tat mir recht und Gott allein hat recht! ... Du hast / Mich mit mir selbst bekannt gemacht, ich weiß / Jetzt wer ich bin ..." (W. I, 262). Even in the *Nachspiel* the riddle reappears as a motivating force in the dramatic action.[20] The thematic concept of hidden mystery is clearly a conjunctival device despite the complex range of its variations. The beginning, middle, end and even the epilogue of the *Genoveva* tragedy are connected to each other via this motif. The recurring challenges and tests are hopeless attempts of certain characters to ascertain the mysterious. But the real world offers little insight into these riddles. Only when reality is temporarily suspended does the starting point for personal action seem to reveal itself. An interval of this kind occurs during sleep: Hebbel's heroes see their own destinies in the oracular dream. Upon awakening, they believe that the nocturnal vision has disclosed what should be done; ironically, however, the course of action suggested and subsequently embarked upon only aggravates an already precarious situation, making the impending tragedy inescapable.

In *Genoveva* — in contrast to most of Hebbel's plays — the fate of a central figure is not revealed in a nocturnal vision. Nevertheless, Genoveva does speak of an "edles Bild" that is often transfigured before her eyes (W. I, 122). She describes the dreamlike vision of her sister's death and in so doing suggests the course of her own life. A knight pursued her sister "mit ungestümen Werben"; she fled in terror and committed suicide because: "Sie wollte nur den Weg / Nicht wandeln, welcher sie mit Schmach bedroht" (W. I, 122). Her statements are indicative of the future situations in the play itself — under parallel conditions Genoveva will choose a similar course of action. The evil Margaretha has two dreams which show the direction of the tragedy. In the third act she says to Genoveva:

> Hochedle Gräfin! Wenn Ihr mich nicht ganz
> Geblendet seht von Eurer Schönheit Licht,
> So ist's, weil ich im Traum Euch schon erblickt,
> Doch eine goldne Krone trugt Ihr da. (W. I, 132)

Her words actually transcend the time boundaries of the depicted poetic reality since Genoveva's future canonization is anticipated in this description. In the fourth act Margaretha recounts the main features of another dream shortly before Siegfried arrives at her home. She summarizes her sinister past, particularly the murder of her illegitimate child, anticipating the future: "Kind, willst Du bitten für das and're Kind? / Da bittest Du umsonst!" (W. I, 211). In the dream past events are telescoped and co-ordinated with the future on a microcosmic scale. At the beginning of the fourth act Golo tells his nurse about his terrifying dream: he saw Genoveva, blood pouring from open wounds, first standing in front of him and then moving toward him in a gesture of sympathy. Even though he has caused her untold suffering, he recognizes for the first time here before the dream figure how much he has debased and destroyed himself: "Aus allen Adern blutete ich selbst" (W. I, 189). In this way his own destiny is predicted both in a spiritual and a physical sense. In the *Anhang* (*Genoveva-Brocken*) Hebbel declares: "Der Traum ist die Pforte des Werdenden zum Seienden" (W. I, 405). With this he indicates the dream's twofold function of looking into the past and revealing the future. On 26 February 1842 he noted in his diary:

> — Man öffnet
> Die Augen, schließt sie wieder und nimmt das,
> Was man erblickt, hinüber in den Traum.
> Das ist das Leben!   (Tgb. 2495)

A short time earlier he had written: "Das Leben ist ein Traum, der sich selbst bezweifelt" (Tgb. 2490). In this conceptual framework, the dream and life itself blend together forming a unity of human experience. Thus it can be demonstrated that the idea of mystery supplies the motivation for the dramatic action; the challenge, i.e., test, represents the desperate attempt of the individual to solve the riddle he is confronted with; and the dream reveals the course of ensuing events often via a reference to the past. Hebbel's *Genoveva* is not derived exclusively, yet to a very large extent, from the combination of these structure-producing elements.

The dream is, of course, not all unusual in the drama. Many dramatic artists write first and last scenes which take place in a "poetic reality," whereas the play itself transpires in a different context. Goethe uses the dream at the end of *Egmont* to transcend the concrete events depicted in the play and to forecast the future.[21] A year before the completion of *Genoveva* (published two years later), the book edition of Grillparzer's *Der Traum ein Leben* (1834, published 1840) appeared; here the hunter Rustan experiences a dream, revealing the extent to which his desire for glory and adventure can destroy him. Hebbel, by contrast, does not utilize the dream in order to create a second plateau of dramatic reality. He attempts no transition into the dream world and never allows a dream figure to appear on the stage. The function of one character describing his dream to another lies in co-ordinating the significant events in a given speaker's past and foreshadowing the direction the entanglement will take. Goethe developed a similar stylistic device, but made use of it primarily in the novel,[22] not in the drama. In *Die Leiden des jungen Werthers*, for example, Werther tells his friend Albert the story of a young girl who was so in love with a suitor that when he left her, she took her own life. "Das ist die Geschichte so manches Menschen," concludes Werther, thereby foreshadowing his own tragic fate. Hebbel's dream configuration in the drama is similar to Goethe's technique of the inserted anecdote in the novel, in as much as both represent attempts at foreshadowing future events on a smaller scale. As an epic device this artistic procedure has a long tradition; Hebbel, however, was able to integrate the dream as a seemingly independent little story into the structure of the closed dramatic form. The nocturnal vision makes possible a coalescence of individual motifs and, at the same time, an expansion of the foreground into a larger frame of reference.

This is not to suggest that earlier German playwrights had avoided utilizing the dream to foreshadow the future. Baroque dramatists in particular created many dream scenes and dreamlike visions in order to reflect in a smaller world the contours of coming events. The terrifying dream experienced by *Leo Armenius* in the third "Abhandlung" of Gryphius' play (1650) and Nero's nightmare in the fourth "Abhandlung" of Lohenstein's *Agrippina* (1665) are well-known examples. Hebbel's technique is very different. The Baroque playwrights brought the dream world and the dream figure onto the stage to foreshadow either future historical events relating to the action or the direction the play would take. Despite the forewarnings contained in the dream the protagonist often continues on his tragic course, presenting himself as an exemplary figure. Unlike the steadfast hero of the Baroque *exemplum*, Hebbel's character must first interpret his nocturnal vision which, like the oracle of antiquity, frequently gives ambiguous predictions. Especially in the later tragedies, the protagonist interprets the dream as a revelation of a beneficial course of action. He soon discovers that he has succeeded only in deepening his tragic entanglement; the action he has initiated has trapped him. In his diary Hebbel noted: "Die Alten wollten aus dem Traum weissagen, was dem Menschen geschehen würde. Das war verkehrt. Weit eher läßt sich aus dem Traum weissagen, was er *tun* wird" (Tgb. 4702). The dream as an ambiguous oracle, often suggesting a course of action detrimental to the hero, is Hebbel's innovation. A technique of this kind had rarely been used in German stage productions and probably had never been seen before in the classical theater.

The close ties between the dream device in Hebbel's plays and the use of dreams in his prose fiction has been outlined by Herbert Schueler. Schueler emphasized Golo's "psychological dream"[23] and demonstrated the extent to which the characters of the "Erzählungen" experience similar visions during sleep. The links between Hebbel's prose creations and his stage productions are even stronger, however: the hero in his stories often desires to penetrate the mysteries of the world which seem to unfold before him in his dreams; in order to gain a deeper insight, he often puts his fellow man to the test. Fourteen of the short stories preserved were written by Hebbel in the decade 1830-1840. Only *Der Rubin* (1843), *Herr Haidvogel und seine Familie* (1848), *Die Kuh* (1849) and the novel fragment *Ein Leiden unserer Zeit* (1851) were created after the completion of *Genoveva*. The poet himself regarded these attempts at prose fiction as his "Jugendwerk." In the preface to the edition of 1844 he calls them "ein zurückgelegtes Stadium meiner schriftstellerischen Entwicklung" (W. VIII, 420); in a letter to Gutzkow dated 15 November 1857 he describes the stories as "die ersten schüchternen Versuche eines sich selbst noch nicht verstehenden Talents" (Br. VI, 80). Nevertheless, these creations contain the essential structural characteristics which will be found later in his great tragedies and comedies. Certain "Erzählungen" are obviously precursors of his dramas: the character of *Barbier Zitterlein* (1836) shows a marked resemblence to Meister Anton of *Maria Magdalena*. *Der Rubin* is the earlier epic counterpart to the "Märchenspiel" of the same title.

"Nachtgemälde," the subtitle of Hebbel's first story, *Holion* (1830), hints that the experiences of the central character, Holion take place in a dream. The narrative also contains the motifs of challenge and riddle, although they are still in an early stage of artistic development. Holion stands before the thick darkness which encompasses the earth. The spirit challenges him three times, threatening to destroy him. But, as the conclusion reveals, Holion has had these experiences only in a dream. It is precisely this physical projection into another dimension which Hebbel later shunned when writing his masterpieces for the stage. The trial and the riddle appear again in the *Räuberbraut* (1833).[24] As if he had never written these early stories, Hebbel calls *Barbier Zitterlein* (1836) his first prose creation.[25] The element of mystery appears initially in the report of Herrn Tobias concerning "das seltsame Leben des Barbiers" (W. VIII, 39 f.). With the arrival of the gypsy woman the thematic concept is expanded: she understands "das geheimnisvolle Spiel der Karten" (W. VIII, 49) and forecasts Zitterlein's "grauenhaftes Schicksal." During the laying of the cards, the barber believes he is permitted "einen tiefen Blick...ins innerste Getriebe des Lebens" (W. VIII, 58). The "geheimnisvolle Schrift" (W. VIII, 51) enables the gypsy to see Zitterlein's daughter as a bride. But he would rather see her dead than married, particularly to Leonhard (W. VIII, 52). The image of his daughter appears to him nightly in mortifying dreams. He sees her with Leonhard, bride and bridegroom, on the way to church and envisions the two of them looking down at him mockingly. In one dream, for example, he beholds the following scene:

> ...die Orgel, der Chorgesang verstummte, der Prediger trat vor den Altar, er wollte die Einsegnungsworte sprechen. Da sprang er selbst, Zitterlein, mit einem gräßlichen Fluch auf die Braut zu, und zog ein Messer, um sie zu ermorden; doch, er hatte das Messer ungeschickt gezogen und das Heft gegen seine Tochter gekehrt, die Klinge aber in der Hand gehalten; die Tochter war unbeschädigt geblieben, sich selbst hatte er in den Finger geschnitten. (W. VIII, 54 f.)

This dream can be interpreted in a number of ways: Schueler was interested in the psychological implications; Ingrid Kreuzer regarded the vision as the respite of the deranged individual "im Stadium der Unzurechnungsfähigkeit" (*HNS*, p. 156). The technical function remains unmistakable nonetheless — an ironic prognosis of the future is contained in the dream: Leonhard and Agathe will soon marry, yet remain "unbeschädigt"; Zitterlein's ensuing challenge will cost him his sanity, if not his life.

In *Die beiden Vagabunden* (1837, printed 1847) Hans and Jürgen claim to be "einem Geheimnis auf der Spur" (W. VIII, 119). They are intent on deriving the maximum benefit from Meister Jakob's challenge to make gold out of worthless material. As a result of their chicanery, Hans begins to have nightmares. He dreams of monsters and demons which break all his bones (W. VIII, 131). The three dreams of Jakob's mother are especially important since they contain hints concerning the direction the story will take (W. VIII, 136). As she foresees in her dreams, Meister Jakob is indeed a "Gerstenkorn," but for Hans and Jürgen he becomes "eine Perle." The strange dream experienced by *Matteo* (W. VIII, 202) at the beginning of the story of the same name is particularly important with regard to his future. In the course of the narrative, he does actually lose something and is really not sure what he has lost. An overwhelming fear will seize him, just as in the dream, whenever he hurries through the streets of the city at night. A yearning for the woman he loves will follow him everywhere. Furthermore, he regards the sickness from which he recovers as "eine bestandene harte Prüfung" (W. VIII, 203). He too believes he is confronted by an impenetrable mystery: "Der unergründliche Widerspruch des Lebens packte ihn, wie mit Krallen..." (W. VIII, 209). Almost every "Erzählung" contains these three thematic-structural units. They are the essential creative motifs in Hebbel's works, representing the archetypal human situations in the poet's complex thought process.

The prose narratives themselves are seldom original works: they were influenced to a very great extent by the fiction of the day.²⁶ This helps to explain why the three structural units are not as conspicuous in his prose as in his dramas of the following decade. In connection with *Holion*, R. M. Werner pointed out the similarities with Jean Paul's "sentimentale Aufsätze."²⁷ The title is also reminiscent of the short stories of Chr. Kuffner.²⁸ Hebbel modeled his fiction after the works of E. T. A. Hoffmann,²⁹ Ludwig Uhland,³⁰ and Heinrich von Kleist.³¹ But popular contemporary writers exerted an even greater influence: Werner demonstrates that Hebbel incorporated whole passages from the works of the extremely popular writer, C. W. Contessa, into *Barbier Zitterlein* (W. VIII, p. XVIII). Many stories reveal Hebbel's attraction to the "Räuberromantik" — particularly revealed in such titles as: *Die Räuberbraut, Mirandola* and *Eine Nacht im Jägerhaus*. Parallels have been drawn with Zschokke's *Aballino, der große Bandit* (1794), Vulpius' *Rinaldo Rinaldini* (1798) and Hoffmann's *Nachtstück: Ignaz Denner* (1817).³² Although we cannot be certain what Hebbel read as a youth, the readily discernible similarities illustrate Hebbel's ability to utilize and rework the material he found in light reading and magazine literature. The challenge or trial, mystery or riddle, and the dream are essential components in fiction of this kind, particularly in the trivial novel of the day,³³ which appealed to the phantasy of the reader by describing mysterious surroundings and strange, supernatural events. Yet even in the great *Entwicklungsroman* of the period a main character is often put to the test. In the narrative fiction of Arnim, Keller, Stifter, and, later, Freytag and Raabe the protagonist is called upon to come to terms with cultural and social mysteries. A secret society or a rich patron may wish to test him. In many instances, the hero will challenge the invisible powers that prevail in his universe, seeking to obtain some sign from them. Hebbel was very familiar with this literature; he took up the basic situations of fiction at this time and fashioned them into his own dramatic form.

But are *challenge* and *mystery* "purely" epic concepts? Are they not, like the dream, found in plays prior to those of Hebbel? Certainly there are numerous earlier examples. The herald's words in the twentieth scene of Kleist's *Penthesilea*, for example, represent an unmistakable challenge.³⁴ Penthesilea is confronted by the mystery of her growing attraction to Achilles. The Kurfürst puts his "son" to the test in *Prinz Friedrich von Homburg* by forcing the prince to decide his own fate. When the officer demands his sword, Homburg is faced with the bewildering mystery expressed in his questions: "Träum' ich? Wach' ich? Leb' ich? Bin ich bei Sinnen?"³⁵ Thus challenge and mystery are not unknown to earlier playwrights. Kleist is typical of dramatists before Hebbel who employed one or more of these motifs at some specific point in the dramatic action. Hebbel's technique differs in that he uses them repeatedly in the same play.

There is an interaction between dramatic and narrative production in the case of Kleist similar to that already observed in the works of Hebbel. Emil Staiger remarked that Kleist's *Novellen* are essentially dramatic creations in which the action did not attain "die nötige Schaubarkeit."[36] Hebbel's attempts in each genre are separated by as much as a decade; Kleist's epic and dramatic works were written almost simultaneously. *Penthesilea* appeared in 1808; *Prinz Friedrich von Homburg* (pub. 1821) was written between 1809 and 1811; the *Erzählungen* were collected and published 1810/11. The motifs of challenge and mystery are found in the narratives too: *Michael Kohlhaas* (begun 1804) eventually challenges an entire state; *Die Marquise von O...* (1808) is faced with the riddle of her mysterious pregnancy. As we have seen, Hebbel was attracted *first* to Kleist's stories which he used as models for his own fiction. Here as well as in other epic productions of the time he discovered these basic concepts. As fictional patterns the challenge and the mystery underwent a development in contemporary narratives not found in earlier dramas.

In fictional prose the challenge and the mystery became significant structural devices. The story writer employed them frequently at central points in the plot in order to sustain the action and intensify the suspense. When Hebbel integrated these patterns into the structure of his *Genoveva*, he placed them at focal points in the dramatic action. The characters are confronted repeatedly by a mystery; their challenges and tests are periodic attempts to solve the riddle. On the one hand, as we have seen, the skillful integration of these components supply the drama with symmetry and coherence. On the other hand, the recurrence of the same basic thematic units tend to divide the action into episodes. In *Genoveva*, Hebbel does not constrict the action; he does not pass judgement on a character or an idea; he does not "prove" anything. We are not dealing — to borrow a word from Emil Staiger — with the question: "Worumwillen?"[37] Instead we ask: what will Golo do next? The dramatist simply demonstrates. The principle at work in *Genoveva* is *addition*. Any tension which develops is a result of "Überbieten". Hebbel intensifies the action by having Golo outdo his previous attempts at seducing Siegfried's defenseless wife. "Addition," "Überbieten" and "das Episodische" are characteristics of the epic, not the dramatic genre.[38]

Staiger's illuminating discussion helps to emphasize the essential "epic" nature of the *Genoveva* tragedy in yet another way. In his description of "Dramatischer Stil," Staiger explains: "der Held eines Dramas [soll] tätig sein...; ein leidender Held sei undramatisch" (p. 185). Genoveva is a suffering heroine in the strictest sense. She does little or nothing to bring about the tragic conclusion. For this reason, interest in the play has invariably shifted from her fate to Golo's diabolical personality. But he too is a "static" figure. He undergoes no basic transition. At the outset he formulates a monstrous plan and continues to carry out a premeditated crime despite occasional setbacks. The pangs of remorse do not suffice to change him. Thus his "story" comprises a series of episodes in which he goes ever further in an attempt to fulfill one passionate desire. The story ends when Golo realizes that he has failed.

We see then that challenge and mystery belong to the repertoire of dramatic motifs konwn to earlier playwrights. However, Hebbel utilizes them as structural components in keeping with epic practices common in contemporary narrative fiction. They are not the only "epic" features of the drama; later we shall examine others. By integrating these fictional patterns into a dramatic structure, Hebbel created an "episodic" play, displaying characteristics felt by earlier dramatists to belong properly to the epic sphere. In many respects, Schiller's description of the epic writer in his letter to Goethe (25 April 1797) characterizes Hebbel's efforts with regard to *Genoveva*: "Da er [der Epiker] uns nicht so auf das Ende zutreibt wie dieser [der Dramatiker], so rücken Anfang und Ende in ihrer Dignität und Bedeutung weit näher aneinander, und nicht, weil sie zu etwas führt, sondern weil sie selber etwas ist, muß die Exposition uns interessieren."

To be sure, the three structural units outlined here are not the only elements occupying important positions in Hebbel's plays. A thorough account would have to mention a number of others. The use of "topoi" is especially widespread in his works. He is notably fond of the topos: "die verkehrte Welt."[39] There is also a significant arsenal of rhetorical devices: by means of aposiopesis, anacoluthon and hyperbole, he illustrates the confusion, insecurity and irrationality of his characters. His imagery, which he had already developed to a sophisticated level in his stories, plays an unusual role in his dramas. Heinrich Dieters examined Hebbel's metaphors, dividing them into five categories.[40] But he did not observe that certain images recur frequently, while undergoing a change in meaning. In *Genoveva,* for example, Hebbel repeatedly employed the image of the eye; at least twenty-six times in the play a character makes reference to the visual organ. In the course of the tragedy, moreover, the signification of the metaphor becomes increasingly broader.

In the first act the eye is a body member completely in man's service, capable at most of reflecting the inner being or state of a given character (W. I, 98). By the second act, the eye exerts a degree of independence and begins to loosen itself from the body. Against Golo's will it perceives his desire and the impending ordeal he has planned for Genoveva. According to the stage direction, Golo is to grasp at his eyes, while formulating his sinister plan. He then exclaims: "Weg, Sündflut vor der Sünd'! Du kömmst zu früh!" (W. I, 115). Golo is irritated by his eye in the third act: "...die hellen Funken zieht / Mein Aug' aus Allem, was mich rings umgibt" (W. I, 153). In the fourth act the eye is used with a different connotation: Siegfrieds "inner eye" fails him (W. I, 216) as he is totally deceived. In this context the eye symbolizes the complete lack of empathy on Siegfried's part. A theological aspect is added to the metaphor when the spirit tells Margaretha about God's relationship to Genoveva: "Auf Genoveva schaut sein Auge jetzt / Herab und sieht die Andern alle nicht" (W. I, 227). By the fifth act the eye has lost its physical dependence. Balthasar says: "Man lös't wohl besser ihr die Augen aus" (W. I, 235). The eye is subsequently liberated from its dependence on the body, as is illustrated by its power to avenge —

Katharina flees in terror, screaming: "Wohin ich schau', / Da stiert es mich, als wär's mit Augen an!" (W. I, 249). At the end of the play, Golo's eyes are to be put out: "Die Augen hier, die viel zu viel auf sie / Und viel zu wenig auf den Herrn geschaut, / Sind auszustechen" (W. I, 272). In the course of the dramatic action the individual image evolves gradually to complete autonomy: that which at first served man at his command, detaches itself in stages from the main characters and begins to lead an independent metaphorical existence. The figurative significance of the eye image is emphasized by the paradox that as it mounts in intensity the characters in the play reveal more clearly their essential blindness. By the conclusion, a main figure has reached the deepest point of despair and tragic entanglement; at the same time, however, the metaphoric representation has reached the highest level of symbolic connotation.

By employing images in this way, the dramatist indicates that he is not concerned with the creation of a *single* tragic destiny but also with man's general condition. The symbolic language supplies new perspectives and points beyond the illusion created on the stage. The image which gradually becomes autonomous breaks throught the confines of the stage illusion, expanding the dramatic action to an archetypal situation. The tragedy of Golo, Genoveva and Siegfried thus becomes a universal human experience.

In his analysis of the *Genoveva* tragedy, Fritz Martini focuses attention on the inherent contradiction between the epic legend and the character tragedy centering around Golo created by Hebbel: "Ein romantischer Stoff, der, epischer Struktur, lyrisch getönt, mit wenig Handlung die Einfalt der christlichen Legende wiedergab, wurde von Hebbel zur metaphysischen und psychologischen Tragödie umgewandelt. Das konnte nicht gelingen."[41] Martini opened a new path of inquiry by touching upon a weakness in *Genoveva* which holds true for Hebbel's works in general: Hebbel preserves the basic features of the classical form, yet the integration of epic structural elements gives rise to an internal strain not found in tectonic plays of the preceding decades.

R. M. Werner analyzed Hebbel's statements concerning the essential characteristics of the different categories of endeavor in an effort to explain the dramatist's assertion that it is possible to unite dramatic and lyric creativity, but impossible to combine the dramatic and epic styles.[42] But Werner failed to recognize that in practice Hebbel never held rigidly to the strict norms of the various genres despite all his theorizing and commenting. Instead he strove throughout his productive career to rework the popular thematic concepts and structural elements found in the epic literature of his day for use on the stage. One of the first scholars to detect a blending of categories in Hebbel's plays was Karl S. Guthke. He was interested primarily in the dramatist's mixture of tragedy and comedy; yet in conjunction with his studies of the tragicomedy, Guthke emphasized Hebbel's "apriorische Formbedingung" and demonstrated that in practice the playwright failed to meet the requirements of the model.[43] To be sure, Guthke believed that in this regard the *Trauerspiel in Sizilien* (1851) was the exception rather than the rule in Hebbel's works.⁴⁴ Later, in a second essay concerning Hebbel and the tragi-comedy, Guthke described the disintegration of traditional dramatic forms and the degeneration of established genres in the nineteenth century; at this point, Hebbel and Dehmel: "...ergriffen nämlich das Wort für die Gattungsverschmelzung als eine neue Norm, für ein gemischtes Genre von eigener Formgesetzlichkeit, das sie als Tragikomödie bezeichnen."⁴⁵ But this "Gattungsverschmelzung" was not reserved, as Guthke surmised, for the tragi-comedy alone; on the contrary, it cleared the way for a new dimension of the theater which was to become a significant creative force on the German stage in the ensuing decades.

Earlier, in the eighteenth century, it was Lessing who had come to grips with the question of "mixed genres." In the 48th piece of the *Hamburgische Dramaturgie*, he wrote: "Was geht mich es an, ob so ein Stück des Euripides weder ganz Erzählung noch ganz Drama ist? Nennt es immerhin einen Zwitter; genug, daß mich dieser Zwitter mehr vergnügt, mehr erbaut, als die gesetzmäßigsten Geburten eurer correcten Racinen, oder wie sie sonst heißen. Weil der Maulesel weder Pferd noch Esel ist, ist er darum weniger eines von den nutzbarsten lasttragenden Thieren?"⁴⁶ Additional examples of the early dissatisfaction with the classical norms can be found in the exchange of letters between Goethe and Schiller.⁴⁷ Among Hebbel's contemporaries, Friedrich Theodor Vischer underscored the possibilities of synthesizing the epic and dramatic genres in his lectures on aesthetics: "Innerhalb der großen Zweige der Poesie ist die reichste Stoffquelle eröffnet in der epischen für die dramatische Gattung: der epische Stoff hat auf höherer Stufe genau noch das Unreife, von geistigen Willensbestimmungen Undurchdrungene, massenhaft Ausgebreitete, Sächliche für den dramatischen Dichter, was der Naturstoff für die Phantasie überhaupt hat; schon das griechische Drama ruht auf dem griechischen Epos, Shakespeares Quellen sind Erzählungen (sagenhafte Chroniken, Novellen)."⁴⁸ Hebbel's dramatic productions anticipated Vischer's aesthetic adjuration by at least a decade.⁴⁹ In this respect he had followed Shakespeare's example.⁵⁰ Additional impulses came by way of Richard Wagner and the German opera. The composer Rubenstein asked Hebbel to write librettos; he complimented Hebbel on his good use of innovations devised initially for the opera.⁵¹

To a certain extent Hebbel's successors carried the trend outlined here even further. It has been shown already that "Poetic Realism" with its analytical approach to milieu and man's psychic nature gravitated away from the norms of the classical theater toward a more narrative style in the dramatic genre.⁵² Otto Ludwig, for example, remarked as follows: "Die dramatischen Stoffe, die ich bebrüte, werden mir zu Romanstoffen, während jede Einzelheit in ihnen für eine dramatische Behandlung geeignet ist."⁵³ Ludwig's drama signifies the transition to the historical "Bildungstheater" of the literary epigones which dominated the German stage until the advent of naturalism, without making any substantial or particularly lasting contribution.⁵⁴ The essential difference between Hebbel and Ludwig[55] lies above all else in their respective relationships to stage illusion. On the one hand, Ludwig called for: "...nicht ein Stück Welt, sondern eine ganze, geschlossene, die alle ihre Bedingungen, alle ihre Folgen in sich selbst hat."[56] On the other hand, Hebbel's dream technique and symbolic language tended to broaden the individual story into a representation of man universally. Under the influence of Ludwig, playwrights returned to the utilization of a closed, neatly organized poetic illusion. Nevertheless, Hebbel had acted as a mediator between classical form and epic breadth for the nineteenth-century German theater by transforming certain elements from contemporary narrative prose into dramatic structures.

This "Stiltendenz" became increasingly more significant as a number of playwrights in addition to Hebbel and Ludwig experimented in their dramatic works with other fictional patterns. Emanuel Geibel returned to the origins of the epic form by assimilating source material from the Norse sagas for his stage production *Brunhild* (1857). In *Die Fabier* (1859), Gustav Freytag amassed such a wealth of detail that the play becomes an epic "Abbildungspanorama" in which exaggerated mannerisms, action and words replace suspense and coherence. Ferdinand von Saar turned to the chronicles and historical novels centering on Kaiser Heinrich IV as the basis for his dramatic episodes *Hildebrand* and *Heinrichs Tod* (1863/67). Ludwig Anzengruber adapted scene techniques from the Viennese "Volksstück," falling into an almost totally narrative style at various points in *Die Trutzige* (1878). Those playwrights in the last half of the nineteenth century preoccupied with psychological sketches and episodic portraitures of man and milieu gradually produced a more pronounced novelistic structure in the drama. In modern times the novel was rediscovered for the theater and brought onto the stage according to new maxims, theories and, in certain cases, widely heralded programs. Ulrich Weisstein has pointed out recently that Bertolt Brecht reworked Lion Feuchtwanger's contemporary novel, *Thomas Wendt* (Munich, 1920), for his play *Trommeln in der Nacht* (1922).[57] In at least this one way, the trend of the nineteenth century received new impetus in the twentieth.

For far too long Hebbel's anticipation of this stylistic innovation has been overlooked. For far too long Hebbel scholarship has honored Hebbel within the strict confines of a very narrow German theater tradition. Critics have been content to place the dramatist's stage productions at the end of a development, stretching from the German classical theater across Hegel's metaphysics and aesthetics to the degeneration of the tectonic form. But Hebbel does not simply close ranks with the "Form der deutschen Klassik."[58] We have seen a new direction in his artistic creativity which will not come into its own until the twentieth century. The assimilation of epic thematic concepts and stylistic devices into the structure of the drama will lead to a loosening of traditional norms and suppositions. Of course, certain earlier dramatists like Büchner and Grabbe will act as catalysts by breaking radically with the established rules of the genre.

By contrast, the uniqueness of Hebbel's attempts lies particularly in his strongly marked tectonic creative impulse. Yet from a literary historical perspective, he too mapped out the new direction by bringing fictional patterns which were extremely popular in the epic literature of the nineteenth century onto the German stage. Future generations would revive this practice in connection with themes borrowed from modern prose fiction. However, it was not until a half century after Hebbel's death that the integration of the epic produced new aesthetic principles and set new standards for the German theater.

NOTES

1 A detailed analysis of the Hebbel literature is not possible here. A survey of the present state of research is available in Anni Meetz, *Friedrich Hebbel*. 2nd ed. (Stuttgart: Sammlung Metzler, 1965); complete bibliographical references, pp. 5 f. Cf. the continuous research reports (especially by Heinz Stolte) in: *Hebbel Jahrbuch* [H-Jb.], ed. Detlef Cölln and Ludwig Koopmann (Heide/Holstein, 1951 ff.).
2 Characteristic of the older approach to the dramatist's works is the attempt to derive Hebbel's concept of art from a single metaphysical "Grundidee" As early as 1903, Arno Scheunert, *Der Pantragismus als System der Weltanschauung und Ästhetik Friedrich Hebbels* (Hamburg, 1903), p. 10, applied the label "Pantragismus" to the entire system of Hebbel's concept of life and art. See also: E. Lahnstein, *Das Problem der Tragik in Friedrich Hebbels Frühzeit* (Stuttgart, 1909); G. Hallman, *Das Problem der Individualität bei Friedrich Hebbel*, Beiträge zur Ästhetik, 16 (1921); Walter Schnyder, *Hebbel und Rötscher*, Hebbel-Forschungen, 10 (1923).
3 Cf. Friedrich Zinkernagel, *Die Grundlagen der Hebbelschen Tragödie* (Berlin, 1904), p. V: "Das Ziel der vorliegenden Untersuchung war es ... zu zeigen, wie das gesamte Hebbelsche Gedankensystem von einer alles befruchtenden Grundidee ausgehend ... sich organisch aus sich selbst entwickelt, um schließlich in einem neuen Dramentypus dem ganzen den krönenden Abschluß zu geben." See also: P. Sickel, *Friedrich Hebbels Welt- und Lebensanschauung*, Beiträge zur Ästhetik, 4 (1912); H. Glockner, "Hebbel und Hegel," *Preußische Jahrbücher* (1922); Elise Dosenheimer, *Das zentrale Problem in der Tragödie Friedrich Hebbels*. Buchreihe der *Deutschen Vierteljahrsschrift* [DVjS.], IV (1925).
4 Klaus Ziegler, *Mensch und Welt in der Tragödie Friedrich Hebbels* (Berlin, 1938).
5 *Ibid.*, p. 189.
6 The metaphysical aspects are emphasized also in the study by F. Koch, *Welt und Ich, das Grundproblem von Hebbels Theorie des Dramas* (Berlin, 1940). See also Ludwig Marcuse, "Der Hegelianer Friedrich Hebbel — gegen Hegel," *Monatshefte*, 39 (1947), 506 ff.; 40 (1948), 157 ff; also the following essays by Wolfgang Liepe, "Der Schlüssel zum Weltbild Hebbels: Gotthilf Heinrich Schubert," *Monatshefte*, 43 (1951), 117-132; "Hebbel zwischen G. H. Schubert und Ludwig Feuerbach," *DVjS*, 26 (1952), 447-477; "Hebbel und Schelling," *Deutsche Beiträge zur geistigen Überlieferung*, ed. Arnold Bergsträsser (Munich and Chicago, 1953); Helmut Kreuzer, *Die Tragödien Friedrich Hebbels* (Diss. Tübingen, 1956); also von Wiese, "Der Tragiker Friedrich Hebbel," *Zwischen Utopie und Wirklichkeit* (Düsseldorf, 1963), pp. 142-162.
7 Cf. Oskar Walzel, *Hebbel Probleme* (Leipzig, 1909). Walzel points out that Hebbel turned away from Hegel and metaphysics in the first years of his artistic creativity; by 1847 he had gone over to a completely empirical approach to reality and art

(pp. 61 ff.). In addition, Edna Purdie, *Friedrich Hebbel* (London, New York, Oxford University Press, 1932) severely criticized the one-sided metaphysical approach (see pp. 265 f.). For a more recent discussion see, Sten G. Flygt, *Friedrich Hebbel* (New York: Twayne, 1968).

[8] Cf., e.g., Benno von Wiese, *Die deutsche Tragödie von Lessing bis Hebbel*. 6th ed. (Hamburg, 1964), pp. 554-639.

[9] Peter Michelsen, "Das Paradoxe als Grundstruktur Hebbelschen Denkens," *Hebbel in Neuer Sicht* [*HNS*], ed. Helmut Kreuzer. 2nd ed. (Stuttgart, 1969), p. 81. Cf. also Peter Michelsen, *Friedrich Hebbels Tagebücher* (Diss. Göttingen, 1951); Wolfgang Liepe, "Hebbels Tagebuchpräambel und ihr Ideenhintergrund," *Gedenkschrift für F. J. Schneider*, ed. Karl Bischoff (Weimar, 1956), pp. 241-253.

[10] Joachim Müller, *Das Weltbild Friedrich Hebbels* (Halle, 1955), pp. 10 ff.

[11] Heinrich Dieters, *Stilistische Studien zu Hebbels Tragödien* (Diss. Berlin, 1911), p. 10.

[12] A. M. Wagner, *Das Drama Friedrich Hebbels*. Beiträge zur Ästhetik, 10 (1911).

[13] Marga Bührig, *Hebbels dramatischer Stil* (Diss. Zürich, 1940); reprinted in: *Wege zur Dichtung*, ed. Emil Ermatinger. Züricher Schriften zur Literaturwissenschaft, 35 (1940) pp. 60-64.

[14] The most important specimens of his approach (especially those of the 1950's) were collected in an anthology (*HNS*) by Helmut Kreuzer in 1963. These studies represent interpretations of the individual dramas.

[15] In an audience with the Bavarian king Maximilian II in March, 1850, he elucidated the idea and construction of this "Jugendwerk" and remarked that he had been occupied for some time with its complete revision. Cf. Emil Kuh, *Biographie Friedrich Hebbels* (Wien, 1877) II, 470.

[16] *Friedrich Hebbels Sämtliche Werke*, ed. R. M. Werner (Berlin: Bahr, 1901 ff.) I, 409-431. Volume and page number in the text refer to this edition; W. = Werke, Br. = Briefe; diary entries are indicated by their respective number next to Tgb. The orthography has been modernized throughout.

[17] Wilhelm Emrich, "Friedrich Hebbels Vorwegnahme und Überwindung des Nihilismus," *Akzente*, 9 (1964), 221-237.

[18] See also Kurt May, "Friedrich Hebbels opus metaphysicum 'Genoveva'," *Euphorion*, 45 (1950), 337-364.

[19] For a detailed analysis of intuitive sensitivity as the motivating force behind Hebbel's dramatic action, see Helga Frisch, *Symbolik und Tragik in Hebbels Dramen*. Abhandlungen zur Kunst-, Musik- und Literaturwissenschaft, 16 (Bonn: Bouvier Verlag, 1961).

[20] See also W. I. 281 f.: Schmerzensreich attempts to solve a riddle; the doe disappears at the right moment in a mysterious way; Siegfried keeps his longing for Genoveva secret, etc.

[21] O. Spieß, *Die dramatische Handlung in Goethes Clavigo, Egmont, und Iphigenie. Ein Beitrag zur Technik des Dramas* (Halle, 1918).

[22] R. Riemann, *Goethes Romantechnik* (Leipzig, 1902).

[23] Herbert Schueler, *Hebbel and the Dream* (New York, 1941), pp. 29-35.

[24] Mystery: "Gewißheit will ich haben, und wäre es auch die Gewißheit ewiger Vernichtung!" (W. VIII, 16); "... seine geheimnisvolle Lebensweise — ich wagte es nicht zu ahnen" (W. VIII, 32). Challenge: Gustav demands Emili's love (W. VIII, 17); Gustav is put to the test by the robbers (W. VIII, 27).

[25] Tgb. 87; in a letter to Bamberg dated May 7, 1847 Hebbel contradicts this entry, when he calls his narrative *Anna* his "dichterischen Erstling" (Br. IV, 35).

[26] R. Ebhardt, *Hebbel als Novellist* (Leipzig, 1916); A Tibal, *Hebbel, sa vie et ses oeuvres de 1813 à 1845* (Paris, 1911).

[27] *Euphorion*, 6 (1899), 804.

[28] Cf. "Helions mythisch-allegorische Miniatur-Erzählungen," Chr. Kuffner, *Sämtliche Erzählungen* (Wien, 1827) II, 235.
[29] Tgb. 2425.
[30] Cf. Kuh, *Biographie*, I, 229.
[31] See: "Über Theodor Körner und Heinrich von Kleist," W. IX, 31.
[32] Cf. W. VIII, p. XV.
[33] A. Killen, *Le Roman Terrifiant* (Paris, 1923).
[34] Heinrich von Kleist, *Sämtliche Werke*. dtv Gesamtausgabe, ed. Helmut Sembdner (München, 1964 ff.), II, 234.
[35] *Sämtliche Werke*, III, 248.
[36] Emil Staiger, *Grundbegriffe der Poetik* (Zürich, 1946), p. 155.
[37] *Ibid.*, pp. 182 ff.
[38] *Ibid.*, pp. 89-153.
[39] In the second act of *Genoveva* the Jew expresses his hopes in the following words: "Dann ist das Maß der Zeit erfüllt, dann dreht / Der Herr die Welt, daß unten oben wird..." (W. I, 125). Margaretha says in the fourth act: "Denn Bös' ist Gut und Gut ist Bös'" (W. I, 221). In the fifth act Golo exclaims, as Genoveva falls at his feet: "Die Welt / Ist umgekehrt. Sie knie't. Sie knie't vor mir!" (W. I, 242). In Hebbels prose fiction we find the topos also; see, e.g., *Herr Haidvogel und seine Familie* (W. VIII, 220).
[40] Dieters, *Stilistische Studien*: "Vergleiche aus der Natur," pp. 92-98; "Vergleiche aus der Tierwelt," pp. 99-105; "Gegenstände aus der Umgebung des Menschen," pp. 106-112; "Vergleiche aus dem Leben des Menschen," pp. 112-132; "Der episch eingefügte Vergleich," p. 133 et passim.
[41] Fritz Martini, *Deutsche Literatur im bürgerlichen Realismus*. 2nd ed. (Stuttgart: Metzler, 1964), p. 154.
[42] R. M. Werner, "Einleitung," W. VIII, p. XI f.
[43] Karl S. Guthke, "Hebbels 'Trauerspiel in Sizilien'. Zur Frage der Gattung," *H-Jb.* (1957), p. 92.
[44] *Ibid.*, p. 79.
[45] "Dehmel, Hebbel und die Struktur des Mischspiels," *Revue des Langues Vivantes*, 24 (1958), 487.
[46] *Lessings Sämtliche Werke*, ed. Karl Lachmann and Friedrich Muncker (Stuttgart, 1893) IX, 390.
[47] See especially Schiller's letters of 26 June and 1 December 1797 and Goethe's letter of 12 August of the same year.
[48] Friedrich Theodor Vischer, *Ästhetik oder Wissenschaft des Schönen* (Reutlingen und Leipzig, 1851) Part III, Paragraph I, pp. 164 f.
[49] Concerning Vischer's influence see Br. IV, 34; also Werner Zimmermann, *F. Th. Vischers Bedeutung für die zeitgenössische Dichtung* (Berlin, 1937).
[50] Cf. O. Brües, "Hebbel und Shakespeare," *Das Nationaltheater*, 4 (1931/32); Paul Graham, "Hebbel's Study of King Lear," *Smith College Studies in Modern Languages*, 21 (1939/1940) 81-90; Fritz Rau, "Hebbels Shakespeare-Bild," *Wirkendes Wort*, 2 (1951), 228-31.
[51] See Adolf Stübing, *Friedrich Hebbels Dramen als Opern* (Hanau, 1911), p. 4 ff.; also *Friedrich Hebbel in der Musik* (Berlin, 1913).
[52] Martini, *Deutsche Literatur*, p. 197.
[53] *Nachlaßschriften Otto Ludwigs*, ed. M. Heydrich (Leipzig, 1874) I, 338.
[54] Martini, p. 199.
[55] Cf. Friedrich Bruns, *Friedrich Hebbel und Otto Ludwig*. Hebbel-Forschungen, V (Berlin, 1913).

56 *Otto Ludwigs Gesammelte Schriften*, ed. A. Stern (Leipzig, 1891) V, 525.
57 Ulrich Weisstein, "From the Dramatic Novel to the Epic Theater," *Germanic Review*, 38 (1963), 257-271. Brecht's theory was influenced to a large extent by Feuchtwanger's novel. See the discussion by Johannes Jacobi of *Der aufhaltsame Aufstieg des Arturo Ui, Die Zeit* (1 July 1960), p. 6.
58 Ziegler, pp. 191 ff.

GERHART HAUPTMANN'S *VELAND*: TOTAL TRAGEDY AS FAILURE OF TRAGEDY

E. Allen McCormick

A reading of Hauptmann's version of Wayland the Smith is full of curious difficulties. One discerns several strands, sometimes quite distinct but often disconcertingly interwoven. It is as though the author's "proteische Wandelbarkeit"[1] had concentrated itself in this one play without achieving the unity evident even in such a puzzling work as *Und Pippa tanzt*. The main facts of *Veland*'s compositional history may be briefly noted: the work was written over a span of some twenty-five years, marked by no less than six periods of actual composition, of which the earliest is from about 1898 to 1901 and the last from 1921 to 1923.[2] Both premiere and publication were in 1925; a "trotzige Ehrenrettung" was attempted in 1941/42 in the Schillertheater in Berlin,[3] but since then one may fairly speak of a silence having descended upon *Veland*.

These two facts, the prolonged period of composition and the relative failure of the play in the eyes of audience and critics,[4] offer a suggestive starting point for our reading of *Veland*. Hauptmann's earliest interest in the legendary smith, aroused by his study of Simrock's heroic poem (1835) and the *Edda*, and presumably also by a knowledge of Wagner's dramatic sketch (1849), falls in the period of his fairytale plays (*Hanneles Himmelfahrt* [1894]; *Die versunkene Glocke* [1896]; *Und Pippa tanzt* [1905]); and the work was completed in the period that brought Hauptmann's immersion in classical antiquity, his interest in mythological subjects, and the publication of *Die Insel der großen Mutter* (1924), which a contemporary critic referred to as "Gott sei Dank zu griechisch, als daß das Volk sie verstehen würde,"[5] and *Till Eulenspiegel* (1928). However, the fairytale-mythical "Stoff" and Hauptmann's Hellenism fail to account fully either for the variety of tendencies and elements evident in the play or the generally problematic reaction to it. We cannot, for instance, dismiss outright the startling claim that *Veland* continues in some ways the naturalism of *Die Weber*. Such a view as Steinhauer's — "both plays depict the tragedy of modern industrial civilization," and "Veland and Harald symbolize the urban proletariat and modern capitalism respectively"[6] — should not, even in its absurdly extreme formulation, blind us to the social implications of *Veland* or even its socialistic overtones.[7] Other '-isms', notably symbolism and surrealism,[8] may claim their place in *Veland*'s complex heritage, as altogether such vital Hauptmann concerns as the "Urdrama", the dualism of world and individual, and the presence of agony and terror in all tragedy make this play a repository for the poet's countless turns of mind and heart in the quarter-century of its composition.

But extreme richness and variety are no explanation for *Veland*'s problematic position in Hauptmann's overall dramatic achievement. Rather we must look to the ideas that have been implanted in or inevitably arise from a sometimes reluctant mythological subject. Two of these appear central, the designation "Tragödie" as subtitle and the introduction of Christianity as an antipode of the pagan Germanic, with the obvious intent in the latter instance to create one of the essential and irreconcilable oppositions which make "Urdrama" possible. To Hauptmann tragedy and "Urdrama" were in fact synonymous, although neither term is ever fully defined. *Die Insel der großen Mutter* contains the much-quoted assertion, "Am Anfang der Dinge stehen zwei Kräfte. *Eine* Kraft gibt es nicht," (V, 882) and one might easily range Hauptmann's entire dramatic production along a scale of polarities that moves from socio-naturalistic 'determinism' to the cosmic forces of the later, symbolic plays. The common denominator is, of course, that basic conflict which Hauptmann defines as the cosmic process and which, as one critic rightly remarks, is a life principle and hence comes before all art.[9] The well-known line from the *Dom* fragment, "Urdrama. Die Brüder Satanael und Christus," (VII, 1011) gives the "zwei Kräfte" a specificity that permits us to include by analogy not only Lucifer, Dionysus, Heracles and Prometheus but also the demi-god Wieland.[10]

As "Urdrama," then, *Veland* is a play of basic opposites within a tragic framework and with an unsatisfactory (or at least puzzling) conclusion. Since this is in no wise exceptional for Hauptmann — other fairytale plays, we recall, offer fascinating but troublesome endings[11] — we are justified in directing our attention to the way in which art and theory, the play as tragedy and the concept of cosmic drama as pantragism, are combined.

Hauptmann's adherence to the broad 'facts' of the Wayland myth is remarkable to the extent that only one new character, the shepherd Ketill, is introduced, while Veland himself suffers for the same reasons (in terms of plot) as in the myth, takes his revenge in the same manner, and flees on self-made wings. The events of the play cover the second part of the saga, Veland's capture and mutilation and his revenge and escape. Beyond this, however, no further reference to mythological sources is useful,[12] since Hauptmann moves quite early in the play towards the 'interiorization' that marks modern tragedy. After an audience-directed conversation between two watchmen on Veland's island prison in which we learn the details of the smith's capture and the long years of suffering and servitude at the hands of King Harald, Veland appears and curses all creation — earth, sea, and sky. The two components of his rage,

> Und du, du, Erde, wüster Schauplatz einer Wut,
> die sich in Zeugung spaltet und Vernichtung! (III, 21)

are the first of many polarities; appropriately, they point ahead to the two aspects of his revenge and at the same time prepare the reader to accept additional paradoxical pairings, the "Urgegensätze" that move the play forward. "Weh! Wehe! Wer nimmt auf sich meine blut'ge Tat?" (III, 22), uttered right afterwards, complements the rage that will feed and make possible his vengeance; but "Weh und Wut" are of course contradictory and, moreover, reduce the space that should be left for free action.

Creation and destruction, or conscience ("Weh") and creature rage, suggest a modern and very human Veland. His captors see him differently, yet there are qualifications (usually unconscious) in their rich invective and more than a hint of what the king is later to call his own black bird of conscience. Veland's guards refer to him as "Untier," "Nachtgeburt," "gelähmtes Scheusal," "Höhlenbär," "Unhold"; and Harald's daughter Bödwild is even more imaginative: "aberwitz'ger Höllenhund," "unflät'ger Krüppel," "ruß'ges Scheusal," "wahnschaffenes Untier" — the list is virtually endless and her disgust as keen as her desire to see more and more of Veland's finely wrought ornaments. Yet Hauptmann himself suggests that Veland is something more than "Untier." His stage directions when Veland is first introduced speak of him not as "Untier" but as a mighty "menschliches Urtier"; and Harald's men constantly refer to the smith's human aspects, even as they seem to deny them Bui sees him as a beast, "das einem Menschen kaum von ferne ähnlich ist" (III, 15), while Boddi recognizes that he is "zum Tier entartet," the result of having been maimed by the king's men. More important, the king himself will have occasion later to stress the human side and thus restore by convenient overemphasis the balance of extremes that constitute Veland's character: "Bist du vertiert heute, warst du einmal doch ein Mensch und fühltest; deiner Menschheit drum erinnre dich" (III, 35).

Our early view of Veland is of a man reduced by suffering and the desire for vengeance — both are "unvernarbte Wunden" — to little more than a beast capable of inspiring disgust and awe. Against this essentially realistic background even his magical powers are open to question. Harald has come to Veland's island to plead for help in finding his missing sons; he is led by desperation and the possibility (not the certainty: "Denn zauberrunenkundig, sagt man, sollst du sein"; [III, 32]) that the smith has such powers. And Gunnar, Bödwild's betrothed, chooses to deny this "Scheusals Sehergabe" outright. Only the guards, presumably ignorant and superstitious, and Veland himself believe in his powers of prophecy."[13]

Veland's view of himself in the first act offers an enlargement and emendation of his captors' version. He tells Ketill that he is immortal but not his agony; moreover, he determines to create with Bödwild a god like himself, condemned to eternal suffering and debasement. This is modified during the confrontation with Harald —

> ich war noch mehr als nur ein Mensch, o Drost,
> und das Verhängnis hatte längst den Halbgott schon
> gestreift, als es dich endlich zum Gehilfen nahm (III, 35) —

and a short time later he alludes to his "gottentsprossenem Leib," now debased and made into a worm writhing in the mud. Veland is not to rise again from this condition until late in the final act, when the emptiness he feels after his revenge renders the issue of identity pointless:

> Tiergott, Gottier, genug der schwarzen Raserei!
> Halt inne, horche lautlos nun in dich hinein,
> ob nicht in dir ein neuer Tropfen sich gebiert. (III, 94)

However, a major part of the dramatic action depends largely on this duality of god and beast; which is to say, it is not the synthesis or resolution of polarity — we must reiterate our skeptical view of the way in which Hauptmann ends his symbolic plays — but the space between the two extremes, the diminishing area in which the protagonist's and antagonist's humanity are evident, which must create the conditions for tragedy.

In a special sense, then, the poles of god and beast, man and beast — and in fact all other dualisms in this play — are converted to the triad of god-man-beast. And so such an assertion as Fiedler's, "Immer unerbittlicher kristallisieren sich seine inneren Pole heraus: Gott-Tier! — Nach Velands Abgang gewinnt das Göttliche noch einmal volle Gewalt"[14] has at best a limited validity simply because there is scant possibility for tragedy in such a polarity and hence little promise of an artistically convincing extension into cosmic or total tragedy. We need no reminder that the "Überdimensionalität" of such figures as Lucifer and Prometheus rests ultimately on human proportions. The attempt to keep the character of Veland in proportion, i.e., credible by raising at various points in the action the specter of human suffering is thus the principal problem in Hauptmann's modernization of the Germanic legend. The bloodthirsty sorcerer, once part god and now less man than animal, breeding cruel and unnatural revenge, must be balanced against the wronged and tormented creature whose best instincts are at some level still intact. It is at once appropriate and confusing that "Brunst," Veland's ardor, becomes the central image accompanying the attempted balance. The term first occurs in Veland's explanation to Bödwild that ardor or passion's creative force:

> die Brunst der Wildnis schuf das Roggenfeld.
> Die Brunst des Meisters, sie allein, schmilzt rotes Gold
> und knetet es zu köstlichen Gebilden um.
> Die Brunst der Liebe nicht nur, auch des Hasses Brunst. III, 27)

This sort of passion sustains the will to vengeance but it also brings Veland precariously close to renouncing or forgetting that very vengeance. It is evident that Veland loves his hate and hates his love. This is true at least until the moment for revenge comes, but at that late point Veland has passed beyond consideration as a tragic figure, just as the Gott-Tier issue has by then become a matter of indifference.

Love and hate, when turned in to each other as they are in Veland, form an irrational equation, which is made all the more confusing by indications that "Liebesbrunst" is not only "Rachelust" (and certainly not mere love of art, "Goldschmiedekunst") but also love itself, in spite of Veland. Harald's twin sons touch the smith deeply. Ingi's "Ein armer Hinker bist du" and Ai's "Du bist ja kindgut, wie ein armes, krankes Tier" (III, 51) bring a groan, a "Wehe, oh!," and the command to help themselves to the treasures and leave the island. The agony passes, only to return with equal force at the beginning of Act III, when Bödwild's metamorphosis reveals a hardness against her parents that forces Veland to confess his sudden compassion for their distress. There is even greater danger of breakdown. The part of Veland's mind that makes choice still has its overwhelming task before it, but Bödwild's love is a narcotic — "wer Glück geschmeckt, wie ich... Er lebt, lebt ewig, Veland, schon im Augenblick" (III, 74) — that softens and weakens, raises the island prison to a "sel'ges Eiland," a paradise, and causes Veland to ask why his giant wings were ever woven.

There are other, lesser instances of Veland's susceptibility to love and pity, the sum of which heightens the dramatic tension but fails to leave the outcome in doubt. Nonetheless, some doubt remains as to the real causes of Veland's passionate state of mind, and here again one senses a quarrel between Hauptmann's overall intention and the natural course of the play. For whereas the first is clearly given with the legend and Hauptmann's concept of "Urdrama," the second constantly reminds us that revenge is not easily or gladly taken. Veland himself speaks of his "hartes Werk" (ironically it is in another context of anguish, when he is moved by Bödwild's childish innocence), and in a later soliloquy he unconsciously ranges himself against a power and destiny outside himself:

> Bin ich ein Gott, entrinn' ich doch mir selber nicht
> und nicht dem Schicksal, das zum Spielzeug mich erkor. (III, 74)

Clearly, Veland does not mean to say that he cannot escape his own responsibility for murder; he is attempting rather to pile up arguments *for* retribution. He is destined to take revenge by fate, whose plaything he is, and by what he himself is in his innermost. Yet the events of the play, which is to say Veland's "Brunst" as it manifests itself in love-hate, put this matter of answering to himself in a different light. The ambiguity is presumably unintentional; what Veland is at his center is not at all what he will achieve. Or to anticipate our conclusion, total tragedy can never be tragic.

Pushing the relationship between love and hate a step further, we may ask what the "heilandartige" figure of the shepherd Ketill means first of all to Veland, then to the way tragedy works or fails to work in the play. Critics are in agreement as to his chief function: he represents Christianity and, to a considerable degree, the voice of Gerhart Hauptmann. He is, moreover, a contrastive figure to the smith or a personification of certain emotions in Veland's breast.[15] More to the point than these (basically correct) equations is the simple fact that Ketill appears at two critical points in the play and but for minor variations utters the same words, raises the same objections, and offers the same consolation — until it becomes clear during his second appearance that Veland has placed himself finally beyond reach.

Beyond reach of what? If we reject as too simple the view that Ketill is the voice of Christianity, of God the "Allvater," then the answer is far from easy. Something of Veland's happy past, something of his stifled humanity, an alternate solution to the agony of hate and passion for revenge — all these are surely present in Ketill, and in combination they suggest precisely the condition that does not diminish man but makes him ripe for tragedy. The play itself allows us to resolve the question of Ketill's identity in a satisfactory way; for in the case of a character who appears twice and but briefly identity is really function. His first visit to Veland comes just after Ai and Ingi have pleaded vainly for their lives; Veland thrusts them into a cagelike room and thus seals their doom. He had nearly succumbed to their innocent pity, we recall, but was able to summon his hatred just in time. Ketill interrupts the smith's preparations but seems totally ineffectual in his pleas to bless those who curse you and love those who hate you. Veland's defiance and scorn are aimed less at the substance of what Ketill says than at the fact that it comes too late. Yet the shepherd did not come unbidden, despite the opening words of this and the second encounter in Act III:

> *K.:* Erlaube, daß ich dich besuche, fleiß'ger Schmied.
> *V.:* Du kamst zu mir und hast mich nie deshalb gefragt.
> *K.:* Ich kam, wenn du mich riefest aus gequälter Brust.
> *V.:* Hab' ich dich je gerufen, tat ich's ohne Laut,
> nie hörte jemand Veland um Erbarmen flehn. (III, 57-58)

The silent summons is not merely a matter of man's conscience crying out for succor; it is a command given to interrupt, is the breaking out of the quarrel between love and hate, memory of the past and lust for vengeance soon to be realized. It seems unnecessary to argue the source of such a command. Ketill's music is Veland-inspired; it comes from a flute which the smith himself carved long ago from a willow branch "auf dem Herware saß und sang / und strählte ihres schweren Haares goldenen Strom" (III, 60). The connection to Veland's lost wife points to an interweaving of three motifs, Ketill, the swan maiden Herwar, and music. Surprisingly, the last of these is the most important inasmuch as it comes closest to expressing Veland's basic condition. Positioned carefully at several points in the play, music appears to be a symbolic statement of the smith's inner reaction to a conscious stance or an external action. Legend has it — so we learn from the island guards early in the first act — that once a man hears the Veland-music he is henceforth consumed by yearning,

> gleich als hätte er
> am Tisch der Götter einmal nur gesessen
> und wäre nun gestürzt in Finsternis. (III, 24)

There is to be sure this aspect of the music: it rises from within Veland's smithy and falls sweetly from the air like the sounds of strings of golden harps, filling the world with sun, song of birds, greenness and blossomy fragrance. But mingled with these sounds is that of "klingend Erz," of pounding and rolls of thunder. Music sounds shortly after Veland expresses for the first time his anguish but then formulates (and thereby strengthens) his resolve to do murder; it is followed straightway by Bödwild's arrival on the island.

Veland-music is heard again in the scene with Harald's captured sons. Here it is preceded by the expression of anguish at Ai's and Ingi's compassion and a sudden reversal — Veland rips the bandages from his festering wounds and regains his resolve: Hauptmann describes him as "verändert" — and followed by the appearance of Ketill. The music, unearthly sounds of "Erz und Saitenspiel ... dazwischen Pochen wie von Hammerschlag" (III, 54), rises directly from Veland's brow and breast. He has withdrawn into a trancelike state, overcome by the memory of Herwar, who is kept as an active force in the play by the chorus of female voices singing brief stanzas from the *Volundarkvida*.

It is impossible (and fortunately unnecessary) to separate these motifs neatly, for only together do they assume meaning in the play. Herwar is Veland's happy past but also his great loss, Ketill (and to some extent Bödwild) the presentness of that past, the gentle balm that argues for love and yet remembers and accepts Veland's suffering ("denke mein in aller deiner Not," [III, 60], and music the deepest, most direct expression of Veland himself. Veland-music is, finally, all three together, and it too suffers the same polarity of love and hate, creates the conditions of Veland's suffering, and ultimately represents the amalgamation that makes tragedy possible. "Erz," the substance which the smith takes from the darkness of the earth, works into fabulous designs that cast reflected light and indeed live and glow only by the power of light, is that part of the "Brunst des Meisters" which fashions revenge. "Erz" is, finally, Veland's servitude, Bödwild-bait, the wealth upon which his enemy's power is built, and his means of liberation. "Saitenspiel" is of course the other kind of ardor, whose origin is in the light, the past, the former ecstasies of an unfettered god-man, and his constant anguished memory as well. Ketill's formulation is the polarity of lamb and wolf, but his plea that Veland be one and not the other is a refusal to see that he is both and that both are in fact interchangeable. Since Ketill functions only when and as Veland would have him do so, we cannot expect his opposition to prevail. Our answer to the question: what has Veland placed himself beyond reach of? — must therefore be — Veland himself, as defined by the images, motifs, and characters throughout most of the play.

Walter Reichart writes convincingly of the inner involvement or entanglement of Hauptmann's tragic characters. He reminds us that one of the bases of this concept of tragedy is, in Hauptmann's words, "Haß und Liebe als Lebenswut."[16] "Urdrama," according to Reichart, is for Hauptmann a "Selbstgespräch des gespaltenen oder doppelten Ich,"[17] and surely no better explanation could be given for the struggle throughout the play between retribution and martyrdom. To this extent *Veland* is a "Seelendrama" and its affinity to such a revenge play as *Hamlet* striking.

If we return to our earlier assertion that Veland is actually a triad, the outer limits of which are god and beast, we may now affirm that the essential movement of the play takes place almost exclusively within the central character as *man*, in whom the relations between the ideals and goals in the mind and their corresponding or opposing actions in the soul are examined dramatically. That Veland could not bring himself to accept as united what he unconsciously — but sometimes consciously, as we have seen — felt as inalterably separated, leads to his downfall. At least our reading of the play to this point demands as much; Hauptmann's refutation, the play's ending, will be shown to be inappropriate insofar as it violates *Veland*'s own definition of the human condition.

At this point we may re-enter the play in order to include King Harald in our consideration of *Veland* as an exposition of human suffering. In youth Harald had incurred guilt by the capture and subsequent laming of the smith, who was poaching the king's game, taking gold from his streams, and refusing to pay tribute. Harald knows that his measures were disproportionate; he resorts to reminding Veland of these transgressions only after his initial apology fails: "Ich tat dir unrecht, Veland, sprich nicht mehr davon" (III, 32). Yet his self-evaluation rings true: "grausam unbedacht," pampered by the gods, he felt that the entire world was his until tragedy struck. With the disappearance of his sons the king has learned the meaning of pain, and with pain has come an appreciation of the suffering of others. His offer to share crown and realm with the smith in exchange for learning the whereabouts of his children is spurned. The king cannot offer what is already Veland's, he must give him Bödwild instead. Harald agrees, but Veland demands first that his "Brunst" be cooled in Harald's royal blood. The reference is to his intended mating with Bödwild, yet the very notion of blood brings to our mind the words spoken earlier, "Aus Mordgestöhn erblüht / die Welt! ... Was lebt, harrt seines Mörders!" (III, 23), and hence doubts about the smith's sincerity. Harald accuses him of cunning, which Veland answers by accusing the king of lying and by repeating his conditions. In a fit of rage Harald orders his men to seize and strangle the smith, and so the pact never comes to be.

Despite evidence that the king's word is worthless, it is impossible to maintain that Veland for his part ever intended to let his revenge stop at this point; indeed, his earlier monologue (as well as the events of the legend) point to the slaughter of the sons. Both men, in other words, are in a sense willing to fulfill the terms of such a pact but neither is able to defy what has become inner destiny. Just as Veland is committed to vengeance through the execution of a plan long nourished and well laid, Harald is likewise trapped by his past. His duality is father-ruler, the self-assured tyrant ("der dich in Wolfstal überwand") and the anguished parent who swoons with pain when Veland evades the soldiers and flees into his cave.

Harald too will wrestle with his ambivalent nature until the final horror is thrust upon him. His anger and defiance at Veland's balking are not an expression of untrustworthiness but rather the revelation that he is unable to remain only the agonized father. But suffering transfigures as well as brutalizes, and it is not difficult for the reader to accept with fullest sympathy Harald's present distress and weigh it favorably against Veland's history of suffering. Seen this way, *Veland* is less a study of revenge than a dramatic statement on the intricate interweaving of the fate of two human beings. Crime and punishment are here a curse and its removal; both men are cursed, one by a past deed, the other by the fateful necessity to avenge it. King Harald is a worthy antagonist throughout the entire play.

His suffering, more direct and therefore more forceful, reaches such intensity in the "last supper" of Act III that only recourse to dream and illusion keeps him and his men from total insanity. A transformed Bödwild appears as Veland's willing mate and "Magd" and serves the quivering hearts of Ai and Ingi — two large red apples — to the king. Hermann Weigand is right in observing that the "mental torture to which the king is subjected borders on the unendurable," but his elaboration of this point seems questionable: "It is made endurable only by the realization that, paradoxically, in the triumph of retribution — itself a measure of Veland's accumulated agonies — the avenger himself shares to the full the unspeakable torture endured by his victim. The slaking of his vengeance is in itself the most acute stage of the martyrdom of the god."[18] This is admittedly true if we accept the play's conclusion as fitting the prior events or if we are willing to grant that *Veland* is primarily about divine martyrdom. But we fail to see this emphasis as Veland struggles with deeper elements within himself on the way to final retribution.

What can be said, however, is that once Veland succeeds in goading King Harald into momentarily breaking his oath — in order to create hastily a counterforce against the threat of Harald's sincerity and the proffered pact — his further course of action is virtually guaranteed. Harald missed his opportunity, we have seen, because of what he is and because Veland is understandably eager to have his grand design, his "Rachelust," fed by his enemy's tyranny and betrayal. To this extent we may agree with the sense of inevitability which Weigand stresses,[19] but we are disposed to see two examples rather than one. Harald's steady movement toward ruin remains approximately parallel to Veland's progress toward revenge and liberation. This creates two centers of tragic weight, about which one must ask, does Veland's really match that of his victim? Liberation, as noted before, leaves Veland empty; his flight is not upwards toward the summit of the human spirit but into nothingness, and what he has left behind is less a failing "Allvater" than a melodramatic shambles.

The accusation of melodrama needs justification. Veland's wedding feast offers several warnings that the effective tensions built up during more than two-thirds of the play are about to be dissipated. The interplay of love and hate, admirable if not always totally clear, is given up, at least in Veland's case. While Harald's suffering reaches peaks that thrust to the limits of what is artistically acceptable, Veland finally *enjoys* his long-awaited revenge. But as a dramatic character he has abdicated. His final preparation for liberation is a monologue that fortifies resolve. He begins by saying

> Veland, nun bist du Veland wiederum und ganz, (III, 75)

but soon changes this to

> Und nicht mehr heiß' ich Veland, bin nicht Veland mehr,
> nicht Leib, nicht Seele mehr: nur Rache bin ich noch. (III, 75)

If Veland has become solely an instrument, then the play as Veland-tragedy is over. There is additional evidence that this is the case. Harald begs Veland to forgive and forget — "Dein Herz verzehrt dich selbst, Veland" (III, 78). Veland's reply, "Du irrst, du irrst, ich liebe dich gar sehr, o Jarl" (III, 78), repeated and elaborated upon, is not merely out of keeping with his actions — which we might expect in the case of a revenge taken in agony — it is also at variance with the calm, deliberate, almost kindly manner in which Veland stages his "Hochzeitsfest." For 'kindly' here means essentially the sort of detachment that makes of his protestation of love a mockery. We sense this most strongly in the lines

> O Jarl, ich liebe dich mehr, als ich sagen kann,
> denn nie, nie tatst du an mir Böses. Aber stets
> tatst du mir Gutes, Gutes ohne Maß und Ziel.
> Und so ergreife den Pokal, der vor dir steht. (III, 82)

This cannot be seen as a total conversion of hate into love. Our earlier claim that Veland hates his love (as weakness and as deterrent *to* revenge) and loves his hate (as chief nourishment *for* revenge) might serve to support the smith's outrageous deception if it were possible to read a degree of emotion, of "Mit-leiden," into the lines. But the spirit that moves these words is neither love nor hate nor any new combination which might reveal a human Veland caught in the tragic process. "Tücke" and "Lüge" now belong to Veland alone.

To express fully the demonic magnitude of a victorious Veland Hauptmann has had to go beyond tragedy. Ketill and Bödwild both confirm this, the former by vision and the latter by direct participation. The final dialogue of the play is reserved for Veland and Ketill, who attributes a "deeper reason" to his final visit. The shepherd's message is hope for salvation "aus diesem Grab, das so viel bittre Qualen birgt" (III, 96), and his image is the polarity of darkness and light. But promise of redemption comes too late; Harald is told to endure patiently, but Veland mocks this as senseless since imbecility now "bleats" from the face of the ruined king; and Veland is admonished to feel remorse, for revenge cannot bring escape from night to day, "zur lichten Weite." Yet for Veland too the proffered help is an impotent gesture by a babbling "Allvater" whose day is really a deception.

If the note of tolerance and remorse at the end is wry it is because Veland reacts in a way consistent with his "Rachelust" *after* it ought to have been quenched! Certainly, remorse and need for pardon are not to be expected; beyond a fearful sense of emptiness, all Veland can feel after his final deeds of vengeance is nausea. Bödwild is now a scurf, to be rejected and hated by her despoiler. And the sound of wings passing overhead (Ketill: "als flögen Schwäne, schien es, übern Velandsholm," 97) cannot be Herware, who will never return to a Veland rendered unacceptable by his "Schmach". Since the word is used by the smith himself to describe his condition, and since all possible causes for his ardor of hate have been removed, it would seem that defeat in victory (or vice versa; both belong to the conventions of tragedy) should introduce, if not tragedy and if not love, an elegiac mood as testimony to life as eternal torment on a polluted earth. The last term is only accidentally topical; we borrow it from Strindberg's *Till Damaskus* (1898-1904), which offers many striking parallels to Hauptmann's *Veland*, especially in regard to the interweaving of love and hate and the impossibility of reconciliation.[20] Some of this notion of eternal torment remains with the creation of Veland's offspring (the "Zeugung und Vernichtung" of the opening monologue), but the play ends on a note of defiance which in effect strikes a new note:

> Trau nicht Allvatern, denn er ließ ja dies geschehen
> in seiner Tücke. Doch geschah es ohne ihn
> und gegen seinen Willen, wer ist mächtiger,
> ich oder er? ...
> Nicht du, nicht Folterqual, auch meine Rache nicht
> erneuert mich in diesem ungeheuren Augenblick.
> Es ist ein anderes, das ich dir nicht nennen kann. (III, 100)

"Tücke" is shifted — all too neatly, it would appear — from Veland to an "Allvater" with dubious omnipotence. More fateful still is the unnamable "anderes," the roots of which we fail to find in the play itself. Veland disappears in a flash of brilliance, carrying his own light with him into darkness, much as does a defeated bellfounder (*Die versunkene Glocke*) and a blinded Hellriegel (*Und Pippa tanzt*).

One may justifiably claim that suffering and loss have given these figures from Hauptmann's symbolic plays a special gift of vision and thus a new kind of freedom which is at once exhilarating and non-tragic. At one level it would seem a meaningful choice: love and hate, and all possible dualities are rejected because they enmesh man in the endless human cycle and in "innere Verstrickung." As W. Emrich puts it, Veland and Bödwild "sind durch ihr Leid, durch diese ungeheuerliche Entmenschlichung, herausgetreten aus allen menschlichen Bindungen und Verhängnissen, in eine neue, höhere, göttliche Sphäre gerückt." But as Emrich also notes, there is a tragic paradox in man's having on the one hand to fulfill the fate of creation, which demands that each dehumanization bring forth another, and each guilt a new guilt; and on the other hand to become "hellsichtig" through suffering, to confront fate as a free man who has become a god, and to destroy the "irdische Schicksalsordnung" itself.[21] No better formulation of cosmic tragedy in *Veland* could be given; the ending of the play abandons the interplay of myth and psychology in favor of myth. That the abandonment means also a refutation of the basic terms of the play — tragedy as the state of things as man is called upon to live them — points not only to pantragism but to the inescapable fact that Veland's god-like liberation from his vale of tears is a problematic resolution to an otherwise deeply human and therefore compelling drama. For Veland's "Verlust der Mitte" through conversion to one of the poles produces a pure state essentially lacking in interest. We prefer criminals and victims to gods, and it is this that Hauptmann fails to take into account in his symbolic extension of a human dilemma into impersonal dimensions.

NOTES

1 Hans Heinrich Borcherdt, "Gerhart Hauptmann," *Deutsche Literatur im 20. Jahrhundert.* 5th rev. ed., ed. Otto Mann und Wolfgang Rothe. (Bern, München, 1967), II, 257.
2 Gerhart Hauptmann, *Sämtliche Werke in zehn Bänden. Centenar-Ausgabe zum 100. Geburtstag des Dichters,* ed. Hans-Egon Hass (Berlin, Frankfurt, Wien, 1962 ff.), III, 10. All quotes in the text are identified by volume (roman numeral) and page number (arabic numeral) and refer to this edition.
3 Hans Daibler, *Gerhart Hauptmann oder Der letzte Klassiker* (Vienna, 1971), p. 197.
4 Noticeable in this regard is the paucity of secondary literature on *Veland*. The bibliography by Walter A. Reichart, *Gerhart Hauptmann Bibliographie* (Bad Homburg, etc., 1969) lists but two entries, one of them a doctoral dissertation, the other a Marxist interpretation. Other critics deal with the play, e.g., Ralph Fiedler, *Die späten Dramen Gerhart Hauptmanns* (Münich, 1954), pp. 21-26; Hermann Weigand, "Gerhart Hauptmann's Range as Dramatist," *Monatshefte,* 44 (1952), 331-32; P. Jolivet, *Études Germaniques,* 9 (1954), 41-43; W. Emrich, *Protest und Verheißung,* (Frankfurt, 1960), pp. 200-202, but, as the pagination will indicate, only briefly and in connection with other works or themes.
5 Fr. Muckermann, in *Der Gral,* 30 (1925), 332. Quoted by Felix A. Voigt, *Gerhart Hauptmann und die Antike* (Berlin, 1965), p. 92.
6 H. Steinhauer, "The Symbolism in Hauptmann's *Veland,*" *Modern Language Notes,* (1935), 259.
7 Cf. Philippe Jolivet, "La légende de Wieland le Forgeron," *Études Germaniques* 9 (1954), 43: "dans la forme offerte par l'Edda il a versé les bravades des Titans du *Sturm und Drang,* et un assez faible écho des revendications du socialisme auquel il avait adheré."
8 Cf. Ernst Alker, "Neue Sicht auf Gerhart Hauptmanns Schaffen," *Neophilologus,* 30 (1946), 69-77.
9 Benno von Wiese, "Gerhart Hauptmann," *Deutsche Dichter der Moderne* ed. B. von Wiese (Berlin, 1965), p. 28: "Dieses eigentliche, 'wahre Drama' liegt noch vor aller Kunst; es ereignet sich als ein ununterbrochener, nie abgeschlossener, rätselhafter Zwiespalt zwischen aufbauend schöpferischen und vernichtenden vitalen Gewalten..."
10 For an account of Hauptmann's eristic figures from mythology and his debt to Böhme and Schelling, see Robert Mühlher, "Prometheus-Luzifer. Das Bild des Menschen bei Gerhart Hauptmann," *Dichtung der Krise* (Vienna, 1951), pp. 257-290.

11 Perhaps the most striking instance is Heinrich's "Morgenröte" at the close of *Die versunkene Glocke*, which illustrates the consistency of Hauptmann's metacosmos as fully as it does the artistic inadequacy of the ending. Cf. my essay, "Rautendelein and the Thematic Imagery of the "Versunkene Glocke," *Monatshefte*, 54 (1962), 322-336, esp. 334-35.
12 For a detailed account of 'sources', see Karl Hemmerich's dissertation, *Gerhart Hauptmanns 'Veland'. Seine Entstehung und Deutung* (Würzburg, 1937).
13 The entire first act is reminiscent of Act I of *Und Pippa tanzt*, especially in the manner in which the characters are seen primarily as human beings in a realistic setting. The old glass blower Huhn is in fact Veland's ancestor, scarcely more human in countenance or behavior, particularly when the more or less everyday setting of "Rotwassergrund," as opposed to the mythical island of *Veland*, is taken into account. Moreover, Huhn exerts much the same irrational power over Pippa as Veland over Bödwild. Admittedly, the analogy should not be pushed too far, but the notion of a creature sharing something of two worlds is common to both plays, as is the steady progression from reality to a sphere which is super-natural and, to one critic at least, surrealistic. See also n. 8.
14 Fiedler, p. 21.
15 Hemmerich, p. 42. Fiedler cites Hemmerich in this context also and points out the inconsistency of viewing Ketill both as contrast and as part of Veland. To Fiedler, Ketill is the "fleischgewordene Stimme seines ringenden Menschentums" (p. 24).
16 W. Reichart, "Grundbegriffe im dramatischen Schaffen Gerhart Hauptmanns," PMLA, 82 (1967) 146-47.
17 Reichart, 146.
18 H. Weigand, "Gerhart Hauptmann's Range as a Dramatist," *Monatshefte*, 44 (1952), 331.
19 Weigand, 331.
20 Strindberg's *Till Damaskus, Ett drömspel* (1902), and *Spöksonaten* (1907) all fall within the period of *Veland*'s composition. The problem of parallels, echoes, and influences remains to be explored in detail, despite indications that aspects of Hauptmann's symbolic plays are often strikingly similar to Strindberg's work during the same period.
21 Emrich, p. 201.

STERNHEIM'S 1913 AS SATIRE:
FANTASY AND FASHION

Edson M. Chick

Carl Sternheim (1878-1942) protested, in response to theater reviews, that he was no satirist: "Also nicht Ironie und Satire, die als meine Absicht der Reporter festgestellt hatte und die Menge nachschwatzte, sondern vor allgemeiner Tat aus meinen Schriften schon die Lehre: daß Kraft sich nicht verliert, muß auf keinen überkommenen Rundgesang doch auf seinen frischen Einzelton der Mensch nur hören, ganz unbesorgt darum, wie Bürgersinn seine manchmal brutale Nuance nennt."[1]

Notwithstanding these protestations and some more recent critical opinions that uphold them, Sternheim must be judged a satirist. His occasional writings, essays and autobiography, reveal the same aggressive impulse and savage indignation that impelled Juvenal ("Difficile est saturam non scribere.") and Swift to attack their coevals. Among these same writings there are also some helpful self-interpretations which provide a glimpse into his workshop and give us a starting point for demonstrating that his *1913* (published 1915, allegedly completed in February, 1914) is not satiric comedy like *Die Hose* (1911) and *Der Snob* (1914) but rather thoroughgoing satire castigating political, social and cultural evils of the time and employing devices characteristic of the kind of writing that is, by general agreement in the Anglo-American literary world and increasingly in Germany, called satiric.[2]

What has made Sternheim and his readers wary of the term and what has consequently made *1913* unnecessarily hard to understand is the standard German definition — drawn from Schiller's *Über naive und sentimentalische Dichtung* (1795) — of the satirist as the poet who points out the flaws in the material world by juxtaposing it to the ideal as highest form of reality.[3] Sternheim saw no need to express an ideal, and he admired Flaubert's *L'Éducation sentimentale* precisely because it applies no labels and "alles ist Urteil in sich selbst."[4] Schiller himself would have accepted Flaubert's and Sternheim's work as satire. To his often cited pronouncement about the real and ideal he immediately adds the sentence: "Es is übrigens gar nicht nötig, daß das letztere [das Ideal] ausgesprochen wird, wenn der Dichter es nur im Gemüt zu erwecken weiß..." And it is characteristic of recent satiric drama that the ideal of order and the inherent rightness of things are made evident only through their opposites: chaos, futility, folly, villainy.

The best of modern satire is, in this sense, undirected or "figural."[5] And Sternheim notes that he has no firm standard by which to measure: "... ich [hatte] keinen 'Standpunkt,'... als daß ich in jedem das Besondere antippte; ihm in Bezug auf sein Unvergleichliches ohne Werturteil gerecht wurde! Ich mußte erkennen, nicht 'entlarven,' mich nicht als 'Satiriker' über sie 'lustigmachen'; zeigen, wie wesentlich traurig, komisch, heldisch, überlegen jeder an sich war!"[6]

Satire deals with reality, real people, situations, places, and ways of thinking. *1913* has historical authenticity. It presents and analyses the laws that Sternheim saw governing human relationships: "Das moderne Gefühl: ich kann auf keine andere Weise mich auszeichnen, als wenn ich als Mitmensch besonders gut angepaßt bin, zerstörte jedes Bedürfnis der Isolation, indem im Gegenteil Vorstellung derer, mit denen ich ringend lebe, vom Kampf ums Dasein unzertrennlich, ja dessen Voraussetzung ist" (VI, 116).

Sternheim noted with anger and dismay that men's actions were dictated by unconscious attitudes, received ideas, and group fantasies and that these actions were leading to a catastrophic, suicidal end. Some of these ideas can be covered by the term "social Darwinism." The phrases "Kampf ums Dasein" and "gut angepaßt" make this obvious.

The other side of the coin, or the psychic impetus behind the dreams of vitality and order, struggle and adaptation, is another closely linked pair: impotence and aggression. Sternheim describes his modern man of the *juste milieu*: "Der Mensch, in gewaltigen unentrinnbaren Naturmechanismus gefesselt, ohne Rest eigener Aktion im Entscheidenden, betäubt sich innerhalb starrer Scharniere durch Fessellosigkeit, die ohne Beispiel ist" (VI, 118). Sternheim's characters fight their battles for prestige.[7] To gain it they must conform to the accepted standard of behavior in the struggle for existence, or *bellum omnium contra omnes*. Success is nothing more than an enhanced public image; and what sets the prominent bourgeois off from his fellows is his brutal "Nuance," that is, his peculiar ruthlessness, astuteness, and capacity for chicanery. He recognizes no limits to his predatory acts, but these acts cannot be decisive because they are confined to the paper realm of journals, public relations, and mere appearance. Like Tantalus and Sisyphus, he is condemned to fail and fail again.

The satirist, having recognized the frenetic yet constrained villainy and folly of those around him, needs merely to record what he sees: "Hinter noch so forscher Geste, keckem Wort hob als lächernder Schatten sich steil eine eherne Wirklichkeit, die es zum Witz, zur Metapher schlug. Nichts mehr zu gestalten hatte im Grunde ja der Mensch, nur aufzupassen und sich Ereignendes mit einem Schlagwort zu prägen" (VI, 118). In *1913* that laugh-provoking shadow is the hard reality of death and war. It makes the most grandiose, pretentious undertakings look puny and the entrepreneurs seem like marionettes. Sternheim thought nothing need be added. The truth should be obvious without any overt pronouncement.

Finally, in his ssay on Molière (1917), Sternheim reveals his satiric method and aims in terms which would well satisfy Schiller's full definition. Speaking primarily of himself, he says:

> Ein Dichter wie Molière ist Arzt am Leibe seiner Zeit. Des Menschen sämtliche, ihm von seinem Schöpfer gegebene Eigenschaften blank und strahlend zu erhalten, ist ihm unabweisbar Pflicht.
> Zur Erreichung seines hohen Zieles bedient er sich wie der medizinische Helfer der allopathischen oder homöopathischen Methode. Er kann den Finger auf die bedenkliche Stelle des Menschtums legen und den Helden eine dagegen mit Einsetzung seines Lebens eifernde Kampfstellung einnehmen lassen (Wesen der Tragödie), er kann aber auch die aufzuweisende Eigenschaft in den Helden selbst senken und ihn mit fanatischer Lust von ihr sinnlos besessen sein lassen (Wesen der Komödie). Der Eindruck auf den Zuschauer ist in beiden Fällen der gleiche: ihn überwältigt zum Schluß die Sehnsucht nach einem schönen Maß, das der Bühnenheld nicht hatte, zu dem er selbst aber durch des Dichters Aufklärung nunmehr leidenschaftlich gewillt ist. (VI, 31)

By "Komödie" Sternheim means something other than the kind of play in which boy loves, loses, and gets girl once, by happy chance, certain blocking figures have been removed. He means undirected, homeopathic satire. The heroes of the seven plays he wrote between 1907 and 1914 are not, nor were they intended to be, ideals. They are infected with the vices and prejudices of the bourgeois *juste milieu*. The plays, in their ironic objectivity, employ the conventional satiric praise-blame inversion.

The satirist has always felt duty-bound to speak out, and his pose is that of plain speaker. If one did not keep in mind the idea of homeopathy, one could misread the first part of the statement Sternheim makes on his dramatic intent:

> Ich entfachte zu keiner Erziehung; im Gegenteil warnte ich vor Kritik göttlicher Welt durch den Bürger und machte ihm Mut zu seinen sogenannten Lastern, mit denen er Erfolge errang, und riet ihm, meiner Verantwortung bewußt, Begriffe, die einseitig nach sittlichem Verdienst messen, als unerheblich und lebensschwächend endlich aus seiner Terminologie zu entfernen...
> Im Grund aber hoffte ich, der Arbeiter sähe statt des ihm frisiert hingesetzten Mannes des *Juste Milieu* daraus endlich den wahren und echten Jakob ein; hinter dessen literarischem Entgegenkommen und geschminkten Mätzchen seine Wirkliche, noch allmächtig lebendige, brutale Lebensfrische und messe an ihr als an formidabler Wirklichkeit statt an verblasenen Theorien Wucht bevorstehender Entscheidung, der ich mit dem einzigen Verlangen gegenüberstand, es möchte sich aus ihr, gleichviel auf welcher Seite, der Zeit Wahrhaftigkeit offenbaren. (VI, 140)

In other words, Sternheim proceeds by giving his bourgeois "hero" the courage of his convictions and letting him drop the façade of "metaphor," that is, of received ideas and clichés provided by the press and the literati. He is then free to realize his true, brutal "Nuance," i.e., his perfect, conscienceless self-interest, according to which he acts and which, he assumes, guides all his fellows. The true Jacob emerges, and the spectator must judge for himself.

Sternheim's straight-faced encouragement of his hero as well as his brilliant rendering of received ideas and clichés in the rhetoric of his plays puts a heavy burden on spectator and critic. Almost all have agreed that he is no satirist and many assume that he intends to put his leading figures in a favorable light.[8] Some go so far as to charge him with insanity and immorality. The most violent accusations come from W. G. Sebald who rightly detects the destructive madness in Sternheim's characters and their ideas but, failing to note the full statement and intent of plays like *1913*, proceeds to pillory Sternheim as a traitor to literature and humanity.[9] Every polemic, *ad hominem* argument Sebald adduces against Sternheim's ideas and style can better be used to demonstrate that his best plays, those from the years 1907-1914, are good satirical comedies (*Die Hose, Der Snob, Bürger Schippel*) or straight, effective satiric drama (*Die Kassette, 1913*).

The foregoing passages from Sternheim's prose were published after 1914. Yet I believe they refute Sebald's contention that he was unaware of what his dramas were saying and was guilty of unwitting self-contradiction. The negative ambiguity inherent in the concept of "die eigene Nuance," the antinomies within each work, the absence of dialectic[10] and resolution, the destructively aggressive character of the plays, the absence of a fixed standpoint for value judgment, the apparent diffuseness, and the mixing of banal and exalted elements can all be reckoned as virtues if one reads the dramas as satires.[11] *1913* in particular mirrors faithfully the madness, waste, and futility Sternheim saw about him in that "dreadful decade from 1897-1907" when Kaiser Wilhelm II ruled over a materially flourishing German Reich (VI, 217).

On first reading, *1913* can easily pass for a bona fide melodrama about a family crisis. Sternheim demands a discerning audience, for he is sparing with overt signals as to his intent. The events of the play are far closer to our experience than, say, the outlandish mixes and exaggerations of Wedekind's Lulu-Tragedy or Bertolt Brecht's *Aufstieg und Fall der Stadt Mahagonny*. The travesty, or "fantastic vision of the world transformed," is there but it is not immediately apparent.[12] It lies in the excitement about haberdashery which looks at first like comic embroidery on the main action.

Not that Sternheim ever tired of making elsewhere explicit statements about his literary intents, namely: to represent the anarchy of the times, in which every man claims to be his own microcosm, and to do this by showing the bourgeois completely possessed by his own being and running amok (*Vorkriegseuropa*, p. 139). In "Das gerettete Bürgertum" (1918) he states: "Sieben Komödien schrieb ich von 1908-1913. Die letzte, die des Vorkriegsjahres Namen trägt, zeigte, wohin, in aller Einfalt womöglich, des Bürgers Handel gediehen war. Vom Dichter gab es nichts, nur noch von Wirklichkeit hinzuzusetzen. Trotz vielfacher öffentlicher Darstellung und Verbreitung durch Druck hatte niemand bemerkt, wohin mit meinem Werk mein Wille ging" (VI, 46).

1913 is Sternheim's most ambitious and successful satire. It is one of the three plays he was proudest of. It remains to demonstrate how he realized his intentions and why it is a well-made satiric drama.

The drama is anchored in its time and yet has timeless implications. The title ells us that this is Germany on the eve of a calamitous war. Also, in 1913 all Germany celebrated the centennial of the Battle of the Nations and the Wars of Liberation as well as the twenty-fifth anniversary of Wilhelm II's accession to the throne. In October of that year, on Der Hohe Meißner, the German youth movement held its great congress, which was to weld it into a unified, powerful cultural force but failed its purpose. It was a year when most believed that the nation was prospering as never before and that the best was yet to come. D. Sarason, editor of *Das Jahr 1913: Ein Gesamtbild der Kulturentwicklung* (Berlin/Leipzig: Teubner, 1913), fully expected to register further gains in the ensuing editions of his annual, which in fact never appeared.

The scene of the drama is Schloß Buchow, somewhere in Prussia. The details of the milieu are contemporary, and the characters are not pale caricatures but rather recognizable figures patterned after living persons. The play is dedicated to Ernst Stadler, and one secondary figure bears that family name, though he has little in common with the noted poet and scholar. Yet these characters are also types; *King Lear* and *Macbeth* provided some models. And their vices are common to all humanity.

The satire has both political and moral dimensions. The incidents which take place in Baron Christian Maske's household anticipate and act out in miniature the downfall of a nation and of western civilization. Through telephone lines, the mails, and the daily press, petty intrigues within the family are linked with the machinery of world history. The question as to who is to be first dandy to astound the social world by wearing a piece of string for a watch chain can, under these conditions, have apocalyptic implications. This is Sternheim's great travesty, his phantastic yet logical linking of superficial banality with the chaos that looms in the near future and that is already there for those with eyes to see.

Through their skill at manipulation and conforming, the Maskes have risen to power and prominence in two generations. First, Theobald found financial security and limited freedom by aping the respectable bourgeois (*Die Hose*). Then his son, Christian, succeeded in business and made it into the aristocracy by adopting its costume and mannerisms (*Der Snob*). Now he has assumed a new guise, that of the astute captain of industry and unscrupulous arms magnate. He has built an empire on the courage of his convictions and has acquired great prestige (I, 225). Yet in a single day his daughter Sofie is about to rob him of it all. "Ein Tag Abwesenheit kostet mich Prestige, Macht, Vermögen," he complains in admiration of her calculating ruthlessness (I, 226). A simple public

217

relations trick threatens to make him a nobody. His battle to regain his prestige ("Ansehen") through a comparable device supplies the play's main action. Sofie says of him: "Diese von sich besessene Natur verträgt nichts Bedeutendes neben sich und wird uns, coûte qui coûte, niederwerfen" (I, 257).

Sternheim's point is that Christian Maske has brought on his own demise. He has created this world and dictates the selfish, materialistic rules by which it operates. He has realized his own brutal "Nuance" and is sufficiently powerful to boast of his unscrupulous greed. It is a virtue in a world where only two forces count: "Magenhunger des Pöbels. Machthunger der Reichen. Sonst nichts" (I, 230). This is the sum of Maske's wisdom. He orders his affairs and acts on the assumption that all others think as he. If they do not, they are lost. His talk of self-realization is merely a euphemism for his self-interest and brutality. By reducing human relationships to this formula, he is able to devote his considerable energy to the exploitation of others and the enhancement of his prestige. Therein resides his power, that intangible fluid that owes its force to the fear and respect of others, can be cultivated by public relations experts, gives a man leverage for financial and political manipulation, and can be gained or lost in a moment.

Maske possesses nothing real. He is possessed by himself, and this self, or nuance, is no more than his public image. All the aggressive characters in this play are possessed and obsessed by their "Ansehen." It is their only strength and their fatal weakness. They fight for it tooth and nail, for it has supplanted all other values. The superficial mask is their being. Without it they are nothing. Beneath the costume lies no substance.

Maske has projected his fantasies of order and dynamism onto the real world. He has reduced human beings to stereotypes and made aggressive vitality the highest virtue. And his society has accepted these fantasies as truths, unaware they are part of a charade and that these dreams must soon become nightmares.

In his hunger for power, he has reified, impoverished, and emasculated his world and himself. By making others impotent he has aroused their destructive instincts and defeated his own ends. His daughter Sofie is now beating him at his own game; and other, even more pernicious parties are scheming to take over the limelight. Rather than free himself, he has become locked with everyone else in the fetters of a mechanism created by his own estimate of his fellows (VI, 118). According to the psychic mechanism of the *juste milieu*, which enables the bourgeois not only to survive but also to gain self-respect and the admiration of others, the struggle for existence is nothing more than the struggle for prestige. The fittest rise to the top, but not for long.

By advertising herself as a pious Protestant, Maske's daughter Sofie has all but concluded, against her father's will, an arms deal with the Dutch government. Though dying, Maske is unwilling to be pushed aside. With like weapons he conducts a campaign to regain his position at all costs. It is a battle for survival. His grandiose coup is a simple trick: He becomes a convert to Catholicism and announces this in a press release to all important newspapers. Holland drops negotiations and the deal is off. Maske, however, never enjoys the fruits of this victory, which is as hollow as himself. It is all theater, as the words of his penultimate speech indicate. Rushing on stage in search of Sofie, he speaks: "Sie läßt sich nicht finden, will mich um letzte Wollust betrügen. Wo ist sie? Wer ist das? Hört mich, alle herbei! Belechtung, Rampe! *Er schreit*: Aus ist's mit dem Karfreitagszauber!" (I, 292). In satire, a heavily rhetorical kind of literature, each fool and knave convicts himself through his own choice of words. Here it is theater talk. Elsewhere it is the language of the battlefield, of chauvinism, of finance, and of fashion.

Maske is in fact cheated out of his ultimate ecstasy. He mistakes his favorite daughter, Ottilie, for Sofie, curses and ridicules her instead, and then falls dead. True, he has foiled his enemy, but the strain has cost him his life. He leaves behind a family and a world in helpless confusion.

His final performance follows the typically satiric course from purpose to passion to anticlimax, and the punishment reveals Sternheim's central meaning.[13] He has adjusted false appearance to correspond with the true state of things. He has collapsed mask and essence; and we see that they are one and the same, empty and dead. He also shows that the struggle to gain and preserve prestige is not merely self-defeating but also indiscriminately destructive.

On the other hand, Sternheim also shows us the humanity of his satiric protagonist. He lets him suffer defeat, degradation, and, in a strangely impersonal way, pangs of conscience. Maske loves his children and wants them to reap the benefits of his work. In the most mordantly ironic line of the play, he says to them: "Gesät habe ich. Die himmlischsten Ernten könnt ihr sammeln" (I, 241). He means his fourteen factories, but the crop from his seed is and will be anything but divine.

Shortly before his end he has a moment of insight into the mass-producing monster he has created: "Es geht mir schlecht. Ich mache Bilanz und fühle, von menschlichen Gefühlen mehr als von eigenen besessen: möchte es diesem oder einem anderen gelingen, von Grund auf Zustände zu erschüttern, die wir geschaffen" (I, 286). Sofie points out that he has created these conditions and bequeathed them to her generation: "Jedes Rezept habt ihr uns und das Hauptbestandteil aller Rezepte übermacht. Skrupellosigkeit. Wir gründen wie ihr, weit vorsichtiger und geschäftskundiger sogar, ohne freilich irgendwie sehen zu können, wohin das alles geht" (I, 285). The machine is running ever more efficiently but is out of control and headed for war. "Nach uns Zusammenbruch!" cries Maske. His concern for the fate of mankind is an alien sentiment; he himself is incapable of emotion. And before the scene is over, he is once more totally possessed by the question of his prestige and hurls a bitter curse at Sofie (I, 289).

Maske is a self-obsessed monomaniac; yet he is far from an integral figure. He is full of inconsistencies. He is moribund, calls himself "der gepflegte Kadaver" (I, 229), and yet he preaches ruthless vitalism, "Lebendiges, ungezügeltes Lebens-bewußtsein!" (I, 228). He is a sentimental idealist and a hard-nosed exploiter. He loves Ottilie and curses her. He works ostensibly to strengthen his fatherland, his firm, and his family but only hastens the debacle.

His role corresponds closely to that of the conventional primitive satirist. He shifts from one guise to another, railing in public against the evils of his own system and showing fatherly concern for his offspring. The satirist, writes Ronald Paulson, is usually "a wonderfully ambiguous figure — part hero, part villain, part public censor, part private man."[14] Yet he ridicules and belittles others with his sharp invective and plain speaking. Like Gulliver and other great misanthropes of literature, he cannot obscure his kinship with the fools he scorns: and he becomes the object of a more serious satiric attack.

If one views him as the commonest target of satire, the rogue, another ambiguity comes to light. W. H. Auden puts it this way: "The rogue transgresses the moral law at the expense of others, but he is only able to do this because of the vices of his victims."[15] Maske adopts the tacit moral, or amoral, assumptions of his society and puts them into practice, unencumbered by the need to feign Christian virtue.

The forces and qualities that were united in him and made him strong are now breaking apart. They reappear singly in his progeny: his ruthlessness in Sofie, his snobbism in Philipp Ernst, his vital sensuality in Ottilie. Like other seed he has sown, each quality goes out of control, becomes hypertrophied, obsessive, debilitating, self-destructive.

Yet each subsidiary character has his own inconsistencies. Ottilie promises to suppress none of her secret desires and whispers to her father of "Machttaumel! Menschen bewältigen — fressen" (I, 225). But she devotes all this energy to the seduction of his secretary, Wilhelm Krey. Sofie is a canny, heartless businesswoman and does not shrink from cheating her father or brother. Yet she acts in the interests of her husband, whom she loves with total devotion. He is a weak man, incapable of getting children, and she wants to transform him into a powerful figure, at least in the eyes of the world. She explains her motives: "Es geht für dich, Otto, für dein Ansehen, deine Größe nach seinem [Christian Maskes] Tod. Dein schlagender Erfolg und sein platter Abgang müssen vor der Welt zusammenfallen. Läßt er über deiner Katastrophe eine Gloriole von sich in der Welt zurück, wandelst du für den Rest deiner Tage ein Schemen in seinem Licht. Das will ich nicht" (I, 258). Her tricks misfire, however, and her fears are realized. Otto, and the rest, remain at the end no more than shades in hell.

And finally, Wilhelm Krey, the eloquent anticapitalist and propagandist for Teutonic virtue and the "neue deutsche Idee," (I, 220) proves in the end to be more concerned for the impression his clothes make on Ottilie than for the cause of patriotic revolution.

Sternheim provides further inconsistencies that call for second thounghts. The opening scene of the third and final act begins with a rendering of Schumann's "Mondnacht," that setting of Eichendorff's jewel of Romantic and Catholic piety. It is applauded with cries of "Himmlischer Schumann" and "Großer Eichendorff" (I, 276). This song of death, peace, and harmony is utterly inappropriate to the situation. Maske has just completed his cynical conversion to the Catholic faith; and the remainder of the scene reveals the vicious battle going on within the family. Sofie defrauds her brother, Philipp, of his inheritance (I, 278-280); Wilhelm Krey promises to liquidate his capitalist enemies once he is in power (I, 281-282); and Christian Maske anticipates Holland's reaction to the news reports. In his accustomed military language he says, "...in diesen Minuten etwa platzt dort die Bombe" (I, 278). Finally, at the center of the scene Sternheim devotes two pages (I, 279-280) to the incongruous, petty question of whether Philipp Ernst will have the sole right to wear a piece of string in place of a watch chain.

This strident incompatability in a play dealing with the destinies of nations finds its counterpart in Sternheim's rhetorical devices. Through allusion and trope his characters work to exaggerate the trivial and belittle the sublime. The megalomaniacs allude repeatedly to heroic men of the past. Maske invokes Bismarck and Napoleon, and he speaks in words that make him a commanding general on the battlefield of business. Everything he plans and does is part of a life and death struggle and is expressed in metaphors of finance and violence. "Breche ich ihr aber auch noch vor meinem Abmarsch den Hals, ist es dann Gewinn für euch," he says of Sofie to Philipp Ernst (I, 242-243). Each of the main characters uses words, consciously or unconsciously, in an effort to transform impotence into power.

The reverse occurs when their actions expose their essential weakness. Christian Maske also regularly deflates the pomposities of the others. He keeps reminding Otto, Sofie's husband, of his impotence. He cuts down the workings of human society to two appetites: hunger for power and hunger for food, and he reduces human issues to mechanical matters of quantity and count. Germany is sixty-five million "Fresser" confined to 540,000 square kilometers (I, 223). This is the brutal "formidable reality" Sternheim wanted his audience to see in his satiric protagonist (VI, 140). This "reality" is in turn belittled and ridiculed by the ultimate backdrop of death and war (VI, 118).

The mixing of up and down movements, magnifying and belittling, characterizes the movement of the play. On every rise follows a fall. The opening scene of Act I shows us Wilhelm Krey, the paper revolutionary, at his desk, writing as always with a "bessessenen Feder" (I, 252) and intoxicated by his own propaganda slogans. He is attacking the disease of international finance and the crass spirit of capitalism in the cause of "eine heilige, allgemeine, vaterländische Verbrüderung und allgemeine deutsche Ideen" (I, 220).

Krey is as hungry for power as the others. Through his writings he aims to gain control of the revolutionary youth movement and then steal the glory from the Maske family. Resentment and obsession with prestige inform his actions. In a later monolog he says of Ottilie:

> Mißbrauchen für eine Laune willst du mich, und von der anderen Seite bieten mir die prachtvoll begeisterten Jungen Gewalt über ihr Leben und Stoßkraft an. Es erhebt sich einer, da du ihn noch in abhängiger Stellung unter dir siehst, schon über den First deines Lebens; durch seine unbestochen freie Meinung macht er heldenhaft großen Eindruck auf die Zeit, die ihn dafür unsterblich nennt. Unsterblich — Ottilie! Du aber und dein Geld bleibst im Namenlosen. Es kommt der Tag, da mit der zwischen uns aufgehellten *wirklichen* Distanz ich die Freiheit deines bloßen Versuchs heimzahlen werde. (I, 251)

However pernicious his irrational, proto-Nazi diatribe may be, Krey is a weakling, courageous only through his pen and when alone. Adaptation has become his way of life, and he has no more substance than the faded phrases he devises. The first indication that this is so, if the clichés of the opening monolog were not sufficient evidence, is his insecure, obsequious behavior toward Ottilie Maske when she enters in Scene Two. His bow before her is an anticlimax and an overt denial of his fantasies of immortal heroism, power, and prestige.

Wilhelm Krey and Ottilie make a good match. She is the victim of her erotic and ideological susceptibility. In Scene Three, speaking of Otto Weininger's *Geschlecht und Charakter*, she tries the phrase "seelisches Neuland" on her father; and he promptly brings her back to earth with facts, figures, and his philosophy of hunger (I, 223-24). As he does this he also exalts himself, through allusion to Napoleon, for instance; and it becomes clear that he is concerned solely with his public image: "...sie (Sofie) hat einen Saltomortale gesprungen, mich in den Schatten zu drängen" (I, 231). He understands well his daughter's intentions. She is aiming to put him in the shadow and therewith destroy him: "Diese genialen Instinkte sind gegen mich, mein persönliches Ansehen gerichtet" (I, 233).

His paranoid delusions of grandeur reach their pinnacle at the end of Scene Five. He is confident of regaining his earlier control over the nation, of once more blinding the world with his flame (I, 234). The anticlimax follows immediately with the entrance of Philipp Ernst, his foppish son. The latter and Ottilie, Maske's helplessly weak offspring, dominate the final third of Act I. They talk of styles in fashion and sexual conquest.

Why does this empty mannikin, the narcissistic dandy Philipp Ernst, whose only battles are fought with sartorial weapons for the favors of a lady, assume a central role in *1913*? Why does the clothes travesty occupy the very center of the play (II, ix-xiv)? And why is costume so important in the concluding three scenes? Sternheim wants more than to take a sideswipe at phenomena of decadence and conspicuous consumption among the rich. This is his central, satiric, synecdochic metaphor. Everyone in the play strives to build and maintain his "Ansehen." This obsession is their folly, and from it spring their vices.

The pageant and costumes prescribed for the final scenes suggest a grotesquely inappropriate, rather chaotic dance of wild costumes moving back and forth between the library and Maske's corpse in the next room: "Es ensteht durch die offene Tür ein lebhaftes Hin und Her... Ein Diener erleuchtet die Szene. Man erkennt jetzt die modisch übertriebene Pracht der Nachtkostüme, insbesondere Philipp Ernsts und des Prinzen Oels, die wie Wilhelm eine Art Turban dazu tragen, und ihre Übereinstimmung in etwa mit dem Anzug Wilhelms" (I, 292-293).

Now they all look alike in their garish outfits. Krey belongs with them now. He has merely exchanged his phrases for another kind of show. Sternheim inverts the fairy tale and shows that the new clothes are there but the emperor is missing. This is all that remains of their prestige. They have lost control of their destinies and of the machines they are responsible for. As they have feared all along, they are now shades, soulless creatures like the new dead in the dance of death, moving willy-nilly to the piper's tune toward the debacle suggested by the title *1913*. Maske's hour of flaming glory has turned out to be an hour of failure and confusion. The "divine harvest" of egoism stands briefly illuminated for the audience to observe. Then the servant turns off the light and the curtain falls on a darkened stage. The contest is over.

The idea of struggle ("Kampf") obsesses all of Sternheim's characters and saturates the play. Maske and Sofie battle for prestige and power; Ottilie for erotic domination over Krey; and Philipp Ernst for the title of best dressed man. "Es gilt gegen ein Weib," he says to Easton the tailor, challenging him to produce his finest wares (I, 267). At bottom, each is competing for the limelight and to push others off into darkness. To glow or to be in the light is to enjoy prestige. Without "Ansehen" one is nothing.

The contest is over and all have lost. To tell us this, Sternheim gives his last and most striking signal. The final words of the play, the hackneyed phrase "Leuchte zum großen Ziel" is the cue for extinguishing all light on stage. This incongruity, like the other dissonances, exaggerations, and ironies, rather than outright pronouncement, is a device Sternheim uses to draw his audience into the other struggle, namely, his altercation with evil and folly.

By synecdoche, that is, by reducing his enemy to one representative figure or to a single family, and by transposing the basic issue to the realm of fashion, he has won his battle. The final scenes with their parade of nightclothes show the threat for what it is. Turning off the light then disposes of it. The audience can laugh at, reject, despise it, now that it appears so inane and self-destructive.

What is this enemy but the cherished beliefs that determine the audience's own mores and cast of mind? It is the dream of technological power and silent efficiency coupled with its companion, libertarian fantasy of freedom from repression. These dreams are symptomatic of the psychic epidemic not only of the Wilhelminian Era but of other ages of affluence. Sternheim's satire anticipates their transformation into nightmares.[16]

NOTES

1 *Die Hose* (Leipzig: Insel, 1919), p. 7.
2 Most of my ideas about satire are drawn from the following: Christopher Booker, *The Neophiliacs* (Boston: Gambit, 1970); Robert C. Elliott, *The Power of Satire* (Princeton: Princeton University Press, 1960); Northrop Frye, *Anatomy of Criticism* (1957; rpt. New York: Anchor-Doubleday, 1963); Matthew Hodgart, *Satire*, World University Library, 043 (London: Weidenfeld and Nicolson, 1969); Alvin B. Kernan, *The Plot of Satire* (New Haven: Yale University Press, 1965); Ronald Paulson, *The Fictions of Satire* (Baltimore: Johns Hopkins, Press 1967); Edward W. Rosenheim, Jr., *Swift and the Satirist's Art* (Chicago: University of Chicago Press, 1963); J. L. Styan, *The Dark Comedy* (London: Cambridge University Press, 1968); Ulrich Gaier, *Satire* (Tübingen: Niemeyer, 1967); Peter Uwe Hohendal, *Das Bild der bürgerlichen Welt im expressionistischen Drama* (Heidelberg: Winter, 1967); Paul Pörtner, "Die Satire im expressionistischen Theater," *Maske und Kothurn*, 9/2 (1963), 169-181. Seen too late to be incorporated are two further German studies of great theoretical and practical interest: Jörg Schönert, *Roman und Satire im 18. Jahrhundert*, Germanistische Abhandlungen 27 (Stuttgart: Metzler, 1969), and Jürgen Brummack, "Zu Begriff und Theorie der Satire," *Deutsche Vierteljahrsschrift*, Sonderheft Forschungsreferate, 45 (1971), 275-377.
3 *Säkularausgabe*, XII, 194. Ideologically inspired scholars — e.g., Wilhelm Emrich in his introduction to Carl Sternheim's *Gesamtwerk* (Neuwied: Luchterhand, 1963 ff.), I — insist that Sternheim overtly states his ideal and point to passages with the ring of pronouncement. But they overlook others that contradict them. See also W. G. Sebald, *Carl Sternheim: Kritiker und Opfer der Wilhelminischen Ära*, Sprache und Literatur, 58 (Stuttgart: Kohlhammer, 1969).
4 Carl Sternheim, *Gesamtwerk*, ed. Wilhelm Emrich (Neuwied: Luchterhand, 1963 ff.), VI, 53. Hereafter this edition will be cited in the text by volume and page number.
5 See Ulrich Gaier, *Satire*, pp. 414 ff.
6 *Vorkriegseuropa im Gleichnis meines Lebens* (Amsterdam: Querido, 1936), p. 135.
7 Nowadays prestige connotes standing in the eyes of people, power, glory. In earlier times it signified illusion or deception and translated Latin "praestigiae," which means conjurer's tricks. The same ambiguity is inherent in Sternheim's use of the word "das Ansehen."
8 One notable exception is Helmut Karasek, whose *Carl Sternheim*, Friedrichs Dramatiker der Weltliteratur (Velber bei Hannover: Friedrich, 1965), makes a convincing case for the opposite view and accentuates the negative.
9 W. Sebald, *Carl Sternheim, Kritiker und Opfer*.
10 Sternheim's dramaturgical thinking is in fact dialectic, but not in a political or ideological sense. Sebald has in mind dialectical materialism, which demands a positive twist, no matter what. See Friedrich Dürrenmatt, *Monstervortrag über Gerechtigkeit und Recht* (Zurich: Arche, 1969), p. 95.
11 Sebald, pp. 17, 26, 38, 39, 43.
12 Hodgart, *Satire*, p. 14.
13 See Alvin Kernan, *Modern Satire* (New York: Harcourt, Brace, 1962), pp. 177-78.
14 *The Fictions of Satire*, p. 79.
15 *The Dyer's Hand* (London: Faber and Faber, 1963), p. 384.
16 See Christopher Booker, *The Neophiliacs*, pp. 68-80.

CAVE MATREM: THE BATTLE OF THE SEXES IN ERNST BARLACH'S DER TOTE TAG

Henry Hatfield

> *Taceat mulier in ecclesia!*
>
> "Wir haben hier... Ausdruck um jeden Preis, gleichgültig gegen Sinn, Gesetz und Stelle... den tiefen Mangel an Richtigkeit,..."
>
> (Gundolf on Kleist's *Amphitryon*.)

Barlach's *Der tote Tag* (1912) has been discussed rather often; remarkably often if one remembers that this is this first, and by no means his best play. Technically it is not even a passable drama; the third act consists of less than three pages (in the standard edition) relating the killing of the magic steed; the fourth and fifth act show a cast mainly composed of highly neurotic characters who rehash in a more or less *tief* way what the reasonably intelligent reader or spectator has long since known. In general, critics who based themselves on an especially naive *Zeitgeist* theory have overrated Barlach's dramas because he is indeed a fine sculptor and graphic artist; *therefore*, they infer, he must be a fine writer. Others seem to value the plays because they are *teutsch und tief*. The latter criterion was of course used in praising the works of Erwin Guido Kolbenheyer and other heroes of that kidney. On the other hand, it should be noted that Thomas Mann's review of *Der tote Tag*, in the *Dial* of October, 1924, claims that Barlach's play was the boldest and most exciting drama of the Munich season. Mann does not tell us about the competition that year, but presumably it was not negligible.

The (largely extradramatic) appeal of *Der tote Tag* derives, I think, from Barlach's employment of several potent myths — a procedure which may well have been unconscious. Gnosticism, Christianity, the old "Amazonian" theme of the battle between the sexes (which agrees with certain psychoanalyltical insights), all play a part. As we shall see, Barlach came to see his own struggle with the mother of his son Nikolaus in mythical terms.

Lacking complete evidence, one may surmise that Barlach assumed a Gnostic stance not from reading books or hearing lectures — he was hardly an "intellectual" — but from bitter personal experience and from the characteristic expressionistic devotion to *Geist* and the equally expressionistic scorn of mere empirical matter. Be this as it may, we do have in *Der tote Tag* devotion to *Geist* and opposition to matter. Etymologically, almost automatically, matter includes the female sex. *Materia, matrix, mater* are all Bad Things — which does not exclude an occasional grudging sympathy for the Mother in our drama. She is a frightful, vicious person, but very strong. Without any true ally, she defeats the various representatives of spirit until almost the end of the play. (It is very unexpressionistic that the father is exalted far above the mother. Here "The father is God, the son man, the mother anti-God."[1]) Throughout *Der tote Tag*, it is made clear that *Geist*, light, and God pertain to the male sex alone. This "sexist" attitude of Barlach's did not persist; in his next play, *Der arme Vetter* (1918) the heroine, Fräulein Isenbarn, offers herself to her unfortunate fiancé, Siebenmark, not because she loves him but because she feels that "mere" flesh is all he deserves. She becomes a sort of lay nun — a further rejection of the world. How far *Der tote Tag* is from any viable human or dramatic balance becomes especially clear if one briefly compares it — may Mozart forgive me! — with *Die Zauberflöte*. Here too light, reason, and the male principle are arrayed against the hysterical feminism of the Queen of the Night; but the work ends with forgiveness, reconciliation, and indeed a sacred marriage, a *hieros gamos*. Of course there are those who prefer the gloomiest obfuscation to Enlightenment.

Appropriately enough, physical darkness or at best twilight prevails throughout the play: the whole stage is one gigantic metaphor of spiritual gloom. As Edson Chick wittily puts it, this is literally Barlach's most obscure piece.[2] Beneath the large room, furnished in peasant style, lies the black cellar where carcasses are stored — the home of rats, particularly nasty insects, etc. Granted that it would be forcing things — given Barlach's antipathy to psychoanalysis — to equate the cellar with the unconscious, the contemporary reader can hardly help seeing the analogy. At any rate, without going beyond the play, we see the cellar as the epitome of blackness — and of lurking evil. After the killing of the magic steed Herzhorn, the sun averts its face; and the sun is clearly linked with the masculine principle and hence with the divine father of the hero or semihero of the drama. At this point we grasp the full force of the title: if the spirit is overthrown, the result is — death. The Mother, of course, incarnates the power of darkness, and tries in every sense to keep the Son in the dark. Kule's blindness is relevant here, as is the invisibility of the exceptionally grotesque gnome Steißbart. For an artist like Barlach, such a deprivation of seeing and light must have represented an ultimate horror.

Since Gnosticism had many bonds with Christianity, it is not surprising that a Christian element fits rather neatly into the play. It is supplied by the blind wanderer and prophet Kule — incidentally the only human character in *Der tote Tag* who has a name of his own. In literary terms Kule is a Tiresias figure, not to say a cliché: his wisdom seems to derive from his blindness. As he was the Mother's lover or husband before the god took her and begot the Son, he is also a Joseph figure. More importantly, it is his vocation to bear other people's burdens — symbolized by some remarkably vocal rocks which he totes about. He is even willing to assume the guilt for the murder of Herzhorn, but this self-sacrificing deception does not work for long. With his altruistic orientation, he is — though often a bore — the one admirable person in the drama.

In a fierce polemic against Richard Wagner, Paul Henry Lang charged that "the sun of Homer" does not shine on the inhabitants of his artistic world.[3] This is perhaps a bit harsh: is not Siegfried a sort of third-string Achilles? Certainly Homer's sun did not shine on Barlach — who did not profit as an artist from the sun of Paris or Florence either — or on his creatures. Some touches in *Der tote Tag* — the gnomes, the generally "Northern" atmosphere, the occasional alliterations[4] — do suggest Wagner. And the Son is a sort of potential savior, like Siegfried, but he turns out to be pitifully weak.

To touch briefly on one of Barlach's own mythical inventions — the horse Herzhorn, sent by the distant, invisible Father (God, or at least the sun god) to encourage and liberate the Son — this is as obvious a phallic symbol as one is likely to find. "Herzhorn," Barlach tells us, was a place name associated in his mind with his father's life,[5] and as such, we may add, the use of the term is pro-male, anti-maternal. Very well; but why that particular place name? Both "Herz" and "Horn" are highly suggestive. When the Mother murders Herzhorn (the word is not too strong) she commits an act of symbolic castration,[6] and indeed the Son's modest powers are further reduced at this point. Thus there would seem to be a link between *Der tote Tag* and yet another myth — here the term is honorific — the creation of the Great Enlightener and Magician of Vienna. Almost certainly this connection has nothing to do with direct or conscious influence: Barlach reading Freud would seem at least as improbable an event as Hermann Hesse reading Voltaire.

A major component of *Der tote Tag* was furnished by Barlach's own life during the years when he was composing the play. He was engaged in a bitter struggle, which he eventually won, for the possession of his son Nikolaus. According to Barlach, Nikolaus' mother was a very dreadful person, but one never finds her side of the case stated. Indeed, I have never found her name, either in Barlach's writings or in the secondary literature — which seems to be evidence of a truly monumental hostility. Barlach writes with some pride that he has never called his former mistress "low" (*schlecht*), but goes on "Ich wollte ihm [dem Sohn im *Toten Tag*] in der Mutter alles geben, was abstößt und doch nicht losläßt."[7] At the same time, he had no intention of writing a bourgeois tragedy. His working titles were "Der Göttersohn," which may point back toward Wagner, and then — hardly an improvement — "Blutgeschrei."[8] *Der tote Tag* surely was a far happier solution.

Barlach had some trouble with his own mother, who struck him as possessive and emotionally parasitical, as we know from *Ein selbsterzähltes Leben*.[9] However, this problem was contained, if not resolved. There was nothing demonic about it, little to suggest the ferocious possessiveness of the Mother of Barlach's first tragedy, who is a Jungian *Magna Mater*[10] of the most man-eating sort. No, when Barlach talks about "the mother" in connection with the play, he means, exclusively or almost exclusively, the mother of his son.[11]

Barlach explains how the transition to the mythical world took place: "Die

Mutter wollte den Knaben nicht hergeben. Auf diese Weise mußte ich früher oder später notwendig Gott für ihn werden. [!] Das war der Anstoß. Unter den Händen wuchs die Idee von selber ins Mythische."[12]

In a letter to Dr. Julius Cohen,[13] Barlach remarked that his first drama probably owed more to his joy in scenes and pictures than to the desire to state convictions. One wonders: certain convictions could hardly be more emphatically stated; it sounds as if he were retreating in the letter from fanatic anti-feminism. Disarmingly, he adds that it was perhaps arrogant to have built his drama on a mythical basis.[14]

Another letter to Dr. Cohen, written about a month later (22-28 April 1916), contains what is by far Barlach's most important statement on the play. The situation was a humorous one: psychoanalysis had discovered *Der tote Tag* and found — how could it not! — that the play was grist to its mill. Barlach protested that he had no thought of incest, which is certainly true, and that he had read only "little articles" about Freud.[15] With some heat he rejected any sexual interpretation: "Fort vom Mütterlichen, vom Schmeichelnden, Wohlberatenen, Sichaneinander-Genügenden und am Ende (in meinem Falle persönlich) weg von dem ewigen Sexuellen."[16]

"Away from sex!" has at least the virtue of originality, even in a decade supersaturated with slogans. But to denounce sexuality so vehemently does not mean that one is free of it. "When me ye flee, I am the wings," as Emerson wrote in a somewhat different context. In any case, the symbolic castration[17] (the killing of Herzhorn) harmonizes perfectly if painfully with "Away from sex!" After reading *Der tote Tag* Jung remarked that Barlach was more accessible in terms of Jungian psychology than of Freud's: Barlach dealt with a symbolic rather than a concrete mother figure.[18] All depends here on what Nikolaus' mother was really like; we do not know, and we cannot judge how 'real' the mythical Mother of Barlach is. We do know that Jung is more helpful with the Hermann Hesses; Freud with the Thomas Manns. In *Seelenprobleme der Gegenwart*[19] Jung quoted the last sentence of *Der tote Tag* to refute his former master: "Sonderbar ist nur, daß der Mensch nicht lernen will, daß sein Vater Gott ist." Probably this is the best line in the play, but one cannot imagine that Freud felt particularly crushed when he read it.

To turn to the text: the *Personen* comprise the archetypal figures Mother and Son; Kule, as blind prophet, is almost an archetype too; Steissbart "as voice,"[20] Besenbein, another gnome; and the *Alb,* a highly symbolic nightmare figure to whom we shall return. Three humans (if one may include the Mother) are balanced by three representatives of Northern mythology; to the best of my knowledge, Steißbart and Besenbein are Barlach's own inventions. The stage is dark, at least in part. We are in the joyless world of unaesthetic paganism.

Act I

The word "unaesthetic" may seem to betray classicistic prejudice, but the first incident in the play confirms its rightness. The Mother arises from the cellar, like Wagner's Erda from the ground, and at once undertakes physically to determine Steißbart's sex. Yes, he indeed has the appropriate organs. Not unnaturally annoyed by her aggressive researches, he urinates on her. Both Barlach's vehement hatred of his son's mother and his utter scorn of decorum are here vividly and irrefutably illustrated. No one could be blamed, at this point, for throwing down the book and going back permanently to Racine, or at least to Goethe. Perhaps when Thomas Mann called Steißbart "filthy," he was referring to this episode.[21] As far as I know, no one has discussed this cloacal confrontation. This is all too understandable, but the episode is enlightening, especially for those who regard Barlach as a sort of Low German saint.

The incident strikes a note of gratuitous ugliness which is repeated throughout the play. A similar exploitation of the ugly is apparent in Ernst Toller's *Hinkemann*, in Brecht's early plays, and indeed in many dramas written after 1945.

Unhousebroken though he is, Steißbart is a rather important figure in the play. A male, he upholds the paternal principle; scorning the flesh, in Manichaean or Gnostic fashion, he maintains "Daß Männer von Männern herkommen" (14)[22] and that the Son knows too little of his father. Appropriately, the Son is the only one who can see Steißbart; the two seem to be mysteriously linked. Old Kule comes in with his staff and various oracular remarks; the Mother eventually recognizes him. Recalling that the Son's father is a god, he speaks of the Son as a hero — the Mother disagrees — as one who may be breaking out of the world like a bird from the egg. (18) One thinks of Hesse's *Demian*. Kule too believes that divine children do not come from mothers. The Mother admits that the God has announced to her in a dream that he is sending a steed to carry his son into the world.

Kule: Zum Heil der Welt.
Mutter: Zum Tode der Mutter. (20)

Almost immediately, the Son proclaims that the magic steed is there; he too has seen it in a dream. True to her emasculating role, the Mother compares it to a cow. (21) She is also fighting the battle of the generations: "Sohnes-Zukunft ist Mutter-Vergangenheit." (23) There follow a few pages of appropriately vague talk about the future — of course a typical expressionistic theme. Clearly revealing her own wish to make a baby of the Son, the Mother fashions a crude doll in his image; faithful little Steißbart knocks off its head. Shifting the image, the Mother truculently proclaims that she is no cradle: "Bin ich wie eine Wiege? Laß ich ein Kind in mich legen [*sic!*] und von mir nehmen wie aus einer Wiege? Mich zum Gerümpel stecken? Mein, mein, mein Sohn ist es gewesen und mein soll er bleiben." (28 f.)

As the act ends, the Son staunchly maintains that he is no longer a baby.

Act II

This is the decisive part of the action, literally and symbolically. The night is only half-dark; but animal, largely unpleasant images set the tone: carrion, bear, stag, rooster; also manure, mould, slime. Again, Steißbart is linked to a bit of gratuitous ugliness. (32)

Steißbart is gagged because of his previous offense, but not before he warns the Son to guard his divine steed. He however prefers to engage in theological discourse with Kule. Apparently jealous, the Mother objects to their talking late:

Und die Nacht betrügen, die heilige Nacht? (33)

While she is obviously a "night" figure in more senses than one, Novalis' words sound strange in her mounth. At this point the Son seems to be gradually developing in the direction of the expressionistic "new man"; he is fascinated with the life of the gods and aspires to it. Probably there are veiled references to Jesus, Siegfried, and Zarathustra — a peculiar triad.

Splitting wood hurriedly in the dark, a none too intelligent procedure, the Son cuts his hand. The Mother's sense of "triumph" at this is only half concealed; this is not sheer sadism, but is based on her correct calculation that the weaker he becomes, the more he must depend on her. She loves him in her own fashion, like a baby, or better, like a sexless doll.

When the *Alb* appears and the Son eventually battles with him, his wound is obviously a handicap. His curious opponent is a "guter Alb" who plagues men at night: "Weil es sie gut macht, wenn ich sie quäle." (38) The Son remarks that if the *Alb* were slain men would be no worse and still could sleep soundly at night. Essaying the role of hero, as a youth of divine origin, the Son would tear the creature's heart out, and the poor *Alb* would be only too happy to die, like Wotan toward the end of the *Ring*.

Probably the *Alb* is best viewed as the Christian conscience, seen in more or less Nietzschean terms: as a very powerful entity, well-meaning but obsolete and capable of causing great suffering. Of course we associate the idea of being pressed and oppressed with *Alb/Alp* and its compounds. Or it could be associated with remorse, as defined and rejected by Spinoza and Goethe. The two concepts are obviously interrelated; the general significance of the figure is fairly clear. One notes that the altruistic Kule is particularly plagued by the *Alb*; whereas Barlach himself had little use for orthodox religion.

Thus the Son engages in the classic ordeal of the heroes of myth. (Perhaps we may also think of Nietzsche assaulting the whole Christian tradition.) Weakened as he is — obviously we must take his injured hand symbolically — he makes little headway in his struggle. Though the son of a god, he calls on his mother; the *Alb* is amazed: "Mutter, rufst du — ein Göttersohn und rufst Mutter!" (43) Steißbart howls from the rafters, where he has been hung to accelerate his housebreaking. Remembering that he is completely on the masculine side, we tend to see the episode as the absolute victory of the maternal element, and it indeed proves decisive.

What are we to make of a mythical hero who fails in his very first ordeal? Such failure need not be final; Parzival, for instance, also got off to a bad start. The mother, however, will soon make it very sure that the youth will never have a second chance. One should remember also that relatively few "new men" in expressionistic literature really fulfill their potential. On the autobiographical level, Barlach may well have feared that his young son — and perhaps he himself — would fail to stand up to that all too human mother whom he so greatly hated and feared.

At the end of the act, the Mother plays with the idea of letting her son bleed to death; then she could never lose him to the Father. Even for her that would be a bit too much; she will attack Herzhorn instead; of course the steed is part of the Son, in a very real sense. The sun image at the end of the act is enlightening: "Ob ich den Mut hätte, die Sonne wie einen Topf zu Scherben zu schlagen?" (44 f.) she asks herself. Doubtless, Barlach knew *Ghosts*: "The sun! The sun!" It is more relevant, though, to remember that later in the play the sun will turn away from the foul world of *Der tote Tag*. In spiritually destroying her child, she has defeated the sun and the sun god — temporarily.

Act III

This scene (only nominally an act) also is played on a very dark stage. The Mother enters slowly, knife in hand, a Barlachian Lady Macbeth. Of course she has killed Herzhorn. By threatening to put the blame on the helpful *Hausgeist* Besenbein, she forces him to drag in the carcass; it is to be stored — suppressed — in her ghastly cellar. He escapes. Blackmailing the harmless Besenbein is the Mother's lowest deed so far. Fortunately for her, Kule and the exhausted Son sleep through the entire act. Still hanging from the rafters, Steißbart *röchelt im Rauch*; only Wagnerian alliteration remains to him. Yet there is a hint of retribution: the Mother notices that her son is laughing in his sleep: "Sollte er noch immer vom Reiten träumen? Weh mir, wenn du vom Reiten träumst!" (48)

Perhaps the Father will send another magic steed.

Act IV

The action takes place in a pale, livid *Morgendämmer* — possibly we should think of *Götterdämmerung*, for the quasi-divine Son has been defeated and is to be further humiliated. *Tot, sterben*, etc. function as leitmotifs. The act is retrospective and extremely talky: falling action with a vengeance. The grunts and groans of poor Steißbart, who is still being smoked like a ham, furnish a very Barlachian obbligato.

Kule has dreamt of the downfall of the quasi-hero. It is at this point that the sun averts its eyes; the day is like a child born dead, "ein toter Tag." (53) The redoubtable Mother launches a two-pronged strategy: Kule is to assume the guilt for the equicide — or rather the disappearance of the horse, for of course she makes no explicit confession; the Son is to regress to being a small boy. Alas, she is largely successful. Not given to half measures, she strikes her son; he recalls that the *Alb* called him "Muttersohn."

While it is in line with Kule's altruism and his weakness that he refuses to deny his "guilt," this point seems dramatically useless: no one is fooled, and further evidence that the Mother is no lady is surely redundant. When Kule refuses to refute the charges against himself, the Son remarks: "Er hat wohl tiefe Keller in seiner Seele" (57), reminding us of the cellar where Herzhorn is lying, and perhaps also of psychoanalysis, but it is equally possible that no specific source is involved. There is a hint that the Son is a blood relation of the emphatically masculine Steißbart; the Son rightly feels that his Mother wishes to reduce him to the stature of a gnome. Equally strong indications suggest that the Mother is beginning to feel a sense of guilt after all; she becomes less of a monster, and we can almost sympathize with her.

Within three pages, at the end of the act, Kule launches an important prophecy *and* is grossly humiliated. One recalls Gundolf's words "tiefen Mangel an *Richtigkeit.*" Of course, prophecy and humiliation could be meaningfully counterpointed against each other, but such is not the case here. Kule prophesies that things will come to a good end; this is almost certainly untrue. Two pages later, the Son, following a hint given by the Mother, plays hobbyhorse, riding around on Kule's allegedly magic staff. Not content with this infantile regression, he breaks the staff to pieces, to use it for kindling wood. Obviously he has inherited the sadism of his Magna Mater. This is another Wagnerian touch: a greatly reduced Siegfried has broken the spear of a most unconvincing Wotan. The nasty word "castration" again comes to mind. With the breaking of the staff, with a whimper, the act ends.

Act V

Again, the light is dim; again there is far more talk than dramatic development. Winter is approaching. The day is "a dead steed"; the Mother is full of *Angst*. Going out of doors, the Son at once is lost in a sudden fog, which he compares to the dying of a god, and again calls on his mother; he too is symbolically blind. Steißbart, the most intelligent of this remarkable group, realizes that the

Mother has beein lying. His manners, however, leave much to be desired: he repeatedly calls the Son a bed wetter (74, 86) — though the gnome is the last one who should use that term — and the poor boy is too beaten down to react.

To concentrate on Steißbart for a moment: he and his ancestors all had no mothers — an excellent thing from the point of view of this play — they had a form of second sight, and his father, though wingless, was able to rise vertically through the air. To be sure, breaking wind was necessary, to supply the necessary upward propulsion.

What is the function of all this ugliness in *Der tote Tag*, or is it all merely repulsive nonsense, alien corn? In addition to the examples already noted, we find at the end that the Mother has served up the horse: they have been eating Herzhorn unawares. Shades of Atreus and Thyestes! Is this what Barlach is really like? In calling the ugliness gratuitous, I meant that it serves no dramatic purpose, but it must have had a cathartic function. One might compare Goethe's so uncharacteristic nastiness in the *Venetian Epigrams*. Barlach rid himself of much black bile: there are many grotesque and cruel elements in his later plays, but he was not again to sink to these depths, except in *Der Findling*. This is a sick play by a sick man, but he was to recover.

Toward the end of the play, the Son finally calls on his father, twice. Turning at last against the Mother, he bitterly reproaches her for hiding the god from him. He believes that he has met someone in the fog — obviously the Father — but actually he has not left the house. Believing that a messenger awaits him, he tries to leave the room, utterly rejecting the Mother: "Euer Sehen ist mein Blindsein, euer Kopfschütteln mein Nicken." (94) She reacts with total war: she curses him, confesses her crimes, and stabs herself. After a few more speeches, the Son also kills himself. Like Fortinbras, Kule and Steißbart carry on: they will wander through the world, proclaiming the father principle. Steißbart has the last word: "Sonderbar ist nur, daß der Mensch nicht lernen will, daß sein Vater Gott ist." (95) It is one of the few really good lines in the play. How eccentric, however, to assign it to an invisible gnome with no doubt a squeaky voice.

Conclusion

It would appear that an otherwise inferior work of literature may be memorable if it contains a strong charge of genuine passion. Barlach's emotional struggle with his son's mother must have been more intense than one could infer from his letters and autobiography.[23] Although *Der tote Tag* is not one of the handful of truly satisfying German expressionistic plays, it deals with a universal theme: sexual hostility. Most of us overcome this aversion or at least contain it; but as a potential danger, the psychologists tell us, it lies within us all.

NOTES

1. See Herbert Meier, *Der verborgene Gott* (Nuremberg: Glock & Lutz 1963), p. 16.
2. Edson M. Chick, *Ernst Barlach* (New York: Twayne, 1967), p. 30.
3. Paul Henry Lang, "Background Music for Mein Kampf," *Saturday Review of Literature*, 28/3 (20 Jan. 1945), 5.
4. Wolfgang Paulsen, "Zur Struktur von Barlachs Dramen," *Aspekte des Expressionismus*, ed. Wolfgang Paulsen (Heidelberg: Stiehm, 1968), p. 121.
5. See Karl Graucob, *Ernst Barlachs Dramen* (München: Insel-Bücherei, 1963), p. 14.
6. Erich Neumann, *Ursprungsgeschichte des Bewußtseins* (Zürich: Rascher, 1949), pp. 186, 206.
7. Quoted by Willi Flemming, *Ernst Barlach: Wesen und Werk* (Berne: Francke, 1958), p. 182, from letter to Julius Cohen, 23. IV. 1916.
8. Graucob, p. 13.
9. Barlach, *Ein selbsterzähltes Leben*, included in *Das dichterische Werk*, II (Münich: Piper, 1958), p. 42.
10. Neumann, p. 183.
11. For a different view, see Paulsen, p. 111.
12. Cf. *Barlach im Gespräch*, ed. Friedrich Schult, (Munich: Insel-Bücherei, 1963), p. 32.
13. Barlach, *Die Briefe, I: 1888-1924*, ed. Friedrich Dross (Munich: Piper, 1968), pp. 477 f. Letter of 23. III. 1916.
14. *Ibid.*
15. *Briefe*, I, 481.
16. *Ibid.*, p. 480.
17. See n. 6.
18. See Dross, in the notes to *Briefe*, I, 798 f.
19. C. G. Jung, *Seelenprobleme der Gegenwart* (Zurich: Rascher, 1931), p. 74; cited by Dross, *Briefe*, I, 800.
20. Steißbart is visible only to the Son.
21. Thomas Mann, "German Letter (October 1924)," *The Dial*, 77 (1924), 414-19.
22. Page references in the text are to Ernst Barlach, *Das dichterische Werk*, I: *Die Dramen*, ed. K. Lazarowicz (München: Piper, 1956).
23. See however the very bitter letter of 19. IX. 1907 (*Briefe*, I, 286) where he speaks of poisoning the boy's mother.

BRECHT'S *DIE SIEBEN TODSÜNDEN DER KLEINBÜRGER*: EMBLEMATIC STRUCTURE AS EPIC SPECTACLE

Steven Paul Scher

Brecht scholarship during the seventeen years since the poet's death has grown to voluminous proportions. Yet only recently, in summing up the present state of research, Reinhold Grimm was prompted to write: "...die grundsätzliche Forschungssituation ist jedoch die gleiche geblieben. Zentrale Fragen sind weiterhin ungelöst; zahlreiche Einzelprobleme harren noch der Klärung".[1] The critical fate of *Die sieben Todsünden der Kleinbürger* of 1933, Brecht's only ballet and the last fruit of his memorable collaboration with Kurt Weill, seems symptomatic. That this unique, though at first glance unassuming little work has been all but neglected[2] is surprising since critics have examined in considerable detail virtually everything Brecht wrote for the stage, even the short one-act play *Die Bibel* of the 15-year old *Gymnasiast*.[3]

Die sieben Todsünden der Kleinbürger is a hybrid among theatrical genres: a ballet combined with solo and ensemble singing based on Brecht's scenario and poem cycle and set to music by Weill. Framed by a prologue and an epilogue, it is essentially a *Stationendrama* in miniature, consisting of a series of seven scenes each ostensibly depicting one of the seven deadly sins: "Faulheit," "Stolz," "Zorn," "Völlerei," "Unzucht," "Habsucht," and "Neid."[4]

Brecht chose a well-known subject to accommodate the complex theatrical design he had in mind involving no less than three basic artistic media: literature, music, and the dance. Adaptation of the religious concept of the seven deadly (or cardinal) sins, fraught with medieval symbolism, to the twentieth-century milieu of capitalistic exploitation and class struggle — preserving traditional ethical connotations of the topos only in the form of hypocritical pseudo-values and clichés — afforded Brecht the opportunity to develop his own ideological interpretation of the altered social conditions within an overtly didactic framework. For inspiration he must have particularly welcomed the loosely connected scenic portrayals of the sins in the paintings and drawings of Bosch and Breughel[5] which are so akin in spirit and execution to the serial, episodic structure of the spectacle he had conceived. The topic itself was not novel in Brecht's poetic practice: already the opening "Choral vom großen Baal" establishes "Wollust" as the major theme of the early play *Baal*, and the scene in *Aufstieg und Fall der Stadt Mahagonny* in which Jakob der Vielfraß eats himself to death in public is a grotesque example of "Völlerei." No doubt aware of the long and illustrious history of the concept in theology, art, and literature, and thus relying on the traces of the religious and allegorical representations surviving in the universal consciousness,[6] the poet could proceed to construct his own, modern version on the theme.

In *Die sieben Todsünden der Kleinbürger*, a lower middle class family in Louisiana sends its daughter Anna on a trip to try her luck in the big city and earn enough money for building a house back home. To convey the ambivalence inherent in the "sinner," Brecht splits the personality of Anna into Anna I, the cynical impresario with a practical sense and conscience, and Anna II, the emotional, impulsive, artistic beauty, the salable product with an all too human heart. During a period of seven years in seven major American cities, under the strict guidance of Anna I, Anna II confronts and successfully withstands the seven deadly sins of bourgeois society.

Around 1926 Brecht began a systematic study of Marxism. With the help of Karl Korsch, his Marxist philosopher friend and expert teacher, the poet was thoroughly indoctrinated by 1933.[7] Thus the blunt ideological content of *Die sieben Todsünden* comes as no surprise. Spelling out a condemnation of the capitalistic system which not only permits but actively encourages the flourishing of the "American dream" as a practical necessity for survival, the ballet unmasks the uncompromising cruelty of bourgeois society toward human nature; it is a vitriolic satire of the competitive game of "making it." More significant than the straightforward, unambiguous moral, however, is the subtly equivocal conceptual framework Brecht devises to get his message across. By appending the phrase "der Kleinbürger" to "Die sieben Todsünden" in the title, he particularizes the universal connotation of the well-known concept: at once the traditional topos is detached from its familiar context and assumes a novel, sociological reference. But Brecht does not stop at this initial stage of alienation. By adding antithetical explicatory phrases to the individual sins, he further twists the original connotations toward his didactic aim. Through ironic reversals of meaning, what he designates as "sins" turn out to be basic human virtues. "Faulheit" by itself, for example, is one of the traditional deadly sins. Anna II reveals herself as only too human in being susceptible to sloth. But "Faulheit — im Begehen des Unrechts" (*GW* 7, 2858) is only regarded as a sin by the inhuman rules of bourgeois society. Wanting to be lazy in committing injustice, Anna II is in fact being virtuous. Consequently, by preventing Anna II from committing this "sin," Anna I presents herself as a vicious agent of capitalist mentality. In a similar manner, Brecht alters the conventional meaning of one sin after another so that a dialectic pattern of connotations emerges: "Stolz" becomes pride in one's own integrity, "Zorn" anger about the meanness of others, "Völlerei" indulgence in the pleasure of eating normally, "Unzucht" genuine, unselfish love, "Habsucht" excessive greed in robbing and cheating,[8] and "Neid" envy of those who may indulge unscrupulously in being virtuous.

Brecht's text by itself is not among his most inspired. The original version is particularly skeletal and wooden compared to the text the poet prepared for Weill to set to music.[9] But, in large measure thanks to Weill's imaginative musical realization, the work as a whole proves to be remarkably successful; and it bears the unmistakable stamp of the Brecht-Weill collaboration at its "culinary" best. In spite of some shallow lines and occasional embarrassingly bare ideological clichés, the text is not without a peculiar charm and contains several typically Brechtian ideas. For example, Anna I and Anna II as the two aspects of a split personality anticipate Shen Te and Shui Ta in *Der gute Mensch von Sezuan* or the sober and drunk personalities of Herr Puntila. The fact that both Annas are simultaneously and continuously visible, however, is unique. The use of an "exotic" setting (Louisiana) is likewise familiar from other plays such as *Mahagonny* (Southern U. S.), *Im Dickicht der Städte*, *Die heilige Johanna der Schlachthöfe* and *Der aufhaltsame Aufstieg des Arturo Ui* (Chicago), *Mann ist Mann* (British India), and *Der kaukasische Kreidekreis* (Russian Georgia). By transplanting contemporary social problems into a geographically distant milieu, the poet intends to alienate them and thereby bring about fresh awareness. The camouflaged moralist Brecht is clearly in his element in *Die sieben Todsünden*. The religious allusion of the title signals at the outset that this social satire is meant as a serious attack on the hypocrisy of the bourgeois moral code; from beneath the pseudo-religious pretense of decency and humaneness, the cruelty and ruthlessness of competitive capitalistic society emerge.

The stage design, only partially suggested by the initial scenario, is as essential a dramatic component as the combined impact of Brecht's poem cycle, the ballet action, and Weill's music. In Caspar Neher's original setting reminiscent of a circus production, seven gates with paper stretched across them form a semicircle at the back of the stage, labelled with the seven deadly sins. Anna II dances through one gate after the other, ripping through the paper. On one side of the stage the members of the family are seated on a small platform; and as the action proceeds the walls of the house gradually rise around them. Anna I stands across from the family on the other side of the stage.[10]

Scored for a large symphonic orchestra with virtuoso instrumentation, Weill's music is composed in seven melodically and rhythmically self-contained movements. The Introduction and Finaletto, corresponding to the prologue and epilogue sections in the text, exhibit a certain thematic similarity and thus round off the cycle of movements. Climactic musical passages usually occur in the form of orchestral interludes which serve as accompaniment of major portions of the ballet action. A bipartite musical structure within the individual movements is suggested by means of contrasted instrument groups, e.g., woodwinds versus strings. Weill uses the strings especially in soft, slow passages in order to create a nostalgic, bittersweet, sentimental mood. From time to time there are reminiscences of earlier Weill sound-combinations like the blend of banjo, piano, and percussion familiar from *Die Dreigroschenoper*. Recurring in leitmotivic fashion, the double bass or the bassoon signifies the domineering mother while woodwind figurations refer to the rest of the family. Consistently incorporated jazz elements and contemporary dance rhythms are easily recognizable throughout.

A male quartet representing the family parodies the chorus in Greek drama and provides the pseudo-moralizing vocal commentary in mock-biblical language. The family members — the mother in the role of the *choryphaeus* (equipped with a deep buffo bass voice!), the father, and two brothers — alternate between solo arias and choral passages. The major vocal role of Anna I is particularly colorful and varied, combining narrative and commentary in straightforward songs and recitative-like passages reminiscent of the evangelist in oratorios. Diverse forms of musical alienation abound in the score and faithfully complement Brecht's textual "Verfremdungseffekte." Weill successfully parodies a variety of serious and less serious musical styles such as film music, "Gesangvereinstil," grand opera, oratorio and cantata style, "Salonmusik," a-capella madrigal style, "Tingel-Tangel-Musik," and circus and country fair music.

I

Up to the present day there is a remarkable lack of verifiable information concerning the origins and subsequent fate of *Die sieben Todsünden*. Brecht wrote the text in the spring of 1933, presumably in Paris where he spent a few months before settling down in Danish exile.[11] Commissioned by Georges Balanchine's ephemeral "Les Ballets 1933," the ballet cantata was first produced in June 1933 at the Théâtre des Champs Élysées with Lotte Lenya as Anna I and Tilly Losch creating the dancing role of Anna II. Balanchine functioned as choreographer and the sets were designed by Brecht's friend and longtime collaborator Caspar Neher.[12] Entitled *Anna Anna ou Les Sept Péchés Capitaux* but apparently sung in German,[13] Brecht's first original venture in exile met with no success. The English performances in London later in the same year also remained without appreciable critical echo.[14] *The Dancing Times* of London, for example, found "nothing to clarify or elucidate the heavy darkness of the Germano-American text..."[15] Only one critic, Constant Lambert, was sensitive enough to perceive in 1934 that *"The Seven Deadly Sins* marks as great an improvement on *Mahagonny* as *Mahagonny* did on *Die Dreigroschenoper"* and that it is "the most important work in ballet form since *Les Noces* and *Parade*."[16] Put on once more before the Second World War in Copenhagen in 1936, the ballet precipitated a scandal: the Danish king indignantly walked out in the middle of the performance.[17] It was not until 1958 in New York that the work was revived again, this time successsfully;[18] and the first German performance in Frankfurt in 1960 also won over reviewers and audiences alike.[19] Lotte Lenya again sang Anna I in both productions. Since 1961 the work has become part of the standard repertory of several East German theaters;[20] and lately there have also been sporadic revivals in the United States and in the rest of Europe.

In addition to the unfavorable reception of the early productions there are other possible reasons for the relative obscurity which still surrounds *Die sieben Todsünden*. First of all, Brecht's original German text was not published until 1959.[21] The work appeared for the first time in 1933 in French translation.[22] The first English version has been lost, while the second English rendering used in the 1958 New York production was printed only in 1961.[23] But even Brecht's German text — as we have grown accustomed to expect of him — exists in several versions which distinctly differ from the original; and the known stage version contains a great many additional and/or altered lines, especially in the choral passages.[24] The fact that the German text was not printed while Brecht was alive suggests that he considered the work artistically inferior and perhaps wanted to suppress it altogether.[25] Yet it is reasonable to assume, I believe, that in 1933 both Brecht and Weill — already well known as co-authors of *Die Dreigroschenoper* — hoped to launch their careers in exile by capturing Western audiences anew with this unusual stage spectacle.

In spite of the overwhelmingly positive critical reaction after the New York and Frankfurt productions, scholarly opinion on *Die sieben Todsünden* continues to be negligible. Most critics who do mention the work in passing tacitly agree that the ballet is an unimpressive, misconceived, and justly forgotten by-product of the poet's once so rewarding partnership with Kurt Weill.[26] Such a view is myopic, I believe. It is only partially attributable to the persisting confusion concerning origins and publishing history. Most likely it stems from the practice in Brecht studies of concentrating exclusively on works written either before or after 1933,[27] thus disregarding his first year of exile. While it is justifiable to separate Brecht's later period — which culminated in the writing of great plays such as *Mutter Courage und ihre Kinder, Leben des Galilei, Der gute Mensch von Sezuan, Herr Puntila und sein Knecht Matti,* and *Der kaukasische Kreidekreis* — from the plays, operas, and *Lehrstücke* written before 1933, it seems to me essential to focus attention on this first year of exile as a decisive time of stock-taking and creative reflection at mid-point in the poet's career. From this perspective, *Die sieben Todsünden* proves to be far from insignificant. As I shall attempt to demonstrate below, in this work we possess an important milestone in Brecht's maturation process, a coherent and transparent model of his theory in practice. The ballet not only incorporates innovations in dramatic form evolved up to 1933; it also anticipates epic theater techniques which are usually regarded as characteristic only of the later plays, especially of *Der kaukasische Kreidekreis*. I believe that two aspects of the formal design of *Die sieben Todsünden* merit particular consideration: emblematic structure and the combination of artistic media in a moralistic-didactic anti-*Gesamtkunstwerk*.

II

In a recent article, Reinhold Grimm calls attention to Brecht's fundamentally emblematic vision — whether conscious or not — as a decisive poetic strategy whose traces are omnipresent in the playwright's works.[28] Though Grimm omits specific mention of *Die sieben Todsünden* in this connection, it seems to me that this work is perhaps best equipped to illustrate the nature of emblematic vision as a basic formative principle in Brecht's conception of dramatic structure.

Albrecht Schöne's *Emblematik und Drama im Zeitalter des Barock* is to date the most comprehensive study of the profound influence of the emblematic tradition on sixteenth and seventeenth-century theater. In the chapter "Aufbau des Emblems und Funktion seiner Teile"[29] Schöne expounds the basic tripartite pattern characteristic of most emblems included in the various standard collections published since Alciati's epoch-making *Emblematum liber* of 1531. It it customary to distinguish three components in an emblem: the *pictura* or symbolic image or picture, accompanied by the preceding *inscriptio* or motto and the subsequent *subscriptio*, usually an explication in verse of the idea expressed in the combination of the *inscriptio* and the *pictura*. Schöne's analytical results become particularly illuminating when he points to the many structural and functional elements in Baroque dramatic practice deriving from emblematic inspiration.

While to some extent an emblematic orientation is perceptible in most of Brecht's stage works, the unique feature of *Die sieben Todsünden* is that here the correspondences between emblematic intention and the poet's well-known techniques of epic theater go far beyond mere generalities and significantly enhance the effectiveness of his didactic purpose. Moreover, I believe that an awareness of the ballet's tightly-knit double emblematic structure can yield a number of new insights concerning Brecht's overall conception of dramatic form. The following sketch will help to visualize the two distinct, but integrated patterns which emerge:

DIE SIEBEN TODSÜNDEN DER KLEINBÜRGER	INSCRIPTIO I
List of the seven sins with suggested meanings — e.g., "Faulheit — im Begehen des Unrechts"	inscriptiones II
SCENARIO CONCERNING ENTIRE WORK	PICTURA I
STAGE DIRECTIONS WITH BRIEF EXPLANATION OF THEME, PLOT, ROLES, SETTING, PROPS	
PROLOGUE: LIED DER SCHWESTER	SUBSCRIPTIO I/a

I) *Faulheit*
   Scenario
   Lied der Familie
	inscriptio II/1
	pictura II/1
	subscriptio II/1

2) *Stolz*	inscriptio II/2
Scenario	pictura II/2
Lied der Schwester	subscriptio II/2
LIED DER FAMILIE	SUBSCRIPTIO I/b
3) *Zorn*	inscriptio II/3
Scenario	pictura II/3
Lied der Schwester	subscriptio II/3
4) *Völlerei*	inscriptio II/4
Scenario	pictura II/4
Lied der Familie	subscriptio II/4
5) *Unzucht*	inscriptio II/5
Scenario	pictura II/5
Lied der Schwester	subscriptio II/5
6) *Habsucht*	inscriptio II/6
Scenario	pictura II/6
Lied der Familie	subscriptio II/6
7) *Neid*	inscriptio II/7
Scenario	pictura II/7
Lied der Schwester	subscriptio II/7
EPILOGUE: LIED DER SCHWESTER	SUBSCRIPTIO I/c

The larger emblematic pattern (I) constitutes the overall structural framework of the ballet. The smaller pattern comprising the seven deadly sins in individual emblematic tableaux (II) is embedded in the larger pattern. In both patterns the title designations (of the entire work as well as of the individual scenes) correspond to the *inscriptiones*; during performances the scene titles are usually displayed conspicuously in large letters. *Pictura* I encompasses the stage action for the whole ballet including permanent components (e.g., basic setting, roles, stage position of characters and props) and changing ones (e.g., changes of scene, house rising in the background). It represents pictorially the dramatic events which are pantomimically executed to musical accompaniment and take the place of conventional dialogue in a scenic framework. The seven scenarios (*picturae* II) perform the same function with respect to the individual scenes. Providing a continuous moral commentary on the episodically unfolding dramatic action, the ten songs (six sung by Anna I and four by the family quartet) assume the emblematic function of the *subscriptio*. Though musico-poetic emblems in their own right,[30] these songs also supply the forward-driving narrative force by informing the audience about the events. *Subscriptiones* I/a and I/c are thematically and musically connected: the first song sets the scene for the journey and anticipates the moral, while the last song completes the cycle of episodes and supplies — however equivocally — the final moral.

    The clear line of development that connects Brecht's dramatic practices with the emblematically inspired Jesuit theater and Baroque drama need not be demonstrated here.³¹ More important in our context is to specify how Brecht utilizes the emblematic framework underlying *Die sieben Todsünden* to suit his didactic intention. To put it another way, how does the presence of an emblematic structure enhance the effectiveness of Brecht's epic theater techniques? The answer lies in the unique dual role of Anna. Central in every respect, present on the stage from beginning to end, and performing in the multiple role of singer, actor, and narrator, Anna I is the perfect authorial instrument to connect emblematic and epic structure. Singing her songs (*subscriptiones*) she is part of both the larger and smaller emblematic patterns; and through her acting as manager to Anna II, she also participates in the ballet (*picturae*). The role of narrator-commentator, controlling the episodic series of events on stage while also informing the spectators directly about them, once again links her both to the individual scenes (*picturae* II) and to interpreting their moral and social meaning (*subscriptiones* II). The representational and interpretive aspects of the split personality also reflect the emblematic relation between Anna II (*pictura*) and Anna I (*subscriptio*).³²

I fully agree with Andrzej Wirth's observation in his stimulating essay "Über die stereometrische Struktur der Brechtschen Stücke" that in the final analysis "das angestrebte Ziel des Brechtschen Theaters ist die *Erzählung* auf der Bühne."³³ Recognizing in *Der kaukasische Kreidekreis* the most accomplished form of epic theater, Wirth concludes: "Als der Kommentar immer mehr die Oberhand über die Handlung gewann, schließlich zum Mitschöpfer der Handlung selber wurde — da entstand das epische Theater."³⁴ I believe that this statement, while certainly true for *Der kaukasische Kreidekreis*, proves to be applicable to *Die sieben Todsünden* as well, written eleven years earlier. In fact, because of the imaginative fusion of emblematic and epic structure — implied in the basic scene sequence depicting the seven deadly sins and realized in the narrating-commentating role of Anna I and the assisting family chorus — the ballet can be considered the most transparent practical demonstration of Brecht's conception of epic theater. Nowhere else do we encounter a dominating narrator figure that is so consistently delineated: Anna I presents, represents, controls, reports, and interprets the dramatic action while also participating in it herself. A closer look at Anna I and the chorus will show that most of the functions or devices characteristic of the singer and his musicians in *Der kaukasische Kreidekreis* can already be found in *Die sieben Todsünden*. I suggest that the narrative apparatus in the later play — adjusted, of course, to the particular requirements of that play — is only a modified and perhaps more sophisticated version of the authorial instrument for "scenic narration"³⁵ which Brecht conceived and utilized already in 1933.

"Im *Kaukasischen Kreidekreis* verbirgt sich der Erzähler nicht hinter seiner Erzählung — er ist eine Gestalt, die sich dem Zuschauer zeigt," observes Wirth.³⁶ In *Die sieben Todsünden*, too, Anna I unmistakably presents herself to the audience in the narrator's role. But instead of arriving on the scene while the prologue is already in progress, as the singer does, she is positioned onstage from the outset. According to the initial stage directions: "Auf der Bühne steht eine kleine Tafel, auf der die Route der Tournee durch sieben Städte aufgezeichnet ist und vor der Anna I mit einem kleinen Zeigestock steht." (*GW* 7, 2859) This device — reminiscent of the performing *Bänkelsänger* and frequently employed by Brecht — establishes the fundamentally didactic nature of the forthcoming spectacle: we are to expect illustrations of the moral principle suggested by the title of the work. Whereas in *Der kaukasische Kreidekreis* the traditional "play within a play" device conveys the didactic purpose, the ballet presents seven illustrative scenic emblems spanned between the *narrative* framework of a prologue and epilogue.

Anna I begins her singing narration by introducing herself (and her other self, Anna II), giving place and time of the commencing action, and orienting the audience about the circumstances of the moneymaking venture and her own attitude toward the imminent journey.[37] As early as the third line of her first song she establishes contact with the audience by stepping out of her role and turning directly *ad spectatores*:

> Meine Schwester und ich stammen aus Louisiana
> Wo die Wasser des Mississippi unter dem Mond fließen
> Wie Sie aus den Liedern erfahren können. (*GW* 7, 2859)

Repeated verbatim in the epilogue, this type of direct address fulfills a multiple alienating function. First, it identifies Anna I as both narrator and active participant in the action, thereby suspending the theatrical illusion. Second, since both prologue and epilogue employ the present tense, it sets off the narrative framework from the individual episodes which are narrated in the past tense. And finally, by referring specifically to the ensuing songs, it lays bare the epic-emblematic structure of the work: a series of self-contained, pantomimically enacted scenes only loosely connected through the continuous presence of the narrator who provides commentary in the form of sung scenic narration.

Having established direct contact with her audience at the outset, Anna I proceeds to demonstrate the alienating mechanics of her split personality. At the end of each stanza in her prologue she turns to Anna II — who, after all, stands next to her on the stage — for confirmation of the narrated details. But what now ensues dispels any trace of dramatic illusion. Since Anna I herself answers the questions she pretends to pose to Anna II, the expected scenic dialogue becomes narrated dialogue as part of the sustained scenic monologue, e.g.:

> Wir sind eigentlich nicht zwei Personen
> Sondern nur eine einzige.
> Wir heißen beide Anna
> Wir haben eine Vergangenheit und eine Zukunft
> Ein Herz und ein Sparkassenbuch
> Und jede macht nur, was für die andere gut ist
> Nicht wahr, Anna?
> Ja, Anna.   (*GW* 7, 2860)

This type of narrated dialogue regularly recurs in the individual scenes when Anna I reports on "conversations" between herself and Anna II, analyzing the lesson to be learned from a particular experience they have just had. For example, Anna I concludes her song in the "Zorn" scene:

> Immer sagte ich zu ihr: halt du dich zurück, Anna
> Du weißt, wohin die Unbeherrschtheit führt!
> Und sie gab mir recht und sagte:
> Ich weiß, Anna.   (*GW* 7, 2864)

Large portions of Anna I's songs accompanying the journey are addressed in this rhetorical fashion to Anna II, containing analytical reflections and commentary. Instead of describing the dramatic events as presented by Anna II and the rest of the dancers, Anna I enters them as active participant: the practical conscience and guardian angel of her sister. Simultaneously, however, through her reflective generalizations about the action she communicates the humane and appealing character of Anna II who is more than susceptible to the many temptations she encounters. Only Anna I's sober perseverance and calculated interventions enable Anna II to extricate herself from the succession of adverse situations.

In the seventh and final episode entitled "Neid," Anna I reveals once more her total control over Anna II and over the entire preceding dramatic action. After briefly recapitulating the morals learned in the foregoing episodes, she devotes the rest of her song to an elaboration of the overall ideological message, ostensibly for the benefit of Anna II:

> Schwester, wir alle sind frei geboren
> Wie es uns gefällt, können wir gehen im Licht
> Also gehen herum aufrecht wie im Triumph die Toren
> Aber wohin sie gehen, das wissen sie nicht. (*GW* 7, 2870)

In a tone of triumphant jubilation, composed by Weill as an effective marching song with rousing, emphatic rhythms, she no longer refers explicitly to Anna II's predictable, meek confirmation of her self-assured insights. Rather, since the battle is won and the seven deadly sins of bourgeois society have been successfully overcome, she now takes Anna II's approval for granted. Here the two aspects of the split personality seem to be reconciled and fused:

> Iß nicht, trink nicht und sei nicht träge
> Die Strafe bedenk, die auf Liebe steht!
> Bedenk, was geschieht, wenn du tätst, was dir läge!
> Nütze die Jugend nicht: sie vergeht! (*GW* 7, 2870)

The twisted logic of the climactic line "Nütze die Jugend nicht: sie vergeht!," a supreme example of Brecht's dialectic of alienation, clearly establishes Anna II in the final tableau as a helpless victim. She has sacrificed her youth and integrity on the altar of Mammon for the dubious cause of her family's material security. Anna II has, however, not become identical with Anna I; the ambiguity of the split personality is maintained to the very end. In the epilogue the two sisters appear arm in arm about to embark on the return trip to their family and their newly built house in Louisiana.

Compared to the interplay between the singer (narrator and chorus leader) and his musicians (chorus) in *Der kaukasische Kreidekreis*,[38] the narrative apparatus of the ballet seems at first glance less consistently integrated. The primary authorial instrument for scenic narration, Anna I, is physically separated from the male quartet representing her family back home. Also, her dual role as narrator and participant is dynamic, while the chorus remains static throughout. The members of the family, physically restricted to their platform on one side of the stage, cannot become participating actors. They have their own chorus leader in the person of the mother and function as a separate body offering their commentary from a distance. Nevertheless, the family chorus effectively complements Anna I in her capacity as mediator between the ballet's emblematic and epic structures. Three out of the seven scenes — "Faulheit," "Völlerei," and "Habsucht" — receive choral commentary alone. In these episodes Anna I withdraws into the pantomimic ballet action and allows the chorus to provide the moralizing *subscriptiones* II. In the "Lied der Familie" at the end of the "Stolz" scene,[39] the family ensemble interrupts the story to reprimand the sisters for their initial blunders and especially for their lack of promising financial success up to that point in the action; in the overall context of the ballet this song belongs to the larger emblematic framework as *subscriptio* I/b. Leitmotivically recurring epigrammatic choral passages of various length[40] can also be subsumed under the *subscriptio*-network of the larger emblematic pattern. Invariably counteracting the meaning expressed in the individual *picturae*, these ironic choral statements are strategically distributed throughout the work to bring about an overall structural and thematic coherence. For example, the pseudo-moralizing couplet sung by the chorus, "Wer über sich selber den Sieg erringt, / der erringt auch den Lohn," first appears after Anna I's song in the "Stolz" scene (*subscriptio* II/2) to give the sanction of family authority to her "moral" pronouncements. The identical couplet reappears in the same function to interrupt Anna I's song in the "Unzucht" scene and also to conclude the "Neid" scene. Within the smaller emblematic pattern, too, a similar use of the chorus to augment the impact of the *subscriptio* may be observed. In the "Faulheit" scene, for example, every line of the mother's commentary as chorus leader is dutifully seconded by the rest of the family with the axiomatic, pseudo-proverbial refrain: "Müßiggang ist aller Laster Anfang."[41]

The brief choral interruptions of Anna I's scenic narration thus effectively link her moralizing with the family's running commentary. In the four individual songs of the chorus, on the other hand, Brecht provides the audience with glimpses of the family's attitude and activities during the absence of Anna. For example, he includes snatches of a conversation (choral song in the "Faulheit" scene), the family's reaction to Anna's slow progress in making money ("Stolz" scene), a letter they receive from Anna and evaluating remarks on its content

("Völlerei" scene), and shows the family in the midst of discussing Anna's adventures in Tennessee (Baltimore according to the stage version) while reading about them in the newspaper ("Habsucht" scene). To underscore the ambiguity of Anna's split personality, Brecht has the family members refer to her by alternating between the use of singular and plural pronoun forms.

Since direct communication between the chorus and Anna I is carefully avoided throughout, the two instances when a semblance of direct interplay does ensue are all the more telling examples of Brecht's dramaturgical virtuosity. The device of accelerating the dramatic action through the intervention of the narrator — accomplished in *Der kaukasische Kreidekreis* by the singer alone[42] — is ingeniously shared in *Die sieben Todsünden* by the family chorus and Anna I. Back in Louisiana, far away from the sisters' turbulent activities, the family nevertheless proves to be so much a part of the progressing events that it exercises control over the action by admonishing Anna I, however indirectly. At one point the family even manages to speed up the action by eliciting a direct response from Anna I. In her next song she reacts to the indignant warning by using the same phrase:

> *Familie*: Das geht nicht vorwärts!
> Was die da schicken
> Das sind keine Summen, mit denen man ein Haus baut!
> ....
> *Anna I*: Jetzt geht es vorwärts. Jetzt sind wir schon in Los Angeles.
> (*GW* 7, 2863, 2864)

Anna I seems to have overheard the chorus, even though this is, of course, impossible. Ironically enough, in stage reality her reaction is physically possible. Such comic incongruity readily suspends the theatrical illusion. Choral use of a deictic formula provides another instance of alienating mediation.[43] The family addresses Anna directly, as if to bridge over the physical distance:

> Denk an unser Haus in Louisiana!
> Sieh, es wächst schon, Stock- um Stockwerk wächst es!
> Halte an dich: Freßsucht ist von Übel. (*GW* 7, 2866)

Here the irony of the situation stems from the fact that both Annas, sharing the stage with the chorus, can look on as the house gradually rises in the background.

III

"Bismarck hatte das Reich, Wagner das Gesamtkunstwerk gegründet, die beiden Schmiede hatten geschmiedet und verschmolzen, und Paris war von beiden erobert worden."[44] This amusing remark à la Heine is only one of many such jibes scattered throughout Brecht's theoretical writings. Indeed, Wagner's idea of the *Gesamtkunstwerk* became the poet's chief target in his relentless effort to create a radically different theatrical practice.⁴⁵ Brecht regarded the Wagnerian operatic model as a dangerous narcotic and strove to achieve the opposite effect himself. He wanted to activate rather than stupefy:

> Solange 'Gesamtkunstwerk' bedeutet, daß das Gesamte ein Aufwaschen ist, solange also Künste 'verschmelzt' werden sollen, müssen die einzelnen Elemente alle gleichermaßen degradiert werden, indem jedes nur Stichwortbringer für das andere sein kann. Der Schmelzprozeß erfaßt den Zuschauer, der ebenfalls eingeschmolzen wird und einen passiven (leidenden) Teil des Gesamtkunstwerks darstellt. Solche Magie ist natürlich zu bekämpfen.⁴⁶

In order to make empathy and abandonment to sensual pleasure on the part of the spectators as difficult as possible, he proposed — in contradistinction to Wagner's synthesis of the arts — a strict separation of the major components in his theater (text, music, and production):

> So seien all die Schwesterkünste der Schauspielkunst hier geladen, nicht um ein 'Gesamtkunstwerk' herzustellen, in dem sie sich alle aufgeben und verlieren, sondern sie sollen, zusammen mit der Schauspielkunst, die gemeinsame Aufgabe in ihrer verschiedenen Weise fördern, und ihr Verkehr miteinander besteht darin, daß sie sich gegenseitig verfremden.⁴⁷

Die sieben Todsünden is not only an exemplary model of Brecht's creative conception of emblematic and epic structure as a didactic instrument; it is also an instructive illustration of how Brecht envisaged his "Trennung der Elemente."⁴⁸ Propelled in this context more by anti-Wagnerian than anti-Aristotelian considerations — his elements "Musik, Wort und Bild"⁴⁹ correspond, after all, to Aristotle's *melos*, *lexis*, and *opsis* as means and manner of mimetic representation — Brecht's aim at an interplay of these autonomously functioning elements seems paradoxical if not unrealizable. Yet, in his practice interplay becomes counterplay. In our ballet cantata, for example, the scenic tableaux of the ballet action, the poem cycle delivered by the narrative apparatus of Anna I and the family chorus, and Weill's strongly parodistic music are played off against one another in a manner which ensures that each of the three components takes turns in making its contribution to the total effect and thus preserves the autonomy of its individual artistic medium.

I have already discussed the mechanics of interplay (or counterplay) between Anna I, the chorus, and the pantomimic ballet action. Even more successful in this respect is Weill's musical setting which, necessarily related to all elements, provides a unifying superstructure of alienation. Among the various autonomous constituents, Brecht regarded music — especially in its capacity as counterpoint to the text — as the most important contribution to the concerted effort that was to produce the finished work. Weill, himself a theoretician of the new musical theater, agreed: "Das neue Operntheater, das heute entsteht, hat epischen Charakter. Denn da die berichtende Form den Zuschauer niemals in Ungewißheit oder in Zweifel über die Bühnenvorgänge läßt, so kann sich die Musik ihre eigene, selbständige, rein musikalische Wirkung vorbehalten."[50]

To evaluate the numerous practical devices of musical alienation skillfully employed by Weill in *Die sieben Todsünden* would require a separate investigation.[51] Here I can merely suggest a few without further comment, such as the so-called "Gegen-die-Musik-Sprechen," the singer's conscious deviation from the prescribed melodic line, alternation between singing and speaking, underscoring the message contained in key words or phrases of a song by irregular rhythmic accents or unusual intervals, sudden changes in intonation, acting against specific predictable moods created by the music, abrupt modulation within an accustomed harmonic context (e.g., sudden change in tonality), and unexpected switches in musical style for parodistic effect.[52] To give at least one example of the last mentioned device: Weill exposes the sanctimoniousness of the avaricious family by composing its leitmotivically recurring refrains as parodistic male chorales in majestic, pseudo-religious cantata style.

*

I have not been able, nor have I intended, to give a comprehensive treatment of this unique work. At best, my essay breaks some critical ground, while many aspects of interpretation and explication remain undiscussed. I especially regret having had to forego analysis of the all-pervasive humor. My aim has been to call long overdue attention to *Die sieben Todsünden der Kleinbürger* for reasons which I hope have become clear. The last work of the Brecht-Weill collaboration, it is Brecht's only ballet. Written in 1933, it occupies a crucial position midway in the poet's career, summing up his preceding dramaturgical innovations and pointing forward to techniques further perfected in the later plays. Because of its extreme brevity and complex yet rigorous construction, it can serve as a model for the study of Brecht's basic conception of dramatic form. In fact, as a structural model it represents the most consistent realization among Brecht's stage works of an effective fusion of emblematic framework and epic theater techniques, achieved through a particularly imaginative use of the narrator figure and the chorus as integral parts of the authorial instrument for scenic narration. And finally, incorporating various artistic media, the ballet is a conscious and successful attempt to create a moralistic-didactic anti-Gesamtkunstwerk in parodistic attire.

[1] Cf. the 3rd, rev. ed. of Reinhold Grimm's invaluable Sammlung Metzler volume, *Bertolt Brecht* (Stuttgart, 1971), p. 104.

[2] Except for a few shorter review articles in newspapers and journals of theater, dance, and music, and occasional references of primarily descriptive nature in the numerous books on Brecht, the present essay constitutes the first critical assessment entirely devoted to this work. Even the most up-to-date and comprehensive bibliography lists only a handful of brief treatments. Cf. Grimm, p. 57. Cf. also four additional items: anonymous review in *The Dancing Times* (London), August 1933; Horst Koegler, "Getanzte Literatur," *Theater heute*, 1 (1960), 25-29, André Müller, "Zu gut verkäuflicher Ware gemacht. 'Die sieben Todsünden' von Bertolt Brecht und Kurt Weill in Frankfurt/Main," *Theater der Zeit*, 15 (1960), H. 6:65-68; Ernst Thomas, "Brecht-Weill: 'Die sieben Todsünden'. Deutsche Erstaufführung in Frankfurt/Main," *Musik im Unterricht*, 51 (1960), 217-19.

[3] *Die Bibel* was first published in the Augsburg student paper *Die Ernte* in January, 1914. Reprinted in Bertolt Brecht, *Gesammelte Werke in 20 Bänden* (Frankfurt/Main, 1967), 7, 3028-38. Cf. also Reinhold Grimm, "Brecht's Beginnings," *The Drama Review*, 12 (1967), 29-34.

[4] Bertolt Brecht, *Die sieben Todsünden der Kleinbürger*, in Brecht, *Gesammelte Werke in 20 Bänden* (Frankfurt/Main, 1967), 7, 2858. Hereafter references to this edition for quotations from the ballet will be given in the text in parentheses, e.g.: (*GW* 7, 2858).

[5] Cf. Brecht's incisive Breughel commentary "Verfremdungseffekt in den erzählenden Bildern des älteren Breughel," *GW* 18, 279-283. Cf. also Wolfgang Hütt, "Bertolt Brechts episches Theater und Probleme der bildenden Kunst," *Wissenschaftliche Zeitschrift der M. Luther-Universität Halle-Wittenberg*, 7 (1957-58), 821-41. As the author of *Leben Eduards des Zweiten von England*, based on Marlowe's *Edward II*, Brecht must also have known the famous scene in Marlowe's *Doctor Faustus* where the personified seven deadly sins make their appearance.

[6] The literature dealing with the subject is vast In addition to Morton W. Bloomfield's comprehensive monograph *The Seven Deadly Sins. An Introduction to the History of a Religious Concept, with Special Reference to Medieval English Literature* (East Lansing, Mich., 1952), the following titles are especially helpful: Samuel C. Chew, *The Pilgrimage of Life* (New Haven, Conn., 1962); Hanno Fink, *Die Sieben Todsünden in der mittelenglischen erbaulichen Literatur* (Hamburg, 1969); Angus Fletcher, *Allegory. The Theory of a Symbolic Mode* (Ithaca, N.Y., 1964); Marie Gothein, "Die Todsünden," *Archiv für Religionswissenschaft*, 10 (1907), 416-86; Hans R. Jauss, "Form und Auffassung der Allegorie in der Tradition der Psychomachia (von Prudentius zum ersten 'Romanz de la Rose')," *Medium Aevum Vivum: Festschrift für Walther Bulst*, ed. H. R. Jauss and D. Schaller (Heidelberg, 1960), 179-206; and Frederick Rogers, *The Seven Deadly Sins* (London, 1907).

[7] See Wolfdietrich Rasch, "Bertolt Brechts marxistischer Lehrer. Zu einem ungedruckten Briefwechsel zwischen Brecht und Karl Korsch," *Merkur*, 17 (1963), 988-1003.

[8] As a Marxist, Brecht seems to be implying here that taking from the rich should be considered a virtue and that only indiscriminate greed is a sin. This section of the text is unconvincing in its logic.

[9] The fact that the original text of the ballet only faintly resembles the version as it is usually performed presents serious difficulties for any discussion of the work in its totality.

10 Cf. Gottfried von Einem and Siegfried Melchinger, eds., *Caspar Neher* (Hannover, 1966), p. 115.
11 Cf. *GW* 7, Anmerkungen, p. 1.
12 Cf. Bernard Taper, *Balanchine* (New York, 1960), p. 319, and also pp. 152-54; and von Einem and Melchinger, *Neher*, pp. 96-101.
13 According to Harry Graf Kessler who was present at the Paris performance. He reports the occasion in a diary entry to 17 June 1933: "Ich fand [Weills] Musik hübsch und eigenartig; allerdings kaum anders als die der 'Dreigroschenoper'. Lotte Lenya sang mit ihrer kleinen, sympathischen Stimme (deutsch) Brechts Balladen, und Tilly Losch tanzte und mimte graziös und fesselnd." Harry Graf Kessler, *Tagebücher 1918-1937* (Frankfurt/Main, 1961), pp. 723-24.
14 Sung in English, in a translation by Edward James which seems to have got lost. Cf. John Willett, *The Theatre of Bertolt Brecht* (New York, 1968), p. 43.
15 Quoted by Martin Esslin in his *Brecht: The Man and His Work* (New York, 1971), pp. 66-67.
16 Constant Lambert, *Music Ho! A Study of Music in Decline* (London, 1966), p. 197. The book was first published in 1934.
17 Cf. Hans Kirk's review in *Tiden* (Copenhagen), 4 (1936), p. 372.
18 The English translation used for this production was done by W. H. Auden and Chester Kallmann but published only later as "The Seven Deadly Sins of the Lower Middle Class," *The Tulane Drama Review*, 6 (1961), 123-29. There exists another, anonymous English translation (Copyright 1957, Brook House of Music, Inc.) accompanying the 1959 recording of the ballet (Columbia KL 5175) which is printed together with the presumably original stage version of the German text. Lotte Lenya sings the role of Anna I on this recording. Cf. Peter Bauland, *The Hooded Eagle. Modern German Drama on the New York Stage* (Syracuse, N.Y., 1968), pp. 186-187 and 275. Bauland is inaccurate on several details.
19 For contemporary reviews see n. 2.
20 Cf. Werner Hecht, ed., *Brecht-Dialog 1968* (München, 1969), p. 335.
21 First published in a separate pamphlet as Bertolt Brecht, *Die sieben Todsünden der Kleinbürger* (Frankfurt/Main, 1959). Later also in Brecht, *Gedichte*, III (Frankfurt/Main, 1961). Most accessible in *GW* 7, 2857-2871.
22 In *Les Ballets 1933 de Georges Balanchine* (Paris, 1933). Peter Bauland (*Hooded Eagle*, p. 186) is thus incorrect in stating that the text "was never published until 1959."
23 See nn. 11 and 13.
24 Cf. the printed German text accompanying the Columbia recording (KL 5175) which, to my knowledge, is the only published stage version.
25 In his voluminous theoretic writings after 1933, including essays on musical theater such as "Über die Verwendung von Musik für ein episches Theater" (1935), Brecht never refers to *Die sieben Todsünden*.
26 The judgment of John Willett, otherwise a circumspect and reliable Brecht commentator, shall suffice here to suggest the general tenor of critical assessment: "*Die sieben Todsünden*... was a quite conscious regression on Brecht's part. He never cared to print, the songs which he wrote for it, and it seems a plain attempt to earn money in exile by recapturing the spirit of his greatest success." Willett, *Theatre*, p. 136.
27 Cf. the radical periodization in books such as Klaus Schuhmann, *Der Lyriker Bertolt Brecht 1913-1933* (Berlin, 1964); Ernst Schumacher, *Die dramatischen Versuche Bertolt Brechts 1918-1933* (Berlin, 1955); and Walter Hinck, *Die Dramaturgie des späten Brecht* (Göttingen, 1966).
28 Reinhold Grimm, "Marxistische Emblematik. Zu Bertolt Brechts 'Kriegsfibel'," *Wissenschaft als Dialog. Studien zur Literatur und Kunst seit der Jahrhundertwende*, ed. Renate von Heydebrand and Klaus Günther Just (Stuttgart, 1969), pp. 351-79. See especially pp. 372-79.

29 (Stuttgart, 1964), pp. 18-26. Cf. also *Emblemata. Handbuch zur Sinnbildkunst des XVI. und XVII. Jahrhunderts*, ed. Arthur Henkel and Albrecht Schöne (Stuttgart, 1967).

30 The recurring, identically worded stage directions signalling the appearance of each song intercepting the dramatic action in *Die Dreigroschenoper* attest to Brecht's awareness of the emblematic nature of this device, e.g.: "Songbeleuchtung: goldenes Licht. Die Orgel wird illuminiert. An einer Stange kommen von oben drei Lampen herunter, und auf den Tafeln steht: Die Seeräuber-Jenny." *GW* 2, 415. Similarly, in connection with *Mutter Courage* cf. Helene Weigel, ed., *Theaterarbeit. 6 Aufführungen des Berliner Ensembles* (Dresden, 1952), p. 274. Cf. also the following lines from the poem "Die Gesänge" (1950) in *Gedichte aus dem "Messingkauf"*, *GW* 9, 795: "Trennt die Gesänge vom übrigen! / Durch ein Emblem der Musik, durch Wechsel der Beleuchtung / Durch Titel, durch Bilder zeigt an / Daß die Schwesterkunst nun / Die Bühne betritt."

31 Cf. especially chapter IX in Reinhold Grimm, *Bertolt Brecht. Die Struktur seines Werkes*, 5th ed. (Nürnberg, 1968), pp. 77-84. Cf. also Brecht, "Vergnügungstheater oder Lehrtheater?," *GW* 15, 272.

32 Cf. the striking parallel with Schöne's statement about the figure of Gryphius' Leo Armenius: "Sich selber zeigt sie [die Figur] als pictura vor und verkündet zugleich die eigene subscriptio." Schöne, *Emblematik und Drama*, p. 219. Cf. also: "... die dramatische Figur erscheint in der Doppelrolle des Darstellenden und zugleich die eigene Darstellung Deutenden." *Ibid.*, p. 158. For a general treatment see Walter H. Sokel, "Brecht's Split Characters and His Ser.se of the Tragic," in Peter Demetz, ed., *Brecht. A Collection of Critical Essays* (Englewood Cliffs, N.J., 1962), pp. 127-37.

33 In Reinhold Grimm, ed., *Episches Theater* (Köln, 1966), p. 227. First published in *Sinn und Form, 2. Sonderheft Bertolt Brecht* (Berlin, 1957), 346-87.

34 *Ibid.*, p. 228. Writing in 1957, Wirth presumably was not yet familiar with Brecht's ballet.

35 *Ibid.*, p. 222.

36 *Ibid.*

37 Cf. "Der Sänger im *Kaukasischen Kreidekreis* führt in die Handlung auf der Bühne ein, bezeichnet ihre Zeit, ihren Ort, stellt die Helden vor. Mit einem Wort: er berichtet, was man gewöhnlich aus der Exposition erfährt." *Ibid.*, p. 223.

38 *Ibid.*

39 In Brecht's original text this "Lied der Familie" is included in the "Stolz" scene, but in the stage version, it belongs musically and dramatically to the subsequent "Zorn" scene. Cf. the text of the Columbia recording.

40 The longest choral refrain is quoted in the back of *GW* vol. 7, Anmerkungen, p. 1: "Der Herr erleuchte unsre Kinder / Daß sie den Weg erkennen, der zum Wohlstand führt. / Er gebe ihnen die Kraft und die Freudigkeit / Daß sie nicht sündigen gegen die Gesetze / Die da reich und glücklich machen."

41 Cf. in this context Schöne's statement on the role of such didactic axioms in the dramatic architecture of Baroque tragedy: "Die 'emblematischen' Sentenzen sind tragende Elemente im Bau des Trauerspiels: Pfeiler, zwischen denen die szenischen Bilder sich spannen, und Säulen, auf das die Bühnengeschehen als ein exemplarisches Geschehen sich gründet." Schöne, *Emblematik und Drama*, p. 159.

42 "Das Primat des Erzählers im epischen Theater kommt auch darin zum Ausdruck, daß nicht die Handlung das Tempo seiner Erzählung bestimmt, sondern er selber über plötzliche Retardationen entscheidet, etwa über ein Beschleunigen der Handlung oder bezeichnende Verkürzungen." Wirth, *op. cit.*, p. 223.

43 Cf. the striking parallel here with Baroque dramatic practices, though extended in Brecht to include the character on stage: "Deiktische Formeln richten den Blick des

Zuschauers und Lesers auf das dramatische Bild, wenn das Resümee erfolgt: *Schaut oder Seht hier."* Schöne, *op. cit.,* p. 161.

44 Brecht, "Über Bühnenmusik, *GW* 15, 486.

45 Walter Hinck is surely correct in understanding Brecht's attack as also directed against Max Reinhardt's production style. Hinck, *Die Dramaturgie des späten Brecht* (Göttingen, 1966), p. 110. Cf. also Hinck's (p. 128) characterization of Reinhardt's style: "Das unverwechselbare Kriterium der Reinhardtschen Inszenierungen: seine Kunst, Atmosphäre, märchen- und zauberhafte Atmosphäre, zu schaffen, der kongruente Einbau von Musik und Tanz im Sinne eines 'Gesamtkunstwerks', die betäubende Wirkung seiner Aufführungen versetzt den Zuschauer gerade in jenen Zustand völliger Identifikation, der eine Selbsttätigkeit, ein 'Mitspielen' am wenigsten möglich macht. In Max Reinhardts Bühne kulminiert das neuzeitliche Theater, hier erst wird es wirklich autonom. Hier überwältigt die ästhetische Realität der Bühne den Zuschauer ganz."

46 Brecht, "Anmerkungen zur Oper 'Aufstieg und Fall der Stadt Mahagonny'," *GW* 17, 1010-1011.

47 Brecht, "Kleines Organon für das Theater," *GW* 16, 698-99, no. 74.

48 *GW* 17, 1010. Cf. also *GW* 15, 440-41 and 495-96.

49 *GW* 17, 1010-1012.

50 Quoted in Egon Monk, "Der Einfluß Brechts," *Zeitgenössisches Musiktheater. Internationaler Kongress, Hamburg 1964,* ed. Ernst Thomas (Hamburg, 1966), p. 73.

51 A comprehensive and musicologically sound study of the Brecht-Weill collaboration on the model of Fritz Hennenberg's excellent *Dessau-Brecht. Musikalische Arbeiten* (Berlin, 1963) remains to date a serious desideratum in Brecht research. Günter Hartung's article, "Zur epischen Oper Brechts und Weills," in *Wiss. Zeitschrift der M.-Luther-Universität Halle-Wittenberg. Gesellschaftswiss.-Sprachwiss. Reihe,* 8 (1959), 659-73, deals with the partnership up to around 1930.

52 For extensive treatment of these and other devices see Hennenberg, *op.cit.,* especially pp. 204-45.

www.ingramcontent.com/pod-product-compliance
Lightning Source LLC
Chambersburg PA
CBHW020747160426
43192CB00006B/269